KARL MARX'S THEORY OF REVOLUTION

KARL MARX'S THEORY OF REVOLUTION
by Hal Draper

VOLUME IV
CRITIQUE OF
OTHER SOCIALISMS

MONTHLY REVIEW PRESS
NEW YORK

Hal Draper died on January 26, 1990. The manuscript for this volume had already been received by Monthly Review Press. The Special Note C, Bibliography, and Index were not included; they were supplied by Ernest Haberkern of the Center for Socialist History, who relied on extensive notes left by Hal Draper.

Copyright © 1990 by The Center for Socialist History
All rights reserved

Library of Congress Cataloging-in-Publication Data
(Revised for vol.4)
Draper, Hal.
   Karl Marx's theory of revolution.
   Includes bibliographies and indexes.
   CONTENTS: 1. State and bureaucracy. 2v.—
   v.2. The politics of social classes.—[etc.]—
   v.4. Critique of other socialisms.
1. Marx, Karl, 1818-1883.   2. Revolutions and socialism.
I. Title.
JC233.M299D7   321.09   76-40467
ISBN 0-85345-387-X (v.1)
ISBN 0-85345-439-6 (v.2)
ISBN 0-85345-674-7 (v.3: pbk.)
ISBN 0-85345-798-0 (v.4: pbk.)

Monthly Review Press
122 West 27th Street
New York, N.Y. 10001

10 9 8 7 6 5 4 3 2 1

Manufactured in the United States of America

THIS VOLUME IS DEDICATED
to the student and worker revolutionaries
of China
who fought for workers' power
through workers' democracy from below
in the bravest popular upheaval ever seen,
against the bureaucratic-collectivist ruling regime
that calls itself "Communist,"
and who temporarily yielded
before the monstrous massacre of June 4, 1989
executed by the bureaucratic-military dictatorship,
assassins of the people.
The association of this counterrevolutionary tyranny
with the name of Karl Marx
is the biggest Big Lie in history,
systematically falsified by both
the Stalinist world of bureaucratic-collectivism
and the decaying world of capitalism,
and by the apologists of both exploitive systems.
H.D.
June 5, 1989

CONTENTS

Foreword xi

1. **Of Utopian Socialism** 1
   1. Accenting the positive (1)... 2. "Scientific socialism" (6)... 3. Utopianism (9)... 4. First exposition (14)... 5. The meaning of utopian socialism (17)

2. **Of Sentimental Socialism** 22
   1. The meaning of sentimental socialism (22)... 2. The "modern mythology" (25)... 3. Morality and moralizing (31)... 4. Humanism and the power of Love (34)

3. **Of State-Socialism: Lassallean Model** 41
   1. Forerunners (41)... 2. The cult of the state (46)... 3. The state-aid nostrum (50)... 4. State-socialism and social-Caesarism (54)... 5. Marx on Lassalle (58)... 6. Marx and the Lassallean movement (61)... 7. Marx's break with the Lassallean party (63)... 8. Lassalleanism and the Gotha unification (67)... —Note on the suppression of Marx's critique (70)

4. **Of State-Socialism: Bismarckian Model** 72
   1. The Bismarck attack (73)... 2. The Katheder-socialists (75)... 3. The crisis in the party (79)... 4. Flashback: Marx on state intervention (82)... 5. On capitalist statification (85)... 6. Argumentation (90)... 7. More consequences of statification (92)... 8. The issue refuses to go away (97)... 9. Four illustrative cases (100)

5. **Of Anarchism: Proudhonist Model** 107
   1. The reservoir of antistatism (107)... 2. Godwin, Stirner, Hess (111)... 3. Watershed: the "ultimate aim" formulation (118)... 4. In-

terlude: bourgeois anarchism (121) . . . 5. Anarchism's "disguised state" (126)

6. **Of Anarchism: Bakunin Model** 130
   1. On the "principle of authority" (131) . . . 2. Engels on authority (135) . . . 3. Revolution and authority (140) . . . 4. The nature of the Bakunin operation (144) . . . 5. Analysis of the Bakunin operation (145) . . . 6. The nature of the struggle with Bakunin (147) . . . 7. Bakuninist ideology: the state (152) . . . 8. Bakuninism: reformist politics (157) . . . 9. Bakuninism: reformist practice (161) . . . 10. Bakuninism and "authoritarianism" (164) . . . 11. The alien ideology (168) . . . 12. Epilogue: the "Marx-Anarchist" myth (171)

7. **Of the Reactionary Anticapitalisms** 176
   1. The meaning of "reactionary socialism" (176) . . . 2. "Feudal socialism" and the triangular class struggle (178) . . . 3. The third corner of the triangle (182) . . . 4. The case of Thomas Carlyle—I (185) . . . 5. The case of Thomas Carlyle—II (188) . . . 6. O'Connor to Comte (192) . . . 7. The case of David Urquhart (196)

8. **Of Boulangism: The Politics of the Third Way** 204
   1. The political matrix of Boulangism (205) . . . 2. Socialists and Boulanger (207) . . . 3. The Guesdist line on Boulangism (211) . . . 4. Paul Lafargue's Boulangeo-socialism (216) . . . 5. Engels on Boulangism (219) . . . 6. Engels' "third way" (222) . . . 7. The international complication (226) . . . 8. Antiparliamentarism and opportunism (228) . . . 9. War and counterrevolution (232)

APPENDICES 239

Special Note A. Lassalle and Marx: History of a Myth 241
   1. Lassalle's character and personality (242) . . . 2. The Hatzfeldt case as career (244) . . . 3. Friendship: up to 1856 (246) . . . 4. Gustav Lewy's mission (250) . . . 5. Lewy's exposé of Lassalle (253) . . . 6. Who broke with whom? (256) . . . 7. The myth of the creator (259) . . . 8. Engels' campaign against the Lassalle myth (263) . . . 9. The Bernstein/Engels critique of Lassalle (266)

Special Note B. Bakunin and the International: A "Libertarian" Fable 270
   1. Preliminary considerations (270) . . . 2. Bakunin's first takeover operation (274) . . . 3. First round at Basel (276) . . . 4. Bakunin's destructo-clique: the secret Alliance (279) . . . 5. Bakunin declares war (284) . . . 6. Bakunin's split drive (286) . . . 7. Racism and the splitters'

campaign (291)... 8. Bakunin's political pogrom of 1872 (295)... 9. The great smear campaign (298)... 10. The paladin of lies (300)

Special Note C. The Strange Case of Franz Mehring 305
1. Mehring's Circuitous Road to Marxism (306)... 2. The Sonneman Affair (308)... 3. The Morning After (310)... 4. 1882—A Year of Change (311)... 5. Last Stop (311)... 6. Mehring as a Left-winger (314)... 7. Mehring's Biography of Marx and the 1913 Dispute with Kautsky (315)

Reference Notes 319

Bibliography 352

Index 365

FOREWORD

The present volume, *KMTR* 4, is devoted to an important part of any exposition of Marx's views, namely, his criticism of alternative ideas and movements: socialist views and theories put forward by others during his active years. The real content of any line of thought is clarified not only through what it says it is but what it says it is *not*: what it differentiates itself from; what it denies or rejects; what it counterposes itself to and how it criticizes it; and also what it accepts from others' contributions. In fact, all thinkers have to start from this point; the subject they broach is not a *tabula rasa*; their own thinking has to go through an apprenticeship.

As a matter of fact, a good deal of attention has already been paid to this approach in the preceding three volumes. The present volume would have a long chapter on Marx's views about Blanqui and Blanquism, were it not that *KMTR* 3 has already devoted more than one chapter to this subject. There is another very important *ism* missing from the present volume: *reformism*, along with a long list of associated isms, such as gradualism, parliamentarism, opportunism, and several others. All of these terms are aspects of a single subject, often summarized as the issue of *reform versus revolution*, or sometimes the "road to power." Marx's views both positive and negative, that is, both as positively expounded and as counterposed to reformist views, will be the subject of the first half of *KMTR* 5, the volume which will end this enterprise.

Of the isms that *are* treated in the following chapters, several have already come up for partial discussion in the preceding volumes, in connection with other subjects. For example, anarchism in general or Bakunin in particular has been discussed in relation to the peasantry, to dictatorship, and to other topics. Needed now is a general analysis.

Each chapter, devoted as it is to a particular socialist tendency, should not be considered an attempt to sum up the state of historical knowledge about that tendency. My subject is not the tendency itself but the views of Marx and Engels on it. For example, there is a great deal about utopian socialism which is not even broached in Chapter 1; my task was viewed as more limited.

The beginning of Chapter 1, below, points out that some of the isms taken up in this volume tend to interpenetrate; in practice they seldom live entirely detached from each other. In particular, the common practice of affixing the label 'state-socialist' on some figure is seldom justified (as is explained below in the case of Louis Blanc, for example). The more useful task is to define a state-socialist *element* in a viewpoint. In general, the subject of each chapter is not a hard-edged theory or school but rather a more or less pervasive element in socialist thinking.

One element of confusion in socialist history is illustrated by the lack of any agreed-on term for a *non*-state-socialist, with the result that terms get invented to label the confusion itself. For example: "libertarian socialism." Since questions get raised about such fuzzy isms, we may take this one as an example of several that are *not* separately considered here.

'Libertarian' goes far back as simply the adjectival form of 'liberty'; and the checkered career of that much-battered word goes far to explain what happens when a blur of thought is turned into an ism. Some of this history is irrelevant to us: for example, 'libertarian(ism)' once referred to a philosophic doctrine about the freedom of the will. By at least 1830, in English, it was in general use to label any advocacy of "liberty." The Oxford English Dictionary illustrates this usage (between 1830 and 1906) with five cases, none of which is concerned with any shockingly extreme view of liberty. More to the point: the term was eventually expropriated by that school of thought which lives ideologically on various declensions of the word 'liberty'—the anarchists.

An anarchist paper named *Le Libertaire* was published by French émigrés in New York as early as 1858-1861, but its terminology did not take hold. In 1895 a leader of the French anarchists, Sébastien Faure, founded a journal with the same name, and announced that *libertaire* was a "convenient synonym for *anarchist*." He did not explain why a fuzzy word was more "convenient" than one that already had a known ideological content; but he did not have to, for everyone could understand that 'libertarian' was preferable because it was more beguiling and *less* communicative. By *defining* liberty in terms of anarchism, it made it unnecessary to prove the identity by argument.

In a later stage of the term, 'libertarian(ism)' was taken over by some other political currents. One tendency was that of left-wing social-democrats who wanted to distinguish themselves from the 'democratic socialism' vaunted by the European Social-Democracy that ignominiously collapsed in the 1930s. It was now too ambiguous for leftist radicals to call themselves 'democratic socialists' in order to differentiate themselves from the Stalinists. The term 'libertarian socialist' came into some use to fill the need, but only sporadically. Later, 'libertarian' was seized on by an American extension of the so-called bourgeois anarchism that goes back to Josiah Warren. In its degenerate contemporary form it was adopted by a right-wing extrusion from the Republican Party to describe a quasi-anarchist program: the program of minimizing government interference with the profit system ("free enterprise") while the power of capital remains unchecked.

Obviously these terminological vagaries have little relation to the subject of this book. The isms chosen to be the subject of chapters in the present volume are some that actually played a significant role in the development of the socialist movement.

TWO INQUIRIES
INTO MARXOLOGY AND SCHOLARSHIP

The rest of this Foreword is devoted to two supplements. The first is a supplement to *KMTR* 3, dealing with the French Revolution. The other is related to Special Note B in the present volume, but it might be thought digressive there. The real subject of both supplements is one that our Forewords have touched on before: the nature of our contemporary marxological scholarship.

1. MARX AND THE FRENCH REVOLUTION: A SUPPLEMENTARY NOTE

This subject has been dealt with in *KMTR* as an adjunct of other issues, especially the question of 'terror' and 'terrorism.' A brief explanation of Marx's views on the so-called Reign of Terror in the French Revolution was given in *KMTR* 3 as part of Special Note C (pages 360-367). For other aspects of the French Revolution, see the indexes of *KMTR* volumes.[1]

An interesting addendum to this Special Note deserves space here.

In two letters written in the last years of his life, Engels recalled a long-forgotten article on the revolutionary Terror that had clearly made a great impression on him and on Marx, in their youthful days. Writing in the centennial year of the Revolution, on December 4, 1889, Engels gave his friend Victor Adler an educational summary of the meaning of the French "Terror," and we have already quoted from this letter in the aforementioned Special Note.[2] At the end of this letter, Engels referred his correspondent to what he considered an especially enlightening article: "The explanation of how the battle of Fleurus [June 26, 1794] overturned the reign of terror was given in 1842 in the (first) *Rheinische Zeitung* by K. F. Köppen, in an excellent critique of H. Leo's *Geschichte der französischen Revolution*."[3] In 1895 Engels made the same recommendation—only more emphatically—in a letter to Mehring, to guide the work the latter was then doing in collecting Marx's early writings. Clearly Engels was directing attention to material that had impressed the young Marx, not simply himself:

> One of the best writings in the *Rh[einische] Z[eitung]* is still, in the feuilleton section, a long critique of the history of the French Revolution by Leo. It is by Marx's friend K. F. Köppen...and gives (for the first time in any language) the correct explanation of the Terror period.[4]

What was this explanation for the Terror that was so impressive in 1842 and was still impressing Engels at the end of his life? What was "the correct explanation of the Terror period" that it put forward?

Köppen, then a very close friend and comrade of Marx, did have a critique of Heinrich Leo's just-published book, in the *Rheinische Zeitung* of May 1842. (Marx, already active as a contributor, was not yet editor of the new left-democratic organ.) Köppen, like Marx himself at this time, was a revolutionary democrat, not a communist; and in attacking Leo he was polemizing against a well-known champion of Junkerdom, absolutist reaction, and anti-Semitism.

Now here hangs a tale of bibliographical confusion, which has helped to keep this material from being better known. For despite Engels' latter-day recollection, in *this* long book review Köppen said nothing about an explanation for the Terror; the piece did not deal with this subject. Engels' memory had played a trick on him. But Köppen did publish another long critique of Leo—only it came the following month, and appeared not in the *RZ* but in the *Deutsche Jahrbücher*. It was, in fact, this latter work that Engels recalled with praise in 1889 and 1895.*

---

*The mixup was first elucidated in an article by Helmut Hirsch in 1936; a recent (1989) article by Walter Schmidt has brought all the facts together. For these two, see the Bibliography.—The clarification of this situation was handed to me on a platter, when I was barely conscious of the problem, as soon as I asked for copies of the *RZ* article from the Karl-Marx-Haus of Trier (letter by Dr. Hans Pelger, April 20, 1989). The cooperativeness of the K-M-Haus (as well as its associated Friedrich-Engels-Haus of Wuppertal) is unmatched in my experience, and my gratitude is commensurate.

Here, then, one finds the basic thought that later reverberated through Marx's and Engels' references to the French Revolution's period of "Terror," as presented in the aforementioned Special Note. The most cogent passage in Köppen went as follows:

> Not base arbitrary despotism and caprice, not petty intrigues and cabals, not the twinges of conscience of an old and bigoted mistress, and similar trivial causes—not these have been the levers of Terrorism; but rather iron necessity itself, i.e., the mutual abrasion and struggle of the most powerful forces and principles. As is well known, this would never have mounted to its radical heights without the intervention from outside [by the European powers in war coalition]. It began when Europe was ranged in arms against France; it ended as soon as this danger for France was over. For it was not because Robespierre was overthrown but because the cause of the Revolution was, since the battle of Fleurus, no longer in danger from without—this was why the system of Terror came to an end.[5]

What Köppen's interpretation underlines, once again, is that this point of view was not "Robespierrist," in the sense already discussed in the Special Note. Marx and Engels "did not regard Robespierre's political current as the central progressive leadership of the revolution," contrary to the viewpoint currently called "Marxist" especially in France, where the line stretching from Mathiez to Soboul via the CP industriously ignores what Marx and Engels actually wrote.[6]

Let us zero in on the more specific question raised by Köppen and so heartily approved by Marx and Engels, that is, the emphasis on the roots of the original "Terror" in *the danger felt from the European counterrevolutionary war*. What has happened to this thought now, in the two hundredth anniversary of the Revolution?

• • •

Engels' first recollection of the old Köppen article, in his letter to Adler, came while the world was celebrating (or damning) the one hundredth anniversary of the revolution that helped to remake Western society. We have now come another century beyond that point, in 1989, when the society that the French Revolution shaped is losing elements of cohesion. To celebrate the bicentennial, the University of Chicago Press has published Prof. François Furet's work *Marx and the French Revolution*, which should be of special interest to us as a summary of the present wisdom of the academic world on this topic.[7]

Not that Prof. Furet himself stakes this claim. On the contrary, he assures the reader that he is *not* a "Marxologist," much less a Germanist. (In the English version, this comes out: he is not a "specialist on Marx.")[8] That is, even though he is publishing a whole book about Marx's views, he avers that he has not been prejudiced by a surfeit of knowledge on the subject, nor tainted by overexposure to the facts. In truth, his essay bears out his claim to have no special expertise on Marx's work.

Nevertheless, almost every page of Furet's essay assures the reader that everything in Marx is all wrong. Marx's preoccupation was "inventing" a new revolution (the original French said: "imagining" a new revolution). Marx "substitutes politics for religion as the dominant illusion of society..." In Marx's view of the rights of man "citizenship is what is false." He did not have "any concept of democracy other than one of illusion or mystification." He defined the state "as a communitarian lie" (whatever that means). Under French absolutism there was "by definition, no dominant class..."[9] These pearls of sciolism, which I select out only because they can be exhibited concisely, are not supported by textual references or other pedantic modes of verification. Instead, Furet leaves all that to the second half of the book, which is not Furet's product but an anthology of snippets from Marx about the French Revolution, assembled by another person, Lucien Calvié, and not directly linked up with the assertions by Furet. As a non-marxologist, Furet is doing his duty as a historian of the *Annales* school just as competently as when he retailed the Stalinist-ideological line in the 1950s. As a recent critic of Furet has said about his antirevolutionary output on the Revolution, Furet is not primarily a historian but rather an "ideologue."[10]

The result is that, in this year *two* centuries after the event, the academic establishment offers a work of such shoddy scholarship that its perpetrator does not even know that there exists an interesting question about Marx's view of Robespierre and the Terror. Furet thinks that Marx "portrays the opposition to Robespierre (the Girondins and the Thermidoreans) as representatives of the propertied classes" (meaning that they were the *only* such representatives), and is apparently unaware that Marx hailed "the opposition to Robespierre" *on the left*, i.e., the "Enragés" Roux and Leclerc in particular. In this same sentence by Furet, Marx supposedly portrays "the Robespierrist dictatorship as emanating from the only 'truly revolutionary class,' the 'innumerable masses.' " Through a concatenation of assertions, Marx is represented as believing that Robespierre was the "proletarian" paladin of the revolution, even though (as I have shown) virtually every reference to Robespierre by Marx (or Engels) is a hostile or distanced one.

It will occasion no surprise, therefore, if we reveal that Furet thinks that the relationship between the Terror and the outside war danger was *unknown* to Marx—instead of being the essential explanation of the Terror that Marx and Engels hailed at the very beginning of their political lives. Furet writes:

> .... Marx remained rigorously attached to this pure notion of historical necessity [an invention of marxologists], without making the least allusion, for example, to the role that might have been played in the Revolution by external events such as revolutionary France's war against the European monarchs.[11]

"Rigorously attached"—"pure notion"—not "the least allusion": these are the sweeping terms in which the ideologue wraps his sorry scholarship. The very thought for which Furet cannot find "the least allusion" in Marx in fact played a central role in *Engels'* exposition of Marx's views, repeatedly. And now we find that both Marx and Engels grasped this point enthusiastically when Köppen made it way back in 1842.

But the marxologists have learned how to handle such inconvenient facts: by means of the Engels-versus-Marx myth. It is clear how important it often is to rip Engels out of the Marx story, and why this game is so popular with a variety of fantasists who wish to write their own version of "Marxism" whether to refute it or toot it.

Furet is an advanced practitioner: *Engels' name does not even appear in Furet's index.* Engels has become a Non-Person, victim of a modern fate well known to Furet in his Stalinoid days.

2. "PACKING" THE HAGUE CONGRESS: THE FABLE ACCORDING TO HANS GERTH

In Special Note B of the present volume the essential facts are set forth about the rule-or-ruin operation by Bakunin and his wrecking crew, organized around the Hague Congress of 1872. This Note necessarily offers many cases of falsi*fictions* by marxologists (the term distinguishes falsi*fictions* from falsifi*cations*, as we have explained). I have staunchly refused to take space to refute *all* of the innumerable falsifictions that later clustered around this episode, since this would leave no room for other material. If now I make an exception, it is in order to take up the one falsifiction which is most often repeated.

I have seen this fable quoted at least a thousand times—no exaggeration—and one reason it is quoted so freely is that its source looks so authoritative. Professor Hans Gerth is an eminent sociologist, and no one would charge him with deliberate falsifi*cation*. When a set of minutes of the Hague Congress, perhaps made by Sorge, was discovered among the Schlüter papers at the University of Wisconsin, Professor Gerth was given the task of translating the document and editing the book in which it was published: *The First International. Minutes of the Hague Congress...*

Unfortunately, Gerth also felt called on to write the introduction, which should have offered the reader some necessary background history. It hardly even attempts to do so in its scant seven pages, and where it refers to the history of the International it is so confused as to be incompetent. What it does manage to do is devote over half its scanty space to heaving mudballs at Marx. Most of these missiles are standard and have been covered in *KMTR*: the Bakuninists "always denied" maintaining their secret society inside the International, and Gerth endorses their claim *ex cathedra*; Marx persecuted poor Bakunin unmercifully and "set out to destroy him"; and so on. It is evident that Gerth's sources are Guillaume's compendium of Bakuninist fabrications plus Carr's irresponsible biography of Marx.

But only one of these mudballs has generally achieved an independent life of its own as an accusation reference-noted to Gerth himself. Gerth writes:

> .... they [Marx and Engels] did what they could to "pack" the Congress. Engels paid the fare for the five members of the General Council he brought over.

And then he quotes two letters by Marx.[12] The fact that, right on the face of it, this passage has a number of puzzling features has not impaired Gerth's scholarly authority for all the aforesaid people who have quoted his statement with confidence.

Even before we get to the two letters by Marx, the reference to Engels' fare-paying must knit a few brows. To begin with, Gerth's own reference note for the fact is a blunder, a testament to sloppy scholarship.* (But few readers will check it, of course.) Secondly, in *all* the countries where the International had sections, delegates usually had to scrounge up travel expenses as best they could, preferably from their organizations but not infrequently from friends (including political supporters). This is so well known even today, for small revolutionary groups, especially those populated by impecunious workers, that it would be ridiculous to offer evidence. The reader must wonder: since this was done by every group in the International, including the Bakuninists, as well as by every group since the International, why is it a matter of "packing" the Congress?

Part of the answer lies in the way Gerth has twisted the words of Gustav

---

*The note goes: "Gustav Mayer, *Engels*, p.247." Readers would assume that this must point to the one-volume English condensation of Mayer's biography; and so they would be puzzled to find nothing pertinent on page 247. If they looked into the two-volume original edition, they would find their page 247 only after getting to the second volume.

Mayer's biography of Engels, which he quotes. Gerth writes about "the five *members* of the General Council he [Engels] brought over." It sounds as if Engels "brought them over" to the Hague in his pocket. What Gerth actually read in Mayer was that *these five "members" were the regularly elected delegates of the GC, and that the GC's treasury was empty.* There is no implication in Mayer's account that there was anything discreditable in Engels' picking up the tab, nor could there be any such implication. Nor were the five elected delegates of the GC the kind of people who would fit into Engels' pocket. Now one may ask: how did Gerth's mind work so as to impose this twist on the facts? The answer is that Gerth got it, not from the source he footnoted (Mayer), but from his real "authority," viz., the foxy work of Guillaume, who specialized in working out twists for easily confusable marxologists.

This should prepare us for those two letters by Marx. To make the story short, what our eminent scholar exhibits triumphantly, as evidence for the "packing," are a couple of letters by Marx, to comrades in America and Germany, *urging them to make sure that their organizations would be fully and properly represented by delegates at the Congress*, which meant "life or death" for the International.

—*What! that's all? Impossible! How could an intelligent scholar like Gerth fail to distinguish this necessary activity from "packing"?* Couldn't he tell the difference between active efforts to win a majority under the existing rules, on the one hand, and on the other the use of illegal and forbidden methods (as are implied by the term "pack")?

Well, Gerth does not bother to explain where he thought the "packing" came in, or what it consisted of; one supposes that he thought the mere words of Marx's letters were enough to indict him. The suspicion must surface that he simply did not understand what he read and quoted, not because his command of German was faulty but because he understood nothing of what was happening in the International, in particular how delegates were elected. The understanding of one term is particularly in question.

The two comrades to whom Marx wrote (in the letters quoted by Gerth) were not casual vagabonds whom Marx was proposing to "pack" into the Congress by a back door. They were both leaders of their respective local sections; beyond question they would get themselves elected as delegates if they wished. Why shouldn't they wish to go to the Hague? Because Sorge lived in the New York City area, in modest circumstances; and it took a fortune in money and an eon of time (from the viewpoint of a workingman) to journey across the ocean and the continent, and back again, just to cast a vote. The other correspondent, Dr. Kugelmann, lived in Hanover, Germany, which on my globe is only about a centimeter from the Hague;

but it was still a longish and expensive trip for a stay-at-home, across one or two borders, and a physician had to make special arrangements for an absence.

This was why Marx wrote in such urgent terms. First, to Sorge, after telling him the Congress date:

> It will just not do for you to put us off with a memorandum [*Memorial*].* *At this Congress it is a question of the life or death of the International. You and at least one other, if not two,* must come. As for the sections that send *no delegates* directly, they can send *mandates* (delegates' mandates).[12]

Whatever the first sentence means, Marx is obviously telling Sorge not to send any kind of casual document that would not be official. The official kind of document was a *mandate*, a delegate's mandate—a document signed by the proper official, naming a delegate. This concern about following the rules and regulations exactly is seen again in the same letter, in a paragraph *not* quoted by Gerth:

> Naturally every section, no matter of how many members, if not over 500 strong, [gets] only 1 delegate.

It is a reminder about the official basis for mandates, explaining the possibility of two delegates. So far, not a word about "packing."

On the contrary, Marx is trying to "get out the vote," to get representatives of the legitimate strength of the defenders of the International against the wreckers. At this point we can throw in the second letter cited by Gerth, in which Marx merely tells Dr. Kugelmann exactly what he told Sorge: that at the Hague "it is a question of the life or death of the International," and: "Germany must therefore have as many representatives as possible."[13]

Did Gerth understand the meaning of the term 'mandate'? This system of delegates' credentials was seldom used in the later history of the movement, for good reason, though it was unchallenged in the First International. A section or branch, entitled to (say) one delegate, filled out a formal document, signed by the proper officers, giving the essential information about the branch for the use of the Credentials Committee, and naming its delegate. The rules of the organization allowed the branch to

---

* Gerth's quote begins *after* this sentence. Note that in the translation of this letter by Padover, in his compilation *On the First International* (p.567), this entire sentence is unaccountably omitted.—The translation of Marx's letters given above are my own; Gerth's versions are based on an early publication which is unreliable in detail (e.g., emphasis) but fortunately nothing substantive is involved.

name *any member of the International* as the delegate, and the minutes of the Congresses are peppered with allusions to delegates who were *not* members of the branch they represented. (At the only International congress he attended, in Basel in 1869, Bakunin represented Lyons although the Russian then resided in Geneva.) Later, this was sometimes called a "proxy system."

But the branch might also decide to leave the delegate's name blank temporarily, until it found a suitable person to represent it, *one who could in fact get to the Congress*. Blank mandates were publicly discussed and known; they were not illegal, though used as a last resort. Again, we must emphasize, for obvious reasons, that blank mandates were as freely used by the Bakuninist forces as by any other tendency in the movement.

This system was used due to the difficulties that faced every branch about sending delegates to a Congress at a distance. Its drawbacks were obvious, but for too many cases the only alternative was to send no delegates at all, or to allow rich individuals to represent the branch simply because they could afford the trip. Again and again Marx or Engels received letters about supporters who would be unable to go to the Hague because they could not afford it.[14] In any case, the 'mandate' system as described was not controversial at the Hague; whatever the system, all tendencies scrambled to get as many delegates for their faction as possible, and the operating system was used equally by all.

Now it is easy to believe that the average reader of Gerth's introduction would know nothing about the 'mandate' system, but it is hard to believe this of Gerth himself—only because he had (presumably) just translated every word of the Congress minutes he was editing, and nearly the first three days of the Congress were taken up with detailed arguments about delegates' mandates. He had just read pages and pages of discussions at the Congress over the validity of credentials. He had read, for example, about delegates who routinely presented the Congress committee with as many as *three* different mandates from different places! Could he make anything of this?

In citing that "incriminating" letter of Marx's to Sorge, Gerth took the space (in a very short Introduction) to give the whole list of possible delegates that Marx had included for Sorge's use, precisely in order to avoid a blank mandate. Obviously Gerth thought this was somehow damaging, a "smoking gun"! This is a measure of his incompetence in this field.

Now if he had been moderately well acquainted with Marx's and Engels' correspondence, he would not have had to rely only on ammunition supplied by Guillaume. He could have cited, for example, Engels' letter to Liebknecht six months before. It exhorted Liebknecht in the same terms as Marx wrote to Kugelmann, about getting a maximum of delegates, and added that the official forms must be carefully followed, warning: "Since the Bakuninists and Proudhonists will probably do their utmost, the mandates will be strictly examined . . ." Engels alerted Liebknecht that the German organization had to regulate dues payments with care "so that its mandates cannot be contested at the Congress . . ." On the other hand: writing to his loyal supporter Cuno, Engels stressed (repeatedly) that the Italian Bakuninists could do anything they liked within the rules, and their mandates would not be challenged: ". . . the Italians have the right to commit all the idiocies they wish, and the General Council will counteract them only by way of peaceful debate." "So long as these gentlemen remain on lawful grounds, the General Council will gladly let them do as they like . . ." Engels wrote to J. P. Becker that things were going well—"But *only if*, on our part, we muster all forces." And he stressed the danger that the Bakuninists might get a majority "through the negligence of our friends."[15] *That* was the danger: negligence meant doing less than was possible to mobilize a majority at the Hague to defend the International.

While Bakunin's factional correspondence was industriously searched out and destroyed by his friends, as we report elsewhere, the correspondence by Marx and Engels *and* their friends has been industriously collected and published. And every word of it speaks to the care taken by Marx and his friends to win a fair majority at the Hague in open debate. If we were to use the Gerth mode of scholarship, we could quote a number of situations in which the Bakuninists used dirty tricks to gain mandates; for the letters of Marx, Engels and their correspondents are peppered with statements about these goings-on.[16] Fortunately, for various reasons it was not necessary to turn the Congress into a month-long credentials session. But looking at it all in hindsight, there was one basic diference between the two sides that does not depend merely on charges and counter charges: the Bakuninists believed *on principle* in using dirty tricks to defeat the evil Authoritarians in any way possible, and they proclaimed this principle openly as an anarchist mark of honor.

• • •

Now let us return to our original subject: Gerth and scholarship. We submit a test specimen, almost of laboratory quality, using a passage of Gerth's Introduction which is *not* about packing the Hague Congress.

Although Gerth had no space in his Introduction to explain much about the history and functioning of the International, he had space enough to include some other items that appealed to his scholarly soul for the purpose of discrediting Marx. On his second page, he has a relatively considerable passage on the Paris Commune and Marx's defense of it, *The Civil*

War in France. We refrain from commenting on his views about the Commune, since these might provoke us to digressions; but in the middle of this passage is the following demonstration of a mode of scholarship. Gerth writes:

> Marx drew the ire of a hostile European society upon himself and the International, for he published the pamphlet [the address on the Commune] and several addresses in its name without being too scrupulous about prior consent and endorsement.

The ordinary reader will understand Gerth to be saying that the "ire of a hostile European society" was due to—the handling of the Address inside the General Council! Let us try to ignore this absurdity. Gerth has the following scholarly footnote appended at this point as evidence for his substantive assertion about Marx's lack of scruples:

> "Some of the Englishmen whose names, as members of the General Council, were appended to it, afterwards declared that they had not seen its contents until it was published."—Carr, *Marx*, pp. 218, 223.

This refers to one of the less interesting episodes involving some English trade-union leaders' attempts to rid themselves of the revolutionary taint of the Commune. We see that neither of our scholars, Gerth nor Carr, thought it important to mention here that the Address had been endorsed *unanimously* at the regular General Council meeting called for the purpose with due notification to all; that *every* GC document since the beginning had been routinely signed by the entire GC list; and that this format of the publication had been routinely executed by the secretary, John Hales, not Marx. We are interested at the moment in a different aspect of scholarship.

Please note that Gerth's reference footnote to Carr pointed to *two* pages in Carr, five pages apart. It might be supposed that both pages said the same thing. Not so. On page 218 Carr made the statement duly quoted by Gerth. *Five pages later, on page 223, without making any connection, Carr gave the following information:*

> Hales, the new secretary of the General Council, signed a letter to the press explaining that Odger and Lucraft had received a summons to the meeting at which the famous manifesto [the Address] had been unanimously approved, and that it was the custom of the Council to append to its publications the signatures of all its members, whether they had actually participated in their preparation or not.

We leave aside Carr's irresponsible handling of the matter—irresponsible because, as author, he took no responsibility for ascertaining the truth— for we are interested in Gerth. Gerth was aware of Carr's page 223 because he referred to it in his own footnote. But he kept its content a scholarly secret. All the reader learned from his own scholarly pages was that certain unnamed Englishmen later made a complaint which reflected badly on Marx ... And what reader could doubt that the accusation must be true, for otherwise would an eminent scholar like Professor Gerth regurgitate it in this way?

The principle of this scholarship is clear: *Against Marx, anything goes*. To paraphrase Clough's well-known lines:

> *You must not lie, but need not act*
> *Officiously to check a fact.*

For some reason I can't remember the name of the old Anglo-Saxon king who commanded the flood to recede from shore.

• • •

This volume is the same as previous volumes in format and other technical respects. The following reminders may be useful.

Notes. There is a sharp distinction between *reference notes*, which are relegated to the back of the book, and *footnotes*, which are intended to be read as part of the text. The general reader is advised to ignore all the superscript numbers that pepper the pages: the reference notes mainly offer information on sources and some other technical matters, but never affect the line of thought.

Quotes. Inside quoted passages, all emphasis is in the original, and all [bracketed words] represent my own interpolations.

Degree-mark symbol. This unorthodox sign is used to indicate that certain quoted words or passages are in *English* in the original. A double degree mark (°°) at the beginning of a quotation means that the whole passage was originally written in English. Inside a quotation, words or phrases originally in English are marked off using the symbol like quotation marks, °°as here.°° (This is done only when necessary, not in every case.)

Translations. Where possible, I have used English translations from the volumes so far published of the Marx-Engels *Collected Works (MECW)* or from the three-volume Marx-Engels *Selected Works (MESW)*. All translations or revisions of translations not otherwise ascribed are my own.

Single quotes. These, with the punctuation marks outside, are used to indicate that a word is being exhibited—that a term is being used as a term—rather than being either quoted or used as an integral part of the sentence.

Finally, the term 'falsi*fiction* does not mean the same as falsi*fication*, as explained in *KMTR 3*, p.3.

1 | OF UTOPIAN SOCIALISM

The types or schools of socialism considered here are grouped mainly as a convenient way to organize Marx's views on the subject of movement alternatives. They certainly are not an attempt at an exhaustive listing in these pages. They seldom appear as pure schools or consciously organized tendencies. They are often simply common currents or strains or ingredients in the socialist movements of the time.

The names or labels usually assigned to them have most often been given by others—critics, rivals, enemies—rather than by themselves. This is surely true of the ingredient called utopian socialism.

1. ACCENTING THE POSITIVE

When the *Communist Manifesto* was written, the modern socialist movement had been in existence only a few decades, but it already exhibited virtually all of the currents that were to become prominent in the next century in more developed form. The spectrum of possible socialisms was in active creation before anyone could turn around and say Karl Marx. And by the 1840s all the rival tendencies were already heatedly denouncing each other, especially the righteous exponents of unity who denounced everyone else for denouncing them. In other words, the situation was normal; there was a lively forum of ideas. Compared with much of the resulting polemical literature, Section III of the *Manifesto*, which looked critically at the socialist field, was as sober as a dissertation.

This section of the Manifesto presented five schools of socialism that needed discussing, and what it called "Critical-Utopian Socialism and Communism" was only one of these, the fifth and last. Marx clearly did not agree with the later writers on socialist history who lump all pre-Marxian socialism under the label of utopian socialism. The utopian element had to be analyzed out of the picture.

Socialist history, as it is written, has not been fortunate in its account of utopian socialism. Cole's *History of Socialist Thought* (widely quoted) states erroneously that "in 1839, the economist, Jérôme [Adolphe] Blanqui, in his pioneer *History of Political Economy*, characterised them all as 'Utopian Socialists'—a name which was to become lastingly attached to them through its adoption by Marx and Engels in the *Communist Manifesto*."[1] But in point of fact the book by the elder Blanqui did not use the term 'utopian socialist' at all, but only "utopian economists."* Indeed, the term 'socialist' itself was still so new that it appeared here only twice, as a designation for Owen only.[2] The word 'utopian' had already been around for a long time, and had been hitched to a variety of nouns before this; getting hitched to 'economist' was no great innovation. In 1845 a then-noted book by Karl Grün actually counterposed "utopianism" (*Utopismus*) to "scientific socialism."[3]

And the Manifesto itself did not use the term 'utopian socialism' but a hyphenated one, "critical-utopian socialism." This may be taken as quibbling, perhaps, but we point out that all this matters mainly because of the marxological myth that Marx invented the term 'utopian socialism' merely as a contemptuous denunciation. Marx's actual term, "critical-utopian socialism," is at odds with the myth.

If we concern ourselves with what is really in the Manifesto, a characteristic that leaps to the eye is the thoroughgoing distinction that Marx made between the innovative founders of the schools and the sects that later operated in their names. This was especially true of the Saint-Simonian and Fourierist sects, which became active after the founder's death; but it was precisely the writings of Fourier and Saint-Simon themselves that had the greatest impact on the young Marx. Long afterward, as in *Socialism Utopian and Scientific*, Marx and Engels continued to speak with utmost admiration of the contributions made by the germinal thinkers at the same time that they criticized the retrogressive role of the sect followers. This combination is found in full force in the Manifesto.

The combination is signaled to the reader by the hyphenated name that the Manifesto confers on this socialist current: *critical-utopian* socialism (and communism), not 'utopian socialism.' The valuable positive contribution of these socialists, it says, lies in their "critical element":

> They attack every principle of existing society. Hence they are full of the most valuable materials for the enlightenment of the working

---

* This is only one of three factual errors in this single sentence of Cole's. As for the other two: the 'utopian' label was not applied to "them all" but only to Fourier and Owen; and the work was published in 1837, not 1839.

class. Their positive propositions on the future society*... point solely to the disappearance of class antagonisms which were, at that time, only just cropping up, and which, in these publications, are recognized in their earliest, indistinct and undefined forms only. Their proposals, therefore, are of a purely utopian character.[4]

In *The German Ideology* Marx and Engels repeatedly identified the strong side of the utopians: "the Saint-Simonian criticism of existing conditions" was "the most important aspect of Saint-Simonism"; and "The critical side of Fourier" was "his most important contribution."[5] This explains the contrast between the founders and their sect followers, who hardened the fanciful side into a dogma:

> Fourier's orthodox disciples of the *Démocratie Pacifique* [their organ] show most clearly how little the real content of these systems lies in their systematic form; they are, for all their orthodóxy, doctrinaire bourgeois, the very antipodes of Fourier.[6]

The Manifesto further emphasized this contrast: "although the originators of these systems were, in many respects, revolutionary, their disciples have, in every case, formed mere reactionary sects."[7]

No one has praised the contributions of the early utopians more enthusiastically than Engels, who repeatedly wrote that Marxism itself

> rests on the shoulders of Saint-Simon, Fourier and Owen—three men who, in spite of all their fantastic notions and all their utopianism, have their place among the most eminent thinkers of all times, and whose genius anticipated innumerable things the correctness of which is now being scientifically proved by us....[8]

Engels' *Socialism Utopian and Scientific* begins with this appreciation of their revolutionary roles, an appreciation broadly applied not only to the early utopians but also to the Enlighteners who inspired them:

> The great men who in France prepared men's minds for the coming revolution were themselves extreme revolutionists. They recognized no external authority of any kind whatever. Religion, natural science, society, political institutions—everything was subjected to the most unsparing criticism.... [9]

For criticism—uninhibited analysis—was inherently revolutionary.[10]

In *Socialism Utopian and Scientific*, Part 1, the part dealing with the utopians, overwhelmingly accents the positive. After a single paragraph stating

---

* So in Marx's original of 1848. In the English version by Moore-Engels, this became: "The practical measures proposed in them..." I take it that by 1888 Engels wanted to de-emphasize the future-looking aspect, which might discourage practical Anglo-Saxon minds.

their utopian-fantasy side, Engels declares: "These facts once established, we need not dwell a moment longer upon this side of the question, now wholly belonging to the past. We can leave it to the literary small fry to solemnly quibble over these phantasies.... For ourselves, we delight in the stupendously grand thoughts and germs of thought that everywhere break out through their phantastic covering...."[11] And it is to the "grand thoughts" that the rest of this part is devoted.

Without losing sight of their negative sides, Engels shows how the foundations of socialist thought were laid in their writings—in Saint-Simon's historical view of the class struggle, of the economic basis of politics, of the coming abolition of the state; in Fourier's witty and insightful critique of bourgeois society and its miseries, his genial social satire, his dialectical view of the stages in the history of society; in Owen's materialist teachings, his belief in the regenerating power of humanized conditions of labor, his educational innovations, his understanding of the relation between the growing productive forces and the need for rational economic planning and organization, his stimulus to cooperatives.[12] Cabet is not discussed here along with these great innovators, for, coming in the wake of the great three, he rigidified the utopian side without opening new critical vistas.

Marx, like Engels, paid little heed to Cabet as a thinker; he mentions Cabet's name more usually as an example of the ready-made system, the negative side of utopianism.[13] He gave Cabet more attention and respect as the leader of a significant pre-1848 group of French workers.[14] Marx's emphasis on the difference between a founding ideologist and the movement he founds is well expressed in *The German Ideology*, where he explains that the first utopian writings had "propaganda value as popular novels" in the early days. Cabet

> should on no account be judged by his system but rather by his polemical writings [previously quoted, against Buchez][15], in fact his whole activity as a party leader.... As the party [i.e., the movement] develops, these systems lose all importance and are at best retained purely nominally as catchwords. Who in France believes in [Cabet's] Icaria...?[16]

So Cabet's name was separated from the three great innovators. In fact, so heavy was Engels' emphasis on the positive contributions of Saint-Simon, Fourier, and Owen that, when this part of *Anti-Dühring* was taken over into the first part of the booklet *Socialism Utopian and Scientific*, Engels had to write an additional *critical* paragraph to strike a reasonable balance in terms of the modern movement. This addition discussed how the utopian mode of thought fostered the later mishmash of eclectic socialist ideas that rubbed the sharp edges off the revolutionary aims of socialism.[17] The new passage took the place of a couple of pages of *Anti-Dühring* in which Engels forcefully denounced Dühring for his contemptuous attitude toward and ignorant undervaluation of the three great utopians, in language so enthusiastic that one must wonder whether Engels gives them *too much* credit.[18]

Engels has been emphasized here because his *Socialism Utopian and Scientific* is often referred to as if it were mainly a denunciation of the utopians, apparently after an exhaustive study of all four words of its title. This is associated with the marxological myth that 'utopian' is simply a "term of opprobrium" in Marx or Engels, or that they simply "cavalierly dismissed" the utopians.[19] (To be sure, when you run across this sciolism, you know you are looking at a particularly ignorant marxologist.)

Marx's references to Fourier and Saint-Simon were in the same spirit as Engels' encomiums. For example, in a note for publication in the French press, Marx wrote that Proudhon "poured gross insult over the utopian socialists and communists whom [I] honored as precursors of modern socialism."[20] It is easy for us to verify this: Proudhon's *Carnets*, published only in our own times, show that alleged "libertarian" foaming at the mouth as he blackguards Fourier et al.

As Engels wrote, "Marx spoke only with admiration of the genius and encyclopedic mind of Saint-Simon," but this statement occurs in an interesting context. In Volume 3 of *Capital* Marx mentions that Saint-Simon and his disciples lumped workers and capitalists together under the head of *travailleurs* (workers) as distinct from the idle aristocracy. Here Marx reminds us that only in his last work did Saint-Simon address himself to the working class and adopt its emancipation as a goal; his previous writings had been "encomiums of modern bourgeois society in contrast to the feudal order.... What a difference compared with the contemporaneous writings of Owen!" This judgment by Marx is quite accurate; it states a negative side of Saint-Simon's theorizing. Marx had recognized as early as 1844 that Saint-Simon himself never proposed a socialistic form of society.[21]

At this point, as editor of *Capital*, Engels appends a longish footnote, lest a reader think that this passage in Marx's manuscript expressed the sum total of Marx's opinion of the great utopian; and Engels virtually apologizes for Saint-Simon's shortcoming, blunting Marx's critique.[22] So sensitive was Engels to even the appearance of derogation.

Actually, Marx's passage was concerned mainly with the Saint-Simonian disciples who became the manipulators of the Crédit Mobilier and "Bonapartist socialism."[23] Engels, in his excess of pious regard for Saint-Simon's reputation, gives the impression of glossing over the founder's degree of responsibility for the direction taken by the disciples. Or perhaps he did not rightly understand, as Marx did, that Saint-Simon stopped well short of proposing the abolition of bourgeois society.[24] In any case, here Engels was wrong and Marx was right. The irony lies in the fact that Engels tended to be too soft on the utopians, not that he "cavalierly dismissed" them.

While Marx and Engels paid homage to the "critical" (social-analytical) element in these great innovators, *it was the utopian element that was subsequently hardened into sects as socialism took organized form.* We have to separate this utopian element out, especially since utopianism by no means died with its three great exponents.

2. "SCIENTIFIC SOCIALISM"

The counterposition of 'utopian socialism' to 'scientific socialism' has been associated with a widespread misconception. The special difficulty here is that the term 'scientific socialism' is often taken askew, especially in English.

In modern English, more than in the Continental languages, the word 'science' and its derivatives have tended to become specialized as references to the natural sciences. As Raymond Williams notes, "This causes considerable problems in contemporary translation, notably from the French."[25] The case is just as true of German, in particular socialist writings in German—not just Marx's usage. Even where the English 'science' is allowed to refer to social studies, the problem has stimulated hazy debates over something called "scientism" and over the applicability of scientific method to society, or over the mechanical derivation of social principles from physical-scientific analogues. These are not the problems that concern us here.

It is a question of what the term *wissenschaftlicher Sozialismus* (scientific socialism) meant to Marx, as well as to his contemporary world.

The German word *Wissenschaft* means knowledge, hence the learning and scholarship that accumulate knowledge. It *includes* the idea of science, and it tends to get translated as 'science.' But it is by no means limited to the natural sciences; it embraces any body of knowledge that a scholar or researcher might investigate, much more loosely than English writers tend to tolerate. Thus, today as yesterday, a good dictionary will define not only the *exakten Wissenschaften* or *Naturwissenschaft(en)* but also the *historische Wissenschaften* and even the *schönen Wissenschaften* (belles-lettres).[26]

There is a good example, for present purposes, that we have mentioned in another connection: the first society for Jewish studies, established in Germany in the early nineteenth century, called its subject the *Wissenschaft des Judentums*—this in its society title; in English "the science of Jewry" would be a mistranslation.[27] In France too, but later, the Société Scientifique Littéraire was founded to publish materials on Jewish studies.

English shrinks from calling such research by the name of "science"; in German this broad use of *Wissenschaft* and *wissenschaftlich* is normal. It is too bad that the English language does not have a word that is congruent with *Wissenschaft* or even the French *science*. Its 'science' has been narrowed.

Another example is provided by the title of the work by Engels from which his *Socialism Utopian and Scientific* was derived—usually called *Anti-Dühring*. Its full title was *Herr Eugen Dühring's Revolution in Science*, in German ... *Umwälzung der Wissenschaft*. This uses 'science' in the Continental sense; Dühring's field was mainly a complex of philosophy and the social sciences.

Everywhere in German literature, *Wissenschaft* and its cognates are used without strain for *any study adding to the sum total of knowledge*; any subject of (scholarly) study. This is illustrated in Engels' remark that "socialism, since it has become a science, demands that it be pursued as a science, that is, that it be studied."[28] In English this is virtually a non sequitur.

Still it is true that the broad Continental meaning has had an impact in some sectors of English-language literature, beginning with Second International publications (especially translations) and continuing with later Comintern literature. When in such contexts Marx's *Capital* (for example) is called a "scientific work" to distinguish it from Marx's journalistic or propagandist or epistolary writings, this term is *not* a claim that the method of *Capital* is equivalent to a laboratory demonstration. (The meaning of scientific method in the social sciences is not under discussion here.) In this context, socialist usage in English has often made do with the term 'theoretical work,' in distinction from 'propagandist work.'

Well then, it is the broad meaning of 'science' as *Wissenschaft* that became attached to the efforts of socialists to base their program not on dreams, visions, or sentiments, but on a knowledgeable analysis of the real forces operating in society. In the days when socialism was very young, all "modern" thought wanted to be thought scientific, in aspiration at least. The new thinking of Campanella, of Francis Bacon's *New Atlantis*, of the Encyclopedists, of almost anyone you can mention, was more or less imbued with scientific thought; and the new thinking of the socialists took this course just as naturally.

This immediately confronts us with another widespread myth, about Marx's relation to this development. It follows from these facts that Marx was *not* the first, and never claimed to be the first, to set the objective of establishing socialism on a scientific (*wissenschaftlich*) basis.

On the contrary, this objective was already a well-known idea and aspiration when Marx first heard of socialism. The aim of working out *a* "scientific" socialism was fairly common among Marx's predecessors and contemporaries, ranging from academic types like Dühring to socialistic yellow-journalists like Emile de Girardin, who opined that "*La science* is the true name of socialism."[29]

Moses Hess has been credited with being the first,[30] but a decade before Hess, Buchez had called his own tendency "Science Nouvelle" after splitting from the Saint-Simonians and establishing his *Journal des Sciences Morales et Politiques*. A similar magazine title, *Phalanx or Journal of Social Science*, has been vaunted for the American Fourierists of 1843–1845.[31] Before either Buchez or Brook Farm, the Saint-Simonians had looked to "science" as their guide: "Saint-Simon had seen the solution of all social problems in the attainment of an empirical science of man," explains the social historian G. G. Iggers; and the Saint-Simonians "tried to demonstrate the 'scientific' character of society," at a time when the term 'science' (avers Iggers) "denoted the reduction of reality into a system." When Frances Wright was lecturing in America around 1836, her exposition explicitly called for a scientific approach in the explanation of history.[32]

Examples can be multiplied; but Lorenz Stein must not be overlooked. When Stein published his pioneer work on French socialism in 1842, he heavily emphasized that socialism had to be viewed as a part of the science of society (*Staatswissenschaft*, political science if you will), and he refuted the superficial notion that socialist theories were merely "empty dreams of unscientific minds." On the contrary, after several pages of this emphasis, Stein wound up *defining* socialism, in letter-spaced type, as "the systematic science of equality realized in economic life, state, and society, through the rule of labor."[33] "Socialism is a scientific system," he wrote in the 1850 edition of his work. Mengelberg says of Stein that he "elaborated Saint-Simon's interpretation of socialism as the first manifestation of a 'science of society.' "[34] Three years after Stein's first edition, as already mentioned,[35] Karl Grün counterposed "scientific socialism" to "utopianism."

In short, the widespread marxological claim that Marx invented, and imported into socialism, the view that socialism *should* be based on a scientific approach to society gives Marx too much credit, on the one hand, and, on the other hand, obscures any useful discussion about the meaning of science in social analysis. Naturally, aspiration is not achievement; if (say) Saint-Simon or anyone else saw himself as a social scientist, this does not oblige us to agree with him.

Marx was one of many socialist pioneers who aspired to *really* base socialism on a scientific view of society. What defines Marxism is his success—or for enemies, his failure. Given his materialist world outlook, this basis in scientific method was of special and fundamental importance for him. When Engels wrote down his opinion that Marx's was "the only scientific socialism that has ever existed,"[36] this was, after all, only another way of saying that he agreed with him—which is not news.

It is, I think, not hard to show from our present-day standpoint how far Saint-Simon, Buchez, Hess, etc. were removed from a consistently scientific analysis of society. Everyone has the democratic right to argue that the same is true of Marx, and half of them have published on this point, it seems. But, as stressed previously, this is not our present subject. The fact is that some sort of "scientific" socialism, the view that socialism should be wedded to science, was widely accepted in the earliest socialist circles, including those called utopian.

The idea that the term 'scientific socialism' involved some special esoteric claim, beyond what we have explained, was repudiated by Marx when he ran across it. Like many other canards, it was invented by Bakunin— the most prolific inventor of lies and slanders that the socialist movement has ever seen—in the course of a book larded with racist and personal smears against Marx. Marx jotted down some short comments as he made excerpts from Bakunin's tome. At one point Bakunin charged that the "Marxists" look to a despotism under an aristocracy of "learned men," which they called "learned [or academic] socialism" or "scientific socialism." (Bakunin really had Lassalle in mind, but he was not choosy about smears.) Marx's note on this said that the first term had "never been used," and that "scientific socialism"

> has been used only in opposition to utopian socialism, which would like to saddle the people with new chimerical fancies, instead of reserving its science for the comprehension of the social movement created by the people themselves; see my book against Proudhon [*Poverty of Philosophy*]. . . . [37]

This comment, that the idea of a *wissenschaftlicher* socialism should be understood in the context of a critique of utopian socialism, helps to illuminate both sides of the comparison. *It is a question of scientific method, which concerns itself with the real forces and facts of social development and not with mere fantasies and feelings.*

We can now directly address the question of what utopianism as a method meant to Marx, and why this method had to be superseded by an approach based on inquiry into the realities of social relations and the forces governing social change (the "laws of motion" of society)—in short, superseded by a scientific approach in the broad sense of the word.

3. UTOPIANISM

In the course of over three centuries of use in English and other languages, the word 'utopian' picked up a variety of connotations, like barnacles. Long before Marx, 'utopian' might imply any of the following ideas: anything considered *impossible*; anything considered *ideal* or *ideally perfect*; anything *imaginary* or involving the imagination; any concern with the shape of the *future*. The word often suggested adjectives like *visionary, perfectionist, chimerical*. All of these meanings, whether incompatible or not, are "correct"; that is, anyone has the dictionary's authority to tangle thought into knots.

It is therefore child's play to prove that anyone is "utopian" in some unspecified sense. To be sure, this way of proving "utopianism" has a drawback: it is likely to be empty of content. This word game has been played with Marx *ad infinitum*. If nothing else works, Marx was certainly concerned with the future, wasn't he?

The game is further complicated by colloquial uses. As we have emphasized in other cases,[38] Marx had no compunction about using a word both in a scientific and strict sense (in one context) and in a loose or colloquial sense (in another context, particularly in journalistic articles and letters). For example: Marx wrote in his 1848 paper that "our readers have never entertained utopian hopes regarding Vienna," i.e., about revolutionary possibilities there.[39] Here the word seems to connote overoptimistic expectations about impossibilities or improbabilities; though it can be argued that such "utopian" hopes about the Vienna revolution were inconsistent with the real relationship of forces. Again: about the "right to a job" watchword in 1848, Engels explained in a letter that the Paris workers were attracted to it "because it looked so practical, so little utopian, so realizable without any trouble," whereas in reality it could be carried out in capitalist society only in the form of "nonsensical national workshops."[40] This seems to use "utopian" with mostly the colloquial flavor. It is also not hard to find journalistic articles in which Marx, in a "you too" spirit, says that bourgeois schemes for reforming capitalism are "utopian,"[41] apparently meaning impossible—though there is usually the background thought that this impossibility is due to the real forces of society.

Marx was as well acquainted as anyone with the conservative propensity to dismiss proposals for basic social change as "utopian," that is, chimerical and impossible. Summarizing the usual bourgeois-philistine viewpoint in an 1848 article, he commented that in this view "If you demand the transformation of the [socioeconomic] organization as a whole, then you are destructive, revolutionary, unscrupulous, utopian, and you overlook *partial* reforms. Hence the result: leave everything as it is."[42]

This whole sprawling congeries of traditional and casual uses of 'utopian' has to be put aside in order to focus on the central meaning of *utopianism as counterposed to a scientific approach*.

This investigation begins with an elementary step: the rock-bottom need for positive knowledge about the real world of society as the basis for theorizing, as against theory-spinning out of the blue. Marx *began* with this conviction even before he became a socialist. When he was still the militant-democratic editor of the left-liberal *Rheinische Zeitung* in 1842, he was already hostile to the prevalent forms of theory-spinning.

This was one of his charges against a group of ex-friends on the Berlin University campus who called themselves "The Free," and who wanted to get into his newspaper's columns. Marx expressed his opinion after receiving a letter from one of them, "whose favorite category is, most appropriately, what *ought* to be."

> I demanded of them [related Marx in a letter] less vague reasoning, magniloquent phrases and self-satisfied self-adoration, and more definiteness, more attention to the actual state of affairs, more expert knowledge.... I requested further that religion should be criticized in the framework of criticism of political conditions rather than that political conditions should be criticized in the framework of religion.... [43]

Indeed, the "political conditions" were rooted in "the actual state of affairs," whereas the "framework of religion" was then another area for theory-spinning.

The following year, the same concern for actuality-as-starting-point brought about a basic reorientation for Marx, as he began trying to work out a new socialist approach, in an exchange of letters published in the *Deutsch-Französische Jahrbücher*. We have already discussed this under the head of "How to Develop a Movement Program,"[44] but now let us view the same train of thought as part of Marx's critique of utopianism. We note first that Marx, a new-fledged socialist, immediately links the utopianism of the theory-spinners with the doctrinairism of the sect.

No one, Marx argues here, has an exact notion of what the desired new world is to be like. Various sect leaders propose various visions of a new society. Should we compete by imagining new and better Icarias? No, let us take a "new direction" altogether: "we do not dogmatically anticipate the world but rather want to find the new world only through criticism of the old."

> If constructing the future and settling the matter for all time is not our job, yet what we have to accomplish at the present time is all the more certain—I mean *ruthless criticism of everything that exists....* [45]

Instead of raising a new "dogmatic banner" (Marx goes on) we should help the dogmatists clarify their own tenets to themselves. How? Through the actual interests of the people, which center especially about political issues. We must start with "these interests even as they are, and not counterpose to them, ready-made, any particular system like, say, the *Voyage en Icarie* [by Cabet]." With this critical method we can develop, out of the "existing reality," our own idea of what to aim at. We do not confront the world as doctrinaires with a new principle and call on them to kneel before it in admiration: "We develop new principles for the world out of the principles of the world itself." We show the world why it is actually struggling, and from this develop a new consciousness for the world.[46]

And Marx even concludes: "It will be demonstrated that it is not a question of a big hiatus in thinking between past and future but of *carrying out* the thinking of the past."[47] He is clearly trying to bend the stick the other way: away from overemphasis on the miraculous leap from the bad old world of today to the shining new world of tomorrow, and toward emphasizing the *continuity* from struggles over actualities to the reshaping of actualities.

In this argumentation, utopianism is not the center of the problem; but utopianism can virtually be defined as that which Marx is combating here. There is no mystery about where Marx acquired this approach, for it emerges essentially out of Hegel's approach to history. It is heavily stressed in what is perhaps the best-known locus in all Hegel, the preface to his *Philosophy of Right*.[48]

Whereas Marx exhibited no early susceptibility to the utopian mode of thought even in his early period of left-Democratic apprenticeship in politics—or at least no record of it remains—the case was otherwise with Engels. Right after he did his small part of the *Holy Family*—which means, right after he had teamed up with Marx but before the two had associated very much—Engels wrote an enthusiastic account of the utopian community experiments in America, to prove that communism was "feasible in practice."[49]

There can be little doubt that it must have been his further collaboration with Marx that straightened him out on utopian-communitarian forms of socialism. Soon came the first clear statement of the balanced (positive and negative) view of the great utopians, the view they both adopted. For several months in 1845 they discussed the project of publishing a "Library of the Best Foreign Socialist Writers," mainly French and English—an anthology of socialist ideas in texts—and Marx even drew up a list of authors to be translated, naturally including the great utopians.[50] When Engels suggested this idea, Fourier had been in the forefront of his mind, and in fact a selection from Fourier was the only part of the project actually published. By this time, the latter part of 1845, Engels wrote an introduction to the selection which put Fourier into perspective.

Here Engels' main theme is praise for Fourier, especially as against the German theoreticians who take ideas from French socialism and Hegelianize them in the worst sense. What these people find in Fourier is "only what is worst and most theoretical: the schematic plans of future society, the *social systems*." (*Systems* means: artificially constructed systems of speculative thought; we will return to this term.) "The best aspect, the *criticism of existing society, the real basis, the main task of any investigation of social questions, they have calmly pushed aside.*" Within the framework of this balanced appreciation, Engels praises Fourier for "correctly understanding the past and the present," even if he "speculatively constructs the future" along utopian lines. Even when Fourier writes speculative nonsense, like his visions of lemonade seas and "anti-lions," his "cheerful nonsense" is preferable to "the gloomy and profound nonsense of these German theoreticians."[51]

Thus we see that, well before Marx and Engels formulated their opinion of utopianism in terms of the counterposition *utopian socialism / scientific socialism*, their essential criticism was already clear. Its crux was the utopian *leap into abstraction*. The trouble with (say) Fourier was not a failure to present a critique of actuality, a brilliant one at that. But this critique existed on one side of a yawning gulf, on the other side of which was the alternative, bright new world. To get to the other side, the utopian took a great leap into the void, on the wings of speculative abstraction.

Since no two utopian speculators dreamed up the same new world—or leaped over the void in the same direction—it was inevitable that, when their brilliant insights hardened into organizational form, the result was a sect. A sect was a theory-based group which counterposed its specially revealed body of doctrine against that of the next brilliant mind who fluttered a pair of wings and took off. In an article in 1847, Marx reminded that the utopian method was not limited to socialists: bourgeois thinkers, in the days when their new class was struggling against feudalism to change society, also fell into a "more or less utopian, dogmatic, or doctrinaire" pattern as long as they reflected the undeveloped character of the social struggle.[52]

In a draft for the *Communist Manifesto*, Marx addressed the charge (or diagnosis) of utopianism also to the bourgeois ruling class, in the following terms:

> The Communists do not put forward any new theory of property. They state a fact. You deny the most striking facts. You have to deny them. You are backward-looking utopians.[53]

It is just as well that this formulation was stricken; it exaggerated. But what it exaggerated was the contrast between a "new theory of property" which is sucked out of one's thumb and a theory derived from an analysis of "facts," that is, from a study of the actual development of society. This highlighted the difference between the utopian and the scientific approach.

4. FIRST EXPOSITION

The first passage in which Marx clearly counterposed utopian socialism to the scientific approach occurred in his book against Proudhon, *The Poverty of Philosophy*, in 1847. Thirty years later, it was this passage he remembered when he jotted down his brief comment on Bakunin, above-quoted in Section 2.

Marx, writing this work in French, continually used *la science* in the broad sense of *Wissenschaft* that we have explained:

> Just as the [bourgeois] *economists* are the scientific representatives of the bourgeois class, so the *socialists* and the *communists* are the theoreticians of the proletarian class.

The bourgeois economists were here called "scientific" (though they were wrong) but the word was not used for the socialistic "theoreticians" of 1847, who were mostly utopians. The passage continued: so long as the class struggle is still at a low stage of development, "these theoreticians are merely utopians who, to meet the wants of the oppressed classes, improvise systems and go in search of a regenerating science." But as the proletarian struggle becomes clearer, "they no longer need to seek science in their minds; they have only to take note of what is happening before their eyes and to become its mouthpiece." (The expression *to seek science* sounds odd in English, as compared with *seek knowledge*; plainly the word has to be broadened in the sense explained.) "So long as they seek science and merely make systems, so long as they are at the beginning of the struggle," they do not see the revolutionary side of poverty and social conditions. "From the moment they see this side, science—produced by the historical movement [of society] and associating itself consciously with it—has ceased to be doctrinaire and has become revolutionary."[54]

Observe that Marx noted repeatedly that the utopians too *aspired* to "la science," like everyone else. But this aspiration they sought to implement in a utopian way, by a utopian approach. Instead of inquiring into what was actually happening in society "before their eyes," they improvised mental constructs—"systems." This word was a highly pejorative one in Marx's vocabulary, and we must understand why, at the cost of a short digression.

Marx always denied—frequently and indignantly, in late as in early writings—that he put forward any "system," for this was a semitechnical term meaning: a speculatively and artificially constructed fabrication of theory in the German philosophical tradition. (He would have violently rejected the title of Louis Boudin's 1907 book *The Theoretical System of Karl Marx*, though Boudin innocently used 'system' in the popular sense of a consistently interrelated body of views.) The speculative 'system' was counterposed to a really scientific investigation, which is *not* based on any such system. For example, this was what Engels explained in a very early article, on what "Germans" (i.e., German philosophers) meant by thoroughness:

> With a few meager data they are capable not only of concocting any kind of theory, but also of linking it with world history. On the basis of the first fact that happens to reach them at third hand, concerning which they do not even know at all whether it occurred in such and such a way or some other, they will prove to you that it *must* have occurred in this particular way and no other.[55]

Engels wrote this three decades before Dühring published his egregious exemplar of the traditional system-fabricating pattern.*

Like German philosophers, the Utopians also fabricated *systems*, and this was one of their great weaknesses, in Marx's eyes. For the Utopians, *la science* still involved the sterile invention of artificially constructed doctrines, hence they were "doctrinaire"; they did not make an investigation into the process by which society actually revolutionized itself, hence their approach was not "revolutionary." Indeed, as Marx wrote elsewhere in the same work, these utopian socialists "want the workers to leave the old society alone, the better to be able to enter the new society which they have prepared for them with so much foresight."[56]

Proudhon was an example of this pattern: he aspired, Marx wrote, to be "the man of science" soaring above the class struggle, but in fact his petty-bourgeois mentality moved him to oscillate between the polar classes in struggle, borrowing eclectically from both the bourgeois economists and the utopians. "He is in agreement with both in wanting to base himself upon the authority of science," added Marx (again acknowledging the utopians' aspirations in favor of science), but instead of science Proudhon

---

* Two decades before Engels wrote this, Heine had paid his own respects to the "German professor":

> He puts life in order with skill magisterial
> Builds a rational system for better or worse;
> With nightcap and dressing-gown scraps as material
> He chinks up the holes in the Universe.

The presentation of something called 'dialectical materialism' as Marx's "philosophic system" is one of the great hoaxes in history, probably invented by Plekhanov.

in fact substituted something else: "Science for him reduces itself to the slender proportions of a scientific formula; he is the man in search of formulas."[57] (Formulas, like systems, were "doctrinaire.")

In the thinking of the socialist innovators, including the utopians, there was commonly a tension between utopian elements and "critical" elements, that is, scientific-analytical ones. The utopian elements in Fourier, for example, were prominent and pervasive, and so it is easy to sum him up on balance as one of the utopians, even while crediting him with his "scientific" contributions, as Engels did in *Socialism Utopian and Scientific*. On the other hand, Louis Blanc, who is not properly summed up by the label 'utopian,' nevertheless on examination shows utopian elements (especially when his National Workshop scheme is regarded as a theoretical construct). Proudhon, likewise, was not *summed up* by Marx as merely a utopian socialist; but (more than his contemporaries could) we now know, from his *Carnets*, the degree to which he played with utopian construction elements, as he speculatively invented a mutual-credit society that was to take over the world.[58] We can thus properly speak of the utopian elements in Proudhon as considerable. In *The Poverty of Philosophy* Marx noted the essential element in Proudhon's economics which was "both reactionary and utopian," without knowing what Proudhon was writing in his notebooks.[59]

One of the utopian elements in Proudhon was also present in the theories of a number of other early socialists, who were not necessarily *primarily* utopian socialists. This was the "labor-money utopia"—a scheme to replace money with "labor certificates"—which was invented and reinvented by a series of reformers from John Gray and Owen to Rodbertus and Proudhon.

Discussing the form it took in Rodbertus, Engels explained that this German economist was one of several thinkers who deduced socialistic consequences from Ricardo's political economy. The conclusion that the social product *should* belong to the workers who produced it was very attractive to the hard-working petty-bourgeois, who toiled in an artisanal workshop or tavern or shop but whose honest labor was daily depreciated by competition with large-scale capitalist production. They longed for a society which would be recast to give them the "full product of [their] labor" *without* going so far as to abolish the laws of capitalist production. Their ideological representatives tinkered about for some way to arrange a state of affairs that would accomplish this. Thus Rodbertus developed Ricardo's theory of value in one direction (to socialistic conclusions) only to a limited point.

> But he cut himself off from further development in this direction by also developing Ricardo's theory from the very beginning in the sec-

ond direction, in the direction of utopia [the "labor-money" scheme]. Thereby he lost the first condition of all criticism—freedom from bias. He worked on towards a goal fixed in advance, he became a *Tendenzökonom* [economist with a line to push].

Once caught in the toils of his utopia, he cut himself off from all possibility of scientific advance.[60]

Here again, the counterposition of 'utopian socialism' to 'scientific socialism' was used as an analytical device, even though Rodbertus could hardly be summed up as primarily a utopian socialist. It was a question of evaluating utopian elements. The label 'utopian socialist' described a preponderant tendency, like most labels.

5. THE MEANING OF UTOPIAN SOCIALISM

In short, what made utopian socialism utopian, in Marx's view, was its method of approaching the problems of society. For one thing, it meant "the concoction, by means of the imagination, of an ideal society as perfect as possible," instead of relying on "insight into the nature, the conditions and the consequent general aims of the struggle waged by the proletariat."[61]

In a passage summarizing how this contrast was made even before the Manifesto, Marx wrote that, as against utopianism, we "put forward the scientific view of the economic structure of bourgeois society as the sole tenable theoretical foundation, and finally explained in popular form that it was not a matter of carrying out any utopian system but rather of consciously taking part in the historical process of social transformation that was going on before our eyes."[62]

In a draft for *The Civil War in France*, Marx gave one of his best expositions of this point, in his shakiest English:

> °°The utopian founders of sects, while in their criticism of present society clearly describing the goal of the socialist movement, the supersession of the wages-system with all its economical conditions of class rule, found neither in society itself the material conditions of its transformation, nor in the working class the organised power and the conscience [*read:* consciousness] of the movement. They tried to compensate for the historical conditions of the movement by phantastic pictures and plans of a new society in whose propaganda they saw the true means of salvation. From the moment the workingmen['s] class movement became real, the phantastic utopias evanesced, not because the working class had given up the end aimed at by those Utopists, but because they had found the real means to realise them,

but in their place came a real insight into the historic conditions of the movement and a more and more gathering force of the military [*read:* militant] organisation of the working class.[63]

Marx saw socialism as the outcome of tendencies inherent in the capitalist system, just as capitalism had developed out of the social world before its day; whereas the utopians saw socialism simply as a Good Idea, an abstract scheme without any historical context, needing only desire and will to be put into practice.

From this primacy of will it followed that the practical way to demonstrate the superiority of the new scheme was to offer a small-scale working model, either on the margin of existing society or virtually outside of it (as in the wilds of America). Since these communities were arbitrary constructs, not developments, they encouraged the thinking up of precise blueprints for the minutiae of community life, characterized by uniformity and regimentation and by control from above—the control being naturally exercised by the philanthropic do-gooders in charge. Of the large number of utopian communities actually established, all the secular ones failed fairly promptly for reasons easily predictable from Marx's viewpoint. (Religious communities lasted longer, for the same reasons that monasticism has endured since the early centuries.)

Since Marx's approach emphasized the need for society (indeed, capitalist society) to reach a sufficiently high level of production on a society-wide basis, it suggested that socialists should stay in their own countries to fight for the transformation of the whole of society from within, instead of going off into a void with others of the converted flock. One reason why German communists such as Karl Schapper, first in the League of the Just and later in the Communist League, moved toward a rapprochement with Marx (in 1847) was that they had come to this conclusion themselves, especially in a disputatious discussion with Cabet and his "Icarians."[64] One of the best pieces of argumentation against utopian community-building that can be read even today was an article in the September 1847 single issue of the Communist League's paper, probably written by Schapper.[65]

The *Communist Manifesto*, which was written soon after, picked the question up where Marx had left it the year before in his *Poverty of Philosophy*. Since the economic system and the class structure were still undeveloped, the material conditions for proletarian emancipation did not yet exist. The utopians "therefore search after a social science, after social laws, that are to create these conditions."[66] Marx appreciated that the utopians were *seeking* to be scientific, as we have seen; their trouble was that they thought they could concoct this science simply out of their own skulls:

> Society's historical action is to yield to their personal inventive action, historically created conditions of emancipation to fantastic [i.e.,

fanciful or fantasized] ones, and the gradual ongoing class organization of the proletariat to an organization of society specially contrived by these inventors. Future history resolves itself, in their eyes, into the propaganda [for] and the practical carrying-out of their social plans.[67]

As a consequence, the utopians' kind of socialism was nonclass, above-class, and nonrevolutionary; but this was also true of other types of reformist socialism—it did not specifically distinguish the utopian variety. Their fanciful pictures of future society corresponded to workers' aspirations for a "general reconstruction of society,"[68] hence had a revolutionary side, but this way of seeking the future was immediately related to the utopian method. In *Socialism Utopian and Scientific* Engels emphasized the abstract-rationalist side of the utopian method:

> The solution of the social problems, which as yet lay hidden in undeveloped economic conditions, the utopians attempted to evolve out of the human brain. Society presented nothing but wrongs; to remove these was the task of reason. It was necessary, then, to discover a new and more perfect system of social order and to impose this upon society from without by propaganda, and, wherever it was possible, by the example of model experiments. These new social systems were foredoomed as utopian; the more completely they were worked out in detail, the more they could not avoid drifting off into pure phantasies.[69]

As the utopian, following this method, went on his search to discover the new model society inside his own cranium, rather than in the observable tendencies of the real society, he derived his abstract society from other abstractions:

> To all these [utopians], socialism is the expression of absolute truth, reason and justice, and has only to be discovered to conquer all the world by virtue of its own power. And as absolute truth is independent of time, space, and of the historical development of man, it is a mere accident when and where it was discovered.[70]

Socialism thus appeared as "an accidental discovery of this or that ingenious brain"[71] instead of as a historical consequence of society's own development in the real world.

'Historical' was often the key word because to Marx it emphasized the links of development between the realities of yesterday and today and the prospects for tomorrow. For Marx there was nothing utopian in itself in thinking about the future; utopianism was *that way* of thinking about the future which makes the future an arbitrary isolate, which breaks away from the historical-developmental link with reality (i.e., with history-up-to-now). Utopians clothed their aims "in the form of pious wishes of which one couldn't say why they had to be fulfilled right now and not a thousand years earlier or later."[72]

This was illustrated from a new direction when, on the eve of the 1848 revolution, Marx (then living in Brussels) engaged in a little polemic with a Belgian bourgeois-radical newspaper. The *Débat Social* of Brussels was trying to draw a line of separation between the Belgian Democratic Association as such and its left wing, that is, the communist tendency openly grouped around Marx. In this context the liberal editor gibed at the "utopias" pursued by "certain Democrats" (meaning Marx's "Democratic Communists," the term used by Marx) who had no hope of effective reforms in their own country (meaning Germany) and who therefore engaged in "dreaming" about "castles in the air." One could see that these liberals assigned a thin meaning to utopianism: simply dreaming. In his rejoinder Marx took up utopianism from his own standpoint.

"German communism is the most determined opponent of all utopianism," he replied, "and far from excluding historical development in fact bases itself upon it...." Marx pointed to the social realities, in particular the class struggle, and cited Robert Peel and Guizot on the actuality of class conflict. But (he went on sarcastically) the Belgian liberals think that Peel and Guizot are utopians. On the contrary, it is the Belgian liberals who are thinking in the utopian manner when (for example) they dream of introducing a universal suffrage system like the American or like the British Charter into Europe "without great social upheavals." Marx concluded: "In our eyes those people are utopians who separate political forms from their social foundation and present them as general, abstract dogmas."[73]

Marx's target here was utopian liberalism, not utopian socialism—*any* ism that cut the road to the future off from the social-historical realities, and substituted "general, abstract dogma" for a scientific inquiry into political and social tendencies and forces. It may be thought that Marx was merely saying that the liberals' dream of a complete constitutional democracy "without great social upheavals" was impossible, thus making 'utopian' a synonym of 'impossible' in the usual colloquial fashion; but this was not so. Marx was at pains to explain that this dream suffered from *a particular kind of impossibility*, namely, the utopian pattern which "separates political forms from their social foundation," etc. Undoubtedly, 'utopian' here *includes* the connotation of impossibility, but it does not work vice-versa, that is, 'impossible' does not necessarily imply 'utopian.'

In short, utopianism was a much wider pattern than simple speculation about the future in free-wheeling fancy, but, to be sure, it frequently showed up in this guise of future-mongering. And not only in the early (pre-1848) period of the great utopians. Abstract dogmatizing about the future has enjoyed bursts of popularity throughout the history of the socialist movement, especially when coteries of intellectuals entered the movement, not on a wave of class struggle but because of intolerable alienation from the realities of the status quo. They therefore liked to reshape the status quo nearer to the heart's desire with the only means at this disposal—their bare minds.

This happened in the German movement in the 1870s, under Marx's eyes. Indeed, the pioneers of reformist intellectualism in the German party, the Höchberg-Schramm-Bernstein trio,[74] named their organ *Die Zukunft* (The Future). Bad articles inventing socialist futures began appearing in abundance. In a letter to a friend Marx groaned that "*utopian* socialism, the play of fancy about the future structure of society, is again rampant, and in a much emptier form" as compared with the brilliant forerunners. "It is natural that utopianism, which *before* the days of materialist-critical socialism concealed the latter within itself in embryo, can now, coming belatedly, only be silly—silly, stale, and reactionary from the ground up."[75] The latter-day fantasizers no longer had anything useful to contribute, "whereas in the utopias of a Fourier, an Owen, etc., there is the presentiment and fanciful expression of a new world...."[76]

Throughout their lives, as in the passages just cited, Marx and Engels contrasted admiration for the imaginative brilliance of innovators such as Fourier, Saint-Simon and Owen with scorn for the increasingly empty fantasizing of the latter-day utopia-mongers.

2 | OF SENTIMENTAL SOCIALISM

Early socialism, "stripped of utopias, and therefore reduced to phrases pure and simple,"[1] turned into a sorry offspring of the great utopians. The less the epigones had to say and the more banal their content, the more they depended on substituting grandiloquent phrases for stirring ideas, and on replacing revolutionary programs with empty sentimentalities.

1. THE MEANING OF SENTIMENTAL SOCIALISM

Sentimentality? Sentimentalism? Well, what's wrong with sentiment or feelings?

Nothing whatever; the point is quite different. In the first place, it is a question of a *substitution*. Vegetarians aside, you may be put out if you are expecting to be served meat, only to be fed molded bean patties; and the case is worse if this is made a steady diet—and the bean meal is third-grade to start with.

Substitutionism is as important in politics as in gastronomy. In the present case, it is a question of *substituting* sentiment for revolutionary ideas and action. Furthermore, we must know that (in English as in German) 'sentimentality' commonly suggests a sickly or sticky form of 'sentiment': its exaggerated or excessive form, an affected version (according to various dictionaries). Everyone has sentiments or feelings, but 'sentimentality' becomes a derogatory term when sentiments are (1) abstractionized and (2) substituted for, or counterposed to, practical thought and action.

That this pattern is true of a multitude of abstractions is well known to common sense, but when Marx insistently points this out in the field of social ideology, his exposition is sometimes treated as scandalous. Thus, one of the staples of the marxological industry is its indignation at Marx's attacks on the substitution of alleged Eternal Truths for concrete historical truths; on the substitution of abstract invocations of Justice and Morality for concrete analyses of social morals; on the hollow celebration of Freedom instead of the defense of actual and concrete freedoms; and so on. It is possible in English, unlike German, to indicate the abstraction by capitalizing, as we have just done; we will take advantage of this capability, just as did the Moore-Engels translation of the *Communist Manifesto.*

Sentimental socialism is not a school of socialism, but rather an ingredient in various schools, an ingredient that runs through the history of socialism and other isms like a soggy vein of unbaked dough in a loaf of bread. It is often a substitute for something else, and its social meaning may depend on what it is a substitute for. Thus, it should be platitudinous by now that abstract sentimentalities about Peace are today a necessary preparation for war, and in order to fulfill this function they *have* to be abstract and sentimentalized. This can be taken as the model. Analogously, abstract sentimentalities about Morality have historically done a similar service for a host of social evils.

Take the following attack by Marx in 1846—quite early—on "socialistic sentimentality." In a critique of Proudhon, Marx started by stating that they agreed on this point.

> I had, before him, provoked a great deal of hostility by ridiculing mutton-headed, sentimental, utopian socialism. But is not M. Proudhon inviting strange delusions by counterposing his petty-bourgeois sentimentality—I mean his elocution about home, conjugal love, and all the banalities of that sort—against socialistic sentimentality, which in Fourier, for example, is much more profound than the pompous platitudes of our worthy Proudhon?[2]

Marx's own warm regard for "home, conjugal love" and so on is well known, and so we know *this is not the target.* It is not "conjugal love" that is banal; it is banalities about conjugal love that are banal, of course. The fact is that Proudhon elevated his peasant-patriarchal view of home and marriage into a basic principle of his ideal society, as part of his fanatically antifeminist, indeed woman-hating, standpoint. This "libertarian" liked to pose as the Great Moralist, but failed to grapple with the real problems of the marriage institution in present-day society, except by pronouncing anathemas on such abominations as equal rights for women in the family or outside it.[3] Thus he converted Morality into patriarchal sentimentalism, *substituting* this for a social-historical analysis.

During the 1848 revolution, a liberal deputy in the Frankfurt Assembly cried rapturously that this was "the most humane revolution" ever, in its decrees and proclamations. As Engels recited part of the record of ruling-class cruelties and atrocities that had occurred in the course of this humane revolution, he replied that the decrees "represent a compendium of philanthropic fantasies and sentimental phrases about fraternity produced by all the featherheads of Europe."[4] The sentimental phrases about Freedom that churned out of this parliamentary talking-shop represented the counterpart of its practical impotence to enroot any freedom, even for itself. A few months later Engels called attention to another substitution:

> We have pointed out often enough that the sweet dreams which came to the surface after the February and March revolutions, the fantasies of universal brotherhood between peoples, of a European federal republic and of everlasting world peace, were fundamentally nothing more than a cover for the boundless helplessness and inactivity of the spokesmen of that time.... [They tacitly agreed] that the people should merely be given sentimental phrases instead of revolutionary deeds.

Thus the betrayal of the revolution's aims was "concealed beneath the flowers of poetry and the frippery of rhetoric," and we have now learned that the "fraternal union of peoples" will come to pass not by "mere phrases and pious wishes, but only by profound revolutions and bloody struggles."[5]

It was especially in Germany that abstractionized thinking flourished and sentimental gushing was glorified: so Marx thought, along with much of the rest of the world. Basically this was an aspect of Germany's retarded social development: the aspirations which in France and England had been worked out in political and industrial revolutions, in Germany took place only inside the skulls of its intellectuals, becoming "mere phrases and pious wishes" not because of the peculiarities of Teutonic gray cells but because social conditions permitted no other outlet.

This view of the abstractionism of the "German mentality" was made internationally famous in Heine's satirical poem "Germany: A Winter's Tale," written in 1844 in the first months of the poet's friendship with Marx in Paris, and first published in the Paris *Vorwärts!*, with which Marx collaborated. "The German soul" feels free—in dreams: so wrote Heine in Caput 7, and he added:

> The land is held by the Russians and French,
> The sea's by the British invested;
> But in the airy realm of dreams
> Our sway is uncontested.
>
> Here we exist unfragmented,
> And rule without a murmur.
> The other nations of the earth
> Developed on terra firma.

Engels, like Marx, emphasized that it was in Germany "where false sentimentality has done and still does so much damage."[6]

In *KMTR* 2, we briefly discussed "abstractionism and sentimental socialism" in connection with intellectuals in the socialist movement.[7] Let us see some of the more general forms that sentimental socialism may assume.

2. THE "MODERN MYTHOLOGY"

In the first article Marx ever published, before he was even a socialist, he already wrote, "The Germans are in general inclined to sentimentalities and extravagances; they have a fondness for music out of the blue." They "devote a cult of worship" to ideas instead of putting them into practice, instead of seeing them "from a blunt, realistic standpoint derived from the immediate background," derived from actuality. It was necessary "to translate the language of gods into the language of men."[8]

This intellectualist fondness for converting the actualities of people's interests ("the language of men") into the abstractions of idealist sentimentalities ("the language of gods") produced a climate that gave rise to a socialistic version of this mode of thought. It was criticized in the *Communist Manifesto* under its then assumed name of "True Socialism" or "German socialism."[9] French socialism—meaning especially Fourier and the Saint-Simonians—had given a critical analysis of actual society, but the German mind, appropriating the French phrases, emasculated them.

> And, since it [socialism] ceased in the hands of the German to express the struggle of one class with the other, he felt conscious of having overcome "French one-sidedness" and of representing, not true requirements, but the requirements of Truth; not the interests of the proletariat, but the interests of Human Nature, of Man in general, who belongs to no class, has no reality, who exists only in the misty realm of philosophical fantasy.[10]

The difference between truth and Truth was vital to understanding this transcendental "robe of speculative cobwebs, embroidered with flowers of rhetoric, steeped in the dew of sickly sentiment." As against the common view that moral, political, and similar ideas have a life of their own apart from society, that there are "eternal truths, such as Freedom, Justice, etc." that are meaningful even when stripped of social context, the Manifesto expounded its class view of society and its realities ("truths"). The bourgeoisie liked to declaim about Freedom when it really meant its own freedom to buy and sell.[11] The so-called True Socialists "are not concerned with practical interests and results, but with eternal truth," which means they are simply "German theoreticians,"[12] for they *counterpose* their abstractionized Truth to the social truths about practical interests and results.

This "language of gods"—this language which directs the gaze to the misty realms above rather than to the gritty soil of practical struggles—is what Marx later called the "modern mythology," as "a designation for the goddesses of 'Justice, Liberty, Equality, etc.' who are all the rage again."[13] Here Marx had in mind, in the late 1870s, a new clique of reformist intellectuals who (he thought) were introducing a "rotten spirit" into the German party, as they strove to replace its class-struggle approach with an allegedly "higher, idealistic" orientation. This was the *Zukunft* group around Höchberg which has already been mentioned.

"Modern mythology": Marx liked the phrase so much he used it at least three times. A letter to a friend said the *Zukunft* intellectuals wanted to replace the "materialist basis" of socialism "by modern mythology with its goddesses of Justice, Liberty, Equality and *Fraternité*."[14] Their socialism, wrote Marx scornfully, had long ago been criticized in the Manifesto's section on True Socialism. "Where the class struggle is pushed to the side as an unpleasant, 'crude' phenomenon, nothing remains as the basis of socialism but 'true love of people' and empty phrases about 'justice.'"[15]

This is the crux of the *substitution* that takes place in this modern mythology. If socialism is emptied of its "crude" social content, something else has to come in as replacement, if only phrases about something else. With well-carpentered abstractions, one can prove anything—and nothing.

> "Justice," "humanity," "liberty," "equality," "fraternity," "independence"—so far we have found nothing more in the Panslav manifesto [by Bakunin] than these more or less moral categories, which admittedly sound very fine, but *prove absolutely nothing* in historical and political matters. "Justice," "humanity," "liberty," etc. may demand this or that a thousand times over; but if the cause is an impossible one, nothing will happen and it will remain, despite everything, "an empty dream."[16]

Thus, this modern mythology is congenial to the utopian mode of thought. By the same token, it is alien to the scientific approach. In *Capital* Marx took as his example Proudhon (again), since he substituted moral homilies for social analysis as a matter of principle:

> Proudhon begins by taking his ideal of justice, of "eternal justice," from the juridical relations that correspond to the production of commodities.... Then he turns around and seeks to reform the actual production of commodities, and the actual legal system corresponding thereto, in accordance with this ideal. What opinion should we have of a chemist who, instead of studying the actual laws of the molecular changes in the composition and decomposition of matter and on that foundation solving definite problems, claimed to regulate the composition and decomposition of matter by means of the "eternal ideas,"

of "naturalness" and "affinity"? Do we really know any more about "usury" when we say it contradicts "eternal justice," "eternal equity," "eternal mutuality," and other "eternal truths," than the fathers of the Church did when they said it was incompatible with "eternal grace," "eternal faith" and "the eternal will of God"?[17]

Here we see Marx trying very hard to explain in very simple terms the difference between a scientific-materialist approach and an idealist-moralistic one.

There was, to be sure, a practical difference between appeals to Eternal Justice made in different social contexts. On the one hand Proudhon—or Lassalle[18]—liked to make such appeals as a matter of abstract rhetoric; but they were also made in the course of real struggles. The left Chartists, for example, proclaimed Eternal Justice as industriously as anyone, along with other fuzzy moralizing, and Marx grumbled about it since it meant self-deception or self-befuddlement[19]; but the class-struggle activity of the Chartists was concrete enough to give Justice a class meaning despite the abstract oratory. When a mill worker heard invocations of Justice while striking for a bare living, he knew what he meant by Justice, precisely because *his* justice was not Eternal. It had a context other than the oratory. The point of Marx's attacks on the modern mythology was not to forbid appeals to justice (or even Justice) but to anchor such appeals in class struggle. The appeal to justice has always been a staple of any social movement, but it is meaningful only if the movement bases its concept of justice on its social struggle, instead of basing its struggle on an abstractionized Justice.

Anyone who, like Marx, has lived to hear bushels of soggy abstractions, about a mythical Justice, Freedom, Morality, and Truth as substitutes for substantive ideas or programs, tends to become allergic to this type of elocution, since it usually has little to do with (lower-case) justice, concrete freedoms, down-to-earth morality, and scientific truths.[20] There is a case of such an "allergic" response by Marx which has been exhibited by marxologists in (literally) hundreds of books. It is evidently regarded as a major scandal. Here are the facts.

Alarm signals went off for Marx just as a newly founded organization was getting under way in October 1864. An international meeting had just been held in London, and the General Council (as it would later be called) was meeting to draw up a program. This organization was going to be the First International, but at this point it was more likely to turn into a damp squib. Marx, absent through illness, was informed that a windy old Owenite named Weston had read the Council a draft that was a dreadful "sentimental declamatory editorial." So said Marx's friend Eccarius, on the Council; he had just heard it and trembled for the enterprise. Weston, wrote Eccarius to Marx, "confines the sentimental doctrine of the old school to the workmen, to be sure, and hates the oppressors instinctively, but seems to know no other basis for labor movements than the hackneyed phrase, truth and justice."[21]

Then a French member submitted another draft, written with the elocutionary fustian of the Continental left republicans: "an appallingly phrase-filled, badly written, and utterly half-baked preamble, pretending to be a declaration of principles, in which Mazzini peeped out everywhere, crusted over with the vaguest scraps of French socialism." So wrote Marx to Engels, and he trembled with Eccarius. (Anyone who has read the typical agitational declamations of these leftists needs no further elucidation.) The Council voted to adopt the "Sentiments" embodied in this document, but Marx managed to gain time to present a new version. What he wrote, and got adopted, was the famous Inaugural Address plus the "[Provisional] Rules," with its preamble: the unique political basis for the International's career.

> My proposals [Marx informed Engels] were all adopted by the Subcommittee. Only I was obliged, in the Preamble to the Rules, to include two phrases with "duty" and "right," ditto "truth, morality and justice," but so placed that they can do no harm.[22]

This is what the commotion has been about; these words are Marx's crime, about which more has been written in indignant denunciation than about centuries of lying by presidents and potentates. For they mean that Marx repudiated "truth, morality, and justice," do they not? that in fact he sneered at Truth, Morality, and Justice, thereby proving himself an enemy of humanity and civilization. Let us see further.

The passage in the preamble that Marx referred to stated that the International and all its affiliates

> will acknowledge truth, justice, and morality, as the basis of their conduct towards each other, and towards all men, without regard to colour, creed or nationality;
> They hold it the duty of a man* to claim the rights of a man and a citizen, not only for himself, but for every man who does his duty. No rights without duties, no duties without rights; . . . [23]

Thus some of the adopted "Sentiments" were "so placed" as to acquire some concrete content: truth, justice and morality were tied to the proceedings of the International itself, not to Eternity, and specified as apply-

---

* *Menschen* in the German text; whoever put it into English treated 'man' as common gender. Note that this sentence was dropped beginning with the 1871 version of the Rules; the sentences before and after remained essentially the same throughout.

ing against discrimination on account of "color, creed, or nationality." They were further elucidated by the preceding six "Considerations" of the preamble, providing the social and class context. Thus embedded in a clear class setting, the generalities had part of the curse of abstraction taken off them—or so Marx opined.

As mentioned, it has been a principle of the modern mythology of marxology to prove, by dint of Marx's letter, that he did not "believe in" the sterling virtues under discussion, and hence was a moral monster. It does not occur to the mythologists that the point is just the reverse: the problem was that *everybody* "believes in" truth, justice, and morality, provided that they can implement their own versions; and this is why the meaningful content of these abstractions tends to rub off and dissolve away. When the reactionary Villetard published his "history" of the International in 1872, he pooh-poohed its appeal to truth, justice and morality by making precisely this point. It's meaningless, he grumbled; "no society has ever considered itself placed under the protection of injustice, falsehood, and immorality; everybody has a most beautiful desire to conform to the true, the just and the good."[24]

"Everybody" included Marx—only in his own way. *There is a test to be performed.* If it is true that Marx was overcome with revulsion at the idea of writing "truth, justice, and morality" into the preamble, he had ahead of him eight years or so of the life of the International in which to make sure that *he* at least never sullied his pen with these words. (For that matter, since the preamble was revised in detail more than once, he could have got rid of those dread phrases; but we have remarked, instead, that in later versions the last sentence was put in italics!)

• It is seldom or never noted, in view of the to-do described above, that Marx—evidently quite willingly—ended the Inaugural Address of the International with a section on foreign policy, in which workers are exhorted, as against the shameless foreign policy of the great powers,

> to vindicate the simple laws of morals and justice, which ought to govern the relations of private individuals, as the rules paramount of the intercourse of nations.[25]

This occurred not as a substitute for concrete ideas but as the very summary of them. In the Address Marx explained the "simple laws of morals and justice" to be his revolutionary ideas of morals and justice. *Cosi fan tutte.*

• Four days after writing that dreadful letter to Engels, Marx, at a General Council meeting, picked up the phrase that was so placed as to do "no harm," and used it to do good. Criticizing the reports printed in papers associated with the International, he "complained [say the GC minutes] that in such reports one of the fundamental principles of the

Association, viz., truth, had been violated."[26] There was no abstraction or substitution involved; it was a question of garbled published accounts of GC meetings.

• At the congress of the International in Brussels in 1868, Marx as usual gave the Annual Report of the GC to the Congress, and in the course reported on the efforts of the Bonaparte regime to destroy the French section and imprison its executive members. As against the well-known lying and dirty tricks characteristic of Louis Napoleon's government, Marx chose to contrast—the International's insistence on "truth, justice, and morality."

> The [French government] tribunal had the naiveté to declare in the preamble of its judgment that the existence of the French Empire was incompatible with a working men's association that dared to proclaim truth, justice, and morality as its leading principles.[27]

It would appear that Marx had clasped the dreadful phrase to his very bosom.

• Of course it was not just a question of the specific phrases written into the preamble. The myth that Marx did not recognize the existence of anything like "morality" is perhaps more a hoax than a myth; the morality which Marx recognized was that which was (in the short run) consonant with the imperatives of a revolutionary movement, or (in the long run) congruent with the advancement of human development in a free society. Naturally, anyone can disagree with this conception of morality, but it does not help the case to deny that it exists. Marx's writings are peppered, implicitly and explicitly, with appeals to moral concepts, but there is a passage which is of special interest in this connection.

In Marx's annual report for the GC to the Hague Congress of 1872, he attacked the king of Prussia for prolonging the state of siege beyond the war's end and for imprisoning Bebel and Liebknecht. These facts, he said,

> prove the awe in which he, amidst the din of victorious arms and the frantic cheers of the whole middle class, held the rising party of the proletariat. It was the involuntary homage paid by physical force to moral power.[28]

Moral power? The moral power represented by the imprisoned socialist leaders was not the power of addressing homilies to the government about Justice and Morality but, rather, the moral power that accrued to a movement from waging a struggle for a more just society.*

---

* On the other hand, the minutes of the GC offer attractive opportunities for quotation-garbling, since they are very sketchy at best and mixed-up at worst. For example, according to the minutes of February 28, 1871, Marx said that "Moral force was no force." The interested reader can take this as an exercise in trying to

3. MORALITY AND MORALIZING

Marx's view of the relations between ethics and society is not our subject; the remarks in this section are only peripheral to that subject.[30] Marx saw the roots of moral concepts and sentiments lying in historically evolved social patterns; in brief, "every *social form* of property has 'morals' of its own."[31] *Anti-Dühring* summarized part of the thought this way: "Social relations such as morality and law" are determined "by the actual historical conditions of the age...."[32] The reader can go on from these suggestions to a massive and sometimes murky literature on the question.

We are concerned here with a simpler matter, which is known to nonphilosophers as *moralizing*. Just as we have seen that the goddesses of modern mythology are born from the twin process of abstractionizing and substitutionism, so here: *moralizing* is the substitution of abstractions for a concrete analysis of class moralities.

For example, in an 1847 article Marx took up a liberal's explanation of why kings have ruled for centuries: the "moral dignity of man" was lacking. But this explained nothing: "It takes refuge from history in morality, and now it can allow free rein to the whole armory of its moral indignation."[33] (How had man suddenly acquired enough dignity in 1789?) Naturally, this argument did not mean that Marx lacked due respect for the Moral Dignity of Man; it merely asked what your moralizing really means.

In 1872 Engels tackled this question in the course of discussing an economic issue, the housing shortage. He was criticizing the "bourgeois socialists" (social reformers) who substituted exhortations to the Powers That Be in place of struggle.

> ...bourgeois socialism...*dare* not explain the housing shortage as arising from the existing conditions. And therefore it has no other way but to explain the housing shortage by moralizing that it is the result of the wickedness of man....

These social reformers want to move the question—

> from the economic sphere into the moral sphere. And nothing is more natural. Whoever declares that the capitalist mode of production, the "iron laws" of present-day bourgeois society, are inviolable, and yet at the same time would like to abolish their unpleasant but necessary consequences, has no other recourse but to deliver moral sermons to the capitalists, moral sermons whose emotional effects immediately

---

find out what Marx really must have said. He had just been complaining how the GC minutes as well as press reports misquoted GC discussions. The "moral force" in question meant mere formal protests by the English government instead of effective action.[29]

evaporate under the influence of private interest and, if necessary, of competition.[34]

When people begin to feel that conditions are immoral or unjust, their feeling is usually based on realities; no doubt of that. The feeling is a symptom: not a proof, and not a program. When a social system is on the decline and a new social order is knocking on the door, Engels wrote, the inequality of wealth increasingly appears as unjust; and

> it is only then that appeal is made from the facts which have had their day to so-called eternal justice. From a scientific standpoint, this appeal to morality and justice does not help us an inch further; moral indignation, however justifiable, cannot serve economic science as an argument, but only as a symptom.... The wrath which creates the poet is absolutely in place in describing these abuses, and also in attacking those apostles of harmony in the service of the ruling class who either deny or palliate them; but how little it *proves* in any particular case is evident from the fact that in *every* epoch of past history there has been no lack of material for such wrath.[35]

This was written against Professor Dühring, who *was* trying to prove his theories by appeals to Eternal Justice. But one must always observe just what a moral appeal is directed to. (This is the principle of context.) It is one thing if moralizing is presented *instead* of scientific analysis and proof, as Engels has just emphasized. It is quite another if the moral appeal is simply a *symptom* of the perhaps inchoate feeling that social conditions are intolerable. From the standpoint of workers in present-day society, that is, from Marx's standpoint, the conditions *are* immoral and unjust in a definite sense; and when this condemnation appears as the summary of, not substitute for, a concrete socioeconomic analysis and program, it can be an invaluable energizer of social action and a driving force of political protest. This relationship may remind us of one discussed elsewhere, the symbiotic relationship in an individual between intellect and passion.[36]

Engels added the following thought: "If the whole of modern society is not to perish," a social revolution must take place. This "tangible, material fact" is impressing itself on workers' minds, and "on this fact, and not on the conceptions of justice and injustice held by any armchair philosopher, is modern socialism's confidence in victory founded."[37]

None of this gainsays that the philosopher's conception of justice tells us a great deal— especially about the philosopher. A moral evaluation may be quite meaningful, provided one consciously understands what the moral evaluation is based on. Marx's writings, as mentioned, often offer such evaluations, not always explicitly. Take a public tribute to "moral courage," in a *New York Daily Tribune* article by Marx:

> ... I willingly embrace the opportunity of paying my respects to those

British factory-inspectors, who, in the teeth of all powerful class-interests, have taken up the protection of the down-trodden multitude with a moral courage, a steadfast energy, and an intellectual superiority of which there are not to be found many parallels in these times of mammon-worship.

One of the factory inspectors, whose semiannual report Marx was discussing in this article, was Leonard Horner, who covered the industrial center of England. Horner's report urged that, because of the overexploitation of women and children, "the clearest dictates of *moral* principles" call for an end to the evil. (Marx italicized *moral*.) He added:

> In other words, Mr. Horner propounds that, in the present state of society, a principle may appear "sound" on the part of the economist and the classes of which he is the theoretical mouth-piece, and may, nevertheless, not only prove contrary to all the laws of human conscience, but, like a cancer, eat into the very vitals of a whole generation.[38]

What Marx especially applauded in Horner was that he "opposes facts to declamations." What took moral courage was the revelation of the facts, not the declamations. Moralizing sermons about Justice and Humanity were heard by mill owners every Sunday with equanimity; they were useful, to massage the conscience. Horner's facts (with a little assist from analysis) had a thousand times more relevance to social morality.

Marx's writings gave such evaluations also with respect to interpersonal relations, hence "party" matters. (Keep in mind that 'party' meant a political tendency, not necessarily an organization.) One example will do. In a letter to the poet Freiligrath, Marx discussed the difficulties of keeping political life *pure*, in the climate of the 1850s, a period of reaction when the émigré groups and their leading gladiators had little to do except engage in mutual backbiting— when, also, Marx withdrew from all organizational contact with them.

In effect, Marx was discussing *socialist* morality. This is what he wrote— in an unusual passage:

> After all, when one thinks of the immense efforts made against us by the whole official world . . . when one thinks of the slanders mouthed by the "Democracy of dunderheads," which could never forgive our party for having more intelligence and character than itself; [and so on] . . . one concludes that in this 19th century our party stands distinguished by its *purity*.
>
> Can one escape dirt in bourgeois intercourse or °trade°? That is exactly its natural habitat. [Some examples follow.] . . . The honest vileness or vile honesty of ready-cash morality . . . is not a jot higher in my estimation than unrespectable vileness, of which neither the

first Christian communities nor the Jacobin Club nor our former "League" [the Communist League] could keep wholly pure. The only thing is, in bourgeois intercourse one gets accustomed to losing all sensitivity to respectable vileness or vile respectability.[39]

In Marx's eyes, the historical figures to be admired were embodiments of moral good, this term summing up a whole view about historical social progress. Explaining the difference between philosophic idealism and the ordinary use of the word 'idealistic' to honor certain highminded motives, Engels pointed to some of the early French materialist thinkers who held steadfastly to a progressive view of humanity's course—

> and often enough made the greatest personal sacrifices for it. If ever anybody dedicated his whole life to the "enthusiasm for truth and justice"—using this phrase in the good sense— it was Diderot, for example.[40]

4. HUMANISM AND THE POWER OF LOVE

There remain two more sentiments, with their corresponding sentimental phrases, that require a word, only because of the amount of nonsense they have provoked over the years when coupled with the subject of socialism. They are: Humanism and Love. These are great words about great realities, in themselves. What happens to them in ideological transformations is a caution for the ages.

'Humanism' rivals 'democracy' as a joker-word: I mean the joker in a deck of cards, for it has the mysterious property of standing for anything you want it to be. 'Humanism' has had a dozen meanings, and it means *nothing* until you know what it is counterposed to. Nowadays it may usefully mean opposition to statism, if properly defined (the state must be subordinated to human beings, not vice versa). It is also used to counterpose the primacy of Humanity in some global sense as against the individual ego (which may lead to the very opposite of the first sense). But in Marx's early years it meant above all Feuerbach's lately announced humanism: a humanism that counterposed a human-oriented view of the world to a God-oriented one. *This* humanism was an antechamber to materialism and even atheism, at least secularism.

This is the humanism that was referred to in Marx's earliest writings. When Marx wrote in his Paris manuscripts of 1844 that *"positive* humanistic" criticism began with Feuerbach,[41] this was true autobiographically. In *The Holy Family,* where the first two words were *"Real humanism,"* it was laid down that Feuerbach represented the union of materialism and humanism in philosophy just as "French and English socialism and communism" represented this union in the "practical domain."[42]

But at this stage this humanism was mainly negative in content: in the name of a human-centered philosophy it invited one to orient away from the supernatural realm and to reject revealed religion (a giant step forward at the time). But if this philosophical outlook was turned to the "human world," what exactly was meant by the "human world"?

Marx's generation sought to give this a "positive humanistic" analysis, but it did not help much to repeat the words "humanity" and "truly human" a thousand times. Already in *The Holy Family*, by the second hundred pages Marx noted down that "If correctly understood, interest is the principle of all morality, man's private interest must be made to coincide with the interest of humanity."[43] But when "private interest" was understood to be the interest of social groups, Humanity broke up into classes, and the repetition of 'human' and 'humanist' at every opportunity was exposed as a way of glossing over class divisions. The 'human world' was no longer seen as seamless.

In another year, in *The German Ideology*, Marx saw what social-ideological function the term was performing: "All quibbles about names are resolved in *humanism*; wherefore communists, wherefore socialists? We are *human beings*...." And he explained the role of such "highsounding phrases" in Germany, "where philosophic phrases have for centuries exerted a certain power"—the role of obscuring and diluting revolutionary views of the existing social order.[44] Emphasis on 'humanity' was a way of blurring a class understanding of society.

Shortly before writing the *Communist Manifesto*, Marx got into a polemic with a liberal who championed "the party of Humanity" as a way of saying that he did *not* champion the interests of the workingpeople, which naturally were too narrow for his lofty mind. By the "party of Humanity," explained Marx with inhumane candor, this liberal meant "the worthy and highminded dreamers who champion *bourgeois* interests in the guise of *human* ends, without however being clear about the connection between the idealistic phrase and its realistic substance." For him, "all classes melt away before the ceremonial idea of 'humanity.'" The use of "humanity" as a blur was a great convenience for refuting class-struggle ideas.[45]

A few years later, looking back to this early period, Marx and Engels gave a scornful mention to

> *humanism*, the catchword with which all confusionists in Germany from Reuchlin to Herder have covered up their embarrassment. This catchword seemed all the more timely as Feuerbach had just "rediscovered Man".... [46]

Obeisances to "humanistic socialism" became a way of saying nothing—

one of the historic functions of moralistic terminology. Besides, the words 'humanist,' 'humane,' 'humanitarian' have a certain tendency to blur together, as is illustrated in English by the fact that 'humanity' has two different meanings and takes two adjectives, 'human' and 'humanitarian.' Whatever 'humanistic socialism' is taken to mean, it could easily blur into humanitarian (philanthropic) social reform.

Along with Feuerbach's brand of humanism came also his "religion of Love," which was to be the foundation of a new society in which egoism was abolished.[47] Systematized into a sort of socialism by Hess and Grün, it became the "True Socialism" which we have mentioned more than once. "What religion should we all profess? The religion of Love and Humanity. Where is the evidence of this religion? In the breasts of all good people." So wrote Hess in 1844 in a "Communist Confession of Faith,"[48] tastefully stirring a pinch of Humanism and Love into a savory stew of "communistic" abstractions.

In his late essay on Feuerbach, Engels showed how Feuerbach's abstract Love was filled with different contents in actual society. He summarized:

> In other words, Feuerbach's morality is cut exactly to the pattern of modern capitalist society, little as Feuerbach himself might desire or imagine it.
>
> But love!—yes, with Feuerbach love is everywhere and at all times the wonder-working god who should help to surmount all difficulties of practical life—and at that in a society which is split into classes with diametrically opposite interests. At this point the last relic of its revolutionary character disappears from his philosophy, leaving only the old cant:* Love one another...a universal orgy of reconciliation![50]

But Feuerbach's attempt to base a theory of morality on Love, regardless of social and class context, could not succeed. Classes develop their own standards of morality and their own patterns of violation of these standards. "And love, which [in Feuerbach's view] is to unite all, manifests itself in wars, altercations, lawsuits, domestic broils, divorces, and every possible exploitation of one by another."[51] For love cannot be a social determinant in *this* society, which cannot be reformed by Love but rather itself deforms love.

---

* Note this statement, and compare the reference to it in Venable's *Human Nature: The Marxian View*:

"Love," says Engels in at least one reference, is "cant."[49]

But far from saying that love is cant, Engels here wrote that *Feuerbach's* abstract Love reduced itself to cant after awhile! I am moved to cite this notable example of quotation-garbling because the author considered himself an expounder of Marxism.

When Love is made into a social ideology, it is emptied of all real content in order to be abstractly counterposed to Hate, that is, to struggle (especially class struggle). And so social struggle, which humanizes an exploited class, is decried under the label Hate; but the ruling class has no objection to an ideology which proposes to Love it out of existence. Reduced to cant, Love becomes a code word for something else:

> Therefore, the more civilization advances, the more it is compelled to cover the ills it necessarily creates with the cloak of love, to embellish them, or to deny their existence; in short, to introduce conventional hypocrisy....[52]

As mentioned before, it happens that both Engels and Marx were not outdone by anyone in their appreciation of love, including but not only sex love. (This needs saying since there has been another socialist type, from Proudhon and Bakunin to Bernard Shaw, which was pathologically antisex.) But our present subject is not love, but Love, the substitute sentimentalized abstraction.

Engels' essay explained:

> ...Feuerbach himself never contrives to escape from the realm of abstraction—for which he has a deadly hatred—into that of living reality. He clings fiercely to nature and man; but ... He is incapable of telling us anything definite either about real nature or real men. But from the abstract man of Feuerbach one arrives at real living men only when one considers them as participants in history. And that is what Feuerbach resisted [as when the 1848 revolution sent him flying into seclusion]....[53]

What was a weakness in Feuerbach became a plague in the 1840s as "True Socialism" took this weakness as its starting point, "putting literary phrases in the place of scientific knowledge, the liberation of mankind by means of 'love' in place of the emancipation of the proletariat through the economic transformation of production...."[54] Above all, this deification of Love excluded struggle just as the phraseology about Humanity negated classes, thus making class struggle doubly unthinkable for all acolytes. Since love is deservedly popular, invocations of Love became a staple of reformist currents in one form or another. It was a handy burble for anyone, even Weitling, who promised that in the communist state "we will love our enemies as soon as we have conquered them."[55]

The revolutionary workmen in the Communist League, on the other hand, were disgusted by the "slobbering feebleness" of this "sentimental Love-mongering."[56] The original motto of the League had been "All men are brothers," and the replacement of this benevolent watchword by "Workers of the world, unite" was a symbol of its ideological transformation under Marx's influence. A decade later, the left Chartist Ernest Jones, at the height of his association with Marx, explained to a meeting why the motto of Christian love was ambiguous: "Yes, all men are brethren—but some are Abels and some are Cains, and this is a gathering of the Abels of the world against the crowned and mighty Cains who murdered them."[57]

If love is social reconciliation, and struggle is hatred of the class enemy, then—as Engels put it long afterward—"In our country it is hatred rather than love that is needed—at least in the immediate future...." A statement like this, of course, is made to order for quotation-garbling out of context, but Engels was writing a letter to a socialist friend who understood the point. In any case, Engels wanted to bend the stick the other way for "Germany, where false sentimentality has done and still does so much damage."[58]

The "socialism of Love" was given a workout in 1846, in a case which can stand as a model for history: that of Hermann Kriege (whom we have discussed elsewhere in other connections).[59] Having gone to America as an "emissary" of the Communist League, this young intellectual went into business for himself: "he founded a paper in which, in the name of the League, he preached an extravagant communism of Love-mongering, based on 'love' and overflowing with love."[60]

The executive of the Communist League adopted a "Circular Against Kriege" written by Marx and Engels, of which the first section dealt with Kriege's "Transformation of Communism into Love-mongering." The Circular cited dozens of Kriege's effusions about Love presented as political tenets of "communism"—sweet nothings, like "The holy spirit of community must evolve from the heart of love"—all addressed "To Women," who were expected to whimper rather than fight (said the Circular). Kriege counterposed a "country-parson phrase" about living together in peace against any idea of struggle: "Everything may be achieved by love and self-surrender."

> It is in accord with this love-driveling that Kriege ... presents communism as the lovelorn antithesis of egoism, and reduces a world-historical revolutionary movement to the few words: love—hate, communism—egoism.[61]

Kriege orated about "the final realization of the beautiful realm of brotherly love," but then (like Weitling) showed the other side of his love-mongering: "Whoever does not support such a party can be rightfully treated as an enemy of humanity." The Circular quoted this telltale threat, and commented:

> This intolerant statement seems to contradict the "self-surrender to all" and the "religion of love" toward all. It is however a wholly consis-

tent conclusion to this new religion, which mortally hates and persecutes all its enemies, like every other. The enemy of the party is quite consistently turned into a heretic, being transformed from an enemy of the actually existing *party*, whom one combats, into a sinner against a *humanity* that exists only in the imagination, whom one must punish.[62]

Kriege's operation, then, has the earmarks of a sect, religious sect or political sect or both.

Kriege orated: "we want to *unite* humanity through *love*, we want to *teach* it to work communally and enjoy communally, until the long-promised kingdom of joy is finally fulfilled." This was very uplifting, but the Circular pointed past the joyful phrases to the first word: *we*.

> ...then come the Prophets, the "we" who "teach" the proletarians what to do next. These Prophets "teach" their disciples, who here appear remarkably ignorant about their own interests....[63]

Kriege orated further: "We have better things to do than worry about our *shabby selves*, we belong to humanity." With this abstraction, humanism turns into a doctrine that subordinates the individual to some higher order of being, and an individual's struggle for his own interests becomes "shabby." The Circular asserted the opposite:

> With this shameful and disgusting servility before a "humanity" that is separate and distinct from the "self" and which therefore is a metaphysical and in his case even a religious fiction, with this utterly "shabby" slavish abasement, this religion ends up like every other one. Such a creed, which preaches a relish in cringing and self-contempt, is quite fitting for valiant—*monks*, but never for strong-minded men, especially in a period of struggle.[64]

At this point, this discussion of the "transformation of communism into Love-mongering" could well merge into our discussion (elsewhere) of the principle of self-emancipation.[65] Nothing could be more alien to the independent struggle of a revolutionary class than these "chimerical dreamy effusions," this "fantasmagorical mist-apparition," "spun from philosophical and love-happy phrases," these "stylized sentimentalities," confusing communism with communion and "the old religious and German-philosophical fantasy."[66] They were useful to Kriege when he sent them out in begging letters to rich German merchants in New York, signing himself "A Friend of Humanity."[67]

The Circular summed it up when it said that, from Kriege's standpoint,

> the answer to all *real questions* can consist only of some highflown-religious *images* whose meaning is wrapped in fog, in some high-

sounding labels like "mankind," "humanity," "species," etc., and in the transformation of every *real act* into a *fantasmagorical phrase.*[68]

This describes the undeniable appeal of various forms of sentimental socialism over the decades. Their lack of real content is no handicap for certain purposes, but an aid. No one can disagree with these lovely-sounding phrases; they will never frighten the Powers That Be into suppressive action; and they will never discommode the phrasemongers by demanding revolutionary acts. These advantages Marx cannot rival.

3 | OF STATE-SOCIALISM: LASSALLEAN MODEL

As so often before, we must begin with a "political lexicon," an inquiry into the meaning of a term. 'State-socialism' is a protean thing. It has no meaning except insofar as a definition is stated or understood in a particular context. In the history of socialism, 'state-socialism' has been used in three or four quite distinct senses, not infrequently two at a time. We are concerned here only with usages that Marx had to take up.

There was a later usage which was favored by Bakunin and other anarchist writers, and which was sometimes taken over by liberals for their own purposes. This defined 'state-socialism' as *any* socialism that "recognized" a state or aimed at establishing a socialist state or workers' state of any kind—that is, any socialism other than anarchism. This semantic strategy is one way of emptying the term of any useful meaning; but it is of no interest in the present context.

The state-socialism which imposed the term on Marx's attention, and which will be our main concern here, was that which arose in Germany in the 1880s, giving currency to the term *Staatssozialismus* as well as 'Bismarckian socialism,' 'socialism of the chair,' 'monarchical socialism,' and other now exotic labels. This current, which originally arose outside of the Social-Democratic Party and socialist movement proper, will be taken up in the next chapter, In this chapter we discuss related tendencies *inside* the socialist movement, which were retroactively clarified by the Bismarckian phenomenon. (Marx himself did not usually discuss Lassalleanism under the label 'state-socialism,')

1. FORERUNNERS

Once the term 'state-socialism' had established itself in popular parlance and academic treatises as a "type of socialism," attention was directed back to early socialist history to identify its progenitors. As far back as 1850,

Lorenz Stein had pinned the label on Louis Blanc, but (as I read Stein) he did not use the term as if it were original with him. Perhaps it was; but there is no information on the first introduction of the label in political literature.*

Stein had so labeled Louis Blanc because, he said, for Blanc "In the end, the state will gain complete control over production.... This is the basis for state-socialism. The state is the only producer.... The state has a complete monopoly over the economy."[1]

As a definition of state-socialism this was quite clear; but in point of fact it was rather unfair to Blanc, who answered the charge by insisting that he looked to the state only for temporary aid in establishing "workers' associations" that would thenceforth control production. There is no reason to doubt Blanc's sincerity in thus repudiating unlimited and complete dependence on the state; it is enough to note that his earlier writings and ambiguities gave color to the charge, and that there is a difference between insincerity and confusion.[2]

If Stein's definition of 'state-socialism' is used, it may describe an element or ingredient in the socialist movement but not a prominent school or organized tendency. ('Bismarckian socialism' outside the socialist movement is a different case, but of course Stein was writing before this came into being.)

Later it became a fixed dogma of academic history that Louis Blanc was the father of something called state-socialism, without clear definition. Neither Marx nor Engels referred to him by this label; to them he was simply a reformist ("petty-bourgeois socialist" or "opportunist"). But there *were* forerunners of Lassallean state-socialism worth mentioning from Marx's standpoint. It is necessary to look for two programmatic ingredients.

(1) *The demand for state aid to establish socialistic institutions.*

As we will see, the central plank of the Lassallean platform, indeed the shibboleth of the tendency, was the demand on the *existing* state to advance large loans to finance the establishment of producers' cooperatives—cooperatives that constituted the boundary of Lassallean socialism. (Lassalle made no other socialistic demands.) In other words, the old state was to be persuaded, or pressured, to bring socialism into being.

In attacking this approach, Marx pointed out more than once that, in making "state aid versus self-help" the "central point of his agitation," Lassalle "merely took up again the watchword which *Buchez*, the leader of

---

* In 1848 Proudhon was flogging Louis Blanc as a "governmental socialist" (for Blanc was *in* the Provisional Government), and he was using language suggestive of the term, but I have not seen the term 'state-socialism' in his writings. In any case Proudhon did not limit his denunciations of this sort to Blanc.

Catholic socialism, had given out in 1843 sqq. against the genuine workers' movement in France."[3]

Buchez—whom Marx once described as an ex-Saint-Simonian "glorifying Robespierre *and* the Holy Inquisition" both[4]—broke away from the Saint-Simonian school to orient toward the working class as his field of operation, but the group around his organ *L'Atelier* acted as a conservative-religious tendency; in 1848 it was to the right of Louis Blanc. Still, there was a direct line between Buchez's *L'Atelier* and Blanc's program for *ateliers nationaux* (national workshops) as the road to socialism. Blanc developed the collectivist and political side of the program to its practical outcome.[5] The common ground, a common ground that would include the Lassalleans, was this: *they all looked to the existing state for the key assistance in establishing socialistic institutions.*

Louis Blanc put it succinctly in a propaganda question-and-answer piece entitled "Socialism":

°°Q.—How are we to pass from the present order of things to that which you contemplate?
A.—By the intervention of the government.[6]

That was putting it as flatfootedly as you can. The operative aspect of Blanc's state-socialism was that the state which was to perform this service for socialism was the existing state of the ruling class. Workers' movements from below could help only as pressures to convince the tops. Indeed, when in the June Days of 1848 and then again in the Paris Commune of 1871 the French workers moved beyond this role and aimed to set up a different state, their own government, Blanc denounced them, and in both cases supported the massacre of the insurgents by the forces of the same state that was to usher in his "socialism." This was far more important in fixing Marx's view of Blanc than the exaggerated claim that the Frenchman wanted a state monopoly of the economy.

Though Marx and Engels saw Blanc primarily as a reformist and "the representative of sentimental phrasemongering socialism,"[7] yet they also noted the statist orientation of his type of reformism. Even before 1848, when (before the revolutionary experience) they held a hopeful view of Blanc, Engels already commented on his national-chauvinist outlook.[8] In 1854, when Marx explained to his *NYDT* readers the difference between the gathering over which Blanc had presided in 1848 in the Luxembourg Palace, and the labor congress then going on in Manchester which called itself the Labor Parliament, the first distinction he offered was "this great difference, that the Luxembourg was initiated by the people themselves...."[9] The very name Labor Parliament showed that the workers' movement looked to establishing its own government. In short, the basic distinction was (and is) *between the existing government of the present ruling class and a workers' state to be established by a revolution against that ruling class.*

Louis Blanc, Buchez, and the Lassalleans were among the many socialists who overtly put forward demands giving to the existing state the basic role in introducing socialism, while the role of the workers' or people's movement was essentially to pressure the state into fulfilling its historic role. *This was what defined state-socialism, in Marx's view.* At the same time, it meant that this state-socialism was one variety of reformism among others.

(2) *The tendency to glorification of, as against hostility to, the state as such.* (This loose distinction will be tightened up; anyway it is clearer than the vague term 'statism' or *étatisme.*)

Louis Blanc, who was moderate in all things, afforded only a moderate example of state cultism, as in the question-and-answer article previously cited:

> °°Q.—Why is it desirable for the Government to take the initiative in Social regeneration?
> A.—Because it is too vast a work ... to be easily accomplished by isolated individual attempts. It requires nothing less than the united energies of all, powerfully exercised by the most upright and intelligent. The Government undertaking to regenerate society is like the head consulting for the health of the body.[10]

Along the same lines: in his *Organisation du Travail*, which launched his reputation, Blanc described the government as "the born protector" of labor and capital alike.[11] This way of thinking, including the head-body metaphor, was common among reformists; in this sense most forms of pink radicalism have a 'state-socialist' component. For if you do not look for social change to a subversive (transformatory) revolution from below, then is there a good alternative to putting faith in a state power which is seen to hover high above society and its class antagonisms?

This problem—*What power can bring about the desired social change?*—points most reformisms toward reliance on the existing state. But for Marx, the guiding issue is not some desired social reconstruction, but something else: the question of *who controls society*. The crux was the control of society from below, or in Marx's customary language, what class ruled the state power. As *KMTR* 2 explained: "Marx and Engels habitually stated their political aim not in terms of a change in social system (socialism) but in terms of a change in class power (proletarian rule)."[12]

This meant that Marx came at the problem of change in society from an angle entirely different from the reformist's slant. For Marx the political movement was in the first place the movement of the working classes to take over state power, *not* primarily a movement for a certain scheme to reorganize the social structure. Therefore, for Marx, hostility to the existing state was not merely a state of mind or a personal predilection, but the basic element of his theory of revolution. The *first* question of politics which the young Marx clarified for himself, in his 1843 notes on Hegel's political philosophy, was not the program of socialism but rather the rejection of Hegel's exaltation of the state and its bureaucracy.[13]*

When Mazzini, the Italian republican nationalist, denounced the Paris Commune in concert with European reaction, Marx explained to the General Council of the International that this was not a new turn for him: Mazzini had always been a bitter enemy of the "workmen's movements." Marx concluded (in the words of the GC minutes, which are sometimes a dubious secretary's paraphrase):

> °°In Italy he [Mazzini] had created a military despotism by his cry for Nationality. With him the State—which was an imaginary thing—was everything, and Society—which was a reality—was nothing. The sooner the people repudiated such men the better.[15]

True, Mazzini was not a socialist of any kind, hence not a state-socialist. When such state-liberalism as his was combined with the view that the apotheosized state should also intervene massively in socioeconomic life, then the resulting "socialism" had to be repudiated all the sooner. The same was true of what Marx came to call "Bonapartist socialism."

We have seen that in the late 1850s Marx published a good deal of denunciation, particularly in his *NYDT* articles, against the "Bonapartist socialism" or "Imperial socialism" represented by the Crédit Mobilier adventure in economics by Napoleon III and his Saint-Simonian finance-capital operators.[16] This "Bonapartist socialism" was, in a small way, the forerunner of the "Bismarckian socialism" which gained more attention twenty years later. The term 'state-socialism' can be applied to it with as much insouciance as 'state-capitalism,' and with equal vagueness, though neither Marx nor Engels did so.

But this Bonapartist socialism, despite the presence of a clique of Saint-Simonians (or ex-Saint-Simonians), was plainly something engineered by the state from above; it did not pretend to be the work of a people's movement. When glorification of the state was joined to the organization of a workers' movement from below, and the combination was represesented as the embodiment of Social-Democracy, then state-socialism reached a new level. This was the case with Lassalle and the Lassallean

---

* This characteristic of Marx occasionally impinges on the conciousness of marxologists. H.B. Mayo remarks that "at first sight" (that is, when Marx is actually read) "the virtue of Marx's political theory . . . is the entire absence from it of any glorification of the state"; and Rossiter admits that "we must admire his own refusal to glorify the state in any way." But they do not allow this discovery to interfere with the predestined conclusion that Marxism is "statist."[14]

tendency, on the basis of which the German Social-Democracy was originally founded. We turn to it in the next section.

Another preliminary word, about the 'socialist' label: it should be clear by now that neither Marx nor Engels had any inhibition against calling many things 'socialist' which later socialists would probably call pseudosocialist or "socialist" only in quote marks. In part this reflected the early amorphous meaning of socialism,[17] and Marx's lack of attachment to the term (he preferred 'communism'). In part the later "strict" use by socialists reflected the exclusivist thinking of sectist organization: the label 'socialist' was thought of as a seal of approval, an import it never had for Marx.

Furthermore, Marx was aware that 'socialism' was used with different connotations in different countries; thus, in the *Grundrisse* notebooks, written while "Bonapartist socialism" was still making hay, he commented that "Bastiat is right insofar as in France, as a result of its characteristic social formation, many things pass for socialism that in England are political economy."[18] By this he meant state interventions as well as the manifestations of Bonapartist socialism. Perhaps he was more aware than modern marxologists of how the terminology of the social sciences itself reflected the development of different societies.

Lastly on this point, we need only note that Engels' usage was similarly loose. In *The Housing Question* Engels said, of a housing enterprise which was a case of "open association between the Second French Empire and the capitalists of Alsace" that "It was one of Louis Bonaparte's socialist experiments, for which the state advanced one-third of the capital." It was actually a case of "state assistance" to capitalist enterprise.[19] Of the Katheder-socialists (who are discussed in the next chapter) Engels used the appellations "reactionary socialists" and "pseudosocialists" in one letter.[20] But there was no consistency in this usage.

2. THE CULT OF THE STATE

The apotheosis of the state as the predestined master of society was not merely a characteristic of Lassalle's ideology; it was its centerpiece. Lassalle proclaimed this idea; it does not have to be deduced from his writings. There was no other socialist figure who came close to him in this respect. And this was the starting point of Marx's political hostility to Lassalle, as it was the starting point of Lassalle's own politics. (The myth that Marx's critique of Lassalle was due to jealousy or personal hostility is taken up in Special Note A.)

There have been many complaints, including mine, that Marx and Engels failed to produce expositions of a general theoretical character on many important political questions. But this complaint cannot be made in the case of Lassallean state-socialism. There *was* a work, promoted by Engels though not written by him, which presented their analysis in some detail. This work is of great historical value and permanent theoretical ("scientific") value. It has been obscured in part because the name of Eduard Bernstein is attached as author.

It was written by Bernstein in 1891, during his leftist period, writing in London virtually dirctly under Engels' tutelage. It was undertaken to accomplish a political task that Engels was anxious to get done, namely, the education of the German movement in the meaning of Lassalleanism and the exposure of the Lassalle legend. Though the pen was Bernstein's, there can be no question that it closely reflected Engels' views, and by the same token Marx's. To underline this fact, it will be referred to here as the Bernstein/Engels critique, without impugning Bernstein's authorship.

Bernstein wrote this study as his editorial introduction to a new edition of Lassalle's writings. Immediately upon its publication in German in 1892, an English translation by Eleanor Marx appeared under the title *Ferdinand Lassalle as a Social Reformer*. Engels' letters of the time showed how delightedly he greeted this publication; on the other hand, the German party leadership was rather appalled, and the hostility generated against Bernstein exerted great pressure on that far from staunch spirit. Soon after Engels' death and his own promulgation of Revisionism, Bernstein distanced himself from this great study of Lassalle, and later rewrote it. The original work eventually fell into a twilight zone: for the Revisionists it was too hostile to a figure who had much in common with them; for the Marxists it was rendered suspect by Bernstein's by-line. Engels' relationship to the production of this work is further described in Special Note A.

• • •

It is immensely educational to look at Lassalle and his brand of state-socialism through the eyes of this penetrating critique by Bernstein/Engels.

Lassalle took his concept of the state directly from Hegel and Fichte, as if nothing had happened after them to render this old-Hegelian "philosophy of right" (political theory) as backward as the theory of monarchy by divine right. The Bernstein/Engels critique duly traced this current in Lassalle's writings even before the start of his political agitation in 1862, back to his first philosophical work on Heraclitus.[21] But it was in the major political speeches of his 1862-1864 campaign that Lassalle gave this ideology its rounded form and linked it with his political program.

"The old Hegelian ideological concept of the State," said the Bernstein/Engels critique, "induced Lassalle to instill into the workers a semi-mystical reverence for the State at a time when, above all, it behooved them to shake off the police State"—that is, the existing state of Prussian absolute monarchy.

It is no exaggeration to say that of the idea of the State he made a veritable cult. "The immemorable vestal fire of all civilization, the State, I defend with you against these modern barbarians" (that is, the Manchester party), he exclaims to the judges of the Berlin *Kammergericht* (Court of Appeal) in his speech on "Indirect Taxation," and similar passages occur in almost all his speeches.[22]

The context of this speech (the Berlin judiciary) was as significant as its words. Addressing himself to an arm of the absolute-monarchist state, Lassalle demonstratively aligned himself with the state bureaucracy in a united front against the liberal bourgeoisie (the "Manchester party").

He had started along this road with one of his first agitational addresses, in June 1862, published under the title "The Workers' Program." Bernstein/Engels pointed out that, already here, "his ideology leads him to sing paean to the State, to the 'Concept of the State.' " The ideology was given an "ethical" cast: Lassalle asserted that workers have "quite a different conception of the ethical aim of the state from the bourgeoisie." The liberal bourgeoisie's concept was that the sole function of the state was to protect the personal freedom and property of the individual. But this, said Lassalle scornfully, was a "night-watchman idea" of the state.*

Bernstein/Engels summarized Lassalle's idea further:

To accomplish the development of the human race toward freedom, *this* is the true mission of the state. The state is "the unity of individuals in an ethical whole" ... And further, the object of the state is "to bring man to positive expansion and progressive development, in other words, to fashion the human *destiny*—i.e., the culture of which the human race is capable—into actual being"; it is "the education and development of man to freedom." So clearly is this "the true and

---

* This was a sally much quoted by Lassalleans. The Lassalleans picked up the "ethical" approach after the leader's death. Nothing is more obvious, wrote a leading Lassallean Social-Democrat, Karl Frohme, in 1885, "than the recognition that it is the state—that means, the ever-enlarging union of individuals which encompasses all particularized strength in an ethical Whole—which has the function of bringing about the evolution of humanity to freedom and well-being."[23] By this time it was quite evident that the "ethical" approach to socialism was the reformist substitute for a class-struggle approach. Lassalleanism, however, identified the "ethical" approach with state-cultism (since the state was the very incarnation of social morality) whereas Bernsteinian Revisionism substituted highly moral elocution.

higher mission of the state" that this mission "has been more or less carried out by the state through all time, by the force of circumstances, and even without its own will, even unconsciously, even against the will of its leaders."[24]

This Lassallean theory of the state was straight out of Hegel—a pure distillation of Hegelian idealism which provided the theoretical basis for supporting the state of an alien class (alien to the working class). Lassalle ascribed this view to the "workers" (with whom, incidentally, he had never had the least substantive contact)—"workers" who have "the profound instinct that this is, and must be, the destiny of the state," *because the workers were in a helpless position.*[25] The beneficent state must emancipate them because self-emancipation was impossible. For Lassalle the concept of the state was "an eternal one," and classical antiquity was right, as against modern bourgeois liberalism, in viewing the state as "the institution in which the whole virtue of mankind shall realize itself."

But, stated the Bernstein/Engels critique, "the grafting, upon the society of today, of the state concept as understood by the ancients, involves the danger of a modern state-slavery."[26]

The critique then showed that even if Lassalle's intentions were taken to be "democratic and socialist," his view meant the cult of the *existing* state:

> The cult of the state as such, means the cult of every state, and even if Lassalle's democratic and socialist views made it impossible for him to support directly the existing state,* it did not prevent this cult from being exploited later on by the advocates of the existing state in its interest. Indeed, the Achilles heel of all ideology, of all theory built upon preconceived concepts, is that, no matter how revolutionary in intention, they are really always in danger of being transformed into a glorification of existing, or of past institutions. Lassalle's concept of the state is the bridge that was one day to bring together the Republican Lassalle and the men fighting for absolute monarchy, the revolutionist Lassalle and the out-and-out reactionaries. Philosophical absolutism has at all times had a tendency inclining it to political absolutism.[27]

The *existing* state that was guarding the vestal fire of all civilization in Lassalle's Prussia was the state of the absolutist bureaucracy, still aspiring to autonomy from the ruling class of civil society, the bourgeoisie; that is, it was the monarchical state of Bismarckian Bonapartism, still fighting the rearguard action which we have discussed elsewhere.[28] If the state that

---

* As we know now, this gave Lassalle too much credit. The critique was bending over backwards to avoid overstatement.

Lassalle confronted had been a more or less modern state like England's, his ideology might have clothed itself in political forms indistinguishable from other reformisms.

We may add here that eventually Lassalleanism did merge into the main body of reformism. But in 1862 *reformists still had a choice between contending ruling classes*, the old one still in control of the state and the new one dominating the economy. Lassalle chose the power that still visibly monopolized the state machine, whereas other reformists (especially in south Germany) made the other choice, viz., chose the leading-strings of the liberal bourgeoisie.

In this pattern, which will be useful in order to understand subsequent developments, the south German bourgeoisie, being anti-Prussian, was hostile to a German state still dominated by Prussia. Part of the south German condition was the existence of an immature socialist and labor movement that was tail-ending a liberal bourgeois party. When the "Eisenacher" party, led by a young turner named Bebel and the experienced confusionist Wilhelm Liebknecht, opted for unification with the Lassalleans at the Gotha Congress in 1875, Marx's pressure (and other influences) had only recently weaned them away from their collaboration with the South German People's Party, a typical liberal-bourgeois organization that kept its back door open for workers' support. For a whole period before this, Marx had chafed at the choice between, on the one hand, the sectist policies of the Lassallean party, which however at least openly advocated socialism, and, on the other hand, the opportunist line of the Liebknecht-Bebel wing of the People's Party in failing to practise *independent* working-class politics. It is important to understand that until the south Germans broke with their People's Party and formed their independent Eisenacher party, *Marx refused to support them against the Lassalleans*, in spite of his dim view of the latter.

3. THE STATE-AID NOSTRUM

From his cultist view of the state, it was easy for Lassalle to conclude that the state, indeed the existing state—"even unconsciously, even against the will of its leaders"—was destined to bring about the solution of the Social Question, that is, the socialistic reorganization of society. The idea of a "Social Monarchy" had been around for a long time; at bottom it meant the possibility that the Crown-cum-bureaucracy, as the old ruling class, might see its way clear to using the working masses, below and behind the bourgeoisie, as a counterbalance against the growing political power of the bourgeoisie—the new ruling class in civil society which was also reaching out for political power.

The state had to be helped to see its destiny; a clever man could help destiny along, and Ferdinand Lassalle was cleverer than most.

A philanthropic-minded petty-bourgeois Democrat, Schulze of Delitzsch (who liked to hyphenate his name as Schulze-Delitzsch), had tried to solve the Social Question by founding self-help cooperative societies of workers. In part these were simply attempts at producers' cooperative associations such as England and France already knew; but Germany was more backward, and Schulze-Delitzsch's scheme was even more suitable for the small handicraft masters who still abounded. By cooperative management of credit, raw materials and distribution outlets, these obsolescent producers would be enabled to better compete with modern industry.

Lassalle found his own solution in a "statified" version of Schulze-Delitzsch's; for him the key was *state aid*. A massive state loan to provide the capital for founding large-scale productive cooperatives, which would proceed to take over all industry and all branches of the economy in the course of time: this was the key political demand.

This plank was not new. Julius Vahlteich, who became the first secretary of the Lassallean organization, wrote in his history of the movement:

> His proposals—producers' cooperatives with state credit, universal suffrage, and the organizing of a workers' association extending through all of Germany—were in themselves nothing new or startling, but to us were thoroughly familiar. We were aware that the whole plan, including the 100 million thaler state credit, had already been placed before a workers' congress in Berlin in June 1848.[29]

That is, the plan emerged from the 1848 revolution. Later, Engels summarized as follows, but he was reminded of the similar program devised by Buchez's group in Paris (already mentioned by Marx, as related earlier in this chapter):

> ... this was no longer the bold socialism of the Manifesto; what Lassalle demanded in the interests of the working class was the establishment of producers' cooperatives by means of state credit—a new edition of the program of the Paris workers' group which before 1848 adhered to the pure-republican [i.e., bourgeois republican] *Le National* of Marrast, hence a program which the pure-Republicans counterposed to Louis Blanc's "Organization of labor." Lassallean socialism, as one can see, was very modest.[30]

Modest indeed; all that Lassalle really claimed was that it would some day lead to socialism, in a distant future. To obtain this political demand (state aid), the workers had to organize politically, independently of the liberal bourgeoisie, in order to lead the state to its historic mission. To give clout to the workers' political movement, universal suffrage was necessary. Lassalle knew that Bismarck had been contemplating introducing universal suffrage in order to dish the liberals, so the demand was not unrealistic. In this calculation, universal suffrage could be won by a grant from above.

The Bernstein/Engels critique tied this state-aid plank up with Lassalle's economics:

> To convince the workers of the futility of self-help as preached by the bourgeoisie [and Schulze-Delitzsch], Lassalle adduced the law of wages in capitalist production as formulated by the classical political economists ... [especially] Ricardo. The "iron and inexorable law, according to which, under the domination of supply and demand, the average wages of labor remain always reduced to the bare subsistence which, according to the standard of living of a nation, is necessary for the maintenance of life and the reproduction of the species." ... [According to Lassalle] "workers and the wages of labor circled for ever round the extreme margin of that which, according to the needs of the time, constitutes the necessary means of subsistence," and this *"never* varies."

Because of this "iron law of wages" every effort by workers to improve conditions through their own efforts was doomed to fail, not only cooperatives but also trade unions.* The working class must become its own employer, and this could be accomplished only on a large state-sponsored scale. Lassalle insisted (stated the Bernstein/Engels critique) that "the means to do this—the necessary capital, i.e., the necessary credit—must be provided by the *state.*"[31]

Lassalle insisted that his programmatic plank (state aid) did *not* amount to socialism, yet provided the "germ" of it: "I can't understand," he wrote to Rodbertus, "how anyone can fail to see that the association, proceeding from the state, is the organic germ of development that will lead on to all that lies beyond."[32] Yet the state and its rulers were expected *not* to see this (otherwise would they finance their own demise?) and the workingpeople who were not yet ready for socialism were also expected to ignore the "germ." Lassalle's scheme was to organize the movement on a plank which contained the "germ" of socialism without being socialism, so that the movement would be led to fight for socialism without knowing it. The workers were supposed to back up into the future.

---

* The reader may become confused at this point, since he has doubtless read in a number of authoritative books that this "iron law of wages" was *Marx's* idea, and was the basis of the accompanying "theory of increasing misery" of the workers. But, as Bernstein (*cum* Engels) does here, Marx *attacked* the Lassallean theory of the "iron law," and never heard of his alleged "theory of increasing misery." (No such theory has ever actually been cited from Marx, by anyone.) Chalk up two more scores for the Mother Goose version of marxology.

Writing to Rodbertus about the ultimate goal on which they agreed—"supersession of property in land and capital"—Lassalle emphasized that the "mob" must not be made aware of this:

> Certainly, not yet today need one tell this to the mob; for this very reason I have very much avoided it in my brochures. But I believe that if we get the state credit for associations, this is precisely the little finger that must lead thereto, with the logic of self-developing life, gradually, to be sure only in a hundred to two hundred years (even if not five hundred).[33]

The secret goal (socialism) might as well remain secret if it were going to take some centuries of "self-developing"; meanwhile the vestal fire of civilization, the state, would fortunately be around to rule. Socialism was for the distant future; for the present, the road was a statified society.*

The Bernstein/Engels critique commented on this clever scheme to change society before changing mass consciousness:

> The excuse that the "mob" must not be told what this [ultimate] end was, or that the masses were not yet to be won over to it, does not hold. If the masses could not yet be interested in the actual end of the movement, the movement itself was premature, and then, even were the means attained, they would not lead to the desired end. In the hands of a body of workingmen not yet able to understand their historical mission, universal suffrage might do more harm than good, and productive cooperative societies with state credit could only benefit the existing powers of the state, and provide it with a praetorian guard. But if the body of workingmen was sufficiently developed to understand the end of the movement, then this should have been openly declared. It need not have even then been represented as an immediate aim, to be realized there and then.

And the critique ends this passage with an instructive lesson about means and ends:

> Not only the leaders, however, but every one of the followers that were led ought to have known what was the end these means were to attain, and that they were only means to that end.[36]

---

* It was precisely this passage by Lassalle that was selected for quotation with approval by the first programmatic statement of German reformism, namely, the "Manifesto of the Three Zurichers" (Höchberg, Schramm, Bernstein) which Marx and Engels attacked in 1879.[34] Höchberg's Zurich grouplet endorsed Lassalle's suspicion of "the blind fanaticism of the mob for what is traditional," and applauded that Lassalle "was clever enough not to reveal his final goal immediately."[35] This was the first bridge between the state-socialist reformism of Lassalle, which by itself had no future, and the bourgeois reformism of the type that did represent the future of the Social-Democracy. Note that Lassalle is viewed from another angle in the section on " Intellectual Elitism" in *KMTR* 2, Chapter 17.

Thus once more the principle of workers' self-emancipation had to be spelled out, as against the crafty idea of making the revolution behind the backs of the people themselves. (We need hardly comment on the marxological myth that is here added to the Mother Goose list: the myth that Marx and Engels believed in a principle called "the end justifies the means.)

Incidentally, this passage was an advance comment on the aphorism with which a transmogrified Bernstein was going to inaugurate Revisionism a few years later: "the final end [of socialism] is nothing, the movement is everything." Lassalle had already said something similar in his verse drama *Franz von Sickingen*: "Show not the end and aim, but show the way." (The way *to what*? Why, to an end and an aim that your guide does not want to show you.)

Lassalle followed through by asking his followers to think of nothing but universal suffrage: "Don't look either to the right or to the left, be deaf to all that is not called universal and direct suffrage, or is related thereto, and may lead to it."[37] Reformism itself was to be reformed into a single-issue tactic, with blinkers.

To support the expectation that the state—the existing state—could somehow be induced to back its way down the road to socialism, Lassalle developed an argument identifying the state with the working class by means of arithmetic. The "true" function of the state was to facilitate the great forward march of humanity. "For this," he cried, "the state exists, for this it has always served and must serve." But "what then is the state?" He cited statistics to show that over 96 percent of the population were miserable and oppressed. "To them, then, gentlemen, to the suffering classes does the state belong, not to us, to the upper classes, for of them it is composed! What is the state? ... the answer: Yours, the poorer classes' great association—that is the state."[38]

If, after some millennia of the state's existence, 96 percent of the people were miserable and oppressed, ordinary minds would conclude that this was so because the state did *not* belong to the 96 percent, but rather was the instrument of the 4 percent or part of it. Certainly if the state belonged to the masses by definition, there was no need to conquer it.

We must assume that this rather simple-minded demagogy reflected the actual role of the state mystique in Lassalle's mind.

4. STATE-SOCIALISM AND STATE-CAESARISM

Lassalle's dealings with Bismarck at the time were no dark secret, but were heavily rumored and reported in the ranks of the German movement.

Marx heard about them from his friends in the Lassallean organization, and was able to piece together much of what was going on, from reports not only by Liebknecht but also from information gained through Countess Hatzfeldt, Lassalle's patron. But what Marx had to piece together we can now read in a single letter, which was discovered in 1927—the letter sent by Lassalle to the Junker chancellor about a fortnight after the founding of the General German Workers Association (GGWA) in May 1863.

With this letter Lassalle sent Bismarck the statutes of the new organization, to show him how the dictatorial powers of the president were tailored to Lassalle's demands. The new "workers' leader" crowed over

> the constitution of *my* empire, which perhaps you'd have to envy me! But this miniature picture will plainly convince you how true it is that the working class feels instinctively inclined to dictatorship if it can first be rightfully convinced that such will be exercised in its interests, and how very much it would therefore be inclined, as I recently told you, in spite of all republican sentiments—or perhaps on those very grounds—to see in the Crown the natural bearer of the social dictatorship, in contrast to the egoism of bourgeois society, if the Crown for its part could ever decide on the (to be sure, very improbable) step of taking a really revolutionary and national direction and transforming itself from a kingdom of the privileged classes into a social and revolutionary People's Kingdom!

Lassalle then asked Bismarck if it was "really your intention, as Your Excellency expressed it, to move the Crown one day to the turnabout, to the proclamation of universal suffrage and to the alliance with the people..."[39] (The dictatorship aspect of this modest proposal was discussed in *KMTR* 3, Chapter 7.)

The proposed partnership—an alliance of the Crown representing the absolutist bureaucracy with a workers' movement under a Lassallean dictatorship—was based on the desire of the *old* ruling class to dish the aspirations of the *new* economic rulers who were reaching out for political power. This was the reality behind the talk about the prospects of a "Social Monarchy"; this talk was undercutting the liberal-bourgeois pressure for a Constitution.

Lassalle, who had been rejected by the liberal movement as its would-be leader just before he accepted the mantle of "workers' dictator," made no secret of his hostility to the liberal bourgeois forces. He even blurted it out in public, in a court speech. The fight for a Constitution, he sneered, was only that of a "clique" against the monarchy; the Crown could not yield to this clique, but it could "call the people upon the scene," remembering its own origin, "for all monarchy has originally been the monarchy of the people." And Lassalle added:

A Louis Philippe monarchy, a monarchy created by the bourgeoisie, certainly could not do this; but a monarchy that still stands as kneaded out of its original dough, leaning upon the hilt of the sword, might quite certainly do this, if it determined to pursue truly great, national and democratic aims.

Leaning upon the hilt of the sword... "This," said the Bernstein/Engels critique, "is the language of Caesarism."[40]

Lassalle, in this his last year of agitation, went on to spell out the content of his social-Caesarism as he continued to glorify the Crown and the monarchist regime. In his so-called Ronsdorf Address, he publicly boasted, as he had privately to Bismarck, that the entire authority of the GGWA (the Lassallean party) was in his single hand. He represented "his" workers as saying: "We must weld the wills of all of us into one single hammer, and must place this hammer in the hands of a man in whose intelligence, integrity, and good faith we have the necessary confidence, so that he may be able with that hammer to strike!" (This, of course, was what *he* was hammering into the heads of "his" workers.)

Our organization, claimed Lassalle, has reconciled Freedom and Authority. (This meant, translated: *his* authority had been freed—from all control from below.) And "thus [it] becomes on a small scale the prototype of our next form of society on a large scale," he went on to explain. "With us there is not a trace of that malcontent spirit of Liberalism, of that malady of individual opinion and superiority with which the body of our bourgeoisie is eaten up...."

To this proclamation of social-Caesarism, the Bernstein/Engels critique replied with a longish section. There is good reason to quote the whole of this Marxist reply to the aspirations of the workers' dictator; it makes important reading today. But because of practical considerations we give only the essential lines of the reply. It emphasized that mass workers' action does *not* mean "personal dictatorship."

> ...indeed, where the masses abdicate their will, they are already on the road to become, from a revolutionary factor, a reactionary one. In the struggles of modern society, personal dictatorship has invariably been the sheet-anchor of the reactionary classes, seeing their existence imperilled; no one is so ready to renounce "negative acrid individualism" as the modern bourgeois so soon as his moneybags and his class privileges seem seriously threatened.... The classes that feel themselves incapable of self-government do that which Lassalle is here imputing to the workers: they abdicate their own will to oppose any private interests of this person as "restless, malcontent individualism."[41]

The example of Bonapartism followed. The French bourgeoisie attacked its own "malcontents" in this spirit—"until Napoleon [Louis Bonaparte] was strong enough to proclaim himself dictator *against* the bourgeoisie, instead of contenting himself with the role of mere maintainer of law and order *for* the bourgeoisie."

A growing revolutionary class [continued Bernstein/Engels] has absolutely no reason to abdicate its will, to renounce the right of criticism, to renounce its "superiority" vis-à-vis of its leaders.... He [Lassalle] needed the dictatorship in order to be sure of the workers whenever he should require them for his actual ends, and he needed the endorsement of his dictatorship to appear to those in higher circles as a power to be treated with.[42]

That last point was the crux of Lassalle's tactic. "The policy he was pursuing," the critique went on to say, "could only be carried through if the members and adherents of the movement followed their leader without criticism, and did his bidding without a murmur," but this "meant nothing but pure Caesarism; so his adherents also were to be ready, on the word of command, to don the livery of loyalty." Caesarism outside the workers' movement had to be shored up by Caesarism inside it. Lassalle had the GGWA secretary, Julius Vahlteich, disloyally expelled because Vahlteich would not go along without a murmur.[43]

But no one man can serve two masters.... It is doubly a pronunciamento of Caesarism—Caesarism within the ranks of the party, and Caesarism in the politics of the party.[44]

The hours of conversation that Lassalle spent with Bismarck did not prove to be entirely useless—to Bismarck. The sequel showed that the Junker learned a few things about up-to-date demagogic mass politics and state-socialistic façades.

Bismarck did not need to make actual concessions to Lassalle in order to get something out of it. Soon after a good deal of the Bismarck-Lassalle relationship came to light in 1878 through statements from Countess Hatzfeldt and the chancellor himself, Marx told an interviewer: "Bismarck encouraged Lassalle's course at that time in every possible way.... He wished to use the working classes as a set-off against the middle classes [bourgeoisie] who instigated the troubles of 1848."[45]

We saw at the beginning of this section that, in his now notorious letter to Bismarck, Lassalle pretended to convey the feelings of the "working class." That this "working class" was a pseudonym for F. Lassalle was shown by the very similar letter that Lassalle sent to the Catholic-social conservative V. A. Huber a few months later, this time openly as his own opinion. After expressing wholehearted agreement with Huber—and Czar Nicholas—that a constitutionasl monarchy was "ridiculous" and "organized self-destruction," Lassalle went further:

> As I said, I have been a republican from childhood on.
> And despite that, or perhaps just *because* of it, I have come to the conviction that nothing could have a greater future and play a more beneficent role than the *monarchy*, if it could only decide to become a *social* monarchy. I would then carry its banner passionately, and the constitutional theories would be laid on the shelf quickly enough. But where is there a monarchy that has the courage and discernment to lend itself to a *social* monarchy? You yourself will concede that such can hardly be found.

After Lassalle's death, Dr. Julius Frese wrote about Lassalle's belief in the state's omnipotence in his paper *Demokratische Correspondenz*, the organ of the liberal South German People's Party. Frese related: when he would chide Lassalle for expecting the impossible from the state, the man would answer very seriously: "What would you? The state is God!" Coming from an atheist, this was a fitting summary of state-cultism.[46]

5. MARX ON LASSALLE

The point of view embodied in the Bernstein/Engels critique is a necessary guide to the political condemnations of Lassalle which dot Marx's correspondence especially after 1862.

The year 1862 marked Lassalle's last meeting with Marx and the beginning of Lassalle's public political agitation. This meeting is described elsewhere in this volume: Lassalle revealed not only his dictatorial ambitions but also his "Bonapartist" proclivities.[47] Before he left London to go back to Prussia, Marx had told him flatly that "politically we agree in nothing except some far-distant ultimate ends."[48]

Lassalle kept sending copies of his speeches and publications to Marx, who read them with rumbles of disapproval. Marx's dilemma was that he was reluctant at precisely this time to come out publicly with the opinion he had formed of Lassalle, since the man had placed himself at the head of a struggle taking place in Germany to form a movement for the first time in decades. He did not want to undermine this movement, or even seem to be undermining it.

When in April 1863 Marx received a copy of the "Open Reply," Lassalle's opening gun in his political campaign, he grumbled to Engels as he exhibited some of its gems:

> He behaves—with an air of great importance bandying about phrases borrowed from us—altogether as if he were the future workers' dictator. The problem of wage-labor versus capital he solves like "child's

play" (literally). To wit, the workers must agitate for *universal suffrage* and then send people like him "armed with the unsheathed sword of science" into the Chamber of Deputies. Then they form workers' factories, for which the *state* advances the capital, and these institutions °by and by° embrace the whole land.⁴⁹

Since Marx was here writing to Engels, he did not have to enlarge on these points; he simply pointed.

By June 1863 there were already heavy reports about Lassalle's negotiations with the chancellor: "the fellow is now working purely in the service of Bismarck," Engels opined, exaggeratedly.⁵⁰ Marx more than ever became conscious that Lassalle had effected a political switchover from his original attempt to take over the leadership of the liberals; he was now lined up with the Bismarck government *against* the liberal bourgeoisie. "During 1859," Marx wrote to his friend, "he belonged wholly to the Prussian liberal bourgeois party. Now he may find it more convenient, under the °auspices of government°, to fly out against the 'bourgeois,' rather than against the *'Russians.'*"⁵¹

In the course of 1864 Marx received a report, shortly after Lassalle's Ronsdorf speech, which reinforced its effect. Liebknecht wrote to Marx as follows:

> Things are in ferment in the Lassallean workers' association. If Lassalle does not give up his "dictatorial ways" and his "flirting with reaction," there will be a scandal. About this "flirting," a little anecdote: before his departure he gave a dinner, to which about 20 workers were invited. At the end of it he gave a speech, against the bourgeoisie. It was the sole enemy, and we had to swear to him to fight against this enemy to the death, and *in this connection not to draw back even from an alliance with the monarchy*. At these words I sprang up in a rage; he looked at me, taken aback, turned fiery red, and immediately (resuming the speech he had in fact ended) he protested against possible misunderstandings, the monarchy was itself no enemy of the workers, to be sure, but it would also not help them—without revolution no salvation, etc.⁵²

Lassalle had said almost as much in the Ronsdorf speech, but had not openly mentioned an "alliance with the monarchy." In any case, only his sycophants could now close their eyes to the course he had chosen.

Lassalle was "saved" from his own policy by two things: Bismarck's rejection of his overtures on the ground that the "workers' dictator" had nothing substantial to sell; and his death a few months later due to a duel. Lassalle "was very ambitious and by no means a republican," Bismarck explained to the Reichstag in 1878. "He was very much a nationalist and a monarchist. His ideal was the German Empire, and here was our point of contact."⁵³ Bismarck went so far as to say that he did not consider Lassalle a Social-Democrat.⁵⁴

At the time this was the most acute aspect of the Lassallean malady in the movement: the perspective of an alliance with the old ruling classes (called the Reaction, for short, in contemporaneous language) against the upcoming ruling class, the bourgeoisie, which was already economically dominant. As Engels put it later, "Lassalle demanded that, in the fight between royalty and the bourgeoisie, the workers should range themselves on the side of royalty...."⁵⁵

Interesting historical metaphors for Lassalle's role appear in Marx's correspondence. For one thing, Marx liked to bring up the figure of the Marquis Posa, advisor to Philip II of Spain, as depicted in a famous drama by Schiller, *Don Carlos*. For the nineteenth century the Posa character was the very model of the wise statesman who seeks needed reforms by getting the sovereign's ear and filling it with enlightened advice on how to preserve the power of absolutism by bending a little in a "progressive" direction. In Lassalle's last speech, wrote Marx, he "played the part of the Marquis Posa with handsome Wilhelm [of Prussia] as his Philip II, whom he would push to the abolition of the existing constitution, proclamation of direct universal suffrage, and alliance with the proletariat." Since he was writing to Engels, Marx had only to add a grunt: "The modern Redeemer!"⁵⁶

A second model was Lassalle's own character Franz von Sickingen, in the drama so titled; for Sickingen "wanted to force Charles V to 'put himself at the head of the movement'...."⁵⁷ Lassalle dreamt of acting out his own retrogressive hero-figure.

Engels had an even harder attitude on Lassalle's scheme for a deal with the monarchy behind the backs of the workers' movement:

> Subjectively his vanity may have made the affair [with Bismarck] appear plausible to him; objectively it was a rascality, a betrayal of the whole workers' movement to the Prussians.... In addition, it will not be long before the time comes when it will not only be desirable but *necessary* to make this whole business public.⁵⁸

Marx soon echoed this: "now we know, moreover that Itzig [Lassalle]*— what was not at all known to us in *this* way—wanted to sell out the workers'

---

* Itzig: one of Marx's favorite tags for Lassalle, sometimes ignorantly cited as an instance of "anti-Semitism." For its use among Jews as a deflator of grandiose pretensions by a Jew, see the last part of Heinrich Heine's "Jehuda ben Halevy" (in his *Hebrew Melodies*, 1851). In fact, since Heine was Marx's favorite source of allusions, this passage in "Jehuda ben Halevy" was very likely what prompted Marx to use it for Lassalle, who was made to order for a deflating gibe of this sort.

party to Bismarck, in order to become known as the 'Richelieu of the proletariat'...."[59]

In this last reference was a third historical model for an aspect of Lassalle's type: Richelieu had established the absolute monarchy against the old feudal class; Lassalle wanted to help establish the absolute monarchy against the rising bourgeoisie. Still a fourth model was suggested by Engels: "it can be seen that Itzig has given the movement a Tory-Chartist character which will be hard to destroy.... Everywhere this disgusting cringing before the Reaction shows itself."[60] This referred to the Chartist sympathizers who were politically oriented toward the so-called "Tory Democracy" or "Tory Radicals" such as Richard Oastler.

Engels' reference to the need "to make this whole business public" no doubt had in view a proper public exposé of Lassalle's machinations with Bismarck. We know, however, that both he and Marx long held their hands on this, first, for fear of seeming to embarrass the initial steps toward workers' organization, and later because of the pressure of the Anti-Socialist Law of 1878-1890. Engels finally made a move only in 1891, and then under provocation—as we will see elsewhere in this volume.[61] Lassalle's death in August 1864 only shifted the problem to the Lassallean organization that survived him.

6. MARX ON THE LASSALLEAN MOVEMENT

Marx and Engels thought the first need was for political education to counteract Lassallean ideas. Engels, in close collaboration with Marx, quickly wrote, and in February 1865 published, a pamphlet titled *The Prussian Military Question and the German Workers Party*, which was set out at some length in *KMTR* 2 and need not be repeated here.[62] The final part of this pamphlet was devoted to a polemic against the Lassallean position of aligning with the Reaction in opposition to the liberal bourgeoisie.

The work of writing reinforced Engels' revulsion against Lassallean politics: he was reminded what a "vile thing" it was for the Lassalleans to refrain from mentioning "with so much as a word the patriarchal exploitation of the rural proletariat under the whip of the big feudal aristocracy" because of their hope of alliance with the Reaction.[63] Engels had originally started writing this work as an article for the Lassallean organ, but, as Marx pointed out to him, it was "too sassy" to be printed by its targets; that is, it was "impudent" in challenging the Lassalleans' pro-Bismarck orientation too openly.[64]

In the Lassallean organ *Sozialdemokrat*, editor J. B. von Schweitzer was doing worse than ever: he was starting a series of articles actually supporting Bismarck's imperial policy and glorifying the monarchical regime at the expense of the bourgeois liberals. Schweitzer's first two articles especially were along these lines, shocking Marx among others. The concluding article said: "Two factors are alone capable of action in Germany, Prussia and the nation. Prussian bayonets or the fists of the German proletariat—we see no third." Since the said "fists" were still hardly in position to run the country, it took little perspicacity to deduce that only Prussian bayonets were left: that is, the Prussian bureaucratic state.

Marx and Engels sent in their resignations as contributors; a number of others did likewise. Schweitzer was not yet president of the GGWA as well as editor; the presidency was held by the incompetent Bernhard Becker. In November 1865 Becker was succeeded by C. W. Tölcke, known as a quite open monarchist sympathizer, who once embarrassed the organization by publicly calling for cheers for the king. In January 1866 the *Sozialdemokrat* under Schweitzer's editorship posed the following alternatives: either the Social Republic, or else "a strong autocratic monarchy, which, filled with a natural jealousy of the ascendancy of the propertied class, must seek its support in the real people, the propertyless people...." In the 1866 election the GGWA formally supported Bismarck's personal candidacy.

In May 1867 Schweitzer took over the GGWA presidency. On October 18, in the North German parliament, he declared:

> We have perceived that the Prussian nucleus of power has at length brought our German fatherland, so long despised, to a place of prominence and honor among the foreign powers, and will also do this in the future. And be it far from us with them to disown and to criticize in Prussia those very qualities which last year a world at enmity with us was compelled admiringly to acknowledge [in the Austro-Prussian war]. In a word ... we stand with the Fatherland.[65]

As mentioned, Marx and Engels broke with this movement in a public statement, drafted by Marx. "About 10 days ago I wrote to Schweitzer," he informed Engels, "that he must stand up against Bismarck, that even the appearance of a flirtation with Bismarck on the part of the workers' party must be dropped, etc." Not only did the *Sozialdemokrat* "cravenly flirt with Bismarck" but it continued to glorify Lassalle "although they know now what treachery he was secretly harboring." The public statement would declare war "against Bismarck and against the knaves and fools who dream or drivel about an alliance with him for the working class."[66]

The Lassalleans' aim of getting state capital for their producers' associations would only help the government extend its tentacles into the workers' movement, wrote Marx to Engels.

The Prussian state [of Bismarck] can *not* tolerate workers' °coalitions°

[any kind of workers' organizations] and trade unions. This is certain. In contrast, *government support* to a few lousy cooperative societies is just the kind of crap that suits it. It means extending the noses of officialdom, controlling "new" moneys, corrupting the most active of the workers, emasculating the whole movement![67]

In this letter Marx told Engels of his realization that Lassalle was actually *against* trade-union organization, and thus reveals (to us) that he had retained an illusion or two about how bad Lassalle's politics were.

On the same day, Marx wrote to Schweitzer, first about the need to support trade unions,[68] and then about the meaning of the Lassallean state-aid nostrum. About the latter: Prussian governmental aid to cooperatives would be minute in extent and of little economic value, while at the same time "it serves to extend the system of tutelage, corrupt part of the working class, and emasculate the movement" (Marx had already used this language in writing to Engels). More to Schweitzer:

...the workers' party will discredit itself...if it imagines that the Bismarck era or any other Prussian era will make the golden apples just drop into its mouth, by grace of the king. It is beyond all question that Lassalle's ill-starred illusion that a Prussian government might intervene with socialist measures will be crowned with disappointment. The logic of circumstances will tell. But the *honor* of the workers' party requires that it reject such illusions, even before their hollowness is punctured by experience. The working class is revolutionary or it is nothing.[69]

Schweitzer's reply told Marx, in effect, to subordinate himself "in all 'practical' questions" to his (Schweitzer's) tactics: so Marx informed his friend. Schweitzer was telling him (if we translate a bit): *Your job is to spin theories in London; it is my job to operate real politics; stick your nose out of my bailiwick*. At the same time the Lassallean boss proceeded to publish another article in his pro-Bismarck series.[70] Marx and Engels then sent in their joint resignation from the list of contributors to the Lassallean organ.

7. MARX'S BREAK WITH THE LASSALLEAN PARTY

Their letter of resignation was a terse statement. It said that they had "repeatedly demanded that at least equally bold language should be used toward the [Bismarck] Ministry as toward the Progressives." (That is, socialists had to oppose both camps, not ally themselves with one against the other.) The policy of the *Sozialdemokrat* was a "flimflam" which they called "Royal Prussian government socialism." They pointed out that as far back as 1847 they had expressed their opinion about a position "in which an alliance of the 'proletariat' with the 'government' against the 'liberal bourgeoisie' had been proposed," and they were still opposed to this kind of politics.[71]

The 1847 article in question (actually by Marx) was one titled "The Communism of the *Rheinische Beobachter*." It had attacked Feudal Socialism and its goal of "a monarchy relying on the support of the people."[72] Thus they tied the new phenomenon of Lassallean state-socialism to the old form of "Royal Prussian government socialism."

This side of Lassalleanism—its tendency to tie the workers' movement to the existing state—was the most dangerous one at the time, and Marx and Engels recurred to it more than once. The statement of resignation, Engels explained later, was compelled by Schweitzer's attempts "to steer [his paper] into feudal and governmental waters."[73] In a review of *Capital* cooked up by Marx and Engels for a Stuttgart paper, special attention was given to publicly taking a fall out of Lassalleanism:

> While Lassalle's whole socialism consists in reviling the capitalists and flattering the Prussian cabbage-Junkers, what we find here [in *Capital*] is just the opposite. Herr Marx expressly proves the historical necessity of the capitalist mode of production, as he calls the present-day phase of society, and likewise the superfluousness of the landowning Junkerdom which simply consumes. While Lassalle had highflown ideas about Bismarck's vocation of introducing the socialist Thousand Year Reich, Herr Marx disavows his wayward pupil loudly enough.... [Marx] has explicitly stated that he has nothing to do with any "Royal Prussian government socialism"....[74]

To a friend Marx wrote a longish explanation on two aspects of the issue, aside from the fact that (as Marx wrote) he and Engels "did not like the paper's editing, the lickspittle Lassalle cult, and the occasional flirting with Bismarck, etc." The first of these two aspects is the one we have been discussing, seen from another side.

Marx emphasized that the Bismarckian state would never concede the legalization of independent trade unions, whereas a liberal bourgeois government of the Progressive party could be *pressured* into such a reform:

> I had written to him [Schweitzer] previously that the Progressives could be *intimidated* on the "question of [workers'] combinations," but that the *Prussian government* would *not now or ever* concede the complete abolition of the Combination Laws [against workers' organization], because this would bring with it a breach in the bureaucratic system, the workers' coming of age, the smashing of the Regulations on Servants, the abolition of rump-flogging by the aristocracy in the countryside, etc., etc., which Bismarck could never allow and which in general was incompatible with the Prussian *bureaucrat*-state [*Beamten*staat].[75]

This was a continuation of the same argument which Marx had made in his polemics against Feudal Socialism (which we will take up later) and which Engels had made in his unpublished and untitled pamphlet "The Status Quo in Germany" almost two decades earlier.[76] It was a question of understanding what class ruled the state. The Prussian state, Marx emphasized, was still a *Beamtenstaat*; and this meant not simply a "bureaucratic state" (for bourgeois states are bureaucratic too) but, more specifically, the *bureaucracy's state*.[77]

The second aspect of Marx's letter concerns reforms. Legalization of "combinations" or "coalitions"—meaning trade unions or other independent workers' associations for economic struggle—would certainly be an important reform. Schweitzer and the Lassalleans were indeed *reformists*— but reformists of their own brand. Marx made a point about this in terms of "Realpolitiker" types, operators in "practical politics," whose idea of practicality in politics was *to conform to existing conditions*. It was a question in Marx's mind of a type of *shortsighted* reform politics, which sought to gain reforms by giving up the independence of the movement.

Lassalle went astray, Marx explained, because he was a "Realpolitiker" of the same shortsighted variety as the ex-radicals (like a certain Miquel) who hitched themselves onto the wagon of the Prussian liberals in order to advance the interests of the bourgeoisie under the protection of Prussian hegemony. Lassalle wanted to do likewise in the name of the proletariat, only the hitching was to be to the wagon of the *old* ruling class, the bureaucratic ruling class of the Bismarckian state.

The former type, who latched onto the liberal bourgeoisie,

> were more justified than Lassalle insofar as the bourgeois is accustomed to take the interests that lie right under his nose as "reality," and insofar as this class has in fact struck a compromise everywhere even with feudalism, whereas in the nature of things the working class must be straightforwardly revolutionary.[78]

The other type, Lassallean reformism, appealed to a German working class which was still "demoralized" by a long period of reaction, and so was ready "to hail such a quack savior, who promised to get them at one bound into the promised land."[79] This was "Realpolitik":

> I think [explained Marx] that Schweitzer etc. have *honest* intentions, but they are *"Realpolitiker"*. They want to take account of *existing* conditions and not leave this *privilege* of "Realpolitik" to Herr Miquel & Company alone.... They know that the workers' papers and the workers' movement in Prussia (and hence in the rest of Germany) exist only by the grace of the police. They therefore want to take conditions as they are, and not irritate the government, and so on, just as our *"republican"* Realpolitiker are willing to "go along with" a Hohenzol-

lern *emperor*. But since I am not a "Realpolitiker," I have found it necessary, together with Engels, to break off with the *Social-Demokrat* in a public statement. . . . [80]

One way to explain what made Lassalle tick was this: he was a man in a hurry, like opportunists in general. Writing some years later with a judicious evaluation of Lassalle, Marx gave a partial explanation along these lines. Lassalle originally latched on to the state-aid nostrum as a plank with which to counteract the Schulze-Delitzsch "self-help" movement, but—

> Being far too intelligent to regard this slogan as anything but a transitory *pis-aller* [expedient], Lassalle was only able to justify its use on the grounds of its immediate (alleged!) °practicability°. To this end, he had to claim that it was feasible in the *immediate* future. The "state" was, therefore, transformed into the Prussian state. He was thus forced to make concessions to the Prussian monarchy, to Prussian reaction (the feudal party), and even to the clericals.[81]

"He allowed himself to be governed too much by the immediate circumstances of the time," Marx summarized, thereby pointing to the essential definition of the term *opportunism*.

And so, while it was true that Lassalle and Schweitzer were reformists, they were not the traditional type of bourgeois reformists that later dominated the Social-Democracy. The difference is worth repeating still again: the ruling class that the Lassalleans bet on was the old one, the bureaucracy-cum-Crown, whereas the traditional reformists attached themselves to the rising ruling class of the bourgeoisie. Both types of reformism had much in common: in particular, adaptation to the status quo (whatever it was); the reformism of Socialism from Above.

Their difference was historically determined. For a period this difference stood in the way of the full political fusion of the Lassallean current into the Social-Democracy—its homogenization with the bourgeois-reformist current represented (later) by the Bernsteinian Revisionists. The development of Germany had to proceed far enough so as to negate the special class content of Lassalle's state-socialism, a state-socialism oriented to the state of a *pre*bourgeois ruling class, the Prussian *Beamtenstaat*.

"We seem," wrote Lassalle to the social-monarchist Rodbertus, "to have come into the world as Siamese twins in spirit!"[82] The world into which these Siamese twins came in spirit, the little world in which the state bureaucracy still held state power, was a world that was progressively on the wane and which was soon to go by the board. Lassallean state-socialism made sense only in this world, but its fate illustrated many facets of reformism in general.

8. LASSALLEANISM AND THE GOTHA UNIFICATION

The Lassallean-Bismarckian relationship had two sides. From the side of the Bismarck government, there was a role for a movement like the Lassalleans, even though Bismarck claimed to be uninterested in buying it up. In the early 1870s Engels thought he saw Bismarck's state "attempting to organize its own bodyguard proletariat to keep the political activity of the bourgeoisie in check," though this Bismarckian operation did not reach its high point for another few years. What is this, asked Engels, but the "quite familiar Bonapartist recipe which pledges the state to nothing more, as far as the workers are concerned, than a few benevolent phrases and at the utmost to a minimum of state assistance for building societies à la Louis Bonaparte?"[83]

In this case the "bodyguard proletariat," of course, was the Lassallean state-socialist movement. Engels made this explicit fifteen years later when the term 'state-socialist' had become current:

> Orthodox Lassalleanism, with its exclusive demand for "producer associations assisted by the state," was gradually dying away [by the 1870s] and proved less and less capable of forming the nucleus of a Bonapartist state-socialist workers' party.[84]

As we have seen, Lassallean strength declined as the society modernized, that is, as the specific weight of the bourgeoisie in the state power grew greater. Especially in the south of Germany, the "Eisenacher" socialist party led by Bebel (with Liebknecht at his elbow) gained strength; the trade unions that the Lassalleans thought to keep tethered to their own party dictatorship grew restive and broke away; their state-aid nostrums no longer looked like the only practical thing; their organization weakened, and splitoffs joined the Eisenachers. Lassalleanism was in decline.

This was the background of the unity negotiations that led to the Gotha party congress of 1875 and its program. To Marx it meant that the Lassalleans were being forced into a merger out of galloping weakness, as an alternative to their wasting away. Marx looked to a different road toward unification of the two movements, one that did not involve making substantial concessions to Lassalleanism.

In the first place, it was Marx's political view that there was no need to make important political concessions to Lassallean ideology: unity yes, by all means, but not at the cost of the program. If the Lassalleans insisted on their independence, let them continue to exist with their own program, which was proving a dead weight. Marx's positive proposal (to the Eisenachers' leadership) was the establishment of forms of united action between the two social organizations—a sort of united front (to use a later term); this would be possible *without* organic fusion. There could be simply "an agreement for action against the common enemy," while a "period of common activity" prepared for further steps. The vital step to be taken was not agreement on a common program, but rather the advancement of the movement: "Every step of real movement is more important than a dozen programs."[85]

This was the thinking *behind* the critique of the Gotha draft program which Marx sent to the Bebel-Liebknecht leadership of the Eisenachers, before the unity congress itself. But this leadership—in particular Liebknecht—partly out of euphoria over the magic word 'unity,' partly from a lack of understanding of Lassalleanism, and partly out of simple opportunism (get-rich-quick), acted as if the accession of the Lassallean group was the be-all and end-all of strategy. (See the note on Marx's Critique which forms the last section of this chapter.)

Marx's opinion of the Gotha draft program was summarized in these words: "the whole program, for all its democratic clang, is tainted through and through by the Lassallean sect's servile belief in the state...."[86]

There were two essential parts to Marx's objection. For one thing, the state in question was the Bismarckian state resting on the reactionary classes, and this highlighted Lassalle's choice of which class to take as ally. Marx's critique pointed out that "Lassalle, for reasons now generally known, attacked *only* the capitalist class and not the landowners," and that his formulations were devised to "put a good color on his alliance with absolutist and feudal opponents against the bourgeoisie." That was why the "one reactionary mass" formula was "indeed not at all displeasing to Herr Bismarck."[87]

Secondly, and more specifically, the Gotha program enshrined the Lassallean nostrum "cooperatives through state aid." It cannot be overemphasized (for Marx's followers have rarely been clear on this point) that *Marx's objection to the "state aid" nostrum was not to "state aid" per se but to its place in the program.*

After all, it was unquestionable that Marx and Engels thought socialists should support cooperatives; and as for state aid, there were many cases where socialists made demands on the state (including demands they did not expect to win). Why then should Marx *not* be in favor of state aid for cooperatives? or rather, why should they rule it out as a possible demand? No reason at all.

What the Lassalleans did with this plank (as Marx reiterated many times) was to make it a "universal panacea" by itself, as a *substitute* for a rounded socialist program. *This* was what determined the character of the Lassallean approach to basic program. *There was no other socialistic plank in Lassalle's political platform*—this was it. Engels argued

> that the universal panacea of state aid should be, if not entirely relin-

quished, at any rate recognized . . . as a subordinate transitional measure, one among and alongside of many other possible ones.[88]

(Here "transitional measure" meant a measure taken by a workers' state in the transitional period *after* coming to power, as in the ten-point program of the *Communist Manifesto*.[89])

As a matter of fact, a state-aid plank was also in the Eisenachers' program, but Engels stressed that it was only "*one* of many *transitional measures*" and did not figure in the program "as the sole and infallible panacea for all social ailments."[90]

There is a useful analogy with another question that has led to confusion: the meaning of 'reformism.' For Marx, reform*ism* did not mean the advocacy of reforms. Marx advocated many reforms; this did not make him a reform*ist*. Reform*ism* meant assigning a certain all-encompassing meaning to the fight for reforms, its elevation to the be-all and end-all of politics; that is, reformism was defined by *the place of reforms in the program*. That is exactly what we said about "state aid." Still, it is well known that from Marx's time to ours, all sorts of self-styled and would-be Marxists have confused the concept of reformism with the practice of advocating reforms.

This may help us to understand why some well-intentioned followers of Marx failed to understand a similar point when applied to the "state aid" nostrum. The best case in point was Bebel, precisely because he was more clear-headed than the confirmed confusionist Liebknecht. As a disciple of Marx, Bebel had fought the Lassalleans for some years, and was accustomed to condemn the "state aid for cooperatives" proposal as a Lassallean nostrum. Then one fine day in 1885 Engels himself proposed a plan (about the Steamship Subsidy question, which we will discuss later) involving support for *(gasp!)* state aid to cooperatives. Bebel's pained reaction showed that he was under the impression that the demand itself was inadmissible; and even when Engels tried to explain the point in some detail, he failed to grasp it.[91]

Some years later, Engels related of the Lassalleans that "although the masses more and more grasped the necessity for the socialization of the means of production, the specifically Lassallean [watchword of] producers' cooperatives with state aid remained the sole publicly avowed program point."[92] The elevation of a single nostrum to the sole content of a political platform was typical of the *sect*, of the sectist mentality glorying that this platform was theirs and no one else's. "The chief offense," wrote Marx in his *Critique of the Gotha Program*, "does not lie in having inscribed this specific nostrum in the program, but in taking, in general, a retrograde step from the standpoint of a class movement to that of a sectarian movement."[93] In public references to the Gotha program, Marx tried to play down the "state aid" watchword as a mere "concession to the Lassalleans" that did not count.[94]

In his critique, Marx emphasized the relationship of the "state aid" plank to the total revolutionary perspective, as the indicator of the plank's political meaning. The trouble with the Gotha plank was this Lassallean characteristic:

> Instead of arising from the revolutionary process of transformation of society, the "socialist organization of the total labor" "arises" from the "state aid" that the state gives to the producers' cooperative societies and which the *state*, not the worker, *"calls into being."*

Thus Lassalleanism assigned the basic creative role to the state, not the working class. It was the very opposite of the principle of self-emancipation. Marx added: "It is worthy of Lassalle's imagination that with state loans one can build a new society just as well as a new railway!" If the Gotha plank threw in the codicil that the "state aid" was to be "under the democratic control of the toiling people," this was only lip service.[95]

Marx distinguished his own favorable attitude toward cooperatives (an attitude most plainly to be seen in *Capital*, by the way) from the Lassallean-type plank as follows: cooperatives mean that the workers are trying in this way to "revolutionize the present conditions of production," but this "has nothing in common with the foundation of cooperative societies with state aid," for

> as far as the present cooperative societies are concerned, they are of value *only* insofar as they are the independent creations of the workers and not protégés either of the governments or of the bourgeois.[96]

The key word is 'independent'—independent of the state, independent of the bourgeoisie. Lassalleanism was the negation of the principle of self-emancipation: this is what its state-socialism came down to.

• • •

NOTE ON THE SUPPRESSION OF MARX'S CRITIQUE OF THE GOTHA PROGRAM

The facts of this episode are seldom made clear in the literature, though the facts are not controversial—merely embarrassing in some quarters. Liebknecht set out to make sure that not all members of the Executive knew of and saw Marx's blast against the draft program, and the chief target of this suppression campaign was Bebel. Liebknecht was, of the Eisenacher leadership, the most mindlessly euphoric over unity, and rightly feared that Bebel, who was in jail when Marx sent the document, might be susceptible to Marx's argument. Liebknecht, that much-inflated figure, was eminently successful in keeping the document from Bebel's knowledge.[97]

Even in 1891, when Engels finally—by threats—got the critique published, the party leadership tried its best to suppress publication, and would probably have succeeded, perhaps permanently, if Engels had not been still alive to break through the conspiracy of silence.[98] Even so, Engels was punished by being sent to Coventry for a while by the German leaders! Liebknecht was again the chief operator of the conspiracy. Between 1875 and 1891 he had devoted much effort to fabricating his reputation as a disciple of Marx, "Soldier of the Revolution," etc. Later the first edition of the Marx-Engels correspondence, edited in practice by Bernstein and Franz Mehring, was massively falsified by deletion, by decision of the Social-Democratic leadership, in order to suppress passages revealing Marx's true opinion of both Liebknecht and Lassalle, among other things. This was the most massive text falsification in socialist history.[99]

4 | OF STATE-SOCIALISM: BISMARCKIAN MODEL

In the Germany of the 1880s, the question of state-socialism was transformed from a matter of theory to a burning political issue, and then to a veritable crisis in the Social-Democratic Party.[1]

Engels had to deal with it almost alone, for Marx's health was already failing well before his death in 1883; and Engels' main allies in the German party—Bebel in the party leadership, and Kautsky and Bernstein on the journalistic-theoretical side—themselves had to be educated on the issue and bucked up to oppose a swelling tide of opinion in the new and politically untried movement. The 1875 merger of the Lassalleans with the Eisenachers was still fresh: only the latter group had contributed a dash of Marxist influence, and they now faced an influx of Lassalle-type state-socialists.

The crisis brought about a classic test of theories: which could effectively guide a revolutionary workers' party, Lassalleanism or Marxism? But did the Marxist responsibility rest on the shoulders of people who were competent to assume it? As the historian Lidtke says, the situation "offered Karl Kautsky and Eduard Bernstein their first significant opportunity to employ Marxism in a major ideological struggle."[1]

As already mentioned, the term 'state-socialism' had become current in Germany by this time; but Lidtke properly warns that although it "had become part of the common parlance in Germany by 1880, it had no precise meaning, even to those academicians who were knowledgeable in all the relevant literature."[2] In fact, the state-socialistic academicians found its imprecision useful: one could tell the working-class public "We are socialists too," without being committed to anything "precise." In 1881 Professor Adolph Wagner, one of the leaders of this school, ran against Bebel in the Reichstag election and helped to effect a drop in the Social-Democratic vote.[3]

From the imprecise academicians it was adopted by the reformist wing of the Social-Democracy, which tried to get the party to take it seriously, that is, to move closer to the Bismarckian "socialists." Engels pointed to the emptiness of the term when the reformists precipitated a debate on it at a party congress:

> The term 'state-socialism' has been picked up. This term expresses no clear idea whatsoever, but, like "Social Question" and the like, it is a purely journalistic expression, a mere phrase, with which one can mean anything or nothing. To argue about the real meaning of such a term is for the birds; its real meaning consists precisely in not having any.

The last sentence is a key to much of the history of socialist terminology. Engels went on to suggest how the debate should have been handled:

> ... in the political discussion, they did Vollmar an enormous and quite superfluous favor when they wrangled with him about *what* state-socialism is and isn't; you can go round and round on that forever; it is a pointless bit of twaddle. In my opinion, this is what should have been said at the party congress: Dear Vollmar, we don't give a hang about what you conceive of as state-socialism.... [4]

Rather (he went on) attention should have been focused on Vollmar's actual statements about policy, and on his "brown-nosing of [Kaiser] Wilhelm and Caprivi," that is, of the state and its government. In short, what was needed was not confusion over abstract terminology, but exposition of its concrete political meaning.

1. THE BISMARCK ATTACK

In 1878 the Bismarck regime, alarmed by the growing strength of the socialist movement, put through an Anti-Socialist Law to suppress the Social-Democratic Party. By our present-day standards it was a mild suppression: no massacres took place, and above all the parliamentary side of the party's activity remained legal. The nine Social-Democratic deputies elected in 1878 still functioned in the Reichstag, thereby becoming the only legal representatives of the party in the country, and socialist candidates still ran (and won) in elections. In fact, during the twelve years of the Anti-Socialist Law, 1878-1890, the party's vote increased rapidly, especially from 1884 on, thereby proving that the law could not do the job.

But for its time it was a drastic suppression, particularly in the first years of its operation; and all propaganda and organizational activities of the party went underground, with the party organ *Sozialdemokrat* published in Zurich and smuggled into Germany.

Bismarck was too shrewd to depend only on the policeman's club. The stick to the donkey's rear had to be supplemented by the carrot dangled in front.[5] In the course of the 1880s Bismarck brought out a whole bunch of carrots. Familiar to us now, they then looked revolutionary to many: a series of social-welfare measures providing for accidents, illness, old age, and other workers' disabilities.

Bismarck's first proposal, for insurance against industrial accidents, came in 1881 and was defeated in the Reichstag by the bourgeois parties. After all, Bismarck's aim was not only to isolate the working class from the socialists but also to mobilize a "bodyguard proletariat" of its own in order to dish the liberal bourgeoisie and its demands for constitutional liberties, its aspirations for bourgeois dominance in the government and the weakening of absolutism. The new measures being proposed by the Bismarck government were going to be paid for by the class that was the government's main target. The proletariat was not only supposed to come all over grateful to the state but also to turn antagonistic to the state's main political opposition, the Liberals or "Progressive party." But the bourgeois liberal deputies could not resist very long, in this as in anything else.

In 1883 a Sickness Insurance Act was passed, with the workers contributing only a third of the cost. In 1884 an Accident Insurance Law followed, with costs borne by employers alone. In 1889 an Old Age and Disability measure was adopted. In 1903 came a code of factory legislation, with a system of labor exchanges to promote employment. Many of these measures were the first of their kind in the world; by the time of the world war Germany had become the model land of advanced social legislation, under the pressure of the absolutist state, not the bourgeoisie. (However, unemployment insurance was never passed; it took a revolution to achieve this reform under the Weimar Republic.)

There was a connection between this beneficent program and the coming world war, for Bismarck's social strategy had still another side: it was intended to ensure internal unity and class peace while the state intensified an aggressive foreign policy of colonialism and foreign-market penetration, thereby compensating the bourgeoisie (at least its upper reaches) for its social-welfare expenses. This foreign policy was also going to drive a wedge between the right wing and left wing of the Social-Democratic Party, but we will see only the beginning of this process before this chapter ends.

In part to finance the technological substructure for war, Bismarck introduced another installment of "socialism": a state tobacco monopoly in 1882 (a big source of revenue) and the nationalization of the railways. Here was something that began to really look like socialism to many people; at any rate, it was a definite intervention by the state into the economy, even if still on a small scale.

Bismarck himself did not represent this program as socialist. He left this task to others, as we will see in the next section—except when conversing privately with very gullible people.[6] It was presented as a program to succor the poor and disinherited, always with a side glance at the grasping greed of the bad bourgeoisie.

The Junker chancellor spoke vaguely sympathetic words about Lassalle's specific "state aid" nostrum: "the idea itself does not strike me as absolutely preposterous and absurd," he told the Reichstag in 1877; and he suggested it might be advisable to experiment "with respect to human labor" in the same way as with systems of cultivation in the Ministry of Agriculture. This might help "to solve the question which, though usually called Democratic Socialism, I should prefer to speak of simply as the Social Question." The function of the Crown and of the state was to elevate the laboring classes. Had not Frederick the Great said "I am king of the beggars"? The state must provide help to the "weakest of our fellow citizens." As early as 1865 Bismarck had trotted out a workingmen's delegation from Silesia to lay their grievances before the Crown, and he defended this subversive act with the statement that Prussia's kings "have never aimed at being the kings of the rich."[7] It was in this connection that the Lassallean president, Tölcke, led in giving three cheers for the king.

"If the state," said Bismarck, "will show a little more Christian solicitude for the working man, then I believe the gentlemen of the [Social-Democratic Party] will sound their bird call in vain."[8] Thus Bismarck sounded his own bird call, the mockingbird's, in order to achieve three interrelated objectives: undercut the influence of the socialists over the working class; mobilize the working class as a counterpoise against the liberal bourgeoisie's campaign for a constitution; and prepare for imperialist expansion.

For these ends Bismarck was prepared to be flexible in tactics on the "Social Question" (one of those imprecise terms, remember) in order to consolidate the status quo on the political question of the day.

2. THE KATHEDER-SOCIALISTS

Bismarck's program of social-welfare measures and state monopolies was promptly hailed as a kind of socialism by a kind of social theorist, especially by a wing of the academy's economists who rejected "Manchesterism" or "Smithiasmus," that is, rejected the political economy of the liberal bourgeoisie (called "economic liberalism").

Laissez-faire economists had used the term 'state-socialism' pejoratively to condemn the intervention of the state in regulating the economy. The Bismarckian economists adopted the term as their own, and a group of them published an organ called *Der Staatssozialist*.[9] It helped provide a theoretical-scientific label for Bismarck's practical program: social welfare, ad-hoc hole-and-corner nationalization, but *no* political reform of the existing state institutions— no democratization. The state power would not be touched.

It was largely these professors who told the country that Bismarck's measures were "state-socialism," and who wrote as if they were proposing a kind of socialism alternative to the brand favored by the Social-Democratic Party. Thus they constituted themselves the theoretical wing of something that became known, especially journalistically, as "Bismarckian state-socialism," or even "monarchical socialism."

This tendency—with national roots in Fichte and Friedrich List, and with congeners in French "Bonapartist socialism" and British "Tory Radicalism"—had incubated a decade before Bismarck began implementing it. At the end of 1871 a liberal journalist named H. B. Oppenheim had given this tendency the derisive name 'Kathedersozialisten': socialists of the *Katheder* (university chair of learning).[10] The Katheder-socialist* tendency organized itself at a congress in 1872 at Eisenach into an Association for Social Politics *(Verein für Sozialpolitik)*, to solve the Social Question through state-oriented economics without political concessions to democratization or constitutionalism. Its luminaries were prominent economics professors: Adolph Wagner, Hermann Wagener, Gustav Schmoller, Rudolf Meyer, Adolf Held, Wilhelm Roscher, and others.

The Katheder-socialists typically argued that all civilized governments are more or less socialistic, since every government activity has something to do with regulating society. The state was viewed as the highest of cooperative institutions, "the grandest moral institution for the education and development of the human race." True, the ideal socialistic state might not be realized for a thousand years or so, but all progress tended to this same end. Adolph Wagner discovered the law of history (long before the humorist Parkinson) that the functions of government constantly increase, and he extrapolated from it to the final socialistic state. The historian Ely summarized:

---

* I use the hybrid (German-English) term 'Katheder-socialist' because of its convenience and connection with the original. The name of the school usually found in English is 'socialism of the chair'; variants are 'academic socialism' and 'professorial socialism.' Although originally intended derisively, the name 'Kathedersozialismus' was generally accepted. Oppenheim also called them "sweet-water socialists," but this name did not stick.[11]

In this socialistic state there would be the same difference in rank as at present between the different governmental employees. At the top of the social ladder there would still be an emperor, and at the bottom ordinary laborers, steadily employed in the service of the state, as, e.g., the workmen on the state railroads now.[12]

This socialism, then, would be as bureaucratic a socialism as the existing Prussian state itself, for it was seen as the spirit of Prussian absolutism writ large without bourgeois contamination. Like most types of socialism that repudiate class struggle, it presented itself as an "ethical" socialism, with an additional emphasis on "Christian" self-denial, self-sacrifice, and similar virtues that are highly praised by pundits, papers, parsons and politicians.

The Katheder-socialist leaders freely admitted that they were reacting to the danger of proletarian socialism. Just as in his "social message" to the Reichstag in 1881 the kaiser explained that a policy of social reform was necessary in order to isolate the Social-Democracy, so too in his opening address at the Eisenach founding congress Professor Schmoller deplored "the open war between masters and workmen, between owners and proletarians, and the danger, still distant but threatening in the future, of a social revolution," which called not for "socialistic experiments" but for the abolition of "the most crying abuses."[13]

The Katheder-socialists discovered their own Marx in the figure of Johann Karl Rodbertus—recently dead in 1875—who in the 1840s had deduced socialistic conclusions from Ricardo (in ignorance of his British predecessors, the so-called Ricardian socialists). But Rodbertus had cast this Ricardian socialism in the mold of a monarchical state-socialism hostile to any form of democracy. As we saw in the preceding chapter, Lassalle had not only corresponded with Rodbertus very warmly but had assured him that they were soul-twins in politics; and indeed the similarity between Lassalle's basic ideas and the views of the Katheder-socialists was unmistakable.

Thus the Katheder-socialists were in a good position to confuse the Social-Democratic public with these dubious relationships. Bismarck praised Rodbertus in the Reichstag.[14] Adolph Wagner published an edition of Lassalle's letters to Rodbertus in 1878; and there was a flurry of publications about Rodbertus well into the 1880s. There was an additional to-do over the claim that Marx himself had "plagiarized" from Rodbertus, a rather silly claim which Engels quashed in a couple of essays.[15]

Marx had dealt with Rodbertus as an economist in his notebooks, especially his *Theories of Surplus Value*,[16] but it was Engels who had to deal with the political impact of the pro-Rodbertus drive on the Social-Democratic Party. This he did, as often, in letters to Bebel, Kautsky, and Bernstein—

the party leader and the two political writers whom he sought to train up to the theoretical tasks of the movement.

Engels complimented Rodbertus' early writings because they "came close on the track of [the concept of] surplus value" though Rodbertus failed to follow through, in part because he went after his "utopia" and in part because, as a Pomeranian landowner himself and an "exploiter of cottagers," he was held back by his own conditions of existence and never broke away. He "might perhaps have become an economist of the second rank if he had not been a Pomeranian," but in the end "The man accomplished absolutely nothing in economics; he had much talent, but always remained a dilettante and, above all, an ignorant Pomeranian and arrogant Prussian." Still, "how can it come to pass for a generally decent fellow to count as the gospel of the careerists of Bismarckian socialism?"[17]

But although as a talented economist Rodbertus was "worth much more than the mass of German vulgar economists including the Katheder-socialists, who indeed live only on scraps picked up from us," his political meaning properly made him "the real founder of specifically Prussian socialism ... now at last recognized as such." He did not have to invent social institutions out of his own head: "For Rodbertus it is much easier. As a good Prussian he appeals to the state: a decree of the state power orders the reform." His whole reform scheme was "adapted to the Prussian state of that time." He simply "refers the whole matter to the decision of the bureaucracy, which determines from above the share of the worker in his own product and graciously permits him to have it."[18]

But the problem was not primarily a scientific evaluation of Rodbertus. This Pomeranian was being used as a stick to beat the Social-Democracy as a movement and belabor Marx as its guide to socialist theory. "Ever since [certain people] have been trying to pit the 'great Rodbertus' against Marx, and now that even Adolph Wagner and other Bismarckians have been exalting him as a prophet of careerist-socialism, we have absolutely no grounds to go easy on this much-trumpeted celebrity," Engels wrote to Kautsky.[19]

The problem was the mounting crisis in the party, as a part of the right wing saw an opportunity to wrench the movement off its class-struggle tracks. (This was the meaning of substituting Rodbertus for Marx.) Publicly and privately Engels, like Marx, remained contemptuous of the scientific attainments of the Katheder-socialist economists; they were merely "slightly philanthropic vulgar economists" who had now become "simple apologists of Bismarck's *Staatssozialismus*," he informed a Russian correspondent.[20] One approach to the problem had to be to educate the party membership, and also the party leadership, to understand why this was so.

3. THE CRISIS IN THE PARTY

The state-socialist development outside the Social-Democratic Party had its inevitable impact inside the party, mediated through the party's academic and intellectual elements who latched onto the new persuasion.

On the one hand, Katheder-socialism was eminently respectable and even government-sponsored: hence Engels' repeated references to it as "career-socialism." It could be very attractive indeed to certain elements as the alternative to an outlawed and persecuted position. Consider the difference: defend Marx, and you might land in jail; cry up Rodbertus, and you might well advance a career in academy or government....

On the other hand, Rodbertus' views purported to offer a theoretical-scientific basis for those party elements that wanted to find a replacement for Marxian politics and a class-struggle approach. Thus there sprang up a wing of the Social-Democratic movement which actually set out to install the monarchist enemy of democracy Rodbertus, taken hand-in-hand with Lassalle, in place of Marx as the "scientific" authority of socialism. (A similar effort had been made before this on behalf of Professor Eugen Dühring.) For a short period it looked as if the only ones standing in the way were the small core of conscious Marxists that Engels was training up. The situation cast a cold light on the common belief that the German Social-Democratic Party was "Marxist."

The leader of the pro-Rodbertus drive inside the party was Carl A. Schramm, whose previous association with Höchberg's group (the "Three Zurichers") we have noted.[21] Schramm's tendency carried on a vigorous campaign—at least up to 1886, when it was clearly defeated—to win the party for Rodbertusism; and in this effort it was the figure of Lassalle that this group glorified above all. (Lassalle was god and Rodbertus was his prophet.)

In 1884 Kautsky warned Engels that Rodbertus

> has a great number of enthusiastic followers in our own ranks. A genuine hatred against Marx and Marxism dominates our educated people, and they eagerly grasp after every non-Marxist socialist, from Louis Blanc to Rodbertus, to play them up against Marx....[22]

Of course the hatred was not personal; Marx had died only the previous year, and it seemed like an opportunity to bury him deeper. These people, grasping at their Pomeranian straw, had for the most part only recently been recruited from the bourgeois intelligentsia, and many had exhausted their intestinal reserves by actually lining up with an outlawed movement. Engels wrote of the situation in a letter to Bernstein: the Rodbertus cult stems from the desire "to pit a noncommunist rival against Marx... For all the people who hang around the state-socialist outskirts of our party, and trot out sympathetic speeches but want to avoid anything contrary to police regulations, his excellency Rodbertus is a godsend."[23]

In the pages of the *Neue Zeit* Kautsky, writing under the tutelage of Engels' letters, was the main stalwart in the theoretical campaign against Rodbertus' political economy. In the *Sozialdemokrat* the editors aimed a little lower. "Why," asked an article in 1884, "are the 'educated' socialists in the universities and the careerists of all sorts enthusiastic about Rodbertus?" And why do they "hate Marx [as Schramm had admitted] and seek to belittle him?" Because with Rodbertus they "can be Bismarckians and make careers for themselves."[24] You had to decide what kind of socialist you wanted to be, the kind that Bismarck encouraged or the kind his police hunted down; and perhaps the latter may be excused for thinking hard thoughts about the former.

The Lassalle connection, already publicized by the Rodbertus-Lassalle correspondence, was further pushed to the fore by the editor of that correspondence, Adolph Wagner. Wagner, disagreeing with Schmoller, indicated that Lassalle's state-credit scheme might be worth adopting.[25] As already mentioned, even Bismarck made statements tending to co-opt Lassalle to the new "monarchical socialism."[26] An undertow of sentiment linked the whole of the still strong Lassallean current in the party to the new "kind of socialism" which made it so much easier to be a socialist of sorts.

There was another important connection. One of the Katheder-socialists, Albert Schäffle, in 1875 published an influential book *Die Quintessenz des Socialismus* (*The Quintessence of Socialism*), which went through thirteen editions by 1891. It discussed the views of Social-Democracy and Marxism with such an attempt at fairness (if without understanding) that many of the party leaders were convinced that it would make a useful party textbook. Höchberg, a year before the "manifesto of the three Zurichers," dipped into his fortune to buy 10,000 copies for distribution to academics and intellectuals. Schäffle's book did qualify as a textbook—a textbook in state-socialism. Once again a cold light was cast on the belief that this was a "Marxist party," that is, cast by the reception given this book.

Even before we look at the politics of Schäffle's book, we should note a nonpolitical side to the affair. The reception was partly due to a feeling of parvenu gratification, on the part of many Social-Democrats, elated that socialism was being "recognized" by respectable professors. Engels, commenting on a similar point made by Bernstein, stressed this: "in what you say about courting praise from opponents you are entirely right. We have often disgracefully worried our heads about happily registering in the *Volksstaat* and *Vorwärts* the pettiest fart of approval by a Katheder-socialist."[27] True, Schäffle himself did not scheme this out; but in fact the party euphoria over the Schäffle book was one of the first demonstrations of the value to the ruling classes of treating the party like a dog: that is, kick it and it became vicious; pat it on the head and it wagged its tail. Engels' thought was that as long as a party reacts in this way, it was still a long way from revolutionary fitness.

That can be considered only a preliminary sidelight. Politically, Schäffle presented Marx's socialism as primarily a view of a future society (precisely what it was not) and he also did Marx the naive favor of portraying this future society as the sort of state-socialism that he, Schäffle, admired. "The Alpha and Omega of socialism is the transformation of private and competing capitals into a united collective capital," Schäffle explained in italics. Everything that centralizes "is very closely allied to socialism." Socialism is "the universal application of the special principle of the State and the municipality," the extension of "the idea of an official public service." The collectivist principle is "essentially a State-principle."

Schäffle did not claim to find this in Marx; he honestly assumed that what he read in much of the Social-Democratic press was "Marxist"—it was a Marxist party, wasn't it? He had no idea that this sort of thing was what Marx consistently attacked. He did not intend to caricature or slander Marxism; he thought he was praising it, presenting it as something really quite reasonable, something worthy of a Prussian professor's attention. The Social-Democrats were not wild men—they "believed in" the State like all other civilized people, even though (as Schäffle explained in another book) their socialism was "impossible."[28] For a generation or two, professors found out what "Marx" taught by reading Schäffle, and the results are still visible in the literature.

As a result of all this, a crisis confronted the Social-Democrats on both fronts, theory and political practice, outside and inside the party. If Bismarck's social-welfare and state-monopoly program was really socialist, then it *was* possible to bring about socialism (or a reasonable facsimile thereof) through this kaiser-state and without a democratization of society and government. A wide swath of leaders and middle figures in the party were ready to assent to this proposition: not only the well-known right-wingers, but persons considered to be more moderate.[29] Standing out against the sweep of this current were Engels and the party leaders he influenced directly.

We will see that there was a tendency—certainly a wish—on Engels' part to underestimate the impact of Schäffle and his similars on the party ranks; and the reasons for this tendency are plain to see in his and Marx's correspondence.

Firstly, they found it hard to believe that politically educated comrades could take this stuff seriously. In the 1870s, before the party crisis matured in reaction to the Bismarckian program, both Marx and Engels in their letters treated the professor's *Quintessence of Socialism* as a butt for ridicule. The book showed, to be sure, that German bourgeois ideologists were being infected with socialistic ideas (wrote Marx to a friend), but it was half a joke, "full of involuntary comedy." Schäffle wrote it for Protestant parsons who wanted to flirt with socialism like their Catholic rivals; he "paints the future socialist millennium so nicely, with true Swabian fancy, that it will be the perfect realm for cozy petty-bourgeois...."[30]

More seriously, Marx objected to Schäffle's invention on his behalf of what he called "Marx's social state."[31] In early 1881 Engels protested to Kautsky that he considered it a sheer waste of time "to refute, for instance, the horrendous rubbish which Schäffle alone has compiled in his many big volumes,"[32] and to Bernstein he wrote that Schäffle was so inane that he "confesses [in his book] that for ten years he pondered over one (the simplest) point in *Capital* before he got to the bottom of it, and then he made it into pure nonsense!"[33]

Secondly, I suspect that Engels was in any case fighting shy of having to do for Schäffle what he had done for (or to) Professor Dühring. In addition he, as well as Marx, perhaps overestimated the theoretical level of the party leadership.

But the problem was going to continue in one form or another all through the 1880s and into the 1890s, and Engels in particular had to deal with it very seriously.

4. FLASHBACK: MARX ON STATE INTERVENTION

Keeping this problem in mind, let us now take a flashback on Marx's views.

Marx had not been previously confronted with the problem of state-socialism in this form or in any clearly formulated way; and so (as usual) his earlier writings had only glancing references to issues that bore on it. We are not concerned now with the overarching question of attitude to the state—hostility to the state as against glorification of the state—but to a more specific issue: what is the meaning for socialists when the state substitutes itself in the economy for private capitalists?

The general answer to this question was clear enough. Marx regularly denied that intervention by the state was *per se* socialistic; when a capitalist state engaged in economic life, it merely generalized capitalist relations. There was a forerunner of this approach as far back as Marx's Paris manuscripts of 1844, where he criticized the "crude communism" of the day for being "the logical expression of private property," in that it "negates the *personality* of man in every sphere." The kind of "community" *(Gemeinschaft)* that this communism dreams up, he wrote, is only a community of labor with equal wages "paid out by communal capital—by the *community* as the universal capitalist."³⁴ At this point, we must remember, he had barely started his economic studies, and he was not grappling with a state-socialist view as such but only trying to show how "crude communism" remained bound by bourgeois relations.

In the 1850 "Address to the Communist League," Marx and Engels took up the economic program of the petty-bourgeois Democrats (called "the Democracy"), which included some demands for state aid. To relieve the pressure of big capital on small producers, they wanted "public credit institutions and laws against usury, by which means it will be possible for them and the peasants to obtain advances on favorable conditions from the state instead of from the capitalists. . . ." The dominance of capital was to be counteracted also by restricting the right of inheritance and "by transferring as many jobs of work as possible to the state." At this point the authors commented:

> As far as the workers are concerned, it is certain above all that they are to remain wage-workers as before; the democratic petty-bourgeois only desire better wages and a more secure existence for the workers and hope to achieve this through partial employment by the state and through charity measures. . . .³⁵

The bourgeois wage-relation remained; whatever these demands were worth as palliatives, they certainly had nothing to do with socialism, no matter how many jobs were transferred to the state payroll.

Journalistically Marx took sharp note of a sort of statification which later became known as "socializing the losses." Writing in the *NYDT* about the 1857 economic crisis, he explained that the Prussian state was (vainly) trying to hold prices up by paying predepression prices.

> °°In other words, the fortune of the whole community, which the Government represents, ought to make good for the losses of private capitalists. This sort of communism, where the mutuality is all on one side, seems rather attractive to the European capitalists.³⁶

Bismarck's later nationalization of the railways was a classic case of "socializing the losses": if private capitalists could not run the indispensable railway system at a profit and as it should be run, the state had to run it on behalf of the capitalist class as a whole. Here and there, when the subject came up, Marx treated "state capital"—capital invested by governments in railways, mines, and other enterprises—as an integral part of the "social capital" of the system as a whole.³⁷

In the 1870s, after the Katheder-socialists made their splash, the record shows direct comments by Marx only on their economic theory. In an unfinished manuscript dating from 1879-1880 Marx criticized a textbook on political economy by Adolph Wagner. He made the following basic point:

> Where the state itself is a capitalist producer, as in the exploitation of mines, forests, etc., its product is a "commodity" and hence possesses the specific character of any other commodity.[38]

The state is a "capitalist producer" when it undertakes a productive enterprise within a socioeconomic framework that is still essentially capitalist. (Such an enterprise may be tagged with that protean term 'state-capitalism,' if you wish, or even with 'state-socialism' in one of its many meanings, but neither term is enlightening by itself.)

The question became more insistent the more industry developed, with pressures for state intervention. On this subject, as on many others in this last decade of Marx's life, it was Engels who wrote directly on the new situation posed before the movement. His first and principal statement was embodied in *Anti-Dühring*, which was written over a period of nearly two years centering on 1877. We will consider this statement in the next section.

To introduce it, it is necessary to re-emphasize a point made in *KMTR* 1, on what is there called the Engels-versus-Marx myth, which often boils down to an effort to separate *Anti-Dühring* from Marx's imprimatur. Since in a preface to *Anti-Dühring* Engels mentioned that "I read the whole manuscript to him [Marx] before it was printed," it is sometimes assumed, for no known reason, that before this final reading the two friends never discussed what was going into the manuscript from week to week and day to day, at any time during those twenty-two months.[39] Yet there is a plethora of evidence that the two of them engaged in long conversations almost every day.

For the period after Engels moved to London in September 1870, Lafargue's reminiscences relate: "From 1870 to the death of his friend, not a day went by but the two men saw each other, sometimes at one's house, sometimes at the other's."[40] Eleanor Marx wrote: "During the following ten years [after 1870] Engels came to see my father every day; they sometimes went for a long walk together but just as often they remained in my father's room... In that room they discussed more things than the philosophy of most men can dream of."[41] A few months after Engels' move to London, daughter Jenny wrote a friend that "Mohr [Marx] and he [Engels] go out for long walks together, whenever Mohr's health permits it."[42]

Some people must assume that the two discussed only the weather, medieval French verse, ancient battle formations, and other subjects known to be dear to one or the other, but that they never talked about the important problems of politics and theory that were occupying their minds and on which Engels was writing during those twenty-two months. To believe this requires a herculean effort of will.

In considering the long and justly famous passage from *Anti-Dühring* which is discussed in the next section, as in other issues in the Engels-versus-Marx myth, we certainly cannot assume that Marx would have written exactly the same thing; but the probability is great that there was a basic identity of views. We will see further that Engels repeated essentially the same view of the matter for the next several years, whenever it came up.

5. ON CAPITALIST STATIFICATION

Engels' exposition in *Anti-Dühring* (slightly revised when this section was included in the popular pamphlet *Socialism Utopian and Scientific*) begins with his explanation that "the socialized organization of production" in the capitalist factory stands in contradiction with the anarchy of production in society as a whole. The pressure of the advancing productive forces demands "the *practical recognition of their character as social productive forces.*" And "this stronger and stronger command that their social character shall be recognized, forces the capitalist class itself to treat them more and more as social productive forces, so far as this is possible under capitalist conditions." One outlet for this tendency is the growth of joint-stock companies, which are a "form of the socialization of great masses of means of production."[43]

In *Socialism Utopian and Scientific* Engels added a passage of explanation on this form of capitalist "socialization of production." The capitalists develop "a trust, a union for the purpose of regulating production." Whole industries are turned into single trusts; competition turns into monopoly,

> and the production without any definite plan of capitalistic society capitulates to the production upon a definite plan of the invading socialistic society. Certainly this is so far still to the benefit and advantage of the capitalists. But in this case the exploitation is so palpable that it must break down.[44]

The bold figure of speech in the phrase "the invading socialistic society" points to the way in which the society's need for a socialist transformation achieves distorted recognition as the capitalist system tries to adapt to the need without going through the transformation. The actual transformation achieved is the change from competition to monopoly, and, as Engels says, the capitalists reap benefits from this. But this screws the original contradiction—the contradiction between socialized production and capitalist anarchy of production—to a higher pitch and brings the end nearer.

But the joint-stock company "form of socialization" is not enough. "At a further stage of evolution this form also becomes insufficient." With trusts or without, "the official representative of capitalist society—the state—must [ultimately] undertake the direction of production." And "This necessity for conversion into state property" is felt first of all in the fields of communication and transportation, post office, railways, etc.[45] That is, it is felt first in those industries that are essential to the operation of the capitalist system as a whole. The qualifier "ultimately" (*schliesslich*) was added in *Socialism Utopian and Scientific*; it represented a slight revision, but was intended to clarify, not to change.[46]

Now Engels hangs his important footnote on the proposition that the state "must [ultimately] undertake the direction of production." For the polemic against Dühring this is a side issue, but of course Engels has in mind the Bismarckian socialist tendency as a whole. The footnote goes as follows.*

> I say *must*. For only in case the means of production or distribution have *really* outgrown their management by joint-stock companies, and therefore their statification has become *economically* imperative—only in this case does it mean an economic advance, the attainment of another step preliminary to the taking over of all productive forces by society itself, even if it is the present-day state that carries this out. But of late, since Bismarck has thrown himself into statifying, a certain false socialism has appeared, and degenerated now and then even into something of flunkeyism, which declares without further ado that *every* statification, even the Bismarckian kind, is socialistic. To be sure, if the statification of the tobacco business is socialistic, then Napoleon and Metternich are to be numbered among the founders of socialism. If the Belgian state, for quite ordinary political and financial reasons, itself constructed its chief railways; if Bismarck without any economic necessity statified the chief Prussian railway lines, simply the better to establish and use them in case of war, to bring up the railway officialdom as voting cattle for the government, and principally to create for himself a new source of revenue independent of parliamentary decisions—this was in no way a socialistic step, directly or indi-

---

* Since the English translation of *Socialism Utopian and Scientific* by Aveling in 1892 was supervised by Engels, it immediately became the standard version, and has remained so. But this version had no English term for *Verstaatlichung* and its forms (statification, statify), which are used repeatedly in the original. This translation is no longer satisfactory for today. My own translation, above, has been kept close to the German text.

rectly, consciously or unconsciously. Otherwise, the Royal Maritime Company, the royal porcelain factory, and even the regimental tailor of the army would be socialist institutions, or even, as was seriously proposed by a sly dog in the thirties under Friedrich Wilhelm III, the statification of the—brothels.[47]

This was probably the first definite repudiation, within the socialist movement, of the view that *statification equals socialism*, or that statification was progressive *ipso facto*, to be supported by socialists more or less automatically as a step in their direction. It was a direct repudiation of the Schäffle doctrine that was even then being promoted by so many in the German party.

The reference to Bismarck in this passage did not primarily concern his social-welfare program; it was his statification measures that were more confusing to many elements in the party. To be sure, such statification—like the joint-stock company "form of socialization"—had "progressive" consequences of a sort that the party was familiar with: it proved how unnecessary the capitalists were. Production went on without them. "All the social functions of the capitalist are now performed by salaried employees. The capitalist has no further social function...."[48]

It also had to be said that the new forms of "socialization of production" under capitalism did not do away with the capitalist nature of the system. This was plain in the case of the joint-stock companies, which were openly owned by capitalists. But the state, which did all this statifying, was also owned by the ruling classes. Therefore this state functioned essentially in the economy as a *collective capitalist* (Engels' term: *Gesamtkapitalist*)—an instrument serving the capitalist class "collectively."

It is unfortunate that the term 'collective capitalist' was eliminated from the standard English translation, along with others thought too difficult for Anglo-Saxon skulls. For that matter, even the German *Gesamtkapitalist* has been shoved into the shadows; the implied thought does not go well with the reformist aspiration to collectivize capitalism and call the result 'socialism.'

Let us restore the illuminating term to Engels' original argument, in the following passage. (The bracketed words were added in *Socialism Utopian and Scientific*.) Engels has taken off from the thought stressed above, that the capitalist no longer has an indispensable social function.

> But the transformation either into joint-stock companies [and trusts] or into state ownership does not abolish the nature of the productive forces as capital. With the joint-stock companies [and trusts] this is obvious. And the modern state, again, is only the organization that bourgeois society takes on in order to maintain the general external conditions of the capitalist mode of production against the

encroachments of both the workers and individual capitalists. The modern state, no matter what its form, is essentially a capitalist machine, the state of the capitalists, the ideal collective capitalist [*Gesamtkapitalist*].* The more it proceeds to the taking over of the productive forces, the more it actually becomes the collective capitalist,* the more citizens it exploits. The workers remain wage-workers, proletarians. But the capitalist relation is not done away with; it is rather brought to a head. But, brought to a head, it topples over. State ownership of the productive forces is not the solution of the conflict, but concealed within it are the formal means or handle for the solution.*[49]

This statement was the key to Engels' approach to both the theoretical and political problems in confronting Bismarckian state-socialism and in dealing with Bismarck's fellow travelers of the *Katheder*. On the theoretical plane, the issue was squarely based on the class nature of the state which was doing the statifying. On the political side, the party was shown how to combine two notions: gratification that the capitalist class and the state are compelled to resort to these measures (for the reasons given by Engels) and, at the same time, *refusal to support them politically nevertheless*.

This statement requires a side remark, at the risk of digression. What we have just seen is a kind of combination that Marx as well as Engels proposed more than once; we will see another case in the next section. The combination is quite simple; yet history shows there must be some difficulty in getting the point. There is a persistent tendency to believe, and to proclaim as a "principle of Marxism," that if an event is considered "progressive" (i.e., accompanied by progressive consequences of some sort), then it is not only desirable, but must be *politically supported*, usually along with its sponsors. In contrast, Marx and Engels thought of this pattern like generals in combat: if your enemy is compelled (for example) to introduce conscription, you may be delighted and gratified because of what this shows about his position, or for other reasons, but you do not consequently conclude that you have to support his introduction of conscription. *That is a matter of political support*, and it does not automatically go along with gratification. For Marx, taking a political position meant literally *taking up a position in the class struggle*, as in a battle, and was not merely the expression of an opinion about the objective or "scientific" meaning of an event or act. (End of digression.)

---

* At the three points marked by an asterisk in this passage, the standard English version edits the text, as mentioned. (1) For "ideal collective capitalist," it substitutes "ideal personification of the total national capital." (2) In the third sentence, for "collective capitalist" it substitutes "national capitalist." (3) For the last words beginning "the formal means," it substitutes: "the technical conditions that form the elements of that solution." No doubt Aveling consulted with Engels on these substitutions.

Engels' exposition in *Anti-Dühring* continued with a passage bearing on the difference between *socialization* and *statification*. As we have seen, there are different kinds of socialization; it depends on what is being socialized. Under capitalism, production is socialized to a high degree both by the joint-stock company and by state ownership, that is, ownership by a capitalist state; and to this, as mentioned before, you may wish to apply the tag 'state-socialism' or indeed 'state-capitalism.' Whatever you call it, it is a socialization of production that stems from capitalist trustification or capitalist statification. It is still bourgeois inasmuch as the bourgeoisie remains the ruling class—at least in civil society, even if the Junker state still controls political power. (The precondition which Engels did not have to make explicit is simply that there still *is* a bourgeoisie, that it has not been abolished.)

What makes the great difference is not any change in the economic forms; it is rather *the conquest of state power by the proletariat*. This is what is highlighted in Engels' analysis; this is its crux. The proletarian state takes production out of the hands of the capitalists on a large scale, and therefore turns it "in the first instance into state property." But this is a step in a new process of socialization, the socialization of *ownership* itself—"the taking over by society of the productive forces."

Here is how Engels presents it. First, the leap in socialization:

> This solution can only lie in the factual recognition of the social nature of the modern forces of production, and therefore in the harmonizing of the modes of production, appropriation and exchange with the social[ized]* character of the means of production. And this can only come about by society taking possession, openly and not roundaboutly, of the productive forces which have outgrown all control except that of society [as a whole].*

As this passage continues, note how the stress is on the social consequences of *political power*:

> The social character of the means of production and of the products today reacts against the producers, periodically disrupts all production and exchange, acts only like a law of nature working blindly, forcibly, destructively; but with the taking over by society of the productive forces, the social character of the means of production and of the products will be utilized by the producers with a perfect understanding of its nature, and instead of being a source of disturbance and periodical collapse, will become the most powerful lever of production itself.[50]

---

* In two places in this passage, bracketed additions give the formulations of the standard English translation, which slightly revises the original.

This brings us to what happens "in the first instance":

> While the capitalist mode of production ... forces on more and more the transformation of the vast means of production, already socialized, into state property, it shows itself the way to accomplishing this revolution. *The proletariat seizes political power and turns the means of production in the first instance into state property.* But, in doing this, it abolishes itself as proletariat, abolishes all class distinctions and class antagonisms, abolishes also the state as state.[51]

This reference to the abolition of the states leads, of course, to another famous question, which is not now our subject.

At this point, it should be clear that what is in the forefront of Engels' thought is *an argument about class political power*. The statification that takes place under capitalism and for nonsocialist motives, he points out, shows the way to accomplishing the real revolution: when the proletariat gains political power, then *its* establishment of state power is a first step toward the general socialization of ownership (which, to be sure, can take place in many forms other than direct state ownership). Since it is only a first step, we will see that what takes place "in the first instance" is followed by other instances.

Now this discussion of statified economy in *Anti-Dühring* was provoked by the contemporaneous issue of Bismarckian state-socialism and the claims of the Katheder-socialists. The latter especially were trading on the well-known fact that state ownership had *something* to do with socialism: so everyone thought. Engels did not stand this on its head and claim that statification had *nothing* to do with socialism. Instead, he set out to show the limits of the connection.

The limits were set especially by the proletarian conquest of power (the class nature of the state) and the tendencies that this class shift unleashed. That is why this argument about state-socialism led, in *Anti-Dühring*, directly into the section on the dying away of the state under socialism.

6. ARGUMENTATION

Even before *Anti-Dühring* was finished and on through the 1880s, Engels wrote a series of letters to German party leaders, bucking them up against the state-socialist attack, and explaining the issues in terms of both basic analysis and ad-hoc political considerations. The party crisis, after all, was not over state-socialism in the abstract—whatever that was thought to be—but over the specific campaign by a specific German regime. A survey of Engels' lines of argumentation shows points made on several levels.

In the first place, it was important to expose the regime's motivations, since Bismarck was posing as the Royal Friend of the Poor. While the overall aim of the Bismarckian program was to offer an alternative to proletarian socialism, it had a number of additional advantages for the regime. "Prussiandom," that is, the Bismarckian state, argued Engels, would get an "enormous increase in power."

For one thing, the state was aided in gaining "complete financial independence from all control"—in particular, from control by the parliament's power to vote taxes—since revenues from the state railways and tobacco monopoly would fill the government's coffers regardless of the bourgeoisie's political institutions.[52] This indicated why "this alleged socialism is nothing but feudal reaction, for one thing, and for another, a pretext for squeezing out money"; for anything that made the government independent of parliament favored feudal reaction. In a letter to editor Bernstein, obviously with press propaganda in mind, Engels urged heavy propagandistic stress on this motive: "With Bismarck it is a question of money, once and again money, for the third time money, and he changes his pretexts to get it from purely external considerations...."[53]

For another thing, the regime gained power "through direct sway over two new armies, the army of railway officials and of tobacco sellers, and the related power of handing out jobs, and corruption." In a letter to Bernstein emphasizing the money motive (state revenue), Engels added that Bismarck had "the additional intention of turning as many proletarians as possible into officials and pensioners dependent on the state, of organizing alongside the regimented army of soldiers and army of officials a like army of workers." He snorted: "Electoral coercion by state superiors instead of big factory overseers—a fine socialism! But there's where you get when you believe what the bourgeoisie itself doesn't believe but only pretends to believe: that the state is = [equal to] socialism." And, into the bargain, "the state's tobacco workers would also be immediately placed under the Anti-Socialist Law [as government employees], and their freedom to organize and strike would be taken away...."[54]

Even leaving these considerations aside, Engels argued, the meaning of statification was ambiguous: "it should not be forgotten that every transfer of industrial and commercial functions to the state nowadays can have a double meaning and double effect, depending on circumstances: a reactionary one, a step backward toward the Middle Ages, and a progressive one, a step forward toward communism."[55] Circumstances showed that Bismarckian statification was reactionary.

With regards to railway statification, Engels stressed what might be called a muckraking argument: "that the railway statification is of use only to the shareholders, who sell their shares above value, and not a bit of use to us [socialists], since we will make a finish of the couple of big companies just as quickly as of the state, supposing first we have it...."[56]

The "muckraking" element Engels wrote up at greater length in an article on "The Socialism of Herr Bismarck" in the French party press, arguing that "The scheme to concentrate all the railways in the hands of the Imperial government has for its starting point not the social welfare of the country but the individual welfare of two insolvent banks." The summary conclusion was that "the German Empire is as completely under the domination of the stock exchange as the French Empire [of Bonaparte] was in its time. It is the stock-exchange speculators who work up the schemes that are carried out—to line their pockets—by the government."[57]

7. MORE CONSEQUENCES OF STATIFICATION

The same article on "The Socialism of Herr Bismarck" devoted its first half, for the benefit of the French public, to a state-interventionist issue that was a part of the Bismarckian program: the protective tariff policy. Engels argued not only that this bit of state intervention had nothing socialistic about it, but also that it was a mistake from the standpoint of modernizing (developing) German industry. He made the same argument in a letter to Bebel: "from our viewpoint protective tariffs are entirely wrongheaded in Germany"; an industry like iron "needs a protective tariff only against the *home* consumers, so as to sell dirt-cheap *abroad*, as the facts show...."[58] The tariff was touted in Germany under the vague heading of "social measures" but it was really a means of exploiting the workers in their capacity as consumers.

Inside the party, the tariff issue intersected the issue of Bismarckian state-socialism. This story illustrates the kind of impact that the latter ism had on the Social-Democrats.

The protective-tariff question arose in sharp form in 1879 when Bismarck proposed tariff legislation. Although formally the Social-Democratic Party had not adopted a tariff policy, and there were opinions on different sides of the question, the Reichstag Fraction of the party (always the fortress of the right wing) allowed Max Kayser, who alone endorsed the whole of Bismarck's tariff program, to be the only party deputy to speak on the floor. Karl Hirsch's Social-Democratic *Laterne* attacked Kayser's pro-Bismarck speech, and was in turn denounced by Fraction leaders. Marx and Engels came vigorously to Hirsch's defense. They devoted Part II of their "Circular Letter to Bebel et al." of September 1879 to a denunciation of the Kayser speech and of the Fraction's indulgence of it. (This was the extremely important Circular Letter which ended with the attack on "The Manifesto of the Three Zurichers," i.e., the Höchberg group.)

Marx and Engels argued that, despite the formal absence of a party position specifically on protective tariffs, Kayser's speech was a violation of two standing party principles: (1) against "voting for indirect taxes, whose abolition is expressly demanded by the party program"; and (2) against "granting money to Bismarck and thereby violating the first basic idea of all our party tactics: to this government not a penny." Engels followed up with another letter to Bebel giving more argumentation against the Kayser line.[59]

In this controversy, the state-socialistic (or state-interventionist) aspect of the protective-tariff question was usually subordinate to the political-strategic, that is, to the principle of all-out opposition to the Bismarck regime and all its works. Subsequently, as the issue of state-socialism developed further, Engels tended to subsume the tariff question under its head.

Aside from the tariff question, there were consequences (side effects) of the Bismarckian program that *were* positive, or "progressive," from the Social-Democrats' angle, and it was necessary to understand this too, *provided that such understanding did not become a pretext for support*. A good example was provided by the new tobacco monopoly, which would help transform the feudalistic conditions in the East Elbian region, where Junker domination was strongest and where tobacco was a domestic (cottage) industry. As we saw above, Engels had stressed that economic activities in the state could have a "reactionary" and retrogressive effect or a "progressive" one, and he continued as follows:

> But in Germany we have just crawled out of the Middle Ages....
> What the highest possible development needs with us, is precisely the *bourgeois* economic regime, which concentrates capital and drives contradictions to a head, especially in the northeast [Elbian region]. The economic dissolution of feudal conditions east of the Elbe is in my view the most necessary advance for us, plus the dissolution of small-scale establishments in industry and trade in all Germany and their replacement by big industry. And this is, in the end, the only good side to the tobacco monopoly—the fact that with one blow it would transform one of the most infamous domestic industries into big industry.[60]

What this shows is that the "good side" did not in the least depend on the fact that it was the state doing it; any bourgeoisification would have a similar effect in this backward region. In fact, it showed that this statification was playing the role not of socialism but of bourgeoisification (modernization). In this context the terms 'state-socialism' and 'state-capitalism' equaled each other in imprecision.

There was another advantageous side, involuntary on Bismarck's side. Editor Bernstein pointed it out in a *Sozialdemokrat* article, and Engels applauded enthusiastically: "very good," he said of "the treatment of the Bismarckian statification mania as a thing which we don't have to come out for but which, like everything that takes place, redounds willy-nilly to our advantage...."[61] (Here again is an example of the combination noted in Section 5 above, in the so-called digression, about political support to "progressive" phenomena.)

What Bernstein's article did was (in Engels' view) to show the other side of the point that Bismarck was aiming to build an "army of workers" dependent on the state. The longer-range consequence of this process must be that these state workers would become "the most effective support of the revolution." This "army" now consists four-fifths of proletarian employees, many of whom already support socialism; and as Bismarck statifies the railways, "he is recruiting for us, exclusively for the Social-Democracy."

> The workers of the Upper Silesian Railway workshops will become firm supporters of our cause the more they are sweated by the state lines. And Bismarck *must* sweat them, for he statifies not in order to give anyone nice ideas but for a very real goal, making money for Saint Militarism.

The state's workers suffer as much from economic pressure as private workers, or more, "but in their case the political pressure which is put on them is far more disgraceful, far more extensive."

> And whatever small difficulties may be encountered by the victorious revolution in taking over social ownership of the big private enterprises and socializing them, the socialization of the state enterprises will be able to proceed—will *have* to proceed—so speedily and immediately as would not be possible for the former. This enormous advantage which flows to us from Bismarck's statification activity should not be left out of account.

The very term "socialization of the state enterprises," used in this passage, was enlightening in view of Engels' repeated insistence that mere statification did not mean socialism. It meant that *state* enterprises still had to be made *socialist* enterprises, just as private industry had to be. The Bernstein article in *Sozialdemokrat* concluded on this subject as follows:

> ... this army of state workers will stand on the side of the revolution ... *yes*. We even go a step further and say: they will not only fight *for* the revolution and not against it, but they will very likely form the vanguard; for they have only one enemy and therefore hate it all the more strongly: the *existing exploiter-state*, the *existing holder of power*.[62]

This went to the heart of the social-revolutionary potential in state-socialism. Far from meaning that the state was instituting socialism, it meant that *the state was setting itself up as the direct and immediate target of revolutionary discontent,* without the intervening screen of private enterprise. The state became not only a political oppressor but the primary economic exploiter. Or to put it in other words: the political and economic ruling classes were fused into one enemy.*

Some aspects of the Bismarckian program, Engels argued, were neither helps nor hindrances, but simply mattered little. Thus, one of the party leaders, Paul Singer, visiting London, appeared to Engels (at this time) to be one of "those who see, in the statification of anything at all, a semisocialist measure or anyway a measure preparatory to socialism, and therefore are privately enthusiastic about protective tariffs, tobacco monopoly, railway statification, etc."

> These measures are humbugs, which are inherited from the one-sidedly exaggerated struggle against Manchesterism and which have supporters especially among the bourgeois and academic elements that have come over to us, because they help the game when they discuss with their bourgeois and "eddicated" milieu.... We should not make ourselves ridiculous over such small considerations, neither politically nor economically.[63]

It was "ridiculous" to base one's politics on getting a good talking point, to wax enthusiastic over the Bismarckian measures simply because they helped one make debaters' points in discussions with bourgeois friends and intellectuals. Engels thought that a measure like the tobacco monopoly "is so trifling a statification that it cannot even serve us as an example in discussion, that besides it's all the same to me whether Bismarck puts it through or not, as either case will finally fall in with our needs." Was it a question of using these measures to prove to bourgeois friends that the capitalist is superfluous? But "the joint-stock companies have already provided the proof how very superfluous the bourgeoisie as such is, since the whole management is carried on by salaried officials, and to this, statification adds no new grounds of evidence."[64] Besides, "one can never derive a declaration of bankruptcy by modern society out of anything done by a creature like Bismarck," who did not represent modern society.[65]

Did the Bismarckian statification program prove that private enterprise was already obsolete? No, warned Engels: this debaters' point could not

---

* The historic meaning of this pattern is seen today, as it applies to the nature of the social struggle within the bureaucratic-collectivist states evolved from Stalinism: the bureaucracy as ruling class fuses political and economic power in its own hands. But it would be digressive to discuss differences and similarities.

be made either, though it was propagandistically tempting. Neither the railway nor the tobacco industry was actually being statified "out of necessity" in this case, as was true of the post office and telegraph; this was shown by the ad-hoc motivations Engels had adduced. There was no reason to favor these new state monopolies simply because "we would have as compensation merely a convenient new phrase in agitation. For a state monopoly which is instituted only out of motives of finances and power, not out of more compelling inner necessities, does not even offer us a proper argument." On the other hand, as soon as the statification backfired—for example, when the regime worsened tobacco quality and raised the price—"the advocates of free competition will point jubilantly to this fiasco of state communism and the people would agree with them perforce."[66]

In short, whatever one's estimate of positive and negative consequences, the crux was that the proletarian socialists must not take *responsibility* for such statification.

Through all these arguments and approaches, Engels sought to reinforce the conclusion which we have already noted more than once: that the equation *"statification = socialism"* was false. He summarized the point for Bernstein:

> It is a purely self-serving falsification by the Manchesterite bourgeoisie to label every intervention of the state into free competition as "socialism": protective tariffs, guilds, tobacco monopoly, statification of branches of industry, the Maritime Trade Company [of the Crown], royal porcelain factory. We should *criticize* this, not *believe* it. If we do the latter and base a theoretical argument on it, then it will collapse along with its premises.... [67]

The basic point, he emphasized in an 1891 letter, was this:

> that so long as the possessing classes remain at the helm, every statification is not an abolition of exploitation but only a change in its form; in the French, American, or Swiss republics no less than in monarchical Central Europe and in despotic East Europe.

Note that this approach bases the nature of the socioeconomic system squarely on the nature of the state power (what class rules).

And in order to drive the possessing classes from the helm, the first need was for a revolutionization in the consciousness of the mass of workers—the kind of change that was brought about by the modern development of industry, the maturing of bourgeois society, and the preparations and preconditions for the political rule of the proletariat. "The other classes are capable only of patchwork or shams."[68]

Workers still backward in consciousness will look for shortcuts, to be sure:

One who is drowning grasps for any straw and cannot wait till the boat bringing rescue pushes off from shore. The boat is the socialist revolution, the straw is the protective tariff and state-socialism.[69]

But the revolutionary socialists in that rescue boat have no reason to urge grasping the straw: so went Engels' view.

8. THE ISSUE REFUSES TO GO AWAY

As we have seen, Engels, looking on from London, tended to underestimate the impact of Bismarckian state-socialism on the German party, in large part because like Marx he saw too clearly the theoretical vapidity of Katheder-socialist ideology. *Could anyone really believe that Bismarck was engaged in introducing socialism? Naw, not verdammt likely....* What Engels especially underestimated was the will-to-believe, or wish-to-believe, on the part of those party circles that looked desperately for some way of making the socialist enterprise more "respectable."

In 1882 German comrades proposed that Engels devote the preface of a coming German edition of *Socialism Utopian and Scientific* to Bismarckian socialism, but he objected that more space was needed; and he countered with a plan for a series of articles on "the spurious socialism spreading in Germany," to be issued later as a pamphlet. The first part, on "Bismarck's socialism," would take up, in successive articles, tariffs, railway statification, the tobacco monopoly, and the social-security measures. But he made clear he was more interested in the second part, "which would criticize a series of unclear ideas that have been adopted through Lassalle and are still parroted by our people here and there; e.g., the 'iron law of wages,' 'the full product of labor for the *worker* (not *workers* [collectively]),' etc."[70] From the standpoint of the party leaders, this reversed the order of importance: they did not want to see an attack on Lassalle from London roiling the internal party waters, after they had suppressed Marx's critique of 1875 with difficulty, only a few years before. In short, Engels wanted to pick up Marx's attack on *Lassallean* state-socialism, while the party leaders wanted to aim him solely against Bismarck.

A few months later, Engels was complaining that the Germans had failed to send him requested materials on Bismarck's proposals, and anyway he was losing interest in Part I of the planned pamphlet, being pulled to other projects. Writing to Bernstein, he seized on some indications to claim that "a special attack on Bismarck socialism is outdated." Enthusiasm for it in party circles had waned, he argued. "So why use cannon to kill fleas? I think we'll let Bismarck socialism bury itself. Then there remains only the criticism of the bad leftovers from Lassalleanism. . . ."[71] It was the Lassallean brand of state-socialism that had stimulated him to attack in the first place, and he was still ready to go after it. In consequence of these cross-motivations, the projected pamphlet got nowhere.

But if (as was dubious) Engels really thought that Bismarckian socialism was a dead dog in the party, the course of events enlightened him. Two weeks after writing the above-cited letter, Engels had to note that state-socialism was even taking root among Italian socialists: he had recently been visited by "one specimen," Professor Achille Loria—"this little man who got his wisdom from the German Katheder-socialists."[72]

In the course of the next years, Engels could see the same tendencies independently at work in France. There was, for example, the case of Paul Brousse, Bakunin's lieutenant turned leader of the Possibilists (right-wing reformists), who was announcing his discovery that *les services publics* offered the road to socialism. Paul Lafargue wrote to Engels that "Brousse who, in the wake of Bismarck, Lassalle, Napoleon [III], etc., has invented the public services, that is, the conversion of certain private industries into state industries, speaks contemptuously of what he calls 'the old Marxist game.'" Later, Lafargue published an attack on Brousse's views, which Engels applauded. "Very good," wrote Engels to Laura Marx Lafargue. °°"It would do good in Germany too, when [*read* where?] the Vierecks and Co. are only too eager to use '*Verstaatlichung*' [statification] in the same bamboozling way as Brousse and Co. use the *services publics*."[73]

In 1884 Engels wrote, to a German party leader who inquired about recommended reading for a friend:

> In England and America, as in France and Germany, the pressure of the proletarian movement has given a Katheder-socialist-philanthropic coloring nearly throughout to the bourgeois economists, and an uncritical, well-meaning eclecticism is dominant everywhere: a soft, plastic, gelatinous mass which lets itself be pressed into any shape you want, and therefore provides an excellent liquid diet for the cultivation of bacteria. The consequences of this enervating, limp mental pap is making itself felt, at least in Germany and here and there among German-Americans, right into the ranks of our party, and is spreading thickly on its boundaries.[74]

Ironically, this letter was addressed to Vollmar, whose own politics were going to turn, in a few years, into that "gelatinous mass" of reformism, and who (as was mentioned at the beginning of this chapter) was going to become a leading exponent of state-socialism at the 1892 party congress.

That Engels had to recognize the spread of this "mental pap" in and around party circles, as well as outside, was further evidenced over a year later in a letter to Bebel. The economic theory of the "Manchesterians" (the "vulgar political economy" of the bourgeois liberals) was disintegrating, wrote Engels, in both England and Germany, though in the former country "it is not so much the [national] state as the municipality which is supposed to intervene."

> The same is proved by the growth of Katheder-socialism, which in one or another form is more and more driving classical economics out of the academic chairs both here and in France. The actual contradictions engendered by the mode of production have become so glaring that no theory can gloss them over any more, unless it be the Katheder-socialist mishmash, which however is no longer a theory but rubbish.[75]

Days before this, Engels had written to another friend about the state-socialistic intellectuals who "hover" between the party and Katheder-socialism, advocate a Social Monarchy, and boost Rodbertus against Marx.[76]

While Engels' attitude remained supremely contemptuous of these "academic softies" *(Kathedersänftlinge)* and "campus tame-cats" *(Universitätszähmlinge)*,[77] the key fact was nevertheless the phrase "growth of Katheder-socialism." So, although in 1883 Engels had wanted to "let Bismarck socialism bury itself," by early 1888 he seems to have been planning to take it up, after all, in the unfinished work now usually called *The Role of Force in History*. At any rate, he made notes for a final chapter, never written, analyzing Bismarck's "social policy à la Bonaparte," in two parts. The first part was to be on the Anti-Socialist Law and Bismarck's crackdown on the workers' movement, and the second on his "social-reform crap"—an irreverent way of describing state-socialism in these rough notes.[78]

The question would not go away, despite Engels' scorn. It is true, the reformist wing of the German party refrained from approving state-socialistic statements, but, on the other hand, it succeeded in getting a specific repudiation of state-socialism stricken from the Erfurt party program of 1891.

So says Susanne Miller's account of this issue in the German party, in her work *Das Problem der Freiheit im Sozialismus*. The party's Election Appeal in 1881, written for an outlawed movement reeling under the shock of the Anti-Socialist Law,

> declared that the Social-Democracy strove for "the organization of labor by the state, the concentration of all economic power in the hands of the state, the utmost intensification of the power of the state." Even though the same Election Appeal previously declared that "genuine state-socialism" was possible only in a *"democratic* state." because "socialism is by its innermost nature democratic; what a police state, military state and class state passes off as state-socialism can at most be a *barracks-economy* and *fiscalism*," yet the view expressed here

is very different from Bebel's, who declared that even in a "socialist-cooperative economy... the state does not have the role of the all-managing god."

Elsewhere Miller records that the draft of the Erfurt Program originally contained a passage strongly repudiating so-called state-socialism, the system of statification for fiscal purposes, which puts the state in place of the private entrepreneur and thus unites in a single hand both the power of economic exploitation and the political oppression of the worker.[79] This did not appear in the final version. Arrayed against it would be the pressure of Lassallean influence, the widespread absorption of Schäffle's teachings, and compromise with Bismarckian state-socialism.

By 1894 Engels was again poohpoohing the whole issue in retrospect. (I think he was still fighting shy of being distracted from his current projects.) In connection with the Jaurès case discussed in the next section, when Engels called state-socialism an "infantile disease" of proletarian socialism, he added that Germany had gone through it in the Anti-Socialist Law period, but that "even then only a negligible minority of the Party was caught in that snare for a short while; after the Wyden Congress [of the party in 1880], the whole thing petered out completely."[80] This is a good example of Engels' minimization of the dispute in the party, for the dates he gives do not jibe with reality.

Besides the press of other work, it must be kept in mind that for Engels the biggest state-socialist danger in the party was always the Lassallean variety, not so much the Bismarckian. But could they be separated for evaluation? In 1882 the worried editor of *Sozialdemokrat* wrote Engels that "in Germany, thanks to the Lassallean agitation, a colossal state cult haunts our ranks, so the danger is always present that these elements will fall for an agreeable but completely unsocialist project, if only the word 'state' plays a role in it."[81] Part of the trouble was that the external state-socialist threat fed on the internal tendency.

9. FOUR ILLUSTRATIVE CASES

As Engels said, the term 'state-socialism' was at bottom a "purely journalistic expression," a vague way of pointing in a certain direction—that is, toward the intervention of the existing state in the socioeconomic structure in a more or less blurry way. But he had no inhibition against using journalistic expressions, as long as they were not confused with scientific ones. Let us see some cases that reminded him of this particular expression.

(A) Czarist "State-Socialism"

Polemicizing with a Russian Populist, Engels argued that, in the crossroads of policy that followed the Crimean War, there had never been any real possibility that the czarist regime would take the path of developing the peasant village communes along communistic lines. He wrote: "Russia could not really be expected to plunge into state-socialistic experiments from above on the basis of the peasant commune."[82]

There is an implicit analogy here: czarist government enterprise and subsidies to develop the peasant commune with "state aid" ("from above") would be similar to Lassalle's notion of developing producers' cooperatives in Germany with Bismarck's state aid. In both cases, otherwise quite different, the existing state was expected to institute measures leading to a sort of alleged socialism—"from above"—in both cases with equal futility.

In the same work Engels made another leap from Russia to Germany. Referring to the communal cultivation of land in the Urals which was "preserved from dying out because of military considerations," he remarked parenthetically that "indeed, we too have [cases of] barracks-communism" in Germany.[83]

(B) "State-Socialism" in Colonial Java

When in 1884 Engels read J. W. B. Money's book *Java* on the difference between Dutch and British colonial policy, he wrote exhilarated letters to both Bebel and Kautsky suggesting that they use Money's material to make educational-propagandist use of this "model of state-socialism" which put Bismarckism in the shade. These two letters and Engels' line of thought were set forth in *KMTR* 1 and need not be repeated here.[84]

It is enough to remind that what Engels here subsumed under the journalistic expression 'state-socialism' was a case of the old village-community system (primitive communalism) that had passed from subjection to an Oriental despotism over to subjection to a Western capitalist imperialism. The British colonialists, in India and during their sway in Java, had tried to introduce modern bourgeois property relations in the system of land ownership; in contrast, the canny Dutch maintained "the old communistic village communities" and "organized all production in so beautifully socialistic a fashion" that they milked the native system very efficiently. "Socialistic" fashion indeed: just as socialistic as Bismarck socialism. "Here one sees," added Engels, "how, on the basis of the old community communism, the Dutch organized production under the aegis of the state," and hence were even more oppressively exploitive.

The case is made more interesting by the wide gap that had to be leaped in Engels' mind in order to make the connection between Java and Bismarck. We can add that what Engels pointed to as an indictment of state-socialism has also figured in some socialist literature as an argument in favor of socialism; for example, not only the primitive society of Java itself but especially the statified economy of the Inca imperium. This is characteristic of the subject, just as the same military barracks that figured in Engels' gibe at "barracks-communism" has also been used as a model of socialism; for example in Edward Bellamy and Robert Blatchford.[85]

Money's book stressed the governmental role in Java. Dutch government capital was laid out on a considerable scale for purposes of development, taking risks that private capital would refuse. When after 1839-1840 the government tried to shift in the direction of private planters, profitability started falling, because the native population reacted hostilely to private exploiters. Money's enlightened conclusion was that, in dealing with "semi-barbarous races of ignorant, idle and suspicious Natives," it is impractical to institute "free, competitive, unprotected, and uncontrolled industry."[86] The suspicious natives were so barbarous that they refused to work well for the profit of private exploiters and had to be deceived into believing that they were laboring for the community. Just the place for state-socialism!

(C) Jaurès and the "Statification" of Grain Imports

We have seen that protective tariffs, being a form of state intervention or "state aid" (to capitalists), figured in the discussions on state-socialism in Germany. In France, in mid-February 1894, a parliamentary debate over the grain tariff saw Jean Jaurès, as leader of the socialist group of deputies, offering a proposal for the establishment of a monopoly on grain imports to be administered by the state.

Engels was appalled: it was "astounding" for socialists to propose "out and out protectionism" for the benefit of the big land owners (since the small ones did not have much grain to sell anyway), thereby raising prices for the working class without even benefiting poor peasants by much. Jaurès—that "peasant of genius" who in Engels' eyes was "ignorant, above all, of political economy"[87]—was bending before the bigger peasants' desire for "state aid" for themselves. Engels wrote indignantly to Lafargue:

> But just take the proposal to make the state responsible for grain imports. J[aurès] wants to prevent speculation. So what does he do?

He makes the government responsible for the purchase of foreign grain. The government is the executive committee of the *majority in the Chamber*, and the majority in the Chamber represents as precisely as possible these very speculators in grain, shares, government stocks, etc. It's like the last Chamber [of Deputies], where they made the Panamists [the guilty politicians] responsible for the Panama [scandal] investigation! And these Panamists, re-elected last August, are the people you want to make responsible for the suppression of speculation! It's not enough for you that they rob France by means of the annual budget and the stock exchange—where at least they use their own capital and their own credit—you want to present them with several billions and the national credit, so that they can clean out other people's pockets more thoroughly by means of *state-socialism*!

Similar state-socialistic measures have popped up in other countries, without revolutionary pretenses, Engels pointed out. The "*petty-bourgeois* socialists in the canton of Zurich" have for years been proposing "a state monopoly in the grain trade," and "*their* state, I may say, is a great deal more democratic than the French Republic." Jaurès was simply proposing "a *state-socialism* which represents one of the *infantile diseases* of proletarian socialism, a disease which was gone through in Germany, for example, more than a dozen years ago, under the regime of the Anti-Socialist Laws, *when it was the only form tolerated by the government* (and even protected by it)."[88]

As chance would have it, exactly a month after Engels reddened Lafargue's ears with this lecture on state-socialism, a Prussian Junker arose in the Reichstag to act out the meaning of his argument in practical politics. A motion for the "statification of grain imports for the purpose of keeping grain prices up"[89] was made

°°by *Count [von] Kanitz*, one of the most shining lights amongst those Prussian Junkers who are, according to Hermann Wagener, their theoretical champion [and leading Katheder-socialist], either *Ochsen von Geburt oder Ochsen aus Prinzip* [oxen by birth or oxen on principle]. This motion, made in the interest of the landed aristocracy of Eastern Germany, *is almost literally the proposition Jaurès* which was to show the way to the socialist world how to use their parliamentary position in the interest of the working class and the peasantry.

The German socialists opposed the Kanitz motion, as did the Reichstag majority. What would Jaurès have done? The same Junker, mentioned Engels, had recently introduced another proposal, whereby the government would turn a profit of some billions by replacing gold coin with silver coin. "Now if I wanted to be malicious," Engels added maliciously, "I might ask M. Jaurès whether, in return for Kanitz's acceptance of his corn [grain] motion, he would not accept Kanitz's silver motion which looks equally socialistic . . . ?"[90]

Engels anticipated the reply: "Ah, but we have a republic in France; in our case it's different, we can use the government for socialist measures!"[91] So he had to go into a discussion of the class nature of the bourgeois republic. The reply assumed a nonclass view of the state that was incompatible with Marx's; and such a nonclass view was a necessary basis for any proposal to use the existing state (however bourgeois-democratic in form) for socialistic measures as distinct from limited reforms.

(D) Bismarck's Steamship Subsidy Proposal

This issue did not necessarily evoke the term 'state-socialism,' but it belongs under that head. In 1884, along with declaring a German protectorate over Southwest Africa, Bismarck proposed government subsidies to build new steamship lines connecting Germany with the Far East, Australia, Africa, and Samoa. This was colonialism in late bloom—just as "socialistic" as the rest of Bismarckian socialism.

The Social-Democratic press attacked this colonialism, though the party had not yet debated the question in general. The reformist wing had not yet come out openly for a colonial policy (except for Karl Höchberg); what appealed to them was the claim that the new steamship lines would provide new markets and new jobs for the unemployed, though some of them translated colonialism into their own language as "bringing the people closer together and removing race hatred" through improved contacts.[92] This right wing had just been encouraged by the party success in the Reichstag elections, for a majority of the twenty-four deputies elected were the type that Engels denounced as "petty-bourgeois elements," in fact middle-class intellectuals for the most part. We have seen what Marx and Engels thought of these elements in general.[93] Now this wing dominated the party's Reichstag Fraction.

A party crisis lasting into 1885 was precipitated when a majority of the Fraction wanted to vote in the Reichstag in favor of the Steamship Subsidy. A determined campaign of opposition was mounted by Bebel, who was willing to make an open fight in the party ranks on this question. The *Sozialdemokrat*, edited by Bernstein as a left-wing voice, mobilized membership protest. The Fraction majority was forced to agree to pose conditions for a yes vote, and this approach eventually resulted in all Social-Democratic deputies voting against the Bismarck proposal in March 1885.

Engels, like Bebel, was appalled at the spectacle that would be presented by the Social-Democratic deputies voting in favor of such a Bismarck proposal—especially the effect of this spectacle on the international movement: "think of the infinite disgrace before the eyes of the whole world!" Whoever voted in favor "must consistently vote for colonies too," he argued (in agreement with Bebel).[94]

But what was the alternative: simply vote against? That would save the party's honor, to be sure. But Engels clearly saw the disadvantages of meeting this proposal—one which purported to help the working class economically—by the simple negation of a no vote. This was a complication typically brought on by the party's successful growth.

It was in response to this problem that Engels developed an approach which was *later* going to be labeled the concept of a "transitional demand" in a special sense.* We will return to the subject of programmatic demands (in connection with reformism) in another place, but a brief explanation is necessary.

The Social-Democrats were used to the distinction between the party's "minimum demands" (realizable reforms) and "maximum demands" (which required the achievement of socialism). But what Engels did was develop the concept of a type of programmatic demand which could not be entirely subsumed under either one. Hence the long-standing confusion. The new type of demand was one which *appeared* to be an immediate reform measure, but which in actuality could never be granted in practice by the ruling class without fatal consequences to itself. It was "transitional" in the sense that insofar as the working class fought for it, it would be carried further to fight for an overthrow of the whole system. In the present case, Engels proposed conditions on the Steamship Subsidy which he thought the government could not accept; he expected that in practice the government would reject the conditions and force even the right-wingers to vote against the project.[95]

But Engels' new idea was not understood by Bebel and Bernstein, who, immersed in the party fight and averse to any appearance of compromise, did not grasp what he was getting at. They thought, in fact, that Engels was yielding too much to the right wing.[96]

On the contrary, how strongly Engels felt on the Steam Subsidy issue was shown by the following fact: *it was in response to the threat that the Fraction*

---

* Historically, this term had already been used for a different idea: demands, or platform planks, applying to a "transitional period" characterized by socialist measures by a workers' state. For example, this term had already been applied to the "transitional program" in the *Communist Manifesto* (near the end of Section II). The new meaning, applying to Engels' position on the Steamship Subsidy, was not going to be so tagged until the twentieth century, and was most clearly explained by Trotsky in 1938. The reader must keep in mind that the two meanings of 'transitional demand (program, etc.)' are entirely different.

majority might vote in favor of the government scheme that he began, in letters to party correspondents, to write about the need for a party split in Germany to separate the reformist wing from the ranks. This is explicable only insofar as he was reacting to the state-socialist content of the subsidy issue.

In the first place, he emphasized how vital the issue was to him. The party Fraction, wrote Engels to an American correspondent, was filled with "petty-bourgeois prejudices: thus, for example, the majority wants to vote for the Steamship Subsidy 'in the interests of industry.'... Fortunately Bebel is there... and so I hope that it will pass off without disgrace." If not? If the reformists win out, "it will be impossible for me henceforth to defend the party abroad," he threatened, writing to Bebel. In subsequent years, too, Engels kept recurring to the reformist threat to vote for the Steamship Subsidy as his prime example of the right-wing danger in the party.[97]

His first suggestions about the need for a split, to separate from the people who wanted to vote for the Bismarckian proposal, came in April 1885, after the issue came to a head in the Reichstag. Whereas at first one of his considerations had been how to prevent "the blowup of the Fraction," now he wrote to Laura Marx Lafargue that "The separation from this element... will come, but I would not like to provoke it as long as the Anti-Socialist Law is in force...." He repeated this to Paul Lafargue: "If there wasn't the Anti-Socialist Law, I would be for an open split."[98] Twice more in June, in connection with the Steamship Subsidy fight, he repeated the split perspective to friends abroad, finally even envisioning the possibility of a split while the Anti-Socialist Law was still in force: we should not *provoke* a split at this juncture, he said, "but if the gentlemen [of the right wing] should themselves bring the split about by suppressing the proletarian character of the party," then it may have to come.[99]

Engels, like Marx, was led to contemplate the need for a split only by issues perceived as basically impugning "the proletarian character of the party." The two had first talked of a split with the reformists in connection with the "Manifesto of the Three Zurichers," the Höchberg operation. Now Engels raised the possibility in connection with the new issue of the day in party work. It was not going to be the last time that Engels projected a split perspective in response to what he saw as *an alien type of socialism taking over the movement.*

In this case the alien ideology that was pulling at the Social-Democracy was that of state-socialism.

5 | OF ANARCHISM: PROUDHONIST MODEL

Anarchism came into existence as a movement and as a distinct school of thought and action only in the last period of Marx's life, when the ingredients came together under Bakunin in the mid-1860s. Before this time, the basic ideas of anarchism had already been developed by the forerunner trio of Godwin, Proudhon and Stirner, but not the idea of a distinctive movement for anarchist power.

This chapter will present Marx's views on the forerunner period, that is, before he and his contemporaries were aware of the ism-to-be. Just as the ism itself was not yet systematically presented, so too the counterposition of views was not yet completely clear.

1. THE RESERVOIR OF ANTISTATISM

One reason it took some time for anarchism to emerge as a separate and distinct viewpoint was that, for a long time, it was part of a much broader and encompassing tendency, which we have noted before: the general reservoir of *hostility to government and politics*.[1]

Viewing the state as an unnecessary excrescence was one of the most ancient ideas in the history of social dissent, older and more primitive than either socialism or anarchism as an ideology or movement. An obvious speculation is that antistatism, including dreams about abolishing the state, naturally arose along with the new burdens on people brought by the state itself and in reaction to the new kind of pressures it produced, and that it long survived as a reminiscence of a stateless Golden Age. In any case, this antistatism was already found at least in ancient Greek and Chinese philosophy. This sort of antistate hostility got a booster shot whenever the state grew more complex and its demands grew more onerous.

All through the history of class society, from the angle of the little man on bottom the state has appeared mainly as a grasping, oppressive force, most particularly to agricultural peoples living a more or less self-sufficient life. To the tiller of the soil, the state takes form in the person of the tax collector, or tribute gatherer, with armed men at his back. "When the French peasant paints the devil," remarked Marx, "he paints him in the guise of a tax collector."[2] The peasant sees the wealth of society produced by the act of his own labor on the breast of nature, and he sees the state as hands outstretched from the outside to take away this wealth that he has produced.

Antistatism has historically flourished best among individual and isolated producers, like peasants and handicraftsmen and home (domestic economy) workers, who do not readily see the connections between their personal labor and the functioning of society. In this limited framework, the state is only an alien intruder. By the same token, the hoped-for "abolition of the state" appears to be a simple matter of will and force only: one slash of the knife and the useless cancer is lopped from the body of productive society. Under these conditions, the aspiration for the "abolition of the state" is an easy commonsense idea, ready for instant execution, needing no theory but only a bold proclamation.

In less consistent form, antistatism may also appear as simply a hatred of laws as such; even more, of lawyers and law men; a hostility to officialdom, and a distrust of "politics" in general, that is, any contamination by the hated state. *Away with laws, down with officials, abolish the state*—these are the oldest and most primitive slogans in the social struggle.

They took on a new lease on life as the revolutionary bourgeoisie fought against the bureaucratically hypertrophied state machines of the absolute monarchies. The resultant hostility to excessive bureaucratization tended to turn into antistate rhetoric, once it was generalized and abstractionized by clever minds. To the bourgeoisie in its Adam Smith phase, the cost of the state machine was too much an unproductive drain on civil society, that is, on the purses of the bourgeoisie.[3] This was the ground on which laissez faire was rarefied into bourgeois antistatism, and Bentham was outbid by Godwin. With Godwin, a full-fledged anarchist theory (not so called) appeared on paper for the first time, as an etherealization of the aspirations of small enterprise. It was the primal scream of the petty-bourgeois in a squeeze.

Early socialism—from the traveling salesman Fourier to the peasant-minded Proudhon, from the fashionable ladies' tailor Weitling to the semiproletarian artisans of the Communist League—was tied by a network of threads to petty-bourgeois producers caught in the act of turning into modern workers. All of socialism began with the tension between hostility to, and hope in, the state. This could be resolved only by a thought-through theory of the state, but the tension lasted for most of the nineteenth century.

There was, then, a vast reservoir of inchoate antistatism, lapping around the borders of the socialist movement, for a very long time, continually renewed as new streams of raw, undeveloped, unclass-conscious workers poured into the reservoir from the sea of peasantry. The history of anarchism—its flare-up and decline in one area after another, from the Jura Mountains to the plains of Andalusia—is one of history's best cases of correspondence between politics and technology.

In *KMTR* 1 it was stressed that pre-Marx socialism usually entailed hostility to politics; it was *social*-ism counterposed to *political*-ism. This early socialism was inhospitable to concern with the major political issues of the day (constitutional democracy above all), which it saw as of interest only to the bourgeoisie or the "politicians." It was a theoretical advance when Marx showed how it was possible to link the "Social Question" up with the "political question" in a single programmatic approach, which he called a "new direction." The primitive state of mind in the movement, general antipoliticalism, was the source of several isms, including pure-and-simple trade-unionism and cooperativism, and only in a specially abstract form did it also show itself as an ingredient of anarchism.[4]

To be sure, this early socialism, for all its antistatism, was never really able to "abolish the state" even in theory, just as in life the state was not abolished no matter how often particular states were overthrown. The reason is clear: the state has been a societal necessity, and primitive discontent has been unable to offer any substitute for the state's indispensable positive functions, no matter how strong its movement or how often it won. The state conquers its conquerors as long as society cannot do without it. As soon as antistatism ceases to be merely negative, as soon as it even raises the question of what is to replace the state as the organizing principle of a functioning society, then it has always been obvious that the state, abolished in fancy, gets reintroduced in some other form.

It is always instructive and sometimes amusing to follow this process in anarchistic utopias, where the pointed ears of a very antidemocratic state poke out as soon as there is a hint about the positive reorganization of society. This law may be tested on the specimens of antistate utopias recommended by the anarchist writer Marie Louise Berneri in her *Journey Through Utopia*—for example, the society imagined by de Foigny; but it is necessary to go to the original, not to Berneri's laundered summary. It is common for historians of socialism to point to Weitling as an "anarchistic" thinker because he breathes fire against the state, in spite of his explicit proposal of a messianic dictatorship as *his* replacement for the "state." And one should not miss the attempt by two French anarchist leaders to describe in detail *How We Will Make the Revolution* through the anarchosyndicalist movement: for you can see the alleged anarchist nonstate turning into a despotic state right in front of your eyes.[5]

The first socialistic utopias often substituted "social" institutions for political institutions without understanding that their proposed new authorities constituted new *states* under disguising labels. Thus Fourier and Saint-Simon have been described as "anarchistic" by some modern writers who get a whiff of their deep animus against the state and are so bemused by this ancient language that they ignore the antidemocratic institutions that fill the state concepts of these utopians.

Since anarchism is indubitably antipolitical, it is sometimes assumed by a lapse in logic that therefore early antipoliticalism was anarchistic. But it does not follow that if all men are animals, all animals are men. For example, no one was more antipolitical than Robert Owen, but not on anarchistic grounds, and he was no anarchist.

Marx's anti-anarchist article "Indifference to Politics" offered a thought on why utopianism tended to reject politics:

> Since social conditions were not sufficiently developed to permit the working class to constitute itself as a militant class, the first socialists (Fourier, Owen, Saint-Simon, etc.) inevitably had to limit themselves to dreams about the *model society* of the future and condemn all such attempts as strikes, organizations and political movements undertaken by the workers to bring some improvement to their lot.[6]

Marx also pointed to the case of J. F. Bray, the early "Ricardian socialist" whose book *Labour's Wrongs and Labour's Remedy* "discovered *mutualism* considerably earlier than Proudhon." Bray, said Marx, condemned working-class political movements along with all other contemporary methods of struggle: this was typical. The early Christians "likewise preached indifference to politics" but *they* "had need of the strong arm of an emperor to be transformed from oppressed into oppressors."[7]

In short, the idea that the future social order would do away with state and politics in some way was one of the common platitudes of early socialism. Obviously the catch lies in what was meant by the state in these discourses. Theorists who understood little about the nature of the state that was before their eyes were not likely to be reliable guides to the nature of nonexistent states.

It leaps to the eye that "the state" was often used to mean only a despotic state, while it was implicitly assumed that a state enjoying democratic freedoms was a nonstate. (We will see, in Section 4 below, that this tendency cropped up even in leading anarchist theoreticians, and points to a bridge between anarchism and reformism.) Insofar as this pattern was followed, fierce talk about "abolishing the state" meant, in actuality, championing democratic reforms, presumably by "revolutionary" methods. This seems to be a question of definition, to be sure, but since definitions were usually lacking, it was usually a question of fashionable rhetoric. "State" was a dirty word, even to theorists who cheerfully proposed dictatorial and hierarchical states of their own devising.

It was also true that this antistatism did not *necessarily* entail anticapitalism, and in fact often did not. Of the three above-mentioned forerunners of the anarchist ideology, Godwin, Proudhon and Stirner, none proposed a socialist type of reorganization of society in a modern sense; they cannot be regarded as basically anticapitalist. It was only after socialism had already established itself as the ideology of social dissent that anarchism (in its Bakunin model) latched onto a consistent anticapitalism. Proudhon and especially Stirner became the patron saints of that school of overtly *pro*capitalist anarchism which became most prominent in the United States, with Josiah Warren and Benjamin Tucker, and whose spirit hovers over a wing of Republican Party conservatism and the University of Chicago.

There was another stream of rhetoric about the state that poured into the reservoir, of special importance to Marx. This was Hegelianism, which, because of its special conception of the state (as explained in *KMTR* 1) allowed his followers to see nonstates in unusual places, like ancient imperial China.[8] Of course there was no question of antistatism in Hegel himself, but it was the special Hegelian *concept* of the state that was so handily abolished by the Young Hegelian, Max Stirner, in 1844 in the convolutions of his book *The Ego and His Own*. Four years before this, Proudhon had made the literary negation of the state well known in advanced circles, and when this idea traveled east across the Rhine, it married into Young Hegelian circles and engendered Stirner in a cloud of philosophizing.

This is the background of the statement made by Engels, looking back in 1871, writing to a pro-anarchist correspondent who thought anarchism was the latest thing down the turnpike. Engels told him that for himself and Marx

> "the abolition of the state" is an old German philosophic phrase, of which we made much use when we were simple youngsters.[9]

Anarchism did not introduce the "abolition of the state" idea; it turned it into a one-sided, abstractionized concept, as we will see.

2. GODWIN, STIRNER, HESS

If we look for Marx's views on anarchism in his early comments on, say, Godwin or Stirner, we will find no such thing. The ism did not yet exist;

it had to be read back into their writings, later, by the anarchist movement. Anarchism was not born in the consciousness of the time simply because in 1840 Proudhon made a stir by using the word "an-archie" in a favorable context, instead of pejoratively. By hyphenating it he wanted to show that, etymologically speaking, it did not mean mere disorder (which had been its only meaning so far). As Engels said a half century later: "Proudhon's innocuous, merely etymological anarchy (i.e., absence of a political power) would never have led to the present anarchistic doctrines" without the ingredients added by Bakunin.[10]

Godwin was the first writer to put forward all the essential anarchist ideas (in his *Political Justice*), but not until long afterwards were these ideas linked to an anarchist movement. This applies not only to Godwin's contemporaries and the subsequent anarchist thinkers, but also to Marx and Engels. Young Engels read *Political Justice*, and made excerpts from it, only three years after Proudhon had included the word "an-archie" in a book in an honorific sense; but he did not tie Godwin up with Proudhon. The link he and everyone saw was with Bentham, the liberal founder of utilitarianism.

In an article published at this time Engels discussed Godwin and Bentham as a single current; and while he stated that *both* of them "attacked the very essence of the state itself with his [Godwin's] aphorism that the state is an evil," this still unmarxified Engels seemed to think that Bentham went even further.[11]

This view of Godwin was held by both Engels and Marx in the next period, in line with general opinion. Engels coupled Godwin with Bentham in a similar way in his book *The Condition of the Working Class in England*, and just as briefly in *The German Ideology*. In the plan for a library of socialist writers that Marx drew up in 1845, Bentham and Godwin likewise appeared together.[12]

Discussing the inclusion of Godwin in the planned "library" (publisher's series), Engels' letter to Marx showed no appreciation of Godwin's anarchism, only his hostility to organized society—which nowadays we connect up with his anarchism in hindsight. His letter reflected how Godwin appeared to contemporaries: Godwin "touches on communism," but "at the *end* of his work, Godwin arrives at the conclusion that people have to emancipate themselves from society as much as possible . . . and in general he is so decidedly anti-*social* in his conclusions." He adds: "But if we include Godwin, we must not leave out his supplement Bentham, although the fellow is deucedly boring and theoretical."[13]

One reason for the general failure to grasp the full import of Godwin's argument was that attacks on "the very essence of the state" as an evil were so commonplace and ancient. *It was not antistatism that marked anarchism as something new*. What initially escaped general attention about Godwin, Proudhon and Stirner was this: they put forward a particular rationale for this attack on the state, a line of thought about "authority." We will see that it is this line of thought that defines anarchism, not mere antistatism.

Proudhon's "an-archie" of 1840 had influence in Young Hegelian circles; but it exerted this influence by the time the tendency was disintegrating, and Marx himself was beginning to face social and political problems as editor of the *Rheinische Zeitung*. In Berlin, a circle of radical campus intellectuals formed around Bruno and Edgar Bauer, calling themselves "Die Freie" (The Free); they developed a solipsistic form of individualism (which was shortly going to be the Bauers' bridge to conservatism). Among the ideas freely tossed around in this circle was a development of Proudhon's suggestions about the devilish nature of "authority." Edgar Bauer announced in December 1842: "The modern man shakes off all authority. He has respect for nothing more than himself." (This anticipated the very essence of anarchism.) There was a spate of philosophizing about the primacy of the *Ich*, counterposing the creative Ego to the dirty Masses (as we noted in *KMTR* 1) and celebrating their own brilliant Egos which incarnated the Absolute Spirit.[14]

In this island of abstraction amidst the Berlin waste land dominated by court and bureaucracy, the repudiation of authority was carried farthest of all, in bold print, by a mousy ex-teacher in a young ladies' academy, named Schmidt, writing under the name Stirner. In an article in the *Rheinische Zeitung* in April 1842 (not yet under Marx's editorship), Stirner drew the extreme consequences for education: only if based on free will would education achieve the full emancipation of people from all authority. In an article written the following year, he applied this view to all states, counterposing an Egoism which alone could realize Absolute Freedom.[15]

On the other hand, the Young Hegelians (and others) who had become seriously involved with the *Rheinische Zeitung*, as an embattled champion of democracy, and with the real problems of the day were repelled not only by the Berlin clique's airy theorizing but also by its irresponsible bohemian life style: its atmosphere of unseriousness, "frivolity," "rowdiness and blackguardism," "compromising the cause and the party of freedom..." So stated Ruge and Herwegh, and editor Marx published their opinion in these terms in his paper.[16]

In a letter to Ruge, Marx explained why he did not want to publish the contributions of these "Berlin windbags": they were worthless, "empty of ideas...a watery torrent of words in the old manner...worthless creations of 'freedom,' a freedom which strives primarily 'to be free from all thought.'" Their writings "find freedom in a licentious, sansculotte-like...form, rather than in a *free*, i.e., independent and profound, content." Marx complained that they seasoned their slovenly articles with "a little atheism and communism" about which they knew little, and "smuggle communist and socialist doctrines" into theater criticisms and such, instead of offering a "thorough discussion of communism" and its new world outlook.[17] If "The Free" also sprinkled some antistate seasoning into their stews, Marx made no mention of it: *that* would be commonplace.

This was probably the first time Marx ran into the practice of replacing "thorough discussion" by exercises in parsing the words 'free' and 'freedom,' an activity that was going to be the stock in trade of anarchism. An analysis of prestidigitation with the word 'free' was going to be important also for understanding the language of political economy: free labor, free trade, free enterprise, and so on.[18] This understanding was still to come, but even in the first article Marx wrote for the *Rheinische Zeitung* in 1842, he rejected vague manipulations of Freedom, in particular objecting to the counterposition of freedom to law (authority): one must not think that necessarily "what is lawless is free, that freedom is lawless."[19]

In hindsight the counterposition was this: freedom through and in laws that facilitate freedom, or freedom viewed as the eternal enemy of all law. In the latter case, which was the case of anarchism, 'freedom' took on a special meaning.

Stirner's contribution was to carry this tendency out to a bizarre end: with Egoism unleashed, everything disappeared from social morality except the demands of the individual Ego. His book (entitled *The Ego and His Own* in English translation) enjoyed a flare of notoriety. This was perhaps the first exposition of an anarchist doctrine which was recognizable as a distinctive ideology, though not yet called anarchism. The view, often expressed, that Stirner's influence was "insignificant" in the development of anarchism is not justified: his book had an impact on Bakunin just when the latter was being radicalized for the first time in Young Hegelian circles.[20] (Marx and Engels were correct in repeatedly ascribing Bakunin's anarchist initiation to the joint influence of Stirner and Proudhon.)

Many replied to Stirner's work; Marx and Engels were among these. Their criticism occupied about 65 percent of their unpublished *German Ideology*, which discussed Stirner's views on society and philosophy in turgid detail, but there was not a single sentence clearly taking note of what we would now see as Stirner's anarchism. Stirner's antistatism was evident enough, but it was lost amidst the critics' reaction to his discourses on other matters—his virulent anticommunism, for one thing.[21] Indeed, *The German Ideology* has a couple of passages in which the abolition of the state enters, but it comes in as a *communist* idea, not Stirner's![22]

Stirner's *Ego and His Own* itself has no clear statement about the abolition of the state as a goal; there is one unclear reference which is tucked away in swaths of philosophizing. Indeed, in one passage he even seems to be ascribing the idea to the communists he is attacking.[23] He does not align himself with Proudhon's newly notorious "an-archie"; he has nothing but hostile criticism for Proudhon, and uses the word "anarchic" only to describe bourgeois liberalism. He rejects political or social revolution—in favor of his ego-rebellion—and, true to his principles, he went through the revolution of 1848-1849 observing events through cigar smoke and a wet glass in Hippel's Weinstube: the very image of the detached Ego and of his own *Idiotismus*.[24]

At the time, "egoism"—the "principle of self-enjoyment"—was associated with Bentham's utilitarianism and its theory of individual happiness as the guide to social right; and, like Godwin, Stirner appeared to many readers to be screwing Benthamism up to a new pitch. Certainly when young Engels first read Stirner's book, he saw it as another offshoot of Benthamism. Stirner's principle, Engels wrote to Marx, "is Bentham's egoism, only carried out more consistently on one side and less consistently on the other." This egoism was "only the essence, brought to consciousness, of present-day society," the end-product of bourgeois thinking along Benthamite lines. This line of thought (as we mentioned in *KMTR* 1)[25] eventually led to its own caricature in the "bourgeois anarchism" we will encounter below.

Engels thought that, propagandistically, Stirner's argument could be turned against itself, in good dialectical fashion: it could be shown that egoism, understood as self-interest and "driven to its highest point," could not remain one-sided "but must turn straightway into communism." The reply to Stirner might go this way, he thought:

> his egoist people must necessarily become communists out of pure egoism.... the human heart, from the start and directly, is unselfish and self-sacrificing in its egoism, and thus he still ends up with what he is combating.... we are communists out of egoism, we want to be *human beings* out of egoism, not simple individuals.... We have to take our departure from the "I," the empirical living individual, not in order to get stuck there but to advance from there to the "human being."[26]

This was a valiant attempt to show that Stirner could be turned on his head: that individualism and self-interest, when properly understood in social context, might turn into their apparent opposite, communism, since only in society could the individual's interests be safeguarded. "Egoism" *could* be given a social content; but for Stirner it was simply unbridled individual will.

A more important man than Stirner, Moses Hess, was the main figure in the *Rheinische Zeitung* circle who was first influenced by the new ideas from France. Even before the appearance of Stirner's book, Hess published two essays picking up Proudhon's new use of "an-archie." He combined the trinity of atheism, communism and an-archy into a single view, linking the components respectively to Fichte, Babeuf and Proudhon. While he freely praised Proudhon's "anarchy" for its "negation of all political rule, the negation of the concept state or politics," he did not systematically develop an anarchist doctrine, and soon dropped this approach as he developed toward "True Socialism."[27]

A few months before the publication of these articles, Hess had expressed some of his anarchoid ideas in an article about political centralization in the *Rheinische Zeitung*,[28] and a fellow contributor was stirred to write a reply. This was Marx, not yet editor of the paper. We have only the first paragraphs of an unfinished article answering Hess.

Hess had begun his article, in philosophic fashion, with the idea that "in general every external law" and "any central state power" becomes "superfluous" if one considers the matter "from a higher standpoint." The crux of Marx's comment on this passage seems to be: *Kindly come down to earth.*

> ... we are told that from this high standpoint, all laws, positive institutions, the central state power and finally the state itself, disappear.... Philosophy must seriously protest at being confused with imagination. The fiction of a nation of "righteous" people is as alien to philosophy as the fiction of "praying hyenas" is to nature. The author substitutes "his abstractions" for philosophy. [*Here the ms. breaks off.*][29]

Marx, we see, was not willing to accept an easy imaginative solution without searching analysis. This was where the unfinished article was probably heading; but as a matter of fact Marx himself did not yet have the theoretical tools for accomplishing the task. Perhaps abandoning the attempt at an article was the better part of valor.

When in 1843 Hess published two articles developing what Cornu has called his "anarchistic communism," Marx praised the articles in his preface to his own Paris manuscripts of 1844, as one of the few *"original* German works of substance" *on political economy*.[30] Wasn't he interested in the anarchoid views expressed by Hess? There is no indication that he was, or that he even considered those views specially noteworthy. In any case, Hess's assumption that communism was *ipso facto* antistate helps to underline Engels' quoted remarks, later, about the commonness of these ideas when they were "simple youngsters."

It is sometimes overlooked that among the simple youngsters who were subjected to the impact of Stirner's ego-anarchism and Hess's invention of a sort of anarchocommunism (sans name) was a young Russian named

Bakunin, who had participated in a Moscow study circle on Hegel (the conservative Hegel) and who had arrived in Berlin in mid-1840. Bakunin was converted to Young Hegelianism by the beginning of 1842, and by October had published an article in a Young Hegelian journal, on "Reaction in Germany," which gained much notice. (Its final words did not yet sound ominous: "Let us put our trust in the eternal spirit which destroys and annihilates.... The passion for destruction is also a creative passion.") When Stirner's book came out, Bakunin was in Paris, where he did Proudhon the disservice of introducing him to shards of Hegel. There can be little doubt that the Russian discussed the writings of Stirner and Hess like the rest of the people in the circles he moved in.[31] This was his most impressionable period.

We may mention at this point that Engels in an 1893 conversation made the connection between Bakunin and the Young Hegelian circles of the early 1840s. A Russian visitor named Voden related in his later published "Talks with Engels":

> When I drew attention to the remarkable similarity of the views of the "Free" and the "Critical Critics" [Bruno Bauer's group] with the ideology of the Russian subjectivists [Narodnik theorists], Engels explained that the resemblance was due not to an unconscious reproduction of the German pre-March [1848] ideologies by the Russian intelligentsia, but mainly to a direct adoption of these ideologies by Lavrov and even Bakunin.[32]

Returning to the early 1840s, we must point to another simple youngster who was impressed with this new rhetoric about Freedom: Engels himself. We saw some of the results in *KMTR* 1 in connection with two articles of his from the 1843-1844 period.[33] In another article of this period, young Engels wrote the following then-fashionable nonsense:

> The Christian state is merely the last possible manifestation of the state as such; its demise will necessarily mean the demise of the state as such. The disintegration of mankind into a mass of isolated, mutually repelling atoms in itself means the destruction of all corporate, national and indeed of any particular interests and is the last necessary step towards the free and spontaneous association of men.

There is no use asking whether the new social order was expected to function on the basis of a disintegrated "mass of isolated mutually repelling atoms," for this early variety of anarchoid confusion had no better answer than later anarchists. This article by our simple youngster incorporated other muddles: the rule of the bourgeoisie, it asserted, "was bound to turn first against the state and to destroy it, or at least, as it cannot do without it, to undermine it." This vision of a capitalist class which hesitates only between undermining or destroying the state is touching; but plainly this language is rhetorical, for we are also told that the undermining of the state was begun by Adam Smith by publishing his *Wealth of Nations*.[34]

It should not be thought that this maundering was all derived from Hess. Invocations to Absolute Freedom were strewn all over the literature of Young Germany like punctuation marks, and over young Engels' verse since he was a teen-ager. We saw some examples in *KMTR* 1. The habit persisted to at least 1840: "Patience! A new day's coming—Freedom's day!... I, too, am one of Freedom's minstrel band." In 1840 he tried to get a publisher for a volume of his translations from Shelley.[35] Indeed, his enthusiasm for Shelley outlasted his youth, for after all, in Shelley's case freedom had some substance: *"What are thou, Freedom?... For the labourer thou art bread..."*[36]

3. WATERSHED: THE "ULTIMATE AIM" FORMULATION

We should expect to find, in Marx's early writings, the usual amount of leftist antistatism then current; and we do, but in a more qualified and careful form than in Hess or young Engels. For young Marx too, the "abolition of the state" was a well-known old phrase and a commonplace of early radicalism, but he was not quite as simple a youngster.

We saw that in 1842, the very first year of his career as a political writer, he had refused to follow Hess in a flight of fancy to the point where the state "disappears" in the mists of philosophical abstraction. To be sure, he had not yet declared himself for socialism or communism, but was studying the question. In the following year, as he was making the transition to communism, he brought up a similar question in his manuscript notes on Hegel's critique of right (political theory); and we saw in *KMTR* 1 that he still refused to accept the presto-changeo disappearance of the state in the theories being imported from France. The "modern French" view had it (he jotted down) that "in true democracy the *political state disappears*," but this (he added) was only partially correct: in "true democracy" the state dwindled to its proper, limited sphere.[37]

This was essentially the view of the matter that remained with Marx permanently, even if it was later expressed in different formulations.

In *KMTR* 1, in context, we noted other occasions when young Marx reflected the antistate language and ideas of the day. The next notable case came in 1844, after the Silesian weavers' revolt: the social ills of society were seen as resulting from "the principle of the state," instead of the other way round. Marx had not yet developed a socioeconomic theory of the state, and this formulation did not last long.

But at the same time he stated a long-lasting idea: after the revolution, which is a political act, when socialism's "organizing activity" begins (to construct a new society), "there socialism throws away the *political* husk."[38] It was a seminal thought; but one should not read into it Marx's mature theory about the dying away of the state; there were still too many questions hidden in mist.

In early 1845 he drew up an outline of a projected book on the "modern state," and its last point read: "*Suffrage*, the struggle for the *abolition* [*Aufhebung*]* of the state and bourgeois society."[39] This suggests that, at this early point, Marx regarded universal suffrage as necessarily antistate—a common enough leftist illusion of the time, one which was related to the anarchist pattern of identifying the concept 'state' only with the despotic state.

A basic point was clarified before 1844 was over: it is not the state that creates the social order, but rather it is the social order that underlies the state; the "principle of the state" is *not* the primary factor in society. This view, which by itself refutes anarchism, emerged in Marx's thinking as part of his development of a materialistic conception of history. The idea was stated fairly clearly in *The Holy Family*: "Only *political superstition* still imagines today that civil life must be held together by the state, whereas in reality, on the contrary, the state is held together by civil life."[40]

The decisive reformulation of the "state principle" was written down in *The German Ideology*. Marx ridiculed "the old fancy that the state collapses of itself as soon as all its members leave it . . . this proposition reveals all the fantasy and impotence of pious desire." A fundamental overturn was needed, one that was guided by the productive forces. Whereas "previous revolutions within the framework of division of labor [e.g., the French Revolution] were bound to lead to new political institutions," and to a new state, the case was different with "the communist revolution, which abolishes the division of labor, [and] does away with [*beiseitigt*] political institutions in the end . . ."

The key phrase was "in the end" (*schliesslich*, ultimately). It was a question of what happened to the state "in the end." The "abolition of the state" was not the first word of the revolution but one of the last. This theory of the abolition of the state "in the end" showed up in *The German Ideology* because it was in this work (as *KMTR* 1 explained) that Marx first clearly put forward his characteristic theory of the state, as well as of social evolu-

---

* From here on, wherever Marx or Engels is cited on the "abolition" (or dying out, etc.) of the state, the original German term will be routinely mentioned, for the reader's information.

tion, together with his thesis that the revolutionary proletariat must seek to conquer political power, that is, establish its own state.[42]

In particular it flowed from the understanding that the state performed a necessary function for society, and was *not* a mere excrescence or cancer, and that *therefore it could not be "abolished" until society was able to perform this function with different institutions.* This is the stumbling block over which anarchism breaks its neck theoretically.

The perspective of establishing a new state—a workers' state—as the outcome of the revolution represented a clear break with the primitive antistatism of the time, a wing of which later congealed into anarchism. When, many years later, Marx and Engels re-encountered the primitive notion in its latter-day Bakuninist dress, it was not news.

Marx's theory of the state had now crossed a watershed. There were still several points wrapped in fog, but it was now possible to make progress toward clearing them up.

When in 1847 Marx devoted a book to Proudhon, he (and his contemporaries) looked on the Frenchman primarily as an economist who offered a special basis in political economy for socialistic conclusions of a sort. Besides, by 1847 Proudhon had still said very little about either "an-ar-chie" or the abolition of the state; and after all Marx wrote his *Poverty of Philosophy* as a reply to a particular book, Proudhon's *System of Economic Contradictions or Philosophy of Poverty.* In this book of Proudhon's there was no statement about anarchy, not even as much as the few pages of his 1840 work. Proudhon's *System of Economic Contradictions* was a polemic against establishment economics and in part against religion, but it had little of a positive view on any subject.[43]

Nevertheless Marx ended his *Poverty of Philosophy* with a positive statement of his own about what was *not* in Proudhon's last book, for the latter had become known for his "an-archie" bit. Marx's last chapter opened fire on Proudhon's bitter opposition to trade unions and strikes, that is, to the elementary "struggle—a veritable civil war" of the working class. Once this struggle reached a classwide extent, "association takes on a political character." And "the emancipation of the oppressed class implies necessarily the creation of a new society."

> Does this mean that after the fall of the old society there will be a new class domination culminating in a new political power? No.
>
> The condition for the emancipation of the working class is the abolition of all classes, just as the condition for the emancipation of the third estate, of the bourgeois order, was the abolition of all estates and all orders.
>
> The working class, in the course of its development, will substitute for the old civil society an association which will exclude classes and their antagonisms, and there will be no more political power properly

so called, since political power is precisely the official expression of antagonisms in civil society.[44]

Although Marx later referred back to this passage more than once as a statement of his views, it is plainly far from clear on all points, taken by itself. The idea which in *The German Ideology* had been expressed by the qualification "in the end" (or ultimately, *schliesslich*) was here represented by the phrase "in the course of its development." It was not even clear that this meant "in the course of its development" *after* the revolution, but it fortunately happens that precisely the same phrase was used, a few months later, in the corresponding passage in the *Communist Manifesto*, this time in a clear context.

This passage came right after the Manifesto's ten-point program, on how "the proletariat will use its political supremacy":

> When, in the course of development, class distinctions have disappeared, and all production has been concentrated in the hands of a vast association of the whole nation, the public power will lose its political character. Political power, properly so called, is merely the organized power of one class for oppressing another. If the proletariat during its contest with the bourgeoisie is compelled, by the force of circumstances, to organize itself as a class; if, by means of a revolution, it makes itself the ruling class, and, as such, sweeps away by force the old conditions of production, then it will, along with these conditions, have swept away the conditions for the existence of class antagonisms and of classes generally, and will thereby have abolished [*hebt auf*] its own supremacy as a class.
>
> In place of the old bourgeois society, with its classes and class antagonisms, we shall have an association, in which the free development of each is the condition for the free development of all.[45]

The abolition of political power (the state, or state power) in any form was no longer a *slogan*. It was posed as the ultimate aim of the social revolution, and was embedded in a theory of societal transformation that gave it a new sense.

4. INTERLUDE: BOURGEOIS ANARCHISM

In the political lull between the defeat of the revolution in 1849 and the outbreak of the Paris Commune, that is, during the 1850-1860s, there was little reason to pay attention to the anarchoid forerunners; but one distinctive aspect requires attention.

Anarchoid ideas had played no noticeable part in the revolution of

1848-1849, and so Marx's and Engels' writings of 1850-1852 about the revolutionary experience included nothing of prime interest in this connection. In the press and leftist literature, the term 'anarchy' or 'anarchist' was found only with its traditional meaning. 'Anarchist' was an establishment synonym for 'revolutionary' or 'subversive'; to the conservative press, revolutionary people were 'anarchists,' and 'anarchy' was what their struggle brought about. Marx's and Engels' articles ironically reflected this usage from time to time.[46]

Furthermore Marx began to speak of the "smashing" of the state (as we will see) but this meant its replacement by a new kind of state; it was not the old business of the anarchists' "abolition of the state" by fiat.

But the "abolition of the state" did crop up in 1850 from an unexpected source—unexpected if we associate the phrase with revolutionary politics. Emile de Girardin, an early French Hearst-type press entrepreneur, was then going through a socialistic phase, and published a book on *Socialism and Taxation*. It put forward a scheme which might be described as bourgeois anarchist. This could be learned from a review of the book by Marx and Engels in the fourth number of their London magazine, the *NRZ Revue*.

Girardin's book proposed to solve the Social Question by abolishing both taxation and the state through a "mutual insurance" plan. It was a fine example of the historical link between aspirations to abolish the tax collector and to abolish the state; and Girardin plainly represented this link between primitive anarchism and bourgeois radicalism. He recommended his scheme because it meant "the revolution without the revolutionary," and because it abolished the state "without any shock," indeed without abolishing the social relations of capitalism. He was all for "the harmony of labor and capital," of course.

Marx and Engels commented:

> Tax reform is the hobbyhorse of all radical bourgeois, the specific element of all bourgeois-economic reforms. From the oldest medieval philistines to the modern free-traders, the main fight revolves around taxes....
> Reduction, or fair assessment etc. etc. of taxes—this is ordinary *bourgeois reform*. Abolition of taxes—this is *bourgeois socialism*.[47]

That is, it was "bourgeois socialism" in Marx's terminology here (compare the *Communist Manifesto*), but in the same sense (alleged abolition of the state) it was also "bourgeois anarchism." To be sure, the review article showed that Girardin's "abolition" of taxes really amounted to a single-tax capital levy, but Girardin thought he was abolishing the state because he replaced the state power with what he called an "administrative commission." As usual, the state was given a new label, and the real state, having been abolished, returned by the back door.

In the key passage of their review, Marx and Engels went from the present nature of the capitalist state to the morrow's elimination of the state, and in between they showed how Girardin reintroduced the state under another name. They began with the "mutual insurance" metaphor in the scheme: Girardin proposed mutual insurance *instead* of a state, and they replied that the state was *already now* the bourgeoisie's mode of "mutual insurance."

> The bourgeois state is nothing else than a mutual insurance for the bourgeois class against its own individual members as well as against the exploited class, an insurance which must become more and more expensive and apparently more and more autonomous with respect to bourgeois society, since the suppression of the exploited class becomes more and more difficult. Changing the names changes not the least bit in the terms of this insurance. The apparent autonomy which Mr. Girardin momentarily ascribes to the individual with respect to the insurance he must himself immediately abandon.

Now the argument referred to the terms of Girardin's plan:

> Whoever estimates his own wealth at too low a figure incurs a penalty: the insurance office [Girardin's state-substitute] buys out his property at the value set, and even invites denunciations by offering rewards. And more: whoever prefers not to insure his wealth takes a place outside the society and is directly declared an outlaw. Society can naturally not tolerate that a class should form within it which revolts against its conditions of existence. Coercion, authority, bureaucratic intervention, which Girardin wants to eliminate, get back into society. If he has momentarily abstracted himself from the conditions of bourgeois society, this takes place only in order to come back to it by a detour.

It is worth citing this at the necessary length so as to show how the trick was pulled off at both ends: how our would-be bourgeois anarchist sought to abolish the state, and eliminate "coercion, authority, bureaucratic intervention," and how Marx exposed the futility of concealing the return of the state with antistate phraseology. The Marx-Engels review article added:

> Behind the abolition of taxation is concealed the abolition [*Abschaffung*] of the state. The abolition of the state has only one meaning for the Communists: it is the necessary result of the abolition of classes, whereupon of itself the need for the organized power of one class to suppress another ceases to exist [*wegfällt*].[48]

Note that at this early point (1850) they already accepted the "abolition of the state" as the communist aim—with the "ultimate aim" formulation. The claim that they came to this view only because of Bakunin's later anarchist formulation is nothing but a myth. As Engels said, they had taken such a view for granted since youth.

In contrast with the Communist meaning, what was the bourgeois-anarchist talk of the famous abolition? The review of Girardin offered a summary analysis that was going to apply more widely than the immediate subject. When anarchoids talked about abolishing the "state," one had to ask what they understood by the state, and what states they were abolishing.

Take, for example, the view encountered among the anarchoids on the nature of the state in the American republic: the Marx-Engels article pointed out their tendency to speak as if it were a nonstate:

> In bourgeois countries [so thought the bourgeois-anarchist types] the abolition of the state means the reduction of the state power to the scale of North America. Here the class antagonisms are developed only incompletely; class collisions are always glossed over because the proletarian surplus population is drained off to the West; the intervention of the state power, which is reduced to a minimum in the East, does not exist in the West at all.

The same anarchoids tended to think that "abolition of the state" in feudal countries meant the abolition of feudalism in favor of a bourgeois state. In Germany, they hocus-pocused *bourgeois* rights into "absolute independence and autonomy of the *individual*." The article referred to "the Berliners Stirner and [Julius] Faucher" as examples of this "silly" way of thinking.[49]

Look back to the beginning of this passage for the naive idea that *no state* existed in a democratic republic like the United States. This was a very convenient conception of the state, for it made it easy to hocus-pocus particular states out of existence whenever dogma demanded. It was not only Faucher, a German "Manchesterite" free-trade economist who was making antistate noises at the time, nor was it only Stirner who viewed the state in this superficial way; this naiveté was common among anarchist ideologists.

Marx noted this tendency in Bakunin, and it can be found in Kropotkin—to take only the two major theoreticians of anarchism. The pattern appeared in Bakunin's 1873 book *Statism and Anarchy*, in a passage which Marx indeed copied out for his notes. In this passage Bakunin looked on Holland, England and the United States as "a new civilization *antistate in its nature*, but *bourgeois in economics* and liberal." For himself Marx jotted down the observation: "This passage [is] very characteristic of Bakunin; the capitalist state proper is for him antigovernmental..." As for Kropotkin: his basic essay on "The State" declared that "so far as Europe is concerned the state is of recent origin—it barely goes back to the sixteenth century" and apparently did not exist in feudal times! That is, Kropotkin saw the medieval state as nondespotic, *hence not a state*.[50]

Later in 1850, Engels started an article—never completed—on the latest German representatives of this trend. It began by reproducing the last summary passage quoted above from the review of Girardin, and continued:

> Abolition [*Abschaffung*] of the state, *anarchy*, has meanwhile become a general catchword in Germany. The scattered German disciples of Proudhon, Berlin's "higher" democracy, and even the forgotten "noblest minds of the nation" of the Stuttgart parliament and the Imperial Regency have—each in his own way—adopted this wild-sounding catchword.[51]

The "German followers of Proudhon" may have been Ruge and Karl Grün, and the "noblest minds" Ludwig Simon and Karl Vogt, who reportedly published articles favoring the abolition of the state in some sense.[52] Engels expected his readers to know that the gentlemen who were using this fierce language were in fact antirevolutionary, and the sense must have been Pickwickian:

> All these tendencies agree on maintaining the existing *bourgeois society*.... they differ from the real representatives of the bourgeoisie only in the unusual form, which gives them the appearance of "going further," of "going further than anyone else." This appearance vanished before all real conflicts; when faced with the *real* anarchy [i.e., disorder] of revolutionary crises, when the masses fought with "brute force," these representatives of anarchy in every case did their utmost to check the anarchy.

The German source of this tendency, Engels went on, was Stirner:

> Stirner's sermon on statelessness in particular is excellently suited to give Proudhon's anarchy and Girardin's abolition of the state the "higher consecration" of German philosophy. Stirner's book ... is forgotten, to be sure, but its mode of thought, especially its critique of the state, makes a reappearance in the friends of anarchy.[53]

This fragment of an article seemed to be aimed at making Stirner's book its main subject, but before he ever turned to it Engels discussed the confusion of ideas from which it emerged. He linked this up with the tendency of the bourgeoisie—as well as the conservative-feudal party—to make a show of advocating some brand of socialism in order to appeal to workers. Since the censorship imposed an abstract mode of expression—for the censor blue-penciled statements written in plain language—a suitably abstract terminology was provided by Hegelianism. The literary battle shifted to the religious and philosophical shadowland. "The philosophical shadow-boxing that went on below the surface of this confusion was a reflection of the real struggle," and attracted the "educated" public—"a host of idle minds, apprentice lawyers, aspirants to teachers' posts, broken-down theologians, unemployed medicos, littérateurs, etc., etc."[54]

Engels' unfinished article ended soon after this hint of how the etherealization of the state in the form of anarchoid phrases arose from such elements of the "educated classes" lacking social roots of their own.

It was now clear that one of the main defects of these bourgeois "friends of anarchy" was that they did *not* really look to the abolition of the state (any real state). At the same time it was clear that Marx had, in his *Anti-Proudhon*, counterposed a communist conception of the abolition of the state: "it is the necessary result of the abolition of classes, whereupon of itself the need for the organized power of one class to suppress another ceases to exist."

The mere "abolition of the state" was not enough to define anarchism. What else, then? A conception like "the extravagant hocus-pocusing of bourgeois freedom into absolute independence and autonomy of the individual." We will see in the next chapter that the *distinctively* anarchist conception revolved around a thesis about "authority." It involved the absolute sovereignty of the individual Ego as against the imposition of *any* "authority" over it.

Along these lines Marx had arrived at a distinctive approach to the old problem of antistatism. There were still many questions to answer, but this much was plain: the famous "abolition of the state" had to be the end-term of the social transformation, not the first step.

5. ANARCHISM'S "DISGUISED STATE"

Before we leave Proudhonism, we should point out that Marx and Engels themselves considered this approach of theirs to be new and distinctive.

This transpired from an interesting epistolary exchange between them on the publication of a new book by Proudhon in 1851, his *Idée Générale de la Révolution au XIXe Siècle*. Marx read it first, and sent Engels a long summary, with almost no comment, asking for his opinion of the book.[55]

Engels read the first part, and was initially impressed rather favorably: in it he found a more sophisticated theory than in Proudhon's previous writings—and he thought he knew where it came from. Proudhon, speculated Engels, must have seen somebody's translation of the *Communist Manifesto*, for he could not read German; perhaps he had also seen translations of Marx's articles in the *NRZ Revue* (meaning *The Class Struggles in France* and perhaps also the review of Girardin). Engels told Marx:

> A number of points are unquestionably stolen from there—for example, that the *government* is nothing but the power of one class for the suppression of the other, and disappears [*verschwindet*] along with the disappearance of class antagonisms.[56]

Or had Proudhon absorbed this from Marx's early *Poverty of Philosophy?* Engels didn't think so. Now, however Proudhon had come by his "sophisticated" ideas, this much is certain: Engels regarded this approach to the abolition of the state as distinctively Marx's, as Marx's hallmark.

It is probably useless to wonder how Proudhon came by the ideas that impressed Engels; he may have absorbed reasonable facsimiles of these ideas from discussions by other people and through the postrevolution ambience. After all, much later, in his *Grundrisse* notebooks, Marx commented pungently on Proudhon's capacity for keeping an ear to the ground: he "indeed hears the bells ringing, but never knows where...."[57] In any case, Proudhon did not develop any of this any further; nor was a development compatible with the rejection of the "principle of authority" that was prominent in the 1851 book.[58]

Engels' copious notes on Proudhon's book were focused on Proudhon the economist, as before; and also as before, he (like Marx and the left in general) showed little or no interest in what we now see as the basic-anarchist aspect of Proudhon's thought. In these notes, Engels mostly gave a summary of the anti-authority argument that was dotted with grunts like: "dithyramb," "declamation," "trash," "verbose," "general platitudes." The same approach was also evident in the exchange of letters between Marx and Engels in August 1851. In one letter Marx gave a précis of the "principle of authority," and summed up only: "In this state concept carried to the extreme its °nonsense° comes to the fore." After summarizing the Proudhonian *Dissolution du gouvernement,* his sole remark was: "Stirnerian phrases."[59]

In another letter Engels did take note of the concept in connection with Proudhon's rejection of democracy, for he grasped the relationship and was repelled by the anarchist's antidemocratic bias:

> ... on the whole one can read nothing more pretentiously superficial than his critique of politics, for example in the case of democracy.... And what a great idea, that *pouvoir* [state power] and *liberté* are irreconcilable opposites, and that no form of government can give him a sufficient moral basis why *he* should obey it! *Par Dieu,* why then was a *pouvoir* needed?[60]

Still, he was mainly hooting at the idea, not really taking it very seriously.

On the other hand, the Marx-Engels correspondence is often allusive because the two took for granted that ABC matters did not need to be explained.

Even after Proudhon's death, when in 1865 Marx summed him up in an obituary article, Marx felt no need to mention Proudhon's anarchist aspect, let alone discuss it.[61] In fact, Marx and Engels never did class him under the tag 'anarchist' in their own thinking. There was a telltale letter by Engels to Bernstein in 1884 in which the former wrote that "the following passages show that we proclaimed the cessation [*Aufhören*] of the state before there were anarchists altogether," whereupon he quoted from Marx's *Poverty of Philosophy* and from the Manifesto.[62] Plainly, by "anarchists" he meant the movement that appeared with Bakunin.

At the risk of repetition, we remind that the Proudhonist movement did not represent itself as "anarchist" but rather as "mutualist"; and that Proudhon did not call himself an anarchist—not at all until 1863 and then only by exception.[63] When a self-styled anarchist movement did come into being, the Proudhonist current (what was left of it) was *hostile*. These facts account for the usages of Proudhon's contemporaries; they do not impugn his place in anarchist history. Even in the early Bakuninist movement the label 'anarchist' was not yet completely accepted; Bakunin's first lieutenant, Guillaume, who was a twister, wanted to drop 'anarchism' in favor of 'federalism.'[64]

Still and all, Proudhon's anarchism did occasionally crop up, and there was an important point with which we must end. In the 1851 correspondence between Marx and Engels about Proudhon's new book, Engels touched a vital idea—on the fly, so to speak. He had thought that Proudhon "does seem to be making progress"—but only at the cost of a greater confusion. For, *as in Girardin's case*, the alleged antistatism crumbled as soon as real alternatives were put forward:

> *Au bout du compte*, then, Mr. Proudhon also comes down to this: that the real meaning of the right of property consists in the disguised confiscation of all property by a more or less disguised state, and that the real meaning of the abolition [*Abschaffung*] of the state is intensified state centralization.[65]

Not only did the state return by the back door after being "abolished" but in fact it would become more, not less, bureaucratic on the basis of Proudhon's detailed scheme for a mutual-credit bank to solve the Social Question. The mutualist bank "is fused with the state on the sly or under another name," and the objective consequence will be that "all real wealth will be centralized in the hands of the state or the commune [municipality]...."[66]

In his private notebooks, now published under the title *Carnets*, Proudhon spelled out fairly candidly the extraordinarily antidemocratic content of his "nonstatist" scheme for a Mutual Credit Society which would eventually take over society. A useful supplement to the *Carnets* is the biographical information about what happened when he actually set up his bank operation in 1849. It was as tightly controlled a personal dictatorship as could be planned by this champion of Liberty (his own). Alongside this specific scheme, Proudhon's *Carnets* were equally frank about his yearnings for "mastery" over society; the picture is pathological.[67]

The issues about the nature of the anarchist ideology were going to emerge more clearly with the man who turned anarchism into a movement: Bakunin.

6 | OF ANARCHISM: BAKUNIN MODEL

Anarchism as a distinctive doctrine was put together, and made the basis of a movement for power, in the middle 1860s and early 1870s, by Michael Bakunin and his circle. To form this movement, he combined three ingredients, loosely mixed:

(1) A social theory suggested by Proudhon, with at least a dash of Stirner—the anarchist element proper.

(2) A socioeconomic program which was a (changing) version of the anticapitalist collectivism current in socialist circles, including eclectic borrowings from Marxian theory to fill the chinks.

(3) For political strategy, the conspiratorial putschism of the then current left-Jacobin tradition of the B's, that is, Babeuf, Buonarroti, Blanqui, Barbès (what historians nowadays loosely call "Blanquism")—all skewed by a Russian-accented terroristic nihilism.

Later anarchists mixed the ingredients in different ways; also later, anarchosyndicalism offered a different menu, and is not considered here.

Some of the components of anarchism are taken up elsewhere: *KMTR* 3 took up Bakunin's theory of the "secret (invisible) dictatorship," and also the general politics of Blanquism or Jacobin-revolutionism. Marx's *positive* views on the dying away (or "abolition") of the state in socialist society are scheduled for our last volume, though the subject has already been touched on. The personal relations between Marx and Bakunin, a subject that has given rise to a mountainous mass of falsifiction *and* falsification, will be covered only in part. The general subject inevitably raises many of the problems of the history of the International, but this whole history cannot be fit into these pages; some background facts about Bakuninism in the International are given in Special Note B.

In this chapter we will be concerned essentially with the *anarchism* of the anarchist movement as Marx knew it, including the specific nature of Bakunin's ideology and operation.*

As always, terminology is a problem. In this case, one question of terminology lies at the heart of the problem. This is the deliberately fostered confusion about the word 'authority.'

1. ON THE "PRINCIPLE OF AUTHORITY"

For nearly two decades after the summer of 1851, neither Marx nor Engels (as far as I know) mentioned the "abolition of the state" in writing. This hiatus was just about the same as for the term 'dictatorship of the proletariat,' as we saw in *KMTR* 3; and the reason was similar, namely, the subject was not raised by events. Marx, as is well known, was generally reluctant to speculate about the future until experience set the agenda, and these two quiet decades had a different agenda.

When a new period began in the 1870s with a war and a revolution, it also evoked the "abolition of the state" as a catchword in a new context: Bakunin's bid for domination of the international left through the instrumentality of the first anarchist movement. What marked this movement as anarchist was not simply the old catchword. It became a distinctive ideology, for one thing, by proposing that the *first* word of the revolution had to be the abolition of all *authority over the sovereign individual* by any power of any sort outside the individual ego.

It was this ideology, construed with varying consistency by different

---

* Since the publication of Carr's still-useful biography of Bakunin, several scholarly works have added immeasurably to our understanding of Bakunin's antidemocratic mind. For full data on the following works, see the Bibliography.—(1) The book by Eugene Pyziur is the oldest on this list; marred by unclear references. (2) A.P. Mendel's *Michael Bakunin* (1981) has an effective assemblage of evidence, despite its psychiatric overkill. Mendel's introduction relates that he began the work to show that Carr's biography "did not take seriously enough Bakunin's contribution to freedom," and he "finished the book convinced that neither the Carr biography nor other works on Bakunin take seriously enough his threat to freedom." (3) Of prime importance is *Violence dans la Violence*, a collection of documents by Prof. Confino, who discovered (and here publishes) Bakunin's letter to Nechayev of June 2, 1870, and other documents exposing his dictatorial aims and methods. (4) The International's original exposé of Bakunin, *The Alliance of Socialist Democracy and the International Working Men's Association*, plus a mass of further documentation, has been published in English: see *The Hague Congress of the First International* [&c.]. (5) Bakunin's raucously racist and anti-Semetic writings during the International struggle are now available in noxious quantity, in French, in the volumes of the *Archives Bakounine*.

elements, which, for the whole period, made anarchism so destructive (to the working-class movement) and so unproductive (in furthering anticapitalism). The anarchist theory of the state included the doctrine of Instant Abolition, since no "authoritarian" transition was permissible. *This meant that as soon as revolutionaries succeeded in establishing a workers' state, the anarchists set out to destroy it, from within or without.* Marx and Engels, who had scornfully dismissed the "principle of authority" when they had run across it in Proudhon and Stirner, now had to confront it seriously.

By the "principle of authority" the consistent anarchist means principled opposition to *any* exercise of authority, including opposition to authority derived from the most complete democracy and exercised in completely democratic fashion. Indeed, democratic authority is the worst of all since it is the most insidious. Of all ideologies, anarchism is the one most fundamentally antidemocratic in principle, since it is not only unalterably hostile to democracy in general but particularly to any socialist democracy of the most ideal kind that could be imagined. This basic truth is befogged a bit mainly by liberal "friends of anarchy" who like to dream of anarchist assuagements of the bureaucratic states they sponsor in practice.

Let us review what we raised in *KMTR* 3 as a central problem of social organization. Since the anarchist denounces the most ideal forms of decision-making in society as an evil to be destroyed, one should think they must address themselves to the consequential question: *"What do you do when people disagree, in any organized society where individuals have to live in concert?"* If every individual Ego is perfectly sovereign, how do you decide what a social group (any society) is to *do*?[1]

No anarchist thinker has ever really answered this elementary question; and it requires heavy research to find any who even recognizes its existence.

The common anarchist view (which can be called an answer in a sense) is that of the ants. Ants have no problem; they seem to come to an automatic consensus in some way which scientists investigate. Some anarchist theorists have solved the problem handily by assuming that people *will* behave like ants as soon as conditions are made "natural," that is, as soon as the Instant Abolition takes place. To anyone who needs to have this nonsense refuted, we have nothing to say here. We should point out historically that the "magic unanimity" which suddenly descends on humanity, as soon as the decree abolishing the state has been read out, is also an article of faith among totalitarian creeds (like Stalinism).

But if this "magic unanimity" is a fable, as of course it is, *what do you do when people disagree?*

In time societies have devised a host of mechanisms by which societal decisions are made; the large majority were on how to impose decisions made from above, by a small number of rulers, over the mass of people. A very small percentage were on how to come to decision by the mass of people themselves, under optimum conditions for *control from below*. (For our purposes, *control from below* is the operative condition for democracy.) Through all the complexities of the problem, anarchism is basically concerned with only one aspect: everything must go by the board in order not to impose a social decision for a moment on a single Sovereign Individual who does not like that decision, let alone a minority who disagree.

In the anarchists' language, democracy is "authoritarian." It is accordingly of the devil (authoritarianism). Anarchism therefore says it rejects *both* democracy and despotism in any form. The history of anarchist thought, such as it is, has been the search for a third alternative that does away with all authority and yet permits society to exist. No such device has ever been found. There is a substitute: what anarchist theory does is substitute elocution about Freedom.

This invitation to confusion has been institutionalized in the use of the chameleon words 'authoritarian' and 'authoritarianism,' which became current after the rise of anarchism. 'Authoritarian,' of course, started from the root meaning 'involving authority' to become a common synonym for 'undemocratic' or 'despotic,' as if the very existence of authority was 'authoritarian.' This *non sequitur* embedded itself in political jargon.

This development might be considered among the curiosa, like other illogical etymologies, except that the political statement implied has been fostered by liberalism. What was an untenable notion of anarchism became a muddled language habit of liberals, who went along with the soul-gratifying counterposition of Authority to Freedom as happily as they went along with the advance of bureaucratism in society and the state.

By their abstractionized Freedom consistent anarchists (as distinct from liberals) mean an individual's unconditional capacity to live by the motto of Thélème: *Do What Thou Wilt.** The rhetoric is retained by liberals who have no intention of letting anyone Do What They Will, but who find anarchist phrases useful to belabor socialism in general and Marx in particular.

Thus it has become the settled custom in writing about socialist history

---

* In defense of Rabelais, who was not responsible for anarchist nonsense, it should be said that the common acceptance of Thélème as the depiction of an anarchist society or community is self-discrediting, though this was done from Proudhon on. Rabelais makes it quite clear that it is only the small company of ladies and gentlemen who live in "Perfect Liberty" and who Do What They Will. For around them is a horde of servants and artisans at their beck and call, who do as their *masters* will. The whole is bankrolled by Gargantua's fortune. Real anarchism!

to label Marx the advocate of "authoritarian socialism" as against the "antiauthoritarian" doctrine of Bakunin, who is advertised to be a "libertarian." A crude type of marxology exhibits Engels' explanation of democratic *authority* as if it were ipso facto a defense of *authoritarianism*.[2]

The question of authority in its simplest aspect was, as it happened, covered by Marx without reference to the new-baked anarchist movement, when he made notes for what was going to be the third volume of *Capital*. All social production, all cooperation in labor, indeed the very meaning of cooperation, involves the labor of supervision in some form, hence the exercise of a certain authority—to see to it, for example, that a labor gang heaved a load all at the same time (else laborers could be seriously injured), or that lumbermen cut down only trees designated by some authority and not As They Will.

> The labor of supervision and management is naturally required wherever the direct process of production assumes the form of a combined social process, and not of the isolated labor of independent producers. However, it has a double nature.

That is, this need has a technological component and a social one:

> On the one hand, all labor in which many individuals cooperate necessarily requires a commanding will to coordinate and unify the process... much as that of an orchestra conductor.* This is a productive job, which must be performed in every combined mode of production.
> On the other hand... this supervision work necessarily arises in all modes of production based on the antithesis between the laborer, as the direct producer, and the owner of the means of production. The greater this antagonism, the greater the role played by supervision. Hence it reaches its peak in the slave system. But it is indispensable also in the capitalist mode of production....[4]

Thus the difference between the technological and the social component entails a *societal* difference in the role of supervisory authority in production. Under different exploitive systems, there may be a difference in *degree* involved. Under socialism there is another difference of no small importance:

> In a cooperative factory the antagonistic nature of the labor of super-

---

* As it happens, Godwin too had pointed to the example of "concerts of music," as well as "theatrical exhibitions," involving "absurd and vicious co-operation." Musicians and actors are actually (*horrors!*) told what to do by someone else: this is "a breach of sincerity," and above all "evil" authoritarianism.[3]

vision disappears, because the manager is paid by the laborers instead of representing capital counterposed to them.[5]

This case—a producers' cooperative where the supervisor or manager is employed by the workers collectively under his supervision—is naturally not the only form of worker-manager relations envisaged by socialism; but it is particularly good for testing the "principle of authority." The "commanding will" is there, but there is necessarily a qualitative change in the *social relations behind the form* in which authority is being wielded.

Wherever authority is democratized, another change takes place: it is demystified. The young Marx, two decades before, had criticized Hegel's treatment of the state's authority on grounds that included this: the state bureaucracy (of Prussian absolutism) typically has a defective attitude toward authority; authority "is the principle of its knowledge, and the deification of authority is its *mentality*."[6] In contrast, Marx later remarked in the course of discussing constitutions that "government cannot be too simple"—it was made "complicated and mysterious" by knaves.[7] The simplification of politics and state machinery, so demanded, made the real sources of authority a transparent thing. This was the demystification of authority. The demystification of authority was a precondition for effective control from below, of course.

But the anarchist is happily spared any analysis of authority in its social context, for it is all Evil. That makes the conclusion very simple: destroy it, instantly or sooner, and there's an end on 't.

2. ENGELS ON AUTHORITY

Whether or not Engels was then acquainted with the above-quoted manuscript for *Capital*, in 1871 he had to explain much the same thing about how the Bakuninists "misuse the word 'authoritarian.' " A short lexicographical excursus is in order.

The word 'authoritarian' was in early use by Bakuninist critics and followers, both, but it is hard to ascertain how far back this usage can be traced. The Oxford English Dictionary dates the word to 1879 in English; the ism much later. This certainly implies that it made its mark on *English* only after anarchist language had become well known; but just as certainly the word was in use before that date on the Continent.

At the beginning of January 1870, a disillusioned Bakuninist who was now the secretary of the Romance Swiss federation, Henri Perret, wrote to the General Council complaining about the Bakunin group's splitting operation: "These democrats are authoritarians, they want no opposition," he wrote. (Marx, sending Perret's opinions on to a Belgian, reported that the Swiss federation had resolved "to emancipate itself from the dictatorship of the Alliance.") In an article for publication in Spain in 1872, addressed to readers accustomed to Bakuninist language, Engels wrote that in the Alliance "despite all the phrases about *anarchy, autonomy, free federation,* etc., there are in reality only two things: *authority* and *obedience.*" In a circular for the GC in 1872, Engels used 'authoritative' and 'authoritativeness' to mean 'authoritarian' and its cognate: a mistake that showed still uncertain grasp of the usage.[8] Certainly by the early 1870s the basic muddle had been implanted in language itself: authority was now lexicographically (by definition) equated with antidemocracy.

When Paul Lafargue prepared to go to Spain at the end of that year, Engels wrote him an educational letter. First he had to call his attention to the mystique around the word:

> As soon as something displeases the Bakuninists, they say: it's *authoritarian* and thereby they imagine they have damned it forever. If they were workers instead of bourgeois, journalists, etc., or if they had but given a little study to economic questions and conditions in modern industry, they would know that no joint action of any sort is possible without imposing on some an extraneous will, i.e., an authority.

That was the point made in the manuscript for *Capital*. But, Engels continued, there are different sorts of authority:

> Whether it be the will of a majority of voters, of a leading committee, or of one man, it is still a will imposed on the dissentients; but without that single and directing will, no cooperation is possible. Go and run one of the big Barcelona factories without direction, that is, without authority! Or administer a railway without the certainty that every engine-driver, fireman, etc., will be at his post at precisely the time when he should be there! I should very much like to know whether the gallant Bakunin would entrust his large person to a railway carriage if that railway were administered according to principles by which nobody would be at his post if he did not please to submit to the authority of the regulations far more authoritarian in any possible state of society than those of the Basel Congress [of the International]!

This is a form of the same question to which (as we said above) no anarchist has ever replied meaningfully except with elocution about Freedom. Engels concluded this line of thought:

> All these fine ultraradical and revolutionary phrases merely serve to conceal the utter poverty of ideas and the most complete ignorance of the conditions in which the daily life of society is carried on. Go and abolish "all authority, even with consent" amongst the sailors on a ship![9]

Aside from the anthill model, perhaps the most rational anarchist response is to advocate the breakup of modern society into atomized fragments on the land, with no interrelations among them; and while this would not really be a solution of their problem, it was obviously a recourse to an irrelevant utopianism of a backward kind.

All of the examples of "authority" in the real world were going to be repeated by Engels in other writings. Let us note some aspects.

We have already stressed (never too much) that the anarchist position was not simply impractical or destructive; it was very basically antidemocratic. In rejecting "all authority, even with consent," it upheld the right of a small minority to impose *its* conceptions and desiderata on the large majority, if necessary by violence. It announced its intention of destroying the first workers' state that the socialists might be able to establish—in the name of Freedom, the Freedom of an anarchist engineer to run his train onto a track that some despotic authority claimed as due to be occupied by another train.

The antidemocratic nature of anarchism was brought out in the first years of the conflict. It was touched on concisely in one of Engels' more compact presentations of the time, in 1872, in a letter to a comrade:

> In this society [the Bakuninist ideal future society] there will above all be no *authority*, for authority = state = absolute evil. (How these people propose to run a factory, operate a railway or steer a ship without a will that decides in the last resort, without single management, they of course do not tell us.) The authority of the majority over the minority also ceases.[10]

The last sentence made the connection explicit: the anarchist rejection of the "principle of authority" made democracy impossible. By the same token it made any organization impossible—at any rate, any democratic organization.

Engels continued: "Every individual and every community is autonomous; but as to how a society of even two people is possible unless each gives up some of his autonomy, Bakunin again maintains silence." And *this* deduction was acted out by the history of anarchist attempts at organization, all of which self-destructed with practised ease.

If the "principle of authority" made anarchist organization next to impossible, it was wonderfully well suited to destroy other organizations. "Instant Destruction" was not only assured to the first workers' state they came across; it was wielded in the first instance against the International. The Bakuninists were the first radical group that made its *conscious* aim "Rule or Ruin," even before the advent of the criminal-adventurer Nechayev. After doing their all to reduce the International to a shambles, so that their own "International Alliance of the Socialist Democracy" could take over, they quickly found that their own anarchist International was susceptible to the same methods of internal smashup.

In 1873 Engels published a short article in the Italian socialist press, "On Authority," giving a somewhat expanded version of the letters which we have quoted. It is something of a small masterpiece of educational elucidation. Its examples from the real world of production and social living were much the same as what we have seen. Above all, it boldly posed the problem of understanding words that "sound bad."

> Authority, in the sense in which the word is used here, means: the imposition of the will of another upon ours; on the other hand, authority presupposes subordination. Now, since these two words sound bad and the relationship which they represent is disagreeable to the subordinated party, the question is to ascertain whether there is any way of dispensing with it, whether—given the conditions of present-day society—we could not create another social system in which this authority would be given no scope any longer and would consequently have to disappear.[11]

Everywhere in modern society, combined action tends to displace "independent action by individuals," and this implies organization. "Now, is it possible to have organization without authority?" Will authority disappear in a social revolution, or will it only change its form? Well, in production the operation of (say) a cotton mill imposes certain regularities; for example, workers must work when the steam is up and they cannot work when it is down. The steam "cares nothing for individual autonomy"—or, for that matter, for any other slogans.

The workers themselves must make decisions about working hours, and these decisions must be observed by all, otherwise production stops.

> ... whether they are settled by decision of a delegate placed at the head of each branch of labor or, if possible, by a majority vote, the will of the single individual will always have to subordinate itself, which means that questions are settled in an authoritarian way.[12]

"In an authoritarian way": we see that Engels was again trying to demystify the fearsome "bad-sounding" word. This "authoritarian way" involved the exercise of authority—in whatever democratic fashion the workers might decide. *This* "authoritarian" way was the only democratic way: what a terminological tangle had been created!

Engels continued to use words that "sound bad" in order to force a confrontation with the real issue tangled in the terminology. Nature (he went on) subjects people to a "veritable despotism," and "The automatic machinery of a big factory is much more despotic than the small capitalists who employ workers ever have been." This is the source of the "despotism"—constraints imposed on people from the outside. (We fight *this* despotism by conquering the forces of nature.) But where the forces of industry, which we ourselves have created, impose a certain "despotism" on us, we cannot wish this despotism away or exorcise it with better-sounding words. We *can* deal with it democratically, that is, by *democratizing the delegation of authority*.

Here in part Engels was taking his cue from Marx's *Capital*, which discussed how the cooperation of laborers was enforced in modern industry: "practically in the shape of the authority of the ... capitalist, in the shape of the powerful will of another" in a form of control that is "despotic," though "this despotism takes forms peculiar to itself."[13]

Looking back to "On Authority," we find Engels again using the railway example:

> Here, too, the first condition of the job is a dominant will that settles all subordinate questions, whether this will is represented by a single delegate or a committee charged with the execution of the resolutions of the majority of persons interested. In either case there is a very pronounced authority.[14]

In the case of those two railway trains that were due to converge on the same track: who exercised the authority to impose his Individual Will? It might be a trainmaster appointed by capitalist owners, by state owners, by the railway workers, by a committee of workers in the industry—in short, one imposed democratically or not; but such a power *must* be "despotically" exercised by some "very pronounced authority." Engels kept insisting that the anarchist mystique about authority fell away before this simple approach.

There was a last qualification. We noted that the exercise of authority varied, in different social contexts, in quantity and quality, "deified" or demystified, bureaucratically imposed or democratically controlled. There was another question: *the sphere to which it could be confined.*

> ... it is absurd to speak of the principle of authority as being absolutely evil, and of the principle of autonomy as being absolutely good. Authority and autonomy are relative things whose spheres vary with the various phases of the development of society. If the autonomists confined themselves to saying that the social organization of the future would restrict authority solely to the limits within which the conditions of production render it inevitable, we could understand each other; but they are blind to all facts that make the thing necessary and they passionately fight the word.[15]

Here Engels set the social goal of *restricting authority within the limits* enforced by the necessities of production and social life. This was a vital addendum to the very idea of democratizing authority. As against anarchism's Instant Abolition of authority and the state, it suggests a dynamic approach to the problem: for as the necessary conditions of production are changed by socialism, so also are the limits or boundaries within which authority has to exercise its "despotism."

Just as state authority is only one kind of authority in social relations, so also the dying away of the state can be viewed as one stage in a longer drama, *the dying away of authority* per se. This can be regarded as at least a tendency or direction, whether or not some absolute end is visible. But at this point we are peering into a dimmer future than we can probably see.

3. REVOLUTION AND AUTHORITY

In practice, anarchists did not consistently apply their "principle of authority" *to themselves*, since consistent practice on these lines would often be hard to distinguish from plain lunacy. While the Bakuninists inveighed against "all authority, even with consent," they made no bones about trying to impose their own authority over the masses *without* their consent. For example—in a putsch.

A putsch was, to an extreme point, the imposition of antidemocratic "authority." An example that Marx especially liked to use was provided by Bakunin on September 28, 1870: it was the "Fiasco at Lyons." (This is the chapter title in Carr's biography of Bakunin.) Perhaps because there was a certain grimly humorous side to the event, Marx and Engels referred to this story at least six times in letters and publications.[16] Attention should be centered not on the fiasco that resulted but on the "authoritarian" coup that precipitated it.

On the fall of Napoleon III and the Second Empire, a popular uprising in working-class Lyons took control of the city. Bakunin rushed to Lyons to take personal command of his small band of followers. The day he arrived, a new city council was being elected under the auspices of a "Committee of Public Safety," but no one really knew what to do with city hall. Bakunin stepped in—and here is how the International's pamphlet, written by Engels, Lafargue and Marx, accurately explained what happened:

> Bakunin installed himself there [in city hall]. Then came the critical moment, the moment awaited for many years, when Bakunin could carry out the most revolutionary act the world has ever seen—he decreed the *Abolition of the State*. But the state, in the form and nature of

two companies of bourgeois National Guards, swept the hall, and set Bakunin hurrying back on the road to Geneva.[17]

The first sentence of Bakunin's decree was: "The administrative and governmental machine of the state, having become impotent, is abolished." However, it was not the state that was suffering from "the fantasy and impotence of pious desire." The servitors of the omnipotent state not only brushed this putsch away but—worse insult—they did not take it seriously enough to jail the leader securely after rifling his pockets of a few francs.

But let us see what happened to the Principle of Authority in this episode. Firstly, the state that our anarchist abolished by decree was not the old state of Bonaparte and despotism but, rather, that of the provisional revolutionary government just established by the democratic movement. Secondly, the world-historic decree of the abolition of the state as issued by Bakunin was signed by twenty of his friends; it was read to an ebullient meeting that cheered everything; and it was then placarded on the walls. Not only did the revolutionary people have nothing to say about this abolition, but even *Bakunin's own little band had voted against the putsch two days before he pulled it off.*

Bakunin utilized a day of confused demonstrations, with the proclamation from the standard balcony. The whole business reflected his usual autocratic methods. No majority was going to exercise its evil authority over *him*! For only the despot enjoys Perfect Liberty. *"All toil alike in sorrow, unless one were lord of heaven; none is truly free, save only Zeus,"* said Aeschylus.[18]

To be sure, even if a majority of the people *had* somehow supported the "abolition of the state" decree, this would not have done away with the state, and it would still have entailed a massive imposition of authority— even if by a democratic majority. Not even a pure fantasist can describe a revolution without an imposition of authority—as was proved by the rare case when an anarchist fantasy of this sort was written.[19]

Marx made this point strongly in the crucial 1872-1873 period of the fight against Bakuninism. The International's pamphlet on the Bakuninist Alliance did so, not for the first time: the anarchists, it said, like "to decree the abolition of the state, as Bakunin did on September 28th in Lyons, despite the fact that abolition of the state is of necessity an authoritarian act."[20]

The simple observation that the famous "abolition" was an act imposing "authority" could be illustrated from the Lyons events in still another way: Bakunin's decree provided capital punishment for anyone who tried to "interfere, in any way whatsoever, with the activity of the revolutionary communes."[21] Obviously anyone who had his head chopped off for "interfering" with Bakunin's nonstate was likely to feel that his Freedom had been cut short.

Among the issues were these: how was authority gained, and how was it exercised? Putschists like Bakunin necessarily imposed their authority despotically since they were opposed on principle to getting democratic sanction. In the International's circular of 1872, Marx and Engels wrote that when Bakunin installed himself in city hall, he refrained from setting up building guards, "as this would be a political act."[22] To provide for the defense of the revolution against counterattack would certainly have been an act of political *authority*. The establishment of a guard would form the embryo of an armed force to safeguard the people's power, and this would be the first form of a revolutionary *state*. But Bakunin had just "abolished" the state with a proclamation.

Engels presented the same elementary line of thought in terms of the democratic movement of the Paris Commune. He wrote to an Italian correspondent about the obviously "authoritarian" element in revolution:

> I believe the terms 'authority' and centralization are being greatly abused. I know nothing more authoritarian than a revolution, and when one's will is imposed on others with bombs and bullets, as in every revolution, it seems to me an act of authority is being committed. It was the lack of centralization and authority that cost the Paris Commune its life.

It may be mentioned, as one of the curiosa of marxological literature, that this passage, written in protest against the anarchist abuse of the term 'authoritarian,' has been cited to prove that Engels was a conscious advocate of 'authoritarianism' (*in* the anarchist sense) by the simple expedient of failing to explain what it was all about, and allowing the reader to assume that 'authoritarian' means just what the anarchist claims it does. The passage continues as follows:

> Do what you like with authority, etc., after the victory, but for the struggle we must unite all our forces in one *fascio* [bundle, the Roman symbol] and concentrate them at one point of attack. And when I am told that authority and centralization are two things that should be condemned under all possible circumstances it seems to me that those who say so either do not know what a revolution is or are revolutionaries in name only.[23]

In short: a revolution imposes a *new* authority; a truly popular revolution can impose a *democratic* authority, which of course anarchists oppose on principle.

The Italian revolutionist Garibaldi made a similar point when Bakuninists sought to claim him (and his prestige) as a supporter of their "fight against the authoritarian principle." He rejected their honors, and told them: "The Paris Commune fell because [at the end] there was no longer any authority in Paris but only anarchy." Engels cheered Garibaldi's statement. At the Hague Congress of the International, a French and a German delegate made a similar appeal to the example of the Commune to underline the necessity of "authority"—democratic authority.[24]

Engels' article "On Authority" came out the following year, to drive the argument home. Let the revolutionary movement be as overwhelming a majority as one might desire, still in a revolution, as in a war, one side imposes its "will" on the other. By pointing out that a revolution was a sort of war, Engels made another attempt to get readers to understand words that "sound bad":

> A revolution is certainly the most authoritarian thing there is; it is the act whereby one part of the population imposes its will upon the other part by means of rifles, bayonets and cannon—authoritarian means, if such there be at all; and if the victorious party does not want to have fought in vain, it must maintain this rule by means of the terror which its arms inspire in the reactionaries. Would the Paris Commune have lasted a single day if it had not made use of this authority of the armed people against the bourgeois? Should we not, on the contrary, reproach it for not having used it freely enough?[25]

It is one of the marvels of marxology that the defenders of democratic authority are labeled "authoritarian" while the autocratic perpetrators of the typical Bakuninist putsch are ticketed as "libertarian." This might be considered one of the most remarkable hoaxes in history if we did not know its origin.

At the Hague Congress there was a lighthearted moment which however was meaningful enough. Just as a form of this question was being discussed, and when the audience grew noisy at one point, the Bakuninist floor leader rose to demand that the hall be cleared. Calls resounded: "Very authoritarian!"[26] With other people, this would have been a quip. For the Bakuninists, clearing the hall would have been "authoritarian" only if *they* were being cleared out—as they eventually were by a democratic vote.

The crux can be summed up this way: the answer to bureaucratic tendencies in the world is *the democratization of authority, not the abolition of authority*—that is, the imposition of control from below on all authority.

But the anarchist talk about "abolishing authority" was not meaningless. It had an operational meaning. The first place in which this operational meaning was analyzed was in the International's pamphlet on the Bakuninist operation, a substantial booklet entitled *The Alliance of the Socialist Democracy and the International Working Men's Association*. The first-named organization was Bakunin's front.

4. THE NATURE OF THE BAKUNINIST OPERATION

Engels and Lafargue wrote the bulk of this pamphlet, using some materials supplied by others. Marx helped draft the conclusion.

This pamphlet demonstrated for the first time that the anarchist talk about Freedom meant its opposite, if anarchist jargon is dropped. Seeking to ensure the Freedom of the sovereign individual Ego, Bakuninism in operation meant the imposition of its own authority in autocratic forms: the establishment of a special sort of despotism by a self-appointed elite who refused to call their dictatorship a "state." They exemplified the familiar pattern whereby an "abolished" state returned by a back door. (The specific 'dictatorship' aspects of Bakunin's scheme have been set forth in *KMTR* 3.)[27]

The International pamphlet aimed its documentation at the then current Bakunin enterprise, which, as always with Bakunin, involved a dual organization: a public front and a secret cadre of controllers. The public front was called the Alliance (or International Alliance) of the Socialist Democracy; the secret cadre of "invisible dictators" was often called the "International Brotherhood."

It is a recorded fact that some of the marxologists who have celebrated Bakunin's "libertarianism" as against Marx's "authoritarianism" have also claimed that Bakunin's instrument for taking over the International was organized without the "principle of authority." But in fact that sort of talk was for the *goyim*. The latest scholar to investigate Bakunin's operation, biographer A. P. Mendel, tells us:

> ... one could not imagine a more rigidly centralized, authoritarian revolutionary organization than the one Bakunin proposed as the weapon for carrying out this destruction of all authoritarianism [i.e., destruction of the International]: the voluntary, freely federated society formed from the "bottom upwards" was reserved for the new world, after the old world had been destroyed by a rigorously disciplined, martial organization formed strictly from the top downwards....

Bakunin *ipse dixit*: he loved to lay out his scheme for cronies, and Mendel cites enough evidence. The biographer adds:

> Even in its open, public mode, the Alliance was to be a highly centralized organization, with all decisions on the national level approved by the central committee. Since it was the real controlling body, the secret organization was even more tightly centralized than the public organization....[28]

It is true that during his lifetime Bakunin sketched one secret-dictatorial scheme after another—most of them imaginary, as biographer Carr emphasized, apparently in the belief that this excused the pattern. But in his International operation Bakunin had live bodies to work on, a real movement.

The International's pamphlet dealt with the *complot du jour*, and had to take it seriously. Its authors had to bring together a wide variety of materials (including translations from the Russian) hastily pulled together by Nicholas Utin of the Geneva branch, documents turned up by Lafargue's sojourn in Spain, etc. Today there is far more evidence to go on. *The overall picture drawn by the International pamphlet was quite accurate.*

Modern research paints an even more damning picture. Anyone who is still bemused by the fable of the "libertarian" Bakunin can maintain that state of innocence only by averting eyes from the new mass of materials, the very existence of which reflects a slow process of disillusionment with the anarchist myth.

At this point we are interested less in the evidence as such than in the line of argument developed in the International pamphlet.

5. ANALYSIS OF THE BAKUNINIST OPERATION

The International pamphlet first showed that the Bakuninists' pretense of abolishing political power was a fraud, if one considered their prescriptions for a "revolutionary commune." The specific Bakuninist document under consideration here is of no importance now; it was simply what the authors, Engels and Lafargue, had to go on.

> Thus in this anarchistic organization ... we have first the Council of the Commune, then the executive committees which, to be able to do anything at all, must be vested with some power and supported by a public force; this is to be followed by nothing short of a federal *parliament*, whose principal object will be to organize this *public force*. Like the Commune Council, this parliament will have to assign *executive power* to one or more *committees* which by this act alone will be given an authoritarian character that the demands of the struggle will increasingly accentuate.

The important outcome of this exposé was the hollowness of the anarchist claim:

> We are thus confronted with a perfect reconstruction of all the elements of the "authoritarian state"; and the fact that we call this machine a "revolutionary commune organized from bottom to top" makes little difference. The name changes nothing of the sub-

stance... Indeed Bakunin himself admits as much when (in Article 8) he describes his organization as a "new revolutionary state."[29]

No one had ever made this analysis of anarchist claims before.

The state which was thus reconstructed by the anarchists under another label was as contemptuous of democracy as anarchist theory required. To give "anarchy" its proper direction, said the Bakuninist document,

> it is necessary that in the midst of popular anarchy, which will constitute the very life and energy of the revolution, *unity of thought and revolutionary action should find an organ.* This organ must be the *secret and worldwide association of the international brethren.*[30]

This pattern of a secret elite of dictators bossing the revolution behind the backs of the anarchic masses occurred over and over in Bakunin's various drafts for his secret "organ." This element was repeated because it was the practical answer to the problem of how anything ever got done in the midst of the "anarchy." In pointing to this secret, the International pamphlet was the first work to unveil what has long been masked by the traditional-marxological account of the struggle in the International as that of "libertarians" versus "authoritarians."

Just as, in the history of society, anarchy tends to be the complement of despotism—as has been mentioned before[31]—so also is this true in patterns of organization. "This transformation into its opposite," wrote Engels in another connection, "this final landing at a point diametrically opposite from the starting point," is the fate of historical movements that are directed toward "merely illusory goals."[32]

The International pamphlet added more information: the Bakunin scheme called for "a revolutionary General Staff composed of devoted, energetic and intelligent individuals who are above all sincere—not vain or ambitious—friends of the people, capable of serving as intermediaries between the revolutionary idea and the popular instincts." But the number of these had to be kept small. "For the International throughout Europe *one hundred serious and firmly united revolutionaries would be sufficient.*" (Elsewhere the Russian schemer calculated that only fifty to seventy agents would be enough to control the world.)[33]

In short: the crude concept of a hidden circle of a handful of Red Dictators pulling the strings behind the backs of a horde of mindless masses—Heavens! where have we seen this stuff? Isn't it the traditional favorite of red scares about the great Communist Conspiracy to rule the world, unless foiled by James Bond or Bulldog Drummond?... Yet this version does not come from trash fiction, nor was it acted out by Marx's evil authoritarians; it was written down in documented programs by the great Libertarian of anarchism, the same paladin of Freedom who is the favorite of marxologists. As a matter of fact, we do know where we have seen this conspiratorial scenario before: Bakuninism, from its rule-or-ruin pandestruction to its rule-and-rein dictatorship, invented the type of conspiracy which is the model of the worst imagined excesses of the Stalinist-type organization, unreconstructed.

The International pamphlet explained, in its own terms:

> So everything changes. Anarchy, the "unleashing of popular life," of "evil passions" and all the rest is no longer enough. To assure the success of the revolution one must have *"unity of thought and action."* The members of the International are trying to create this unity by propaganda, by discussion and the public organization of the proletariat. But all Bakunin needs is a secret organization of one hundred people, the privileged representatives of the *revolutionary idea*, the general staff in the background, self-appointed and commanded by the permanent "Citizen B" [code name for Bakunin as No. 1]. Unity of thought and action means nothing but orthodoxy and blind obedience. *Perinde ac cadaver* [like a corpse: Jesuitic principle]. We are indeed confronted with a veritable Society of Jesus.[34]

A good deal more from the Bakunin plan was cited by the International pamphlet, which still today has to be rescued from the ignorant contumely heaped on it by dupes of the "libertarian" myth, whose roll call was headed by Franz Mehring. But we must now go on to other myths, in particular the myth that the destructive struggle in the International was over anarchism.

6. THE NATURE OF THE STRUGGLE WITH BAKUNIN

It would have been helpful to our present purposes if the struggle in the International *had* really been over "Marxism versus Anarchism," as historians usually advertised it. It might have been educational in that case. But this was not so, in terms of its formal political content. As it turned out, neither side wanted to make it so, for entirely different reasons.

Bakunin never presented the International with an anarchist issue until the very last stage when his faction was already planning to split. At the sole congress he attended personally—Basel, 1869, when he was at the height of his prestige, and before an open conflict had broken out—Bakunin deliberately avoided posing any anarchist issue whatever, and in more than one case even put forward views that were incompatible with anarchism, for obviously opportunist reasons. His aim was to gather as large a following of malcontents as possible, on any issues, in order to discredit the General Council and fragment the movement, after which the "invisible" manipulators of the International Brotherhood would pick up the pieces.

Marx, on his part, had worked hard to keep the International open from the beginning to the public coexistence of different tendencies, ideologies, and schools within the framework of the one organization. He had been instrumental in establishing a pattern, first outlined in his Inaugural Address, that subordinated clashes of doctrine, which would be inevitably destructive, to practical cooperation on common aims, in order to create a broad *class* movement.

In the International it was taken for granted that individuals would and could publicly advocate their own views *as individuals*, and likewise political tendencies in the movement with compatible programs of their own could speak their mind, as long as they did not speak for the International; but just as the International did not gag any of these people, so too *they* had no need to demand that the organization adopt their special views as against all others. Marx excoriated the sectist principle (already well known) which held that one had to make every organization the mirror of one's own opinions.

Thus Marx never proposed a vote on adopting any distinctively "Marxist" program, for the same reason that he would oppose turning the International into a Proudhonist sect. Marx's principles called for keeping the International an inclusive assembly of the whole range of working-class forces, and in view of the manifold disagreements it was a marvel that this character lasted so long.[35]

How much the organization could adopt in the way of doctrine and still hang together depended on the course of education and experience that the movement went through, and this had to be worked out as the movement went along. The International never even committed itself to any sort of socialistic program or plank at the beginning, in order to carry along both the French Proudhonists and the English trade-unionists. Its congress adopted even a mildly socialistic plank (land collectivization) only at the third congress in 1868, that is, only when it could be done without a racking struggle. When Marx supported the proposal for independent working-class political action in 1871, it was not a "Marxist" property but widely advocated, for example by the Blanquists, French independents, and German social-democrats.

If therefore Marx did not want to make the anarchist creed an issue in the International to be voted on, this was no special policy. But *nota bene*: once the Bakuninists launched their war for the anarchist takeover, Marx made it explicitly clear that *the ideological anarchists belonged inside the International*. In the struggle against the Bakuninist bid for power, Marx and

Engels kept the door wide-open to anarchists who, while agreeing with Bakunin's ideology, might wish to separate themselves from his wrecking drive. *The all-inclusive policy applied to the anarchists as to everyone else.*

This approach can be seen clearly in Engels' appeal to one of Bakunin's leading Italian followers, Carlo Cafiero. First Engels stated the issue in terms of what Bakunin was doing, under the *mask* of anarchism, with

> the *Bakuninist secret society*, the *Alliance*, which, preaching the disorganization of the International to the uninitiated, under the mask of autonomy, anarchy, and anti-authoritarianism, practises absolute authoritarianism with the initiated, with the aim of taking over leadership of the Association; a society that treats the working masses as a flock of sheep blindly following a few initiated leaders, imitating in the International the role of the Jesuits in the Catholic Church.

He then appealed to Cafiero in the latter's capacity *as an anarchist*:

> But I cannot believe that you, an anarchist and anti-authoritarian of the purest kind, have renounced your dearest principles to such a degree....[36]

For he felt confident that no honorable revolutionary who rejected "authority" on principle could fail to be revolted once Bakunin's dictatorial operation was understood. (True, a number of Bakunin's dupes did fail; but by the end of the 1870s Cafiero abandoned anarchism.)

This approach—keeping the International open to ideological anarchists—was likewise embedded in the International pamphlet against the Alliance. The issue was repeatedly put in terms like this passage from the summary in the pamphlet's introduction, which treated the offense as one perpetrated "under the mask of" anarchism.

> Here we have a society which, under the mask of the most extreme anarchism, directs its blows not against the existing governments but against the revolutionaries who refuse to accept its dogma and leadership.... It brazenly substitutes its sectarian program and narrow ideas for the broad program and great aspirations of our Association....

This much Marx always denounced even when he met it in "Marxist" sects. The passage went on with specific reference to the Bakuninist form of sectism:

> ... it organizes within the public sections of the International its own little secret sections which obey the same instructions and in a good many instances succeed in gaining control of the public section by prearranged action... It resorts to any means, any disloyalty to achieve its ends; lies, slander, intimidation, the stab in the back—it finds them all suitable.[37]

Engels reiterated the same view of means-and-ends a decade later, as he denounced "the old Bakuninist tactics, which justify any means—lies, calumniation, secret intrigues."[38]

It was this approach, this effort to keep the door open to anarchism *as a creed* divorced from the boring-from-within of the Bakuninist operation, that partly accounted for the form in which Marx and Engels even stated their view of anarchism itself. Thus, in the oft-quoted declaration which ended their anti-Bakuninist circular of 1872, they stated their position on the abolition of the state as *one* interpretation of "anarchy," which here means not the ism but the future society envisaged:

> All socialists see anarchy as the following program: once the aim of the proletarian movement, i.e., abolition of classes, is attained, the power of the State, which serves to keep the great majority of producers in bondage to a very small exploiter minority, disappears, and the functions of government become simple administrative functions.[39]

This view of the future "anarchy" was put forward as common ground for knowledgeable socialists and anarchists. The authors did not add their disagreements with the doctrines of anarchi*sm*; they did not counterpose their own view to the anarchist view of the instant abolition of the state. Instead, in this passage they chose to counterpose the meaning of the Bakuninist "anarchy" *to the movement*: its aim of "anarchy in proletarian ranks."

> The Alliance draws an entirely different picture. It proclaims anarchy in proletarian ranks as the most infallible means of breaking the powerful concentration of social and political forces in the hands of the exploiters. Under this pretext, it asks the International, at a time when the old world is seeking a way to crush it, to replace its organization with anarchy. The international police want nothing better.... [40]

It was the organization-smashing principles of Bakuninism, not its antistate (anarchist) views, that made this movement incompatible with the effective existence of the International.

If the struggle with Bakunin in the International had begun over a proposal to adopt the anti-organizational ideas and practices of consistent anarchism, the ensuing fight might have been more enlightening. But this is not what happened. In fact, the only proposal Bakunin made in this area was to *increase* the powers of the General Council (as we see in Special Note B).

Bakunin's system was to reserve his demands for the imposition of anarchic disorganizing principles strictly for his opponents, while at the same time seeking to build his own secret nucleating faction under his own hierarchical and despotically disciplined controls. The principles of Freedom and of anarchy in organization were exclusively designed to disorganize the other fellow, not his own band of agents. It was only in the last stage of the fight that Bakunin's faction came out openly with the demand for the *abolition* of the General Council, for its very existence was the "bureaucracy" against which they inveighed.

In the anarchist vocabulary, the *existence* of a central body was called 'centralism,' entirely apart from its powers or policies. In finally calling officially for the abolition of any General Council (while its own Secret Dictators pulled the strings in the dark) the Bakunin faction made plain how its dictionary defined the chameleon word 'autonomy.'

The sections of the International enjoyed, and used, an enormous degree of autonomy. *There has never been any socialist organization, national or international, that rivaled it in this respect.* The fake issue manufactured by the Bakuninists was simply that of the minimal powers accorded to the GC in the Rules. As Engels wrote: "No one, to be sure, disputes the autonomy of the sections, but federation is not possible without ceding certain powers to the federal committees [national bodies] and, in the last instance, to the General Council."[41]

Federal (meaning national) autonomy had been untrammeled in the International even across sharply divided ideological lines. In France, the Proudhonist leadership of the International had run the movement for years, in partisan fashion too, but within the rules; and the General Council had raised not a murmur about it.[42] No one had ever proposed taking organizational measures against the Bakuninists in Switzerland, Italy or Spain for making anarchist propaganda in the name of the International. In many respects the degree of autonomy taken for granted in the International was looser even than that imposed in the later anarchosyndicalist movements.

The Bakuninist issue of "autonomy" must be understood according to the lexicographical theory propounded by the Caterpillar in Wonderland.* A General Council might be a technical bureau supplying post-office services and statistics gathering, but it could have no powers of any sort; a federal (national) committee could have no powers over a section; a section could have no powers over individual members. But all of this applied only to opponents of the Bakuninists; inside the International Brotherhood of conspirators, discipline was draconic.

One of the dreadfully authoritarian questions posed to the Bakuninists

---

* Actually the trick was much older than either Lewis Carroll or Bakunin. In 1856 Marx had taken pleasure in quoting a letter he had dug out of the archives, by Sir George Macartney, on Anglo-Russian imperial strategy to befuddle the Swedes: "our first care [wrote Macartney] should be, not to establish a faction under the name of a Russian or of an English faction; but, as even the wisest men are imposed upon by a mere name, to endeavor to have *our* friends distinguished as the friends of liberty and independence...."[43]

was how the organization could defend itself even against the infiltration of known police spies. Engels tried arguing with an Italian anarchist as follows:

> They [the Bakuninists] do not want any authority exercised through the General Council even *if it were freely assented to by all*. I would very much like to know how without that authority (as they call it) it would have been possible to bring the Tolains, Durands, and Nechayevs to account, and how the intrusion of Mardocheans [police agents] and traitors is going to be prevented by your fine phrase, autonomy of the sections, as is explained in the [Bakuninist] circular.[44]

The Bakuninist cry for "autonomy" made excellent sense as simple demagogy: it helped to suck in all malcontents with an all-purpose slogan against the General Council's alleged "despotism"—never documented—and to strike a pose in favor of Freedom.

7. BAKUNINIST IDEOLOGY: THE STATE

If the conceptions of Bakuninism in the field of organization were on the dark side, the case was not much different with Bakunin's ideology in general. Even today it has to be pieced together from fragmentary writings, with indifferent success. Anarchism as a movement and a creed was going to have its period of bloom in the future, a couple of decades ahead; as yet there was not much to take hold of.

Bakunin himself was, notoriously, incapable of a systematic presentation of his ideas; he was, for example, constitutionally unable to finish any of the propaganda fragments that he did write. Marx knew him well enough to understand that he was not really interested in developing a theory that hung together: "His program was a mishmash superficially scraped together right and left ... For Mr. Bakunin, doctrine (bits and pieces he has cadged together from Proudhon, Saint-Simon, etc.) was and is a secondary matter ..." Engels, though he lived longer into the period of anarchism's international notoriety, always thought of Bakuninism mainly as a "botched form" of Proudhonized Stirnerism, and gave no sign of considering it worth any extended analysis.[45] (The first more or less systematic critique of anarchist doctrine from a Marxist viewpoint came before Engels' death, from a Russian: Plekhanov's pamphlet *Anarchism and Socialism* in 1894.)

Perhaps the nearest Bakunin came to a theoretical presentation was in his 1873 book *Statism and Anarchy* (unfinished, as always); and in fact Marx applied his newly acquired Russian to reading this book and making such copious notes on its contents as to suggest that he considered writing a reply.[46] Such a work, which might have supplied a systematic analysis of anarchist ideas by Marx, did not materialize, along with other writings planned by Marx in these last years.

Besides Marx's failing energies in his last decade, there may have been another factor. It is not often appreciated that Bakunin's own anarchist period was a flash in the pan; he started anarchist agitation only by about 1868 (when he cranked up his take-over drive in the International), and by 1873, only a year after the Hague Congress, he had started to disintegrate politically and personally. How thorough this disintegration was is made clear in Carr's biography. This means: the immediate pressure on Marx for a reply was soon lacking, as Bakunin fell apart and ceased to be a factor.

A systematic consideration of anarchist doctrines can be based only on materials that fall outside of the scope of this work. But there were some aspects of Bakunin's forays into the realm of theory that drew some attention from Marx or Engels. With the warning that the results were not extensive, let us summarize this material for what it is worth.

Bakunin's theory of the state was a very simple one: the state, politics in general, was the devil that engendered all social ills. Engels first stated the theoretical difference in his 1872 letter to Cuno:

> Bakunin has a peculiar theory of his own, a medley of Proudhonism and communism. The chief point concerning the former is that he does not regard capital, i.e., the class antagonism between capitalists and wage-workers which has arisen through social development, but the *state* as the main evil to be abolished. While the great mass of the Social-Democratic workers hold our view that state power is nothing more than the organization which the ruling classes—landowners and capitalists—have provided for themselves in order to protect their social privileges, Bakunin maintains that it is the *state* which has created capital, that the capitalist has his capital *only by the grace of the state*.

We may mention at this point, digressively, that this Bakunin theory of the state came closest to applying to Russia, to *that* state's pattern of "breeding a capitalist class," [47] though the anarchist conclusions did not follow even there. Engels went on to Bakuninist conclusions about the famous abolition of the state:

> As, therefore, the state is the chief evil, it is above all the state which must be done away with and then capitalism will go to blazes of itself. We, on the contrary, say: Do away with capital, the concentration of all means of production in the hands of the few, and the state will fall of itself [*fällt von selbst*]. The difference is an essential one: without a

previous social revolution the abolition [*Abschaffung*] of the state is nonsense; the abolition of capital *is* precisely the social revolution and involves a change in the whole mode of production.[48]

This was by far the main point as far as theory was concerned. For Marx the abolition of the state was an *outcome* of the development of socialist society, some sufficient time *after* a social revolution, but—

> °°The Anarchists reverse the matter. They say, that the Proletarian revolution has to *begin* by abolishing the political organization of the State.[49]

Anarchists often repeated Marxist formulations (or approximations) that the state was the "executive committee" of the ruling class, and so forth, but the content of their state theory was just the reverse of Marx's. Their insistence that the abolition of the state had to be the *first* act of the revolution was the product of pure dogma, simply an unhistorical view of the relation between the state and the social order. Many socialists (including Marx and Engels, as we have seen) had struggled with this question in the early days of the movement, so it had always been a well-known view before it became hardened into anarchist theory.

Since the state was the very devil, revolutionaries must not contaminate their souls by "recognizing" it. To engage in political struggle *against* it was to "recognize" it: this was another anarchist principle. In a letter summarizing Bakunin's programmatic theory for Lafargue, Marx seemed to burble over with astonishment:

> °°As the transformation of the existing States into Associations is our last end [*read:* final goal], we must allow the governments, these great trade-unions of the ruling classes, to do as they like, because to occupy ourselves with them is to acknowledge them. Why! in the same way the old socialists said: You must not occupy yourselves with the wages question [i.e., raising wages], because you want to abolish wages labour, and to struggle with the capitalist about the rate of wages is to acknowledge the wages system! The ass has not even seen that every class movement *as* a class movement, is necessarily and was always a *political* movement.[50]

In this letter Marx formulated the basic theoretical difference in another way:

> °°The whole thing rests on a superannuated idealism [obsolete philosophy of idealism] which considers the actual jurisprudence [legal system] as the basis of our economical [economic] state, instead of seeing that our economical state is the basis and source of our jurisprudence!

The anarchists specialized in refusing to "recognize" the state or its manifestations, though the state usually had little difficulty in recognizing the anarchists. Proudhon had refused to "recognize" nationalities and national struggles—by which he meant that *French* control over subject peoples was the natural state of the cosmos—and even in the International the Proudhonists continued this pseudointernationalist cant. In 1866, when Paul Lafargue was still a Proudhonist sympathizer, Marx wrote Engels about a moment of comic relief during the General Council's discussions on the current Austro-Prussian war:

> The representatives of *"jeune France" (nonworkers)*, by the way, trotted out their view that any nationality and even nations are *"des préjugés surannés"* [outdated prejudices]. Proudhonized Stirnerism. Everything to be broken down into small *"groupes"* or *"communes,"* which in turn form an "association," but not a state. Furthermore, this "individualization" of humanity and the *"mutualisme"* it entails are to proceed while history comes to a halt in every other country and the whole world waits until the French are ripe for making a social revolution. Then they will demonstrate the experiment to us, and the rest of the world, bowled over by the force of their example, will do the same. Just what Fourier expected of his *phalanstère modèle*. Anyhow, everyone who clutters up the "social" question with the "superstitions" of the Old World is a "reactionary."

Writing to Engels, Marx did not dilute the humor by explaining the politics, but he evidently enjoyed his success as a stand-up comic:

> The English laughed heartily when I began my speech by saying that our friend Lafargue and others, who had abolished nationalities, had addressed us in *"French"*, i.e., in a language which nine-tenths of the audience did not understand. I suggested further that by negation of nationalities he appeared, quite unconsciously, to understand their absorption by the model French nation.[51]

With the last sentence the joke darkened over. Proudhon's antinationalism, including his virulent opposition to national liberation, was accompanied by extreme French chauvinism and imperialist yearnings for the greater glory of France—a view somewhat less amusing than the naive conviction that French was the language spoken in all the bistros in Heaven.

National questions were only one kind of political question. Bakunin, remarked Engels in a letter, "is opposed to all political action by the working class, since it would in fact involve recognition of the existing state."[52] The Bakuninist opposition to "politics" not only excluded activity in elections but limited the movement in other respects to two sorts of activity: abstract propaganda, on the one hand, and putsches on the other.

But in fact the main issues raised by the class struggle usually had something to do with "public affairs" (politics).

In his summary letter to Cuno, Engels wrote in an educational vein:

> Now then, inasmuch as to Bakunin the state is the main evil, nothing must be done which can keep the state—that is, any state, whether it be a republic, a monarchy, or anything else—alive. Hence *complete abstention from all politics*. To commit a political act, especially to take part in an election, would be a betrayal of principles. The thing to do is to carry on propaganda, heap abuse on the state, organize, and when *all* the workers, hence the majority, are won over, depose all the authorities, abolish the state and replace it with the organization of the International. This great act, with which the millennium begins, is called *social liquidation*.

Here Engels was being mistakenly kind to the anarchists. No consistent anarchist ever held the view that a majority, let alone "all," of the workers had to be won over before the anarchist boon could descend on humanity. Bakunin in particular recognized no such precondition; respect for majorities violates anarchist principles, since it violates the sovereignty of the individual Ego. It is worth pointing out Engels' error to illustrate how far socialists were as yet from appreciating the enormities of anarchism. Engels' letter to Cuno continued its educational course as follows:

> All this sounds extremely radical and is so simple that it can be learnt by heart in five minutes; that is why the Bakuninist theory has speedily found favor also in Italy and Spain among young lawyers, doctors [i.e., Ph.D.'s], and other doctrinaires. But the mass of the workers will never allow itself to be persuaded that the public affairs of their countries are not also their own affairs; they are naturally *politically minded* and whoever tries to make them believe that they should leave politics alone will in the end be left in the lurch. To preach to the workers that they should in all circumstances abstain from politics is to drive them into the arms of the priests or the bourgeois republicans.[53]

This anarchistic amputation of the political arms of the working class meant the maiming of its revolutionary effectiveness:

> [In Italy where Bakuninism is rife in the movement] all political activity was rejected since it implied recognition of "the State," and "the State" was the epitome of all evil.... On the other hand, we have the command to agitate, organize and conspire for the coming revolution, which, when it drops from the skies, should be carried through solely by the initiative of the working classes (secretly directed by the Alliance) without any provisional government and in the total absence of

state or statelike institutions, which are to be destroyed—"Only, do not ask me how."*[54]

Marx wrote an article for the Italian socialist press on "Indifference to Politics," mainly directed against the Proudhonist version of antipoliticalness, registering the same scorn at "the idealist fantasies that these doctors of *social science* have deified under the name of *Liberty, Autonomy and Anarchy.*" According to these antipolitical thinkers, the workers, instead of struggling against the state power in practical life, must "show their profound theoretical disdain for it by purchasing and reading literary treatises on the abolition of the state..."[55] In a survey of the European movement in 1877, Engels emphasized how the anarchists' political abstentionism had reduced them even in Italy to a tiny sect.[56]

8. BAKUNINISM: REFORMIST POLITICS

Anarchism's theory of the state implies a *reformist* approach to political issues, when push comes to shove. To be sure, this is at odds with the myth of anarchism's fearsomely revolutionary character, but it is fitting from another angle. We have pointed out that anarchist theory does not get rid of political issues by refusing to "recognize" politics, but when unrecognized politics does break through the shell of dogma, it is likely to evoke its crudest form.

Marx was, I think, the first to see that anarchists, despite the apparent fierceness of their vocabulary and the sporadic rage of their outbursts, were essentially bourgeois-minded or petty-bourgeois-minded reformers in despair: another case of the "petty-bourgeois in a frenzy." (The case was somewhat similar to that of the Blanquists noted in *KMTR* 3.)[57] We cannot discuss here the massive historical evidence for this proposition, which is not gainsaid by the sometimes hysterical bourgeois fear of anarchist tactics; after all, the bomb-throwing reformer is a fixture of history. In Marx and Engels themselves, this conclusion generally appeared as an ad-hoc *aperçu*. As Marx once wrote about the r-r-revolutionism of Johann Most's London organ: "We do not reproach Most because his *Freiheit* is *too revolutionary*; we reproach him because it has *no revolutionary content*, but only deals in *revolutionary phraseology*."[58] We limit this section to presenting some of their comments on the subject.

The proposition was easiest to see in the case of Proudhon, and easiest of all in the case of Proudhon's "mutualist" followers who initially domi-

---

* The quotation ends a quatrain in Heine's *Book of Songs*.

nated the French section of the International. At the Geneva congress of 1866, it was especially this wing that stood in the way of the International's adopting so much as a rudimentary socialistic plank (on land collectivization) or even a position of general support to the struggles of organized workers against capital. (Proudhon himself had been in favor of shooting strikers.) A month after the congress, Marx described the Proudhonist delegation in a letter to a friend:

> They spurn all *revolutionary* action, i.e., arising from the class struggle itself, every concentrated social movement, and therefore also that which can be achieved by *political means* (e.g., such as limitation of the working day *by law*). Beneath the *cloak of freedom* and antigovernmentalism or anti-authoritarian individualism these gentlemen, who for 16 years now [under Napoleon III] have so quietly endured the most wretched despotism, and are still enduring it, are in actuality preaching vulgar bourgeois economics, only in the guise of Proudhonist idealism![59]

One could say about some Proudhonists what Marx and Engels once wrote about one Julius Faucher: "Under the pretence of wishing to abolish the state and introduce anarchy he refrained from dangerous opposition toward the existing government...."[60]

Bakunin generally made more ferocious noises, depending on his audience, but the content of his agitation was often no less reformist, when stripped of its berserker rhetoric. As Marx once wrote of another pathetic figure *not* an anarchist: behind him "... no experienced person could fail to see the figure of the buffoon who tries to appear terrifying both to himself and others."[61]

A preliminary explanation is necessary. It has been mentioned that, until the International came on the scene late in his life, Bakunin refused to join up with any socialist or communist organization, reserving his energies for his self-fabricated conspiratorial bands of personal followers; he did not adopt distinctively socialist views until the late 1860s. In this he continued the tradition of Jacobin revolutionism, a tradition that did not rise above the level of left republicanism even in its conspiratorial forms, and that sank back into old bourgeois politics as soon as its windbags were pricked by the coming of a democratic republic. When the International split took place at the Hague Congress, Bakunin had not even been *talking* socialism for more than a few years.

An early case in point may be seen toward the end of 1847. It happened that Bakunin was living in Brussels, at the same time that Marx was there busily building a Democratic Association, a German Workers Educational Association, and a Communist League branch. Note that Marx was promoting three levels of political work. Bakunin was barely willing to join the lowest level (lowest from Marx's standpoint)—the Democratic Association. Marx duly sponsored Bakunin's membership in that group. His Russian recruit attended two meetings, and lost interest—*ho hum, no revolution yet?* As for the movements farther left: Bakunin wrote a friend that he refused to join "their communist artisan society" and "wanted to have nothing to do with that organization." He explained in another letter that Marx was "ruining the workers by making theorists of them," that is, teaching socialist ideas without so much as pulling off a practice putsch. Indeed, Marx was just then finishing the *Communist Manifesto*. Bakunin yawned and found life a bore except for the company of an extreme right-wing general of the Polish emigration.[62]

Marx and Bakunin met again long afterwards, in 1864—on Marx's initiative.[63] Marx hoped that the Russian agitator might help the new International, just founded. Now turned fifty, Bakunin claimed to Marx that he was getting serious about more or less socialistic views. In this friendly conversation he promised that, now that his pan-Slavist enterprises had collapsed, he would henceforth "take part only in the socialist movement."[64]

Nothing of the sort happened. For the next three or four years, while the hard work of building the International was being done, he showed not a flicker of interest in it. In 1867 he did turn his attention to working within an international body: it was the bourgeois-liberal Peace League that he chose for a bore-from-within operation. (More about this in Special Note B.)

To become the left wing of this liberal international, Bakunin's main proposal was cast in terms of "the economic and social *equalization* of classes and individuals" (emphasis added). It is unlikely that he understood this to be a bourgeois-reform demand and not at all socialistic; or, if he understood this was true, then it simply appeared to him as good suckerbait for liberals. Even so, the resolution he presented to the League did not rashly suggest that the League actually come out for this worthy goal: only that it "put on the agenda the study of practical methods of settling this question." This was eminently statesmanlike and impeccably liberal: a *study* was to be put on an agenda. As Carr says, this wording was "studiously moderate, almost academic." The liberals rejected it anyway, study and agenda both.

Repulsed by the liberals, Bakunin turned with about eighteen supporters to the next easiest prey. He now recognized that the International amounted to something of a force; it deserved to become his new borefrom-within target. For this purpose he formed a new nucleating agency of his regular pattern, called the Alliance (or International Alliance) of the Socialist Democracy, fully accoutred with a secret-invisible core of

International Brotherhood "masters," in accordance with the Bakuninist principles of Secret Dictatorship of the last several decades.

What we are interested in at this point is the fearsomely revolutionary program with which Bakunin endowed the Alliance, by virtue of which it was to be the super-revolutionary vanguard of the vanguard. This program was nothing other than the liberalistic formula about "equalizing" classes that had been too radical for the bourgeois Peace League. The Alliance program called for the "political, economic and social equalization of classes and individuals of both sexes, beginning with the abolition of the right of inheritance." This was not even socialistic.

In a letter Marx gave a pejorative summary of the points in the Alliance's "mishmash," as follows:

> ... *equality of classes* (!), *abolition of the right of inheritance* as *starting point* of the social movement (Saint-Simonian nonsense), *atheism* as *dogma* dictated to the members, etc., and as principal dogma the *(Proudhonist) abstention from political action.*[65]

Here Marx ignored the antistate rhetoric in the Alliance program. The operative part of the anarchist theory of the state was not its vision of the wonderful tomorrow but what it did now to keep the movement sterilized from politics.

The "equalization of classes" was liberal-reform rhetoric because it presupposed the continued existence of the antagonistic classes under capitalism, instead of abolishing the system that required the existence of these classes. In a letter to a friend, Marx allowed himself to get indignant about the "shameless ignorance and superficiality" of these new recruits who were setting up to be teachers to the movement. Nor was this liberal language a chance slip-up on Bakunin's part: he was going to cling to it despite all remonstrance, even after admitting in a private letter to Marx that the International's criticism was correct and that a different formulation should have been used. He still continued to defend it in his 1873 book *Statism and Anarchy.*[66]

The other theoretical contribution of the Alliancists was Bakunin's proposal to make a programmatic cornerstone out of the abolition of the right of inheritance.

This proposal was a revival of one of the hoariest planks in the movement, for it had done duty in the 1820s as the only near-socialistic part of the program of the Saint-Simonian sect. This was why Marx called it *"vieillerie St. Simoniste"*—"old stuff" that had been obsolete for nearly a half century. It *had* had a meaning back in the days when the movement was not yet talking about social ownership of the means of production which gave rise to inheritances. Today it had no positive function in a socialist program; but it did have a negative side. It needlessly scared the potential allies of the workers among the peasants and among the middle classes.

Marx argued as follows. *After* you make the social revolution, this plank would make no sense; for you would then take steps to abolish both private property in land and exploitive capital. So after the revolution, you "would therefore have no occasion at all to occupy yourselves with the right of inheritance." *Before* you make the social revolution, it is counterproductive to talk up this plank: °°"the proclamation of the *abolition of inheritance* would be not a serious act, but a foolish menace, rallying the whole peasantry and the whole small middle-class* round the reaction."[67]

The scientific-political meaning of the plank cut no ice with Bakunin: for him it was mainly an issue on which he could hope to drum up a big congress vote against the General Council. This was what explained why he chose to revive an old plank that did not even *sound* very revolutionary. But one must remember how much of a Johnny-come-lately Bakunin was to practical socialist problems. He had spent most of his lifetime working out, on paper, innumerable variations of hole-in-the-corner conspiratorial bands and cliques; and he had spent much time on his hobby of devising unusable codes and ciphers; but he had never been involved in the real problems of socialist mass organization and agitation. When in the aforementioned letter Marx emphasized that Bakunin was a sheer *"ignoramus"* and underlined it, this should be taken as a simple statement of fact.

9. BAKUNINISM: REFORMIST PRACTICE

The Bakuninist movement time and again exemplified the historical tendency for anarchist revolutionism to turn into a hectic kind of reform. Behind its terrible phrases about the dangers of "politics" lay extreme naiveté about reformist politics. We have mentioned the anarchist propensity to use the word 'state' to mean a despotic state only. The other side of this misapprehension is the propensity for the abrupt outbreak of the crudest sort of political opportunism.

In the case of Bakuninism, three cases may be cited.

(1) Switch in Sweden.

The following example is one made striking by biographer Carr's evident astonishment as he recounted it. This episode took place in Stockholm, a year before Bakunin's 1864 meeting with Marx.

In the course of a trip in Sweden, Bakunin had gotten his charisma

---

* When Marx is writing in English, for "small middle class" read: petty-bourgeoisie.

working full-strength and had scored a personal triumph as the incarnation, in Swedish eyes, of Russian revolutionism. He was accorded a private audience with King Charles XV himself, a dazzling honor. At a prestigious banquet attended by politicians, businessmen, ministers of religion, etc., and even three or four nobles, Bakunin amazed everyone with a swingeing speech—in which he championed constitutional monarchy! He even denounced the czar's government as "revolutionary" because it unloosed a peasant jacquerie against Polish landlords and "excite[d] popular passions." Carr relates: "Far from being a revolutionary, Bakunin declared that he and his friends were not even unconditional republicans."[68]

It was a bewildering example of Bakunin's facility for suddenly turning *presto!* into a crude political opportunist. In this case it took a little royal tickling to do it.

(2) Frenzy in France.

In September 1870 a similar pattern was acted out by two of Bakunin's lieutenants in the Alliance: his right-hand man James Guillaume, the Swiss schoolmaster, and Gaspard Blanc. When Napoleon III fell and the Third Republic was established in France, they published an uncritical paean of praise to the new state.

Marx opined that he was not surprised, at least when he wrote about the episode to the Belgian, César de Paepe, who was then a twixt-and-tweener:

> The manifesto printed in the supplement to *La Solidarité* did not surprise me. I was well aware that people who preach absolute abstention from politics—as if the workers were monks who set up their own world outside the big world—will always relapse into bourgeois politics, at the first sound of the historic tocsin.[69]

But Marx *had* to be surprised, nevertheless: few documents ever showed such a gulf between ideological pretensions and real politics. The "bourgeois politics" of the Bakuninist manifesto can be fully appreciated only by reading the whole of it, for its main characteristic was the complete absence of any critical hint that the new republican regime was not the workers' millennium at last descended on earth. It virtually identified the Third Republic with *The Revolution*.[70]

"Republican France represents the liberty of Europe," proclaimed these Bakuninist anarchists—who regularly denounced the very existence of the state as incompatible with liberty, and who at the very same time were arguing that a *workers'* state established by a popular revolution had to be instantly destroyed. Yet all that had happened had been the replacement of Bonaparte with a brace of discredited bourgeois parliamentarians!

Instead of taking advantage of the republican turmoil to bring about the immediate overthrow of the new bourgeois state, as anarchist rhetoric demanded, the Bakuninist leaders hailed the new state in these terms: "The Republic has been proclaimed; the French people have again become master of their own destiny." They gushed: "The cause of the French Republic is that of the European revolution, and the moment has come to give our blood for the emancipation of the workers and all of humanity." "This is the dawn of the new day. . . ."

This fulsome frenzy over the new bourgeois republic should be contrasted with the corresponding statement that Marx wrote for the General Council, an appeal to defend republican France against European reaction. In this "Second Address on the War" Marx warned the French workers not to be "deluded" by republican memories: "We hail the advent of the Republic in France, but at the same time we labour under misgivings which we hope will prove groundless." He cautioned against illusions about the new republic. And then Marx, with the General Council, unleashed a whirlwind of activity to mobilize working-class forces to achieve British recognition of the republican regime and to defend republican France against dismemberment.[71]

The contrast between these two documents illuminates a whole area of socialist politics.

(3) *Spectacle in Spain.*

An even more extreme acting-out of the pattern took place in 1873, when during revolutionary turmoil in Spain the Bakuninists came to power locally here and there in peasant districts. In an article on "The Bakuninists at Work," Engels related how they had junked their anarchist principles about setting up state powers in revolution — in fact, had deserted elementary revolutionary principles by participating in *bourgeois*-controlled governments as powerless captives of the liberals. (This was history's rehearsal for the similar role of the anarchists in the Spanish Civil War of the 1930s.)

What happened was in line with Marx's remark to De Paepe about the manifesto by Guillaume and G. Blanc. When the test of experience made nonsense out of the anarchists' rhetoric about the Instant Abolition of the State, they knew nothing to do except behave like the frenzied liberals they basically were.

Engels' article related the events in the town of Alcoy, one of the centers of Bakuninist influence. The Bakuninist Alliancists, "who here too, contrary to their anarchist principles, formed a revolutionary government, did not know what to do with their power." These enemies of all authority (which is basically evil) introduced passes to prevent people from leaving the city without authorization. In general, they presided over confusion and helplessness. (How can one run a revolutionary state which is not supposed to exist?)

In Cordova, the same Bakuninists who a few months earlier had been arguing that to establish any revolutionary government was a betrayal of the workers "now sat in all the revolutionary municipal governments of Andalusia, but always in a minority," so that the bourgeois republican majority could do what it wished, sheltered behind the anarchists' responsibility. Instead of forming revolutionary governments that were systematically controlled from below by the workers in action, they joined coalition governments they did not control at all.

They had no political guide for a situation that was not supposed to happen; they had been "against politics," and they had no politics—other than the crudest parliamentary politics of the liberals. Since the Bakuninist prescription of "decentralization" proscribed any "centralized leadership" of the revolutionary forces of the various towns, each town in the insurrection was defeated one by one by the counterrevolution, picked off separately.

Engels summed up as follows:

> 1. As soon as they were faced with a serious revolutionary situation, the Bakuninists had to throw the whole of their old program overboard. First they sacrificed their doctrine of absolute abstention from political, and especially electoral, activities.

And so on: Engels listed one after the other the abandoned anarchist tenets—till they were sitting in the municipal juntas, "almost everywhere as an impotent minority outvoted and political exploited by the bourgeoisie."

> 2. ... Thus, when it came to doing things, the ultrarevolutionary rantings of the Bakuninists either turned into appeasement or into uprisings that were doomed to failure, or led to their joining a bourgeois party ....

> 3. Nothing remains of the so-called principles of anarchy, free federation of independent groups, etc., but the boundless and senseless fragmentation of the revolutionary resources, which enabled the government to conquer one city after another with a handful of soldiers, practically unresisted.

Engels' fifth point was all-inclusive: "In short, the Bakuninists in Spain have given us an unparalleled example of how a revolution should *not* be made."[72]

10. BAKUNINISM AND "AUTHORITARIANISM"

The reformist side of Bakuninism showed up most prominently where it gained something like a mass following locally. When it was not putschist, terrorist, or adventurist, it could make contact with reality only by shelving its antistatist rhetoric. For Marx this fact was linked with its class appeal.

We have seen Bakunin's views on class orientation, particularly his hopes of "riding the peasantry," utilizing elements of the lumpen-class (brigands and such), and topping this barricade fodder off with the elite dictatorship of a lumpen-intelligentsia.[73] The International's anti-Bakunin pamphlet pointed out that the "one hundred people" who were to constitute his ruling elite under the name of International Brothers had to come from the ruling classes:

> To say that the hundred International Brothers must "serve as intermediaries between the revolutionary idea and the popular instincts" is to create an unbridgeable gulf between the Alliance's revolutionary idea and the proletarian masses; it means proclaiming that these hundred guardsmen cannot be recruited anywhere but from among the privileged classes.[74]

In some rough notes on the Bismarck government's attempt to justify its Anti-Socialist Law in the Reichstag, Marx commented on the official claim that anarchistic "extremists" were sure to dominate socialist movements because of an alleged law that extreme tendencies always win out over moderate ones:

> The "anarchist" tendency is no "extreme" wing of the German Social-Democracy... In the latter we have the actual historical movement of the working class; the former is a fantasy-vision of the *jeunesse sans issue* [youth with no future] who want to make history, and it shows only how the ideas of French socialism are caricatured in the *hommes déclassés* of the upper classes. Accordingly, anarchism is in fact everywhere defeated, and is only vegetating in those places where no real working-class movement has yet come into existence. This is the fact.[75]

If in Germany a weak anarchist tendency was derived from a lumpen-intelligentsia, if in Italy the Bakuninist group was based on lumpen-bourgeois and professionals *sans issue*, it was a seemingly odd fact that the Bakuninist operation to take over the International was centered in the Jura mountains, where Guillaume led the Jura Federation in Switzerland. But flare-ups of this sort pepper the history of anarchism. Engels explained that "the Jura, with its watch-making carried on just in scattered cottages, seems to be the destined hearth of this nonsense...."[76] It was typical of several areas where anarchism appeared for a while: the cottage craftsmen of the Jura lived in a little world stranded between the old and the new, like the pockets of newly proletarianized peasants that characterized anarchist developments in, say, Italy and Spain.

With class appeals like these, the Bakuninist movement tended to be antidemocratic—"authoritarian," in the vocabulary it was popularizing. A circular written for the International by Engels in August 1872 summed up some facts about the Alliance. Bakunin, it charged, aimed to impose his "personal dictatorship" on the whole movement. It was naturally a startling accusation against the man who presented himself as the very paladin of untrammeled Freedom, especially since Engels did not then have the secret documents, now known to us, in which Bakunin said so repeatedly in his own words.

The charge made by Engels can now be documented ten times over:

°°The same men who accuse the General Council of authoritativeness [i.e., authoritarianism] without ever having been able to specify one single authoritative [sic] act on its part, who talk at every opportunity of the autonomy of the sections, of the free federation of groups; who charge the General Council with the intention of forcing upon the International its own official and orthodox doctrine and to transform our Association into a hierarchically constituted organization—these very same men, in practice, constitute themselves as a secret society with a hierarchical organization, and under a, not merely authoritative, but absolutely dictatorial leadership; they trample under their feet every vestige of autonomy of sections and federations; they aim at forcing upon the International, by means of this secret organization, the personal and orthodox doctrines of M. Bakounine. While they demand that the International should be organised from below upwards, they themselves, as members of the Alliance, humbly submit to the word of command which is handed down to them from above.

The Alliance (went on Engels) separates members into two classes, the "initiated" who lead in secret and the "profane" who are led by the nose, through "an organization whose very existence is unknown to them" (the International Brothers, in Bakunin's scheme). The Alliance imposes the duty of "mendacity, dissimulation and imposture," in the first place to deceive the profane ranks as to the very existence of the secret organization and leadership.[77]

The circular summed up: "What is at stake at this moment is neither the autonomy of sections, nor the free federation of groups, nor the organization from below upwards, nor any other formula equally pretentious and sonorous"—but only the hidden control by a "secret society of dupers" who lead their dupes, like a flock of sheep, through "secret instructions emanating from a mysterious personage in Switzerland" (i.e., Bakunin).[78]

Eventually (Engels wrote later) their dupes realized "that behind the preachment of anarchy and self-rule lay hidden the claim by a few wire-pullers to take dictatorial command over the whole working-class movement." This referred to Italy, where the editor of *La Plebe*, Bignami, was repudiating what was left of the Bakuninist movement. Engels told Marx:

With this split in Italy, the Messrs. anarchist-dictators are kaput. From the brief notes in this issue of *La Plebe* on the "narrow and anarchistic—and at the same time (monstrous contradiction) dictatorial—minds," it transpires that Bignami has gotten to know exactly what kind of people these are.[79]

The Bakuninist conception of their future dictatorship was brought out by the International's anti-Bakunin pamphlet of 1873, largely on the basis of Russian-language documents put out by the Bakunin-Nechayev operation. They were made available to the General Council through hurried work done especially by Utin in Geneva.

One of the main exhibits was a work written by Bakunin's partner Nechayev during the International period. (The myth that Bakunin had no connection with a number of basic writings by Nechayev is treated in Special Note B.) This work brashly presented the anarchist future social order as a nightmare of despotic ("authoritarian") control from above, in which the secret dictators had arranged everything in advance.

"The ending of the present social order," the anarchist utopia explained, involved "concentrating all the means of social existence in the hands of Our Committee, and the proclamation of compulsory physical labor for everyone." Anyone who refused to join a work group "will be left without means of subsistence. All the roads, all the means of communication will be closed to him; he will have no other alternative but work or death."[80] There are further revolting details.

"What a beautiful model of barrack-room communism!" exclaimed the International's pamphlet.

> Here you have it all: communal eating, communal sleeping, assessors and offices regulating education, production, consumption, in a word, all social activity, and to crown all, *Our Committee*, anonymous and unknown to anyone, as the supreme director. This is indeed the purest anti-authoritarianism.[81]

The pamphlet went on to highlight the atrocities: the bosses of "Our Committee"—"Messrs. Bakunin and Nechayev"—have reason to nourish their "competitive hatred of the state and of any centralization of the workers' forces." They have to wipe out every alternative to their own hidden dictatorship, to fragment society so that it is amenable to manipulation by "Our Committee" incognito. They would not be able to succeed "while the working class continues to have any representative bodies of its own," that is, its own democratic political organization.

The International's pamphlet runs over with indignation and runs on with a Gallic sentence structure (it was published in French). Like this:

> This same man [Bakunin] who in 1870 preaches to the Russians passive, blind obedience to orders coming from above and from an anon-

ymous committee; who declares that jesuitical discipline is the condition *sine qua non* of victory, the only thing capable of defeating the formidable centralization of the state—not just the Russian state but any state; who proclaims a communism more authoritarian than the most primitive communism—this same man, in 1871, weaves a separatist and disorganizing movement into the fabric of the International under the pretext of combating the authoritarianism and centralization of the German Communists, of introducing autonomy of the sections, a free federation of autonomous groups, and of making the International what it should be: the image of the future society. If the society of the future were modeled on the Alliance, Russian [Bakuninist] section, it would far surpass the Paraguay of the Reverend Jesuit Fathers, so dear to Bakunin's heart.[82]

The closing reference was to the theocratic, bureaucratic-collectivist community founded by the Jesuits in the seventeenth century, based on the labor of the Paraguayan Indians: a model, by the way, which found admirers in the socialist movement as well as among anarchists. Bakunin often expressed his admiration for, and desire to emulate the example of, the Jesuit system of infiltrating centers of power with trained adepts.[83]

11. THE ALIEN IDEOLOGY

Once the Bakuninist champions of anarchy no longer had somebody else's International to infiltrate and smash, but confronted each other in their very own, they speedily showed the awesome power of the anarchist concept of organization: their International disintegrated in record time before it really came into existence. When Engels heard that even James Guillaume himself had stalked out of the Jura Federation in a huff, he commented: "It had to come to that. The anarchists would not even be worthy of their name as long as anarchy hasn't broken out among themselves."[84] Bakunin himself had started to fall apart politically and personally before the Hague Congress was a year old; and in the spring of 1874 he advised Guillaume to "make [his] peace with the bourgeoisie" as he himself was doing—though he had one last fling at a putsch (the most absurd of all, in Bologna) before setting out to set himself up as landed gentry.[85]

Let us take a brief glance at the next period in order to illuminate Marx's view from another side.

Lying ahead were flare-ups of anarchist influence in limited regional and national situations. The mutation called anarchosyndicalism played out its hand in France by the beginning of World War I; the Spanish afterlife of anarchism lasted much longer into the twentieth century, as a reflection of Spain's relative backwardness; but even these pseudopodial extensions of anarchism remained on the margin of the European working-class movement. The last real battle in socialist ranks ended with the defeat of the anarchist campaign to get accepted as a legitimate faction inside the Second International, that is, to get the opportunity to repeat its triumphant bore-from-within destruction of the First International. When the International Socialist Congress of 1896 voted to exclude them, and they could no longer have a form of existence as a parasitic growth, the anarchists were historically finished as an international working-class current; and even the national exceptions declined one by one.

At the same time that the socialist movement was separating itself from the anarchists, much of the *right-wing* Social-Democracy began to tend toward an attitude about anarchism that was basically different from Marx's. This attitude was largely taken over from liberalism. It was the view that anarchism was merely a lovely and saintly vision of the Good Society which was admirable but unfortunately impractical.

In part this delightful conception was made possible by one-sidedly seeing anarchism simply as an idea about a future stateless society—that is, by equating anarch*ism*, the ideology, with what Marx and others sometimes called *anarchy* when they were referring to a future society in which the state had completed its destiny in ultimately dying away. The more the anarchist movement disintegrated as an organized phenomenon counterposed to the socialist movement, the more the Social-Democrats tended to drop Marx's understanding of anarchism as one of the most antidemocratic currents in the history of society, as the mirror image of bureaucratism.

As against Marx's view, the new Social-Democratic opinion often met was that our increasingly bureaucratized society should be *balanced out* with the injection of a little anarchism, as a sort of antidote. The combination of a lot of state bureaucratism and a little "cultural anarchism" was even put forward by some thinkers as a desirable goal. Anyway, it is nice to have harmless people around talking up a little anarchism (with its *frisson* of revolutionary bravado) as a counterweight to what is *really* happening in society. Alice had a bottle labeled "Drink me" to grow smaller, and a little cake labeled "Eat me" to grow bigger: so, too, one should alternately sip from the bureaucratic bottle and nibble at the anarchist cake in order to keep social "authority" at just the right size. A little later we find in Wonderland that the bureaucratic and anarchist potions are both taken out of opposite sides of the same mushroom; they had turned out to be the same fungal growth.

This common Social-Democratic attitude implied condescending or patronizing smiles at anarchist jesters who had a right to make fools of themselves as long as they supposedly told some home-truths about the bureaucratization of society, which was being nurtured by the Social-Democrats as by the bourgeois rulers. Marx's attitude was quite different.

Marx and Engels had little but scorn for "this clownish caricature" of the real movement,[86] and for the "childish minds" of "the so-called anarchists, who in fact are props of the present order."[87] Here Marx made an advance comment on the later liberal-Social-Democratic practice of showcasing anarchist sages as saints who were, unfortunately, too good and innocent for this world. (Like Prince Kropotkin, who was no Bakunin, to be sure.)

But socialist militants also knew of the role that the anarchist movement played in country after country—as even Kropotkin had done in France in his militant days before becoming an icon in England—in providing the reactionary governments and their police with ammunition to harass and smash the working-class movement. The governments' "black cabinet" (department of dirty tricks against subversives) had a positive need for something like anarchism to be played up as a "social peril' while remaining quite harmless to the real powers: in short, to be used as a bogy. So Marx remarked in a letter to his daughter Laura. As for the image of the Saintly Innocent, he recalled a parable: when Henry VII asked Pope Julius II to place Henry VI among the saints, the witty pope "answered that an *innocens* (otherwise known as *idiot*) is not thereby to be called *sanctus*."[88]

But it was after Marx's death that the movement suffered most from the governments' use of anarchist outrages (indiscriminate bombings, assassination attempts, etc.) to direct blows at labor and socialism. This was why Engels wrote in an 1894 letter, "there is a great gulf between us and the anarchists."[89] By the end of the nineteenth century there was literally a line of blood between.

For Marx anarchism was not a beautiful vision of saintly dreamers but a sick social ideology. Rooted in an idealist theory of the state, it oscillated between opportunism in politics and a frenzied flight from political reality to adventures in individual terrorism. *Above all, it was an ideology alien to the life of modern working people.* In the course of its development it reflected various class elements in a blind alley: artisanal workers fearfully confronting modern industry; recently proletarianized peasants fearfully meeting new societal pressures; lumpen-bourgeois elements fearfully facing an empty future; and alienated intelligentsia fearfully resenting the indignities of a money-obsessed society.

As time went on, the backward-looking labor element tended to fade out of this mixture—finally even in Latin countries—and anarchism as a creed tended to return to its starting point in Godwin and Stirner as an outbreak of bourgeois-idealist desperation, the ideology of a moorless *Intelligenz*. A year before Engels' death, the aforementioned brochure on anarchism by Plekhanov—immediately translated into English by Eleanor Marx—laid heavy stress on anarchism as a product of decadence in bourgeois society. While the brochure had many faults, it was good in conveying the reek of French *fin-de-siècle littérateurs* flirting with anarchist phrases to *épater la bourgeoisie*. "You will remain what you are now ... bags emptied by history."[90] Plekhanov's characteristic rhetoric this time had a fit target.

12. EPILOGUE: THE "MARX-ANARCHIST" MYTH

In spite of the historical facts, marxological literature even today is peppered, or at least spotted, with the revelation that Marx was an anarchist himself, after all. It is usually presented with an air of discovery. The discovery is merely this: that Marx advocated the (ultimate) dying away, or "abolition," of the state, this coming about as the end-product of socialist-communist society. The crux of the discovery is often the passage we have quoted from the International's circular of 1872: "All socialists see anarchy as the following program...."[91]

This revelation assumes ignorance of the real history of antistatism in the socialist movement, that is, of the fact that anarchism developed *out of* a reservoir of antistatism, but that antistatism is not congruent with anarchism. This has already been adequately stressed.[92] In fact, in the 1872 passage Marx did not claim this view as specially his own, but as characteristic of "all socialists." It is difficult to explain why the discoverers of Marx's "anarchism" fail to see that, by the same token, they are discovering that "all socialists" are anarchists.

The discoverers also ignore that knowledgeable anarchists do not define themselves by their views on the abolition of the state (some day) but by their principled stand on the exercise of *any* authority over the sovereign Ego.

The "Marx-anarchist" myth may have taken its start from the Bakuninists' allegation that Marx's *Civil War in France* cribbed from their master's patented antistatism. It should be assumed that the complaints originally came from some honest ignoramus who knew little or nothing about what the socialist movement had taken for granted for decades. The cribbing, for example, was what Carlo Cafiero had been told; and note that it was in an 1871 letter to Cafiero that Engels had to write that the "abolition of the state" was well known to Marx and himself when they were "simple youngsters."[93] One cannot blame young Cafiero for believing that his then master had invented Freedom itself; but modern marxologists are another matter.

Marx's *Civil War in France* reminds us that a distinction should be made that explains part of the history of the "Marx-anarchist" fable. It is hard to see how the aforesaid modern marxologists could take the "Marx-anarchist" fable seriously; but it is easy to see how the contemporaneous public of 1871 might read unlimited antistatism into the International's address, especially those people (like Cafiero) who had been pumped full of Bakuninist myths. Marx's ringing defense of the Paris Commune wanted to stress how new and unprecedented it was, as distinct from the heavily bureaucratized French state that it fought.

What Marx stressed was that the Commune was a "workers' government," and this key designation (which disposed of the anarchist label by itself) appeared more than once in the published version of the address. Pages of the address were devoted to an enthusiastic description of the Commune's machinery of representative government, based on universal suffrage—both of these institutions being anathema to any anarchist who knew what he was talking about.[94]

The address even warned against being misinterpreted in an anarchist direction!

> The few but important functions which still would remain for a central government were not to be suppressed, as has been intentionally mis-stated.... The unity of the nation was not to be broken.... While the merely repressive organs of the old governmental power were to be amputated, its legitimate functions were to be wrested [from the old state, etc.].

And the address went on to *deny* that the Commune aimed to break France up "into a federation of small States."[95] (As we will explain under another head, Marx advocated neither what was called "centralization" nor "decentralization," but rather a course hostile to both: the construction of a central government *from below*.) Certainly, all this was written as if Marx anticipated a "Marx-anarchist" fable.

To be sure, Marx's drafts for the address contained more ambiguous expressions, and, like as not, this was why these formulations did *not* appear in the published version. One example will be enough. In the First Draft, Marx wrote that the Commune "was a Revolution against the *State* itself," not simply against a class—"a Revolution to break down this horrid machinery of Class domination itself." We forbear discussing at this point what Marx had in mind*; for this indubitably ambiguous formulation van-

---

* Mainly because the general subject of Marx's views on the "dying away" of the state is reserved for the last volume of *KMTR*. But see parts of *KMTR* 1, especially

ished even before the Second Draft. Instead, the Second Draft tried out an *anti*-anarchist exposition. (The English is tottery and requires close attention.)

> It is one of the absurdities to say, that the Central functions, not of governmental authority over the people, but necessitated by the general and common wants of the country, would become impossible.

This may well have been cut out because it was *too* clearly anti-anarchist!—for certainly Marx did not want the International address to read like a partisan document.⁹⁶

The "Marx-anarchist" fable poked out in the course of a polemical exchange in 1884 between editor Bernstein of the *Sozialdemokrat* and a writer for the *New Yorker Volkszeitung* who signed himself von der Mark. The latter had put forward anarchoid views on the state, and in response the editor explained the elements of Marx's conception. The reply by von der Mark declared that, by coming out for the idea of the dying out of the state, Engels was making a concession to anarchism—referring to *Anti-Dühring* and to Bebel's book *Woman and Socialism*.

"Concession" to anarchism! Engels was amused or indignant, or both, when he wrote to Bernstein about all this (in a comment already partly cited in another connection). He said that "In case Herr von der Mark or anyone else talks any more about 'concessions' to the anarchists on our part, the following passages show that we proclaimed the cessation of the state before there were anarchists altogether . . ."—and then came the citations previously noted.⁹⁷

Ironically, but typically, when the same Bernstein entered upon his Revisionist incarnation over a decade later, he reinvented or rediscovered the "Marx-anarchist" confusion as if he had just thought of it. Having come to the view ("the movement is everything, the goal is nothing") that Engels' conception of the dying out of the state was "utopian," Bernstein as Revisionist rejected any idea of the *eventual* abolition of the state as—anarchistic. Lassalle, he decided, was essentially right after all: the state and its bureaucracy were eternal: "The administrative body of the visible future can be different from the present-day state only in degree."⁹⁸

It turned out that *not* "all socialists" accepted the old socialist antistatist conception, as Marx had thought in 1872. Indeed, as we know, it was after this time that the meaning of Lassalleanism was borne in on Marx, and

---

Chapters 13–14, remembering that loosely the radical public often used the "state" as a designation of the executive power, particularly in the case of overbureaucratized and overcentralized governments like the French. Throughout *The Civil War in France* the "state" often means simply the old state.

later still that Revisionism brought out into the open a basic split in the nature of socialism. The new social-reformism was the first school of self-styled socialism that overtly and systematically accepted the state as everlasting—and in consequence sought to pin the "anarchist" label on Marx's concept.

This gambit was subsequently rediscovered every few years, perhaps from Bernstein's pages. For example, Hans Kelsen trotted it out in at least two essays proclaiming the slogan "Back to Lassalle!"—only, he improved on Bernstein by calling it Marx's and Engels' "individualist-anarchist view of the future." *Individualist*-anarchist! Kelsen was an internationally known eminent scholar and hence did not feel it necessary to adduce evidence. The thing was screwed to a still higher pitch by one R. R. Pranger, who published a study claiming that Marx was "explicitly apolitical".... [99]

If one collected the published arguments that Marx was not only an "anarchist," but also a Blanquist, a theologian, a Platonic idealist, a Zen Buddhist, a parliamentary reformer, a Mosaic lawgiver, and so on, one would have—a curious book.

• • •

To sum up the basic difference between Marx's views and those of anarchism, at three depths:

(1) For Marx, the "abolition of the state" could come about only at the *end* of a sufficient period of socialist reconstruction of society. For an anarchist, the decree "abolishing the state" must come, by an irrefragably fixed principle, on the day of the revolution, with no "transitional" period or state form. It follows that, from the day that a socialist government takes power, all good anarchists must seek its instant destruction as an "authoritarian" menace.

(2) For Marx, the aim of the socialist movement is the *democratization* of political authority, and indeed of all authority. For an anarchist, any and all authority, however ideally democratic its basis, is the work of the devil, and must be destroyed. Besides, for Marx the abolition (or diminution, etc.) of state power does not yet necessarily entail the elimination of all elements of authority in political and social life, though the latter may become a still-farther goal of societal evolution.

(3) One way of summing up the difference in basic views lies in the definition, or interpretation, of *freedom*—the much exalted freedom whose abstract glorification is the stock in trade, if not the total content, of all anarchist rhetoric.

• The anarchist view of "freedom" is basically *individual-solipsistic*: it depends on the absolute inviolability of the sovereign Ego in relation to the outside world—the total impermissibility of any imposition of any authority, authority of any kind or source, upon the unconditional autonomy of that sovereign Ego. Anarchism is basically a solipsism, whether or not anarchists recognize this consciously in their philosophic outlook. It does not mean freedom *through* democracy, or freedom *in* society, but, rather, freedom *from* any democratic authority whatsoever or any social constraint: in short, not a free society but freedom from society.

• Marx's view of "freedom" is basically *social* in its reference, and depends on the relation of the individual to his membership in the human species, which is historically organized in a society. Briefly, this view of "freedom" makes it a shorthand term for *democratic freedom in society*; and the "problem" of freedom is the interpretation and implementation of this approach. "Democratic freedom in society" means that relationship of the individual to the collectivity which involves the maximum extension of *control from below* (control of the collectivity and all its decisions). This control applies also to the determination through democratic institutions of the extent or degree to which the collectivity of society should exercise *any* control over its individual components. In Marx's view, this last relationship is not fixed by abstract fiat, but is an evolving thing, which, in the course of a socialist reconstruction, may set a series of farther and still farther goals for realization, in the historical process of maximizing individual autonomy in society. In this sense, socialism raises not only the potentiality of the dying-away of the state but also of the farther goal: the dying-away of the role of authority in society, whether or not this can be conceived as reaching an extreme terminus.

This, then, was what Engels, for one, was thinking of in speaking about the leap into the world of freedom, from the world of necessity. But a further exploration of this conception is reserved for the chapter in *KMTR* 5 on the dying-away of the state under socialism.

7 | OF THE REACTIONARY ANTICAPITALISMS

Marx and Engels themselves offered a critique of rival socialisms in Section III of the *Communist Manifesto*. But even as this survey was being written, the scene surveyed was on the point of coming to an end in the general dégringolade of the European revolution of 1848. The more famous the Manifesto became in the subsequent decades, the more customary it became for Section III to be dismissed or ignored as the "obsolete section." This tradition must have still been strong as late as the 1948 centennial of the Manifesto, when I felt called on to argue that Marx's concept of "reactionary socialism" was very much alive.[1]

Still, could there be a *feudal* socialism, a *reactionary* socialism? We remind again that the term 'socialism' later tended to be used as an honorific only, a seal of approval. But this was not true in Marx's broad usage. A censorious modifier could be attached to 'socialism' without difficulty. Besides, Section III referred to socialistic schools that no longer existed and to figures long forgotten.

In truth, the content of Section III has proved to be far from obsolete.

1. THE MEANING OF "REACTIONARY SOCIALISM"

The Manifesto classified different socialisms in its own way—different from other works and other writers that had already published accounts of the socialist movement; for example, Reybaud in France and Lorenz von Stein in Germany. The Manifesto divided existing socialisms under three heads: (1) reactionary socialism; (2) conservative, or bourgeois, socialism; and (3) critical-utopian socialism and communism. That is: the socialisms that looked to the past, to the present status quo, and to the future. Subordinate to this scheme was the class provenance of a socialist tendency.

Engels' draft for the Manifesto, the so-called *Principles of Communism*, followed this outline about two-thirds of the way. His third group was not "critical-utopian socialism" (which he did not label as such) but the "democratic socialists," which meant a part of the class bloc he called the Democracy.[2]

Of the Manifesto's three groups, the first calls for further explanation, especially of its disconcerting title, "reactionary socialism."

The first thing to be pointed out is that Marx and Engels here used the term 'reactionary' with its proper and original political meaning, which later blurred as the word came to be used as an all-purpose cussword like 'fascist.' The Manifesto defined it clearly when it described the old intermediate class strata as "reactionary, for they try to roll back the wheel of history." Engels' draft had applied it in the same way to those who advocate "that feudal and patriarchal society should be restored because it was free from these ills [of bourgeois society]."[3]

'Reactionary socialism' was an ideology hostile to the bourgeoisie but from a standpoint alien to modern (bourgeois) society as a whole, and by the same token hostile to the proletariat. The strict meaning of 'reactionary' was: looking backward to a return to *pre*bourgeois society, hence retrogressive in a societal sense.

Should a reactionary anticapitalism be properly labeled 'socialism'? This was an idle terminological exercise, which Marx eschewed. It has been pointed out that to Marx 'socialism' was a broad term which he commonly used with few inhibitions, though he was more sparing about the use of 'communism.' In 1843, barely converted to socialism/communism, he was already differentiating: see the passage in one of his *Deutsch-Französische Jahrbücher* editorial letters, quoted in *KMTR* 1, stressing that "Abolition of private property and communism are therefore by no means identical."[4]

In the later socialist movement, this idea might be formulated: anticapitalism and socialism are by no means synonyms. Or to spell it out: the abolition of capitalism does not yet entail socialism. Neither Marx nor anyone else could have seen in 1843 how important this notion would become.

Terminologically, 'reactionary anticapitalism' represented a pattern, common since antiquity, in which an upper class under pressure from commercial classes stretched out its hand to the plebs, over the heads or behind the backs of its monied rivals, in order to mobilize in its own support the lower classes threatening those rivals.

A variant of this pattern can be seen as the key to the appearance of antibourgeois utopias from Thomas More on. Absolutism had first developed by mobilizing the developing bourgeoisie in its own support against the feudal nobility. Then, as the old nobility ceased to be the main threat, the bourgeois ally itself had to be contained by placing *its* rear under threat from below (or pressure from its rear). This encouraged ideologies that combined hostility to bourgeois values with an idealization of absolutist virtues, and fostered the typical elitist utopias-from-above that multiplied in the seventeenth and eighteenth centuries.[5] After the French Revolution, this type of antibourgeois ideology tended to fuse with working-class resentments and aspirations, to stimulate some forms of modern socialism.

The same pattern, in new forms, continued to influence later tendencies too. This was involved, for example, when the German absolute monarchy, through Bismarck, tried to reach behind (or below) the bourgeoisie to the working classes, generating talk about a "Bismarckian socialism," its academic reflection in Katheder-socialism, and the illusions of Lassalleanism (in short, the phenomena examined in Chapters 3 and 4).

This pattern was pointed out by Marx to Lassalle himself,[6] when the latter sent him his self-revelatory drama *Franz von Sickingen.*

> ... Sickingen and Hutten had to go under because they were revolutionaries in their imagination [only] ... and just like the *educated* Polish nobility of 1830, on the one hand made themselves organs of modern ideas, but on the other hand in point of fact represented a reactionary class interest.[7]

For the admirers of Rodbertus, the herald of Bismarckian socialism, Engels used the terms 'reactionary socialists' and 'pseudosocialists' interchangeably.[8] We are dealing here with a pattern which, in various forms and under various names, has run all through the history of socialism to our own day.

2. "FEUDAL SOCIALISM" AND THE TRIANGULAR CLASS STRUGGLE

The Manifesto's section on "Reactionary Socialism" was itself divided into three parts: (a) Feudal Socialism; (b) Petty-Bourgeois Socialism; (c) German, or "True," Socialism. Let us concentrate on Feudal Socialism proper.

The portrait of Feudal Socialism was clearly limned in the Manifesto. "Owing to their historical position, it became the vocation of the aristocracies of France and England to write pamphlets against modern bourgeois society." Only this literary battle was possible for them; they were politically impotent. "In order to arouse sympathy, the aristocracy were obliged to lose sight, apparently, of their own interests, and to formulate their indictment against the bourgeoisie in the interest of the exploited working class alone." The socialistic-sounding literature thus produced was "half echo of the past, half menace of the future." But while these antibourgeois critics could draw blood, they had no understanding of historical development, either their own or the bourgeoisie's. "The aristocracy, in order to rally the people to them, waved the proletarian alms-bag in front for a banner," but (the Manifesto asserted) were answered with "loud and irreverent laughter."[9] (Not always, we may add.)

These reactionary antibourgeois critics (continued the Manifesto) "forgot" that they themselves represented an antiquated form of exploitation of the masses, and that the bourgeois world they detested had been generated by their own form of society. They denounced the bourgeoisie for giving rise to a proletarian class because a revolutionary proletariat would cut the ground from under both the old and the new ruling class. "In political practice, therefore, they join in all coercive measures against the working class," and in economic life they did not let highfalutin principles stand in the way of dipping their own fingers into the pot of bourgeois profiteering as much as they could.[10]

About whom was the Manifesto talking?

The period's literature was, of course, impregnated with antibourgeois values stemming from former times and former people, from nostalgic hackwork to German romanticism.* To Marx's generation in Germany, 'romantic' was not only a literary term but also a sociopolitical reference, especially applied to the retrogressive swing in German society and culture taking place after the defeat of Napoleon. When Marx remarked that King Friedrich Wilhelm IV ascended the throne "full of the visions of the romantic school" and full of medieval hankerings, this was not a specially "Marxist" opinion. We will shortly see Engels' reference to the "romantic feudalism" of Young England. There were many such usages in Marx and Engels, as well as in contemporary journalism.[11]

In the economic literature of the time, the "feudal socialistic" trends and moods were visible to Marx when he encountered backward-looking viewpoints. He observed in his *Grundrisse* notebooks: "Complaints about business dealings by means of money as being illegitimate dealings [occur] among a good many writers, who form the transition from the feudal era to the modern era; likewise later among socialists."[12]

In political literature, the manifestations of this tendency "later among socialists" bedeviled the whole period before 1848 while Marx was begin-

---

*I have no intention of getting into the shifting quicksands of general definitions of 'romanticism,' a murky term in comparison with which even 'socialism' is crystal-clear. This passage is concerned only with the German romanticism of the nineteenth century.

ning to find his way. It gave rise to a three-cornered confrontation, hence engendered a ninefold opportunity for confusion. The triangle went this way: *feudal absolutism* (the old ruling class in power) versus the *bourgeoisie* (the aspiring ruling class of civil society) versus the *working classes*, exploited by both.

The first occasion on which Marx performed the service of pointing to this triangular class struggle came quite early, in mid-1844, when the first big antibourgeois revolt exploded in Germany: the Silesian weavers' uprising.[13] As Marx's liberal ex-friends sought to belittle its significance, Marx put a finger on part of the new problem:

> ...the uprising was not aimed directly at the King of Prussia, but against the bourgeoisie. As an aristocrat and absolute monarch, the King of Prussia cannot love the bourgeoisie; still less can he be alarmed if the submissiveness and impotence of the bourgeoisie is increased because of a tense and difficult relationship between it and the proletariat.... In the sphere of politics, the King of Prussia, as a politician, has his direct opposite in liberalism. For the King the proletariat is as little an antithesis as the King is for the proletariat.[14]

There it is: the three-corner problem, the triangular class struggle. How Marx worked his way through it, step by step, we have seen in *KMTR* 2, and there too we saw that in Germany Feudal Socialism took the special form of "True Socialism." This part of *KMTR* 2 is relevant here, but cannot be repeated.[15]

Suffice to say that Marx and Engels had to repeatedly explain the conception of the triangular class struggle, as distinct from a simple duel. The "duel" metaphor is famous from the *Communist Manifesto*, where it was extrapolated for the future. In the triangular class struggle Marx and Engels were confronting their present reality, and trying to deal with its difficult politics.

One of the first works in which they did so in some detail was a pamphlet which Engels tried to draft in 1847, with Marx's advice, but which was never in fact finished. "True Socialism," wrote Engels, "is reactionary through and through." Because of it, the bourgeois liberals mistakenly accuse the Communists of playing into the hands of Reaction, by imputing to them the reactionary politics of the True Socialists. (This, in fact, was an important reason for Marx's and Engels' virulent hostility to that tendency.) He drew a line between the antibourgeois criticism of the Communists and the antibourgeois animus of the "status quo" (this latter term meaning the absolutist regime opposed to constitutionalism).*

---

*Untitled in manuscript, this work has had two different titles conferred on it: "The Status Quo in Germany" (in MEW) or "The Constitutional Question in Germany" (in MECW). The point of the work is that it was about both, as *two* corners of the triangle.

Our attacks on the bourgeoisie differ as much from those of the True Socialists as from those of the reactionary nobles, e.g., the French Legitimists or Young England. The German status quo cannot exploit our attacks in any way, because they are directed still more against it than against the bourgeoisie.

It then went on to state a difficult idea:

If the bourgeoisie, so to speak, our *natural* enemy, is the enemy whose overthrow will bring our party to power, the German status quo is still more our enemy, because it stands between the bourgeoisie and us, because it hinders us from coming to grips with the bourgeoisie. For that reason we do not exclude ourselves in any way from the great mass of opposition to the German status quo. We only form its most advanced section.... [16]

In this framework Marx and Engels had to think their way through the "enemy of your enemy" problem,[17] and the problem merged with that of the permanent revolution, according to which the Communists formed the "most advanced section" of a political bloc which they called the Democracy. These manifestations of the triangular class struggle were part of the problem-complex discussed in *KMTR* 2.

If, for Marx, Communism was *proletarian socialism*, our present subject raised the problem of *nonproletarian socialisms*. In the pre-1848 period one of these tendencies, with clearly prebourgeois characteristics, was constituted by the early incarnations of Christian socialism. The Manifesto referred to "clerical socialism" under the head of Feudal Socialism (this became "Christian socialism" only in the 1872 edition).[18] When the Manifesto was written, Christian socialism as a distinct school did not yet exist; but Marx and Engels may well have had in mind the example of Lamennais, perhaps also Buchez.

Certainly, Lamennais was then the best known among those who sought to "give Christian asceticism a socialist tinge," as the Manifesto put it. Young Engels, in a very juvenile (pre-Marx) article of 1843 for the Owenite organ, had hailed Lamennais—and virtually everyone else in sight—as being "more or less inclined towards the Communist doctrines." When in 1843 Marx and Ruge invited Lamennais to collaborate with their *Deutsch-Französische Jahrbücher*, this was no special invitation—it was extended to all radicals. By 1846 Marx and Engels were of the opinion that communism had left Lamennais "far behind," and of course when Lamennais denounced the June 1848 uprising of the Paris workers as perpetrated mainly by criminals, Marx's *Neue Rheinische Zeitung* replied with a few suitable words. In later years, little was to be found in Marx or Engels on either Lamennais or Christian socialism as a political tendency.[19]

It was the medievalizing aspect of Christian socialism that the Manifesto hit off particularly: "the holy water with which the priest consecrates the heart-burnings of the aristocrat."[20] In the Germany of the 1840s this backward-looking nostalgia was the hallmark of the romanticist reaction. The Manifesto referred in a different section to "the brutal display of vigor in the Middle Ages, which Reactionists so much admire."[21] This amalgam of admiration for the prebourgeois values of medievalism with socialistic sympathy for the lower classes had a future before it in the socialist movement, though not under the name of Feudal Socialism.

3. THE THIRD CORNER OF THE TRIANGLE

But in the Manifesto's section on "Feudal Socialism" the main examples were not tendencies inside the socialist movement at all. The passage quoted above ("loud and irreverent laughter") was followed by this: "One section of the French Legitimists and 'Young England' exhibited this spectacle."[22] It was a question of social appeals emanating from aristocratic circles, circles reflecting prebourgeois values.

Shortly before writing the Manifesto, Marx had had to criticize "The Communism of the *Rheinische Beobachter*," an organ of the Prussian reaction. He pointed the finger at absolutist propaganda that was considered antibourgeois, and to which the communist label was being attached, just because it proclaimed that the monarchy was "one with the people" in calling for social reform. Some socialists were being taken in:

> If a certain section of German socialists has continually blustered against the liberal bourgeoisie, and has done so in a manner which has benefited nobody but the German governments, and if at present government newspapers like the *Rheinische Beobachter*, basing themselves on the empty phrases of these people, claim that it is not the liberal bourgeoisie but the government which represents the interests of the proletariat, then the Communists have nothing in common with either the former or the latter.[23]

Almost two decades later, Marx referred back to this very article when he broke with the Lassalleans as the representatives of "royal Prussian government socialism." In 1847 Engels' draft pamphlet, as cited above, had pointed to the same movements as exemplifications of Feudal Socialism: "the French Legitimists or Young England."[24]

In France the Legitimist champions of the overthrown Bourbon monarchy were quite willing to attack the Louis Philippe regime from the "left," or from any other direction. So Heinrich Heine pointed out in brilliant journalism, which was a model for Marx as for a whole generation:

> It is amusing beyond words [wrote Heine] to hear these masked priests

vociferating in the language of the sansculottes, to watch the coquettish air of savagery with which they sport the red caps of the Jacobins, to note how at times they are seized with a panic lest in a fit of absentmindedness they should have donned the bishop's red cap instead. When this happens, they will remove the borrowed headgear for a moment, to make sure, and everyone can see the tonsure it was hiding.[25]

"Young England" had already petered out as a political group by the time the Manifesto was written, but in the early 1840s it had made a stir, under the leadership of Lord John Manners. Its best-known spokesman was the young Disraeli, whose novels *Sybil* and *Coningsby* can be read as textbooks of the school. Its most effective legislator was Lord Ashley (the later Lord Shaftesbury), who played an important part in winning factory laws. These Tory scions of the aristocracy had an idealistic aim: to counteract the rising bourgeoisie and regenerate the power of the aristocracy by appealing to the working classes of the factories and farms, not simply by social demagogy but by real amelioration of the workers' lot—exclusively at the expense of the rival ruling classes.

There was an interesting nuance in the treatment of Young England, within the space of a few months, by Marx in *The Holy Family* and by Engels in *The Condition of the Working Class in England*. In each case it was a passing comment.

Poking fun at Eugene Sue's hero Rudolph, Marx wrote that "This great lord is like the members of *Young England*, who also wish to reform the world, perform noble deeds, and are subject to similar hysterical fits."[26] Engels, writing from his immersion in the English class struggle, also saw the absurdity of the group's posture, but he added an E for Effort, to recognize that these "philanthropic Tories" are "honorable exceptions" to the general sins of the ruling classes:

> The hope of "Young England" is a restoration of the old "merry England" with its brilliant features and its romantic feudalism. This object is of course unattainable and ridiculous, a satire upon all historic development; but the good intention, the courage to resist the existing state of things and prevalent prejudices, and to recognize the vileness of our present condition, is worth something anyhow.[27]

Although Young England as such did not last very long, the tendency it represented was instrumental in putting through a Ten Hours Bill, in alliance with certain working-class and "Tory Chartist" elements. Writing in 1850, Engels emphasized the "reactionary" wellsprings of this bill, as against the kind of Ten Hours Bill that the labor movement was advocating.

This analysis of Engels' can be read more generally, for its picture of the feudal-social component of the period's politics. On the one side, the alliance fostered by Young England utilized meek, broken-down workers filled with "humble reverence" for aristocrats who deigned to notice their plight, workers who were still imbued with backward-looking anti-industrial animus. The "Ten Hours party" included these "reactionary" workers as well as bourgeois and aristocrats, all united by a class orientation:

> Without exception they were sentimental Tories, mostly fancy-filled ideologues who reveled in memories of vanished patriarchal hole-and-corner exploitation with its train of piety, domesticity, virtuousness and narrowmindedness, with its fixed ways handed down by tradition. Their narrow skulls were overcome with dizziness at the sight of the maelstrom of industrial revolution. Their petty-bourgeois mentalities took fright at the new forces of production growing up with magical suddenness....

These people counterposed the virtues of the old system to the vices of the new:

> These soft-hearted ideologues did not fail to take the field, from the standpoint of morality, humanitarianism and compassion, against the merciless harshness and ruthlessness with which this process of social transformation made its way, and against this transformative process to counterpose, as their social ideal, the stability, quiet coziness and decent respectability of dying patriarchalism.[28]

This tone was quite different from that of five years before, though strictly speaking the content was not much different. What changed was made clear as Engels proceeded: he now saw that the alliance of "these reactionary classes and factions" with the workers was serving to keep the workers "permanently under the influence and to some extent under the actual leadership of these property-owning allies." It was corrupting them, that is, vitiating their consciousness of the class struggle. The reminder that the aristocratic allies were themselves "property owners" was a reminder that their interests lay with bourgeois society.

True, it was natural for the workers in this period to ally themselves with aristocratic and bourgeois elements who did not directly exploit them and who were fighting the industrial bourgeoisie that did exploit them; but there was a price to pay.

> But this alliance adulterated the working-class movement with a strong reactionary admixture which is only gradually fading away; it gave a significant reinforcement to the reactionary element in the workers' movement, namely, those workers whose kind of work still belongs to manufacture [manual fabrication, not machinofacture] and is therefore itself threatened by industrial progress, like, for example, the hand-loom weavers.[29]

Now we are at the roots of what is called today "working-class Toryism," which can be considered in part as a degenerate modern descendant of Feudal Socialism.

4. THE CASE OF THOMAS CARLYLE—I

In the period leading up to the *Communist Manifesto*, the most radical voice of Feudal Socialism in its Young England form seemed to be Thomas Carlyle. In his *Condition of the Working Class in England*, young Engels estimated that Carlyle "goes beyond all those hitherto mentioned" among the Young England types, and he hoped that this "half-German Englishman" would develop further.[30]

Many a Chartist and Owenite was much more enthusiastic than this over the Scottish-born prophet. In those days Carlyle's radicalism seemed to be at its zenith, following the publication of *Past and Present*. Biographer Symons tells us that

> its fervour frightened Radicals ... its criticism of the existing state of affairs angered the ruling class. Like Carlyle's other works, however, it made disciples for him among young men at the Universities who were looking for a new way of life.

One of Carlyle's admirers trembled as he opined that the book "would be very dangerous if turned into the vernacular and generally read." Statesmen and "society" were shocked.[31]

The mystique of Carlyle's "radicalism" has continued to this very day, and after a century books are still being published arguing that he was a prophet of the Left or, alternatively, a herald of fascism.[32] That is, his political position is sought on a left-right line, instead of on the leg of a triangle. But the reactionary anticapitalisms do not range themselves on a left-right line; they go off at right angles to the traditional left-right continuum, precisely because they take up their basic position *outside* of modern bourgeois society.

In no work was this plainer than in Carlyle's *Past and Present*, which specifically counterposed the prebourgeois values of the past to the present and unpleasant world of capitalism. This gave it its antibourgeois gloss, even though the prophet's voice was really crying: *Reform, ye selfish bourgeois, in order to save our/your world from the barbarian hordes from below.*

The revolution of 1848 cleared up many of Carlyle's illusions about himself, and turned him onto the road of conscious reaction. After his defense of slavery in "The Nigger Question,"* and especially after his *Latter-Day Pamphlets*, even John Stuart Mill discovered that Carlyle did not believe in democracy and publicly criticized him.[34]

The contrast between *Past and Present* (1843) and *Latter-Day Pamphlets* (1850) was recorded by two book reviews that concern us. *Past and Present* was reviewed by Engels in early 1844, *before* his association with Marx and while he was still under the influence of Hess's anarchoid radicalism.[35] *Latter-Day Pamphlets* was reviewed in 1850 in an article authored by Marx and Engels jointly (Engels may have drafted it); by this time both had not only developed their basic ideas but had hardened them in the experience of revolution. The difference between the two articles in understanding is very instructive.

We saw in *KMTR* 1 that in late 1843 young Engels, having been converted to what he called "communism," was repeating the anarchoid (Proudhonist) sentiment that "democracy" was a sham like all forms of government.[36] When he reviewed Carlyle's *Past and Present*, all of Carlyle's cynical remarks about parliamentary incapacity and the "national talk-shop" was grist to the mill. Carlyle's book exposed some of the tinsel beneath the show of democratic institutions in England, which "from a distance... looks quite impressive." All English leftists were relishing Carlyle's indictment that "This liberty turns out... to be, for the Working Millions a liberty to die by want of food...." Engels' Chartist and Owenite friends enjoyed what sounded like Carlyle's denunciation of all ruling classes, of a "Parliament elected by bribery," of laissez faire and the dearth of "soul," and so forth. Because of this sort of thing, wrote Engels, Carlyle's book was "the only one which is worth reading" this year; it was "the only one which strikes a human chord." Carlyle, "alone of the 'respectable' class, has kept his eyes open at least towards the facts...."[37]

This enthusiasm Engels shared with his English friends; he was writing for German readers. But he also made a distinctive contribution, a corrective to Carlyle's negativity. The essential aspect was explained in *KMTR* 1: Engels thoroughly rejected Carlyle's orientation toward heroes and aristocrats, and argued roundly that "England's salvation" could come only from the working classes; the aristocracy as well as the middle classes were finished.[38]

More difficult for this new-baked socialist was an analysis of what made Carlyle so peculiar: an analysis of the link between his antibourgeois air and his essentially reactionary (retrogressive, backward-looking) outlook.

---

*Carlyle's defense of slavery became more open in reaction to the American Civil War. In *Capital* Marx footnoted: "Thus, finally the bubble of Tory sympathy for the urban wage-workers—by no means for the rural!—has burst. The kernel turns out to be—slavery!"[33]

That the young man made such an analysis at all, in the midst of the pro-Carlylism of the Left, was something of a triumph.

Engels began by echoing Carlyle's view of Toryism as a lesser evil: "If, by the way, either of the two parties into which the educated section of the English people is split deserves any preference, it is the Tories." The Whigs were tied up with industry, the immediate exploiter of the working class. "The Tory, on the other hand, whose power and unchallenged dominance have been broken by industry and whose principles have been shaken by it, hates it and sees in it at best a necessary evil." This was why the philanthropic Tories of Young England took the part of the factory workers against the manufacturers, and why Carlyle stood closer to the Tories than to the Whigs. "This much is certain: a Whig would never have been able to write a book that was half so humane as *Past and Present*."[39] So far, these sentiments were well known among the English leftists.

Engels then went on to an analysis that was far from common: a critique of Carlyle's hero-worshiping elitism.

Very philosophically, he ascribed it to Carlyle's "pantheism" with "German overtones." One of its roots lay in "vestiges of Tory romanticism." Carlyle's hero worship or "cult of genius" was still on the level of D. F. Strauss, the not-very-left Hegelian. Feuerbach and Young Hegelians had critically killed this pantheism, which leads to elitism because it longs for something higher than itself (divinity). The analysis led him to write the following:

> Hence his [Carlyle's] longings for a "true aristocracy," for "heroes"; as if these heroes could at best be more than *men*. If he had understood man as man in all his infinite complexity, he would not have conceived the idea of once more dividing mankind into two lots, sheep and goats, rulers and ruled, aristocrats and the rabble, lords and dolts; he would have seen the proper social function of talent not in ruling by force but in acting as a stimulant and taking the lead. The role of talent is to convince the masses of the truth of its ideas, and it will then have no need further to worry about their application, which will follow entirely of its own accord. Mankind is surely not passing through democracy to arrive back eventually at the point of departure.[40]

These words went to the heart of Carlylism, probably even more directly than the writer may have wholly understood at the time. In another statement he posed a basic distinction: "Democracy, true enough, is only a transitional stage, though not towards a new, improved aristocracy [as Carlyle thought], but towards real human freedom...." This unwittingly drew a line between two antithetical approaches that would thread their way through the entire history of socialism: (1) Since this democracy is a sham, we must discard democracy; *or* (2) since this democracy is a sham, we must replace it by real democracy, in order to progress toward "freedom." Engels stated the thought positively: "Democracy, Chartism must soon be victorious, and then the mass of the English workers will have the choice only between starvation and socialism."[41]

This 1843 review ended with the hope that Carlyle would draw socialist conclusions from his premises. As mentioned, Engels repeated this sentiment in his *Condition of the Working Class in England,* where the few references to Carlyle differ little from the book review, which incidentally was very favorably greeted by the little public that read it.[42]

5. THE CASE OF THOMAS CARLYLE—II

As a later edition of *The Condition of the Working Class in England* was revised to report about Carlyle: "the February Revolution [of 1848] made him an out-and-out reactionary. His righteous wrath against the Philistines turned into sullen Philistine grumbling at the tide of history that cast him ashore."[43] When Marx and Engels* read the self-revised Carlyle's *Latter-Day Pamphlets* in 1850, all illusions about Carlyle's radicalism had gone.

Engels (if he was indeed the drafter) began by briefly giving a meed of credit to the antibourgeois content of Carlyle's *earlier* writings: he had "come out against the bourgeoisie on the literary field at a time when its conceptions, tastes and ideas completely dominated all of official English literature, and he did so in a way which now and then is even revolutionary."

Then the review immediately stated the reactionary kernel of Carlylism:

> But in all these writings criticism of the present day is closely bound up with a singularly unhistorical apotheosis of the Middle Ages, which is also widespread among English revolutionaries, e.g., Cobbett and a sector of the Chartists. While he admires in the past at least the classical epochs of a given stage of society, the present drives him to despair, and he shudders at the future. Where he does justice to revolution, or indeed exalts it, for him it is concentrated in a single individual, a Cromwell or a Danton. To them he devotes the same

---

*All book reviews in Marx's magazine, the *NRZ Revue,* were unsigned, and have generally been ascribed to Marx and Engels jointly. That certainly does not mean they actually wrote every review in unison. It seems altogether likely that Engels drafted the one on Carlyle (with whatever suggestions or revisions by editor Marx), and this authorship is assumed for present purposes. But little would be changed if this assumption is not made.

hero cult that he preached in his *Heroes and Hero Worship* as the only way out of the despair-filled present, as a new religion.

Carlyle's new book showed a "marked retrogression" from whatever was positive in his earlier writings. "Of the cult of genius that Carlyle shares with [D. F.] Strauss, the genius has been lost in the pamphlets before us. The cult has remained."[44]

The review summarized Carlyle's argument on the impossibility and undesirability of democracy, and proceeded to a rebuttal. To this end it presented a classic critique of elitism, beginning with Carlyle's pantheistic approach to reality.

We would wish that a philosophical excursus could be avoided at this point, but there is an interesting reason why that would be inadvisable. Engels' 1843 review of *Past and Present* had devoted considerable space to Carlyle's pantheism—namely, the tendency to infuse (and confuse) all phenomena with divinity; "God" lives in all nature and man and everywhere else. The later 1850 review appeared about the same time as a three-part article on Carlyle in Harney's left Chartist magazine, *Democratic Review*, written by Helen Macfarlane.* The interesting point is that most of Macfarlane's article was a polemic *in favor* of pantheism as the basis of Red Republicanism and in favor of a socialism based on Christianity. Given this current among the best Chartists, Marx and Engels would indeed have been interested in pointing out, via Carlyle, that pantheism led not to socialist conclusions but to a reactionary elitism. Engels might well have been specially concerned, for he had himself gone through a pantheistic period on first embracing Hegelianism.[46]

In any case, the reviewer showed the relationship between Carlyle's pantheism and elitism. Since the thought is pantheist, Carlyle assumed that the historical process flowed from an eternal and immutable law of nature, which was Eternal Truth. He resolved all class antagonisms of all epochs into "one big, eternal antagonism" between those who have fathomed this eternal law and act on it (the Wise and Noble) and those who have not grasped it (the Fools and Knaves).

> A class difference that is historically engendered is thus turned into a natural difference which must indeed be recognized and honored as a part of the eternal law of nature by bowing down before the noble and wise sent by nature: the cult of genius.

The circularity of this elitist thinking was then demonstrated.

---

*In these same months Helen Macfarlane had published the first English translation of the *Communist Manifesto* in Harney's *Red Republican*; she was will acquainted with Engels and also with Marx.[45]

> Thereupon the old question naturally comes up: who then should really rule? It is discussed with highflown shallowness at the greatest length, and finally answered with the view that the noble, wise and knowledgeable should rule....

Obviously the old leftist illusions about Carlyle are being dissipated. The argument continued:

> But how [according to Carlyle] are the noble and wise to be discovered? No supernatural miracle reveals them; one must search for them. And at this point we get a reappearance of the historical class differences that have been turned into purely natural differences. The noble person is noble because he is a man of wisdom and knowledge. Therefore he is to be sought among the classes that have a monopoly on education—among the privileged classes.... Thereupon, the privileged classes immediately become, if not quite the noble and wise classes outright, at least the "articulate" classes; the oppressed classes are, naturally, the "dumb, inarticulate" classes; and thus class rule is sanctioned anew.[47]

Why then did Carlyle complain about the bourgeoisie? His "grumbling and growling is merely due to the fact that the bourgeois do not allot any place at the head of society to their misunderstood geniuses.... Carlyle offers us striking examples of how here and elsewhere grandiloquent twaddle turns into its opposite, and how the noble, knowledgeable and wise are in practice transformed into the mean, ignorant, and foolish." Intellectuals face a contradiction between the nature of their own capacities and the nature of those talents for which bourgeois society offers its greatest rewards.

Carlyle demanded strong government and denounced anarchy, which he identified with "the cry for liberation and emancipation." In his blustering he lumped all sorts of things into one bag: "Red Republic, *fraternité*, Louis Blanc, etc., along with free trade, abolition of the corn laws, etc." He denounced everything that destroyed the remnants of feudalism, that made for "the reduction of the state to what is unavoidably necessary and least expensive," that encouraged "free competition by the bourgeoisie"— all of which he identified with the *abolition* of bourgeois relations and society.

> What a brilliant reversion to the "night of absolutes" in which all cows are gray!... What strange sagacity, which believes that all relationships among people are abolished along with the abolition of feudalism or free competition![48]

Thus the elite's wisdom turned out to be ignorance, and their noble-mindedness turned into open vileness as soon as they descended from noble phrases into the real world. For Carlyle revealed that the new aristocracy which was to take over the scepter of rule in society was—the "Captains of Industry." Amazing! After blustering for forty pages with noble wrath against egoism, free competition, laissez faire, cash payment, cotton spinning, and so on, "now we suddenly find that the chief representatives of all these shams, the industrial bourgeoisie, not only belong among the celebrated heroes and geniuses but . . . the trump card in all his attacks on bourgeois relations and ideas is the glorification of bourgeois figures."

Before he was through, Carlyle presented an imagined harangue which he wanted to address to the masses of workers—reviling them as vagabonds, slaves, lackeys, vagrants, and what not, and calling them to work in his "Regiments of the New Era" on pain of being flogged or shot.

> The *"new era"* in which genius rules differs from the old era, therefore, mainly in the fact that the whip fancies itself endowed with genius. Carlyle's genius differs from that of any old prison guard or poorhouse warden in his virtuous indignation and in his moral consciousness that he flays the paupers only to elevate them to his *own* level. Here we see our sanctimonious genius, in his world-redeeming wrath, in fancy justifying and outdoing the infamies of the bourgeoisie.[49]

Finally, Engels' (or Marx-Engels') review took up the chapter in which Carlyle's righteous wrath reached its peak of sanctimoniousness: this moral discharge was unleashed in a vile denunciation of people held in the Model Prisons, the criminals and paupers—for these two groups were held on the same footing.[50] Just as at the beginning Carlyle had separated out the Noblest of the Noble, so now he ferreted out the worst of the worst, "in order to lust in the pleasure of hanging him" (said the review). But when the worst has been hanged, another becomes the worst; hang him, and then still others succeed to the head of the list—and the hangman is the Noblest of all. So "at the end no one is left except Carlyle, the Noblest . . . who suddenly turns into the basest of scoundrels and, as such, has *to hang himself*."[51]

In form, black humor; in content, a parable for witchhunters and purgers with or without Noble intentions. Among other things, once the democratic approach was rejected the question was: *Who will elect the Elect?* —just as, many years before, Marx had raised the question: *Who will educate the educators?*[52]

Carlyle in his early years had gone looking for an antibourgeois answer, and in the old society to which he looked back, found nothing usable. "Captains of Industry" was his latter-day attempt to weld the vileness of medievalism to the vices of capitalist society. "Reactionary anticapitalism" had turned into something else.

6. O'CONNOR TO COMTE

The Feudal Socialism discussed in the *Communist Manifesto* was gone as an identifiable tendency by 1848, but, as Marx and Engels had to recognize from time to time, the drive behind it kept cropping up in other forms. For one thing, it was a "socialistic" way of looking back to the Good Old Days. Its spirit was reactivated wherever a revulsion against bourgeois oppression or bourgeois values found no outlet in a forward-looking program. To say this is to point the finger immediately at a class: at the petty-bourgeoisie, the old and declining intermediate class—historically, a fount and reservoir of reactionary anticapitalisms in various guises.

The Engels (or Marx-Engels) review of Carlyle in 1850 had mentioned that an "unhistorical apotheosis of the Middle Ages" characterized a "sector of the Chartists."[53] What Chartists? The reference was very likely, *inter alia*, to the prominent figure at the head of the movement, Feargus O'Connor. About a month later, Marx and Engels published an opinion of O'Connor along these lines, in a final judgment of his land plan.[54]

The Chartist movement, they explained, was divided between a revolutionary wing, represented by G. J. Harney and Ernest Jones, and a reformist ("pure-and-simple democratic") wing reflecting the movement's petty-bourgeois elements and its "workers' aristocracy." This tendency was headed by O'Connor. Their description of this personage is of the first importance for the subject of this chapter.

> Old O'Connor, an Irish squire and alleged scion of the old kings of Munster, is, despite his lineage and his political tendency, a genuine representative of Old England. He is conservative by his whole nature and has a very definite hatred of industrial progress as well as of the revolution. All his ideals are patriarchal-petty-bourgeois through and through. He combines in himself an untold host of contradictions, which are resolved and harmonized through a certain shallow °common sense°. . . . It is clear that a man like O'Connor is bound to be a great hindrance in a revolutionary movement; but such people serve to bring it about that a host of old ingrained prejudices get worked out with them and through them, and when the movement finally shakes these people off it is also rid once and for all of the prejudices they represent.[55]

Another required background reading for this question is the chapter on the petty-bourgeoisie in *KMTR* 2; perhaps most relevant is the section on the "Petty-Bourgeois as Anti-Semite."[56] It is not the Jewish question that is directly involved here, but rather it is the political phenomena that link anti-Semitism with the incidence of reactionary anticapitalism. When in Germany a racialist type of anti-Semitic political movement based on social demagogy sprang up under the leadership of the court chaplain Stoecker, in the wake of "Bismarckian socialism," Engels saw its social base in the prebourgeois elements that were wasting away in a blind alley and that wanted to strike out at an invisible enemy.

These classes "are reactionary through and through," he emphasized, and their anti-Semitism was "nothing else than a reaction of medieval, declining social strata against modern society, which essentially comprises capitalists and wage-workers, and therefore anti-Semitism serves only reactionary ends under a speciously socialistic cover; it is a variety of Feudal Socialism, and with that we can have nothing to do."[57] It cannot be overstressed that this describes the specific anti-Semitic movement of *that* time; later, anti-Semitism provided "cover" for other kinds of political animals.

It was easy for Stoecker's Christian Social movement to imply that it was a Christian Social-*ist* movement, though in Bebel's famous phrase it was the "socialism of fools," the *ersatz*-socialism of shopkeepers, guild artisans, and other little people who were being ground down by the power of Money in some fashion mysterious to them. Even if they tended to be *agin' the system*, that is, even if they were attracted in the direction of anticapitalism, they could easily be steered into reactionary channels. The reactionary anticapitalisms were made for these dupes.

As the Manifesto had said of Feudal Socialism, it was "half echo of the past, half menace of the future." (The critics who called Section III of the Manifesto "obsolete" somehow never remembered the second half of that statement.) Medievalizers had an affinity for anti-Semitism. For example, Carlyle was one of the most virulent anti-Semites of his time, though this telltale fact is seldom mentioned.

Feargus O'Connor and Chaplain Stoecker seemed very different from each other, and Auguste Comte appeared to have little in common with either. What united them all is the subject of this chapter.

Comtism (calling itself Positivism) came onto the social scene as a reactionary ideology apparently hostile in some way to the status quo. To be sure, it was not anticapitalist: as Marx said, the Comtists °°"defend the 'eternity' of capital rule and the wages system."[58] But an anti-status-quo stance is not easily distinguishable from anticapitalism, and the Comtist movement played an ambiguous role, especially in relation to the workers' movement. It was also sometimes an ambivalent role, particularly in England. The Comtists could speak as earnestly as anyone about the "emancipation of the working classes."

Marx began paying attention to Comte only in 1866, when the International ran into a Positivist Club of French workers. (This club was permitted to affiliate after dropping its sect name.) Marx wrote Engels in midyear:

> I am now studying Comte on the side, since the English and French are making so much noise about the fellow. What attracts them in him is the encyclopedic character, the synthesis. But this is pitiful stuff compared to Hegel. . . . And this crappy positivism appeared in 1832![59]

Marx's opinion of Comte's theory evidently stayed at this low estimate. It was simply beneath discussion: "ignorant" stuff, nothing but intellectual "arrogance," "fantastic crotchets," "sectarian doctrines" incapable of comprehending social transformation. Engels was just as complimentary: Comtism was "the Higher Rubbish," he opined; and one day Charles Rappoport was shocked to hear him say flatly that Comte was an ass.[60] Neither Marx nor Engels ever thought it worthwhile to write down a theoretical analysis of Comte's system of thought.

True, shortly before his death Engels remarked in a letter to Tönnies that a "substantial job" ought to be done on this "philosopher" (the skeptical quote marks were Engels'); but he had not changed his opinion. He meant for one thing that Comte's debt to Saint-Simon, which Comte himself tried to play down, should be brought out. In this letter Engels gave something of a comment on the Comtean system as such, though still not much:

> In this system there are three characteristic elements: (1) a number of brilliant thoughts, which however are near-generally spoiled more or less because of insufficient development; accordingly (2) a narrow, philistine mentality sharply contradicting that brilliancy; (3) a hierarchically organized religious constitution stemming from a thoroughly Saint-Simonian source, but stripped of all mysticism and made extremely insipid, with a veritable pope at the head, so that Huxley could say of Comtism that it was °Catholicism without Christianity.°
>
> Now I'd bet that No. 3 gives us the answer to the otherwise incomprehensible contradiction between No. 1 and No. 2; that Comte took all his brilliant ideas from Saint-Simon but ruined them in course of arranging them in his own personally characteristic way. By stripping them of the mysticism inherent in them, he dragged them down to a lower level, reworking them in a philistine way in accordance with his own capacities.[61]

It was the practical-political character of the Comtist, self-styled Positivist, *movement* that Marx thought needed public attention, and he devoted a political criticism to it more than once. In an American newspaper interview he was asked about the Positivists' influence in the International, and in response he separated himself from "their philosophy, which will have nothing to do with popular government, as we understand it, and which seeks only to put a new hierarchy in place of the old one."[62]

Marx originally intended to include a passage criticizing the Comtist movement in his *Civil War in France*. The final version contained only an oblique reference in which Comte was not mentioned by name. This document, issued in the name of the General Council and signed by its members, acidly repudiated "the didactic patronage of well-wishing bourgeois doctrinaires, pouring forth their ignorant platitudes and sectarian crotchets in the oracular tones of scientific infallibility."[63] The first draft of the address had been much stiffer, comprising two critical passages.

Of these two passages, the minor one has already been partially quoted: the Comtists regard capitalism as eternal; they are "completely ignorant" about the present economic system; they oppose "the threatened abolition of 'property,' because in their eyes their present class form of property—a transitory historical form—*is* property itself, and the abolition of that form would therefore be the abolition of property." If the Comtists had lived in earlier epochs, "they would have defended the feudal system and the slave system as founded on the nature of things." (The last point had been made in *Capital* too: the Comtists would "have shown that feudal lords are an eternal necessity in the same way that they have done in the case of the lords of capital.")[64]

Marx's major attack on Comtism in this draft was directed against the principle of dictatorship held by this "sect," at least in its French homeland. He wrote scathingly:

°°Comte is known to the Parisian workmen as the prophet in politics of Imperialism (of personal *Dictatorship*), of capitalist rule in political economy, of hierarchy in all spheres of human action, even in the sphere of science, and as the author of a new catechism with a new pope and new saints in place of the old ones.[65]

(Here "Imperialism" meant Bonapartism; Comte and the French Positivists had supported Bonaparte's 1851 coup d'état, and continued to support the dictator.)

Thus Marx put the spotlight not only on the Comtists' procapitalism but in particular on their conception of an elitist, hierarchical, and dictatorial society in which the Positivist lords of intellect would rule on behalf of "the lords of capital," over a scientifically subjected working class. *Half echo of the past, half menace of the future.*

Marx dropped these two attacks on Comtism from the final version of *The Civil War in France* for more than one reason, in all likelihood. In the first place, the final version probably had to be shortened, and in the second place (already mentioned) the address was not going to be personally signed but, rather, issued over the names of the General Council, to whom it had to be satisfactory. In this connection the courageous stand of the *English* Comtists in defense of the Paris Commune must have played a role.

The English Comtists were virtually the only bourgeois respectables in the country who dared to speak up for the Paris Commune. In the draft Marx had inserted a special paragraph distinguishing the English Comtists from the French, not only because of the former's "personal valour" but because they supported trade unions and strikes, "which by the by are denounced as a heresy by their Paris coreligionists."[66]

One of the most prominent of the English Comtists, E. S. Beesly, had an honorable record as an active friend of the labor movement; and, as such, he had chaired the St. Martin's Hall meeting of September 1864 at which the International had been founded (though he did not join). He subsequently became very friendly with Marx, whose powers of intellect he admired greatly; and Marx returned the sentiment to the extent of rating him higher than his Comtist colleagues. "Professor Beesly is a Comtist and as such obliged to maintain all sorts of °crotchets°," Marx wrote to a friend, "but otherwise he is a very capable and bold man." To Beesly himself Marx wrote forthrightly:

> as a party [i.e., partisan] man I take a thoroughly hostile attitude towards Comtism, while as a man of science I have a very low opinion of it, but I regard you as the only Comtist, in England as well as France, who deals with historical turning points (°crises°) not as a sectarian but as a historian in the best sense of the word.... [67]

But over two decades later, Engels noted that a few years after the Paris Commune "the Comtists cooled off considerably toward the labor movement. The workers had become too powerful ... and since then the Comtists have become altogether silent with regard to the labor question."[68] For it was no longer a question of helping the underdog, but of class power.

7. THE CASE OF DAVID URQUHART

The ideological area covered by this chapter tends to produce maverick types, eccentric rebels who are difficult to classify. Not only may they be outside of the left-right continuum: they may seem alien to rational political criteria. But for precisely this reason they may raise important political issues with an impact damaging to the status quo, since they look at society from an unexpected or uniquely nonconformist slant.

What should be the attitude of a revolutionary to an anomalous dissenter of this sort—one whose theoretical ideas are *formally* reactionary (that is, backward-looking) but who in political actuality plays an objectively progressive role, if only in the sense of exposing the powers that be?

The question does not imply that a single formula-answer exists; the cases tend to be *sui generis*. But we can observe Marx as he dealt with such a problem in the person of David Urquhart. His solution was of greater interest than the personage who precipitated the issue. *Inter alia*, it concerned the question of a united front with someone you disagree with.[69]

Urquhart, following a diplomatic career in the Levant, was a member of Parliament for a few years, and became the leader and Prophet of a movement of opposition to the British government's foreign policy on the ground that it favored Russia's advance in world power. He edited or dominated the London *Free Press*, the *Sheffield Free Press*, *Diplomatic Review*, and other publications at various times, in support of the goal of rolling back Russia's sphere of influence. From Marx's standpoint, this was Urquhart's positive side; for Marx thought that Russia exercised a specially pernicious influence in diplomatic circles and world affairs that made it the greatest bulwark of counterrevolution in Europe, and that czarism's power had to be broken if a European revolution were ever to succeed.

Moreover, Marx came to the conclusion that Lord Palmerston's policies were furthering Russian ambitions in international diplomacy, and found that Urquhart was vigorously pushing the same opinion; though Marx had arrived at this point through his own studies and *not* through reading Urquhart or his press. This opinion, he said repeatedly, was his sole area of agreement with Urquhart, an area strictly limited to this part of the foreign-policy question, and on everything else they were poles apart.[70] This was what created the united-front problem.*

Urquhart's views, to be sure, were by no means limited to foreign policy. When Engels originally called Marx's attention to Urquhart in 1853, he

---

*Marx's opinion that Palmerston acted over a long period to promote Russian aggrandizement is generally regarded as a baseless obsession of his. A softer evaluation is that it suffered from a one-sided emphasis on those aspects of Palmerston's foreign policy in which Britain sought to use Russian power to repress revolutionary tendencies in Europe and Asia. In a late (1892) sketch of Marx's life by Engels, the latter summarized Marx's *Revelations of the Diplomatic History of the 18th Century* as being "on the continual self-interested dependence of English Whig ministers on Russia."[70a] Since I have made no independent examination of Marx's charges or Palmerston's political role, I put this question aside for present purposes. If we assume that Marx was quite wrong about Palmerston's motivations, the political questions raised by Urquhart remain.

labeled the latter "the mad M.P. [really *ex*-M.P.], who denounces Palmerston as being in the pay of Russia"; a "Celtic Scot" who is "by inclination a romantic" (i.e., backward-looking). Urquhart, wrote Engels, after fighting for Greece as a philhellene, went to Turkey and fell in love with the Turks. "He enthuses over Islam"; he would be a Moslem if he were not a Calvinist; the Turks are "the most perfect nation on earth in every possible way"; their language, architecture, manners, etc., are the finest; and so on. Moreover, the Turkish political system is the best there is; religious liberty and freedom in general exist *only* in Turkey; and class struggles are nonexistent in this paradise "for in matters of internal politics all are of the same mind."

This monomania Engels treated as droll, but the serious side was that the Liberals hostile to Palmerston drew their ammunition almost entirely from Urquhart, their fellow free-trader. In a *NYDT* article (sent in by Marx) Engels gave a shorter version of this portrait of the "romantic Highlander" whose "mediaeval and patriarchal recollections of [his Celtic] home" led him to "this strange enthusiasm for the Turks."[71] The Liberals were taking the Turkish side in the Russo-Turkish dispute, and Engels was as emphatic in attacking the belief in Turkey as a paladin of progress as he was in denouncing Russia's role in the East.

When in the fall of 1853 Marx published a longish study of Palmerston's foreign policy, Urquhart was delighted with it and inaugurated contact with Marx, for an exchange of information.[72] During the next few years, up to 1859, Marx occasionally published articles on related subjects of foreign policy in Urquhart's press. They met in person only once, in early February 1854: Marx introduced himself as a "revolutionist" (which in Urquhart's vocabulary meant a devil); concluded that Urquhart was a "complete monomaniac" who really expected to become prime minister and save England; and observed that Urquhart went into play-acting "fits" when contradicted. His account of the conversation, in a letter to Engels, was all-acid.[74] There was no further personal relationship or contact. Through the 1850s Marx occasionally used Urquhart's material on foreign policy in articles or made other journalistic references to his activities and publications.

In his letters to Engels, Marx referred to Urquhart as a droll crackpot who wrote a great deal of nonsense and was useful to rational politics only on one point. He was "Daud Pasha," the "High Priest," "Father Urquhart," "the poor clever child," who often talked foolishly even when not riding his monomania.[74] It will come as a surprise, to those who think that Marx obsessively ascribed all evil to the Russian regime, to find that Marx's and Engels' correspondence often poked fun at Urquhart on precisely this ground: whatever happened, Urquhart would see the sinister hand of Moscow or Muscovite agents.[75]

But just because he occasionally used Urquhart's material and made public references to his work, Marx also repeatedly made sure to publish his criticisms and disagreements with this man who, after all, was known as the leader of a political tendency, the "Urquhartites." Such passages in Marx's *NYDT* articles began almost as soon as did the references to Urquhart's agitation.[76]

Marx especially made clear that Urquhart was antirevolutionary. After reporting a vigorous speech by Urquhart against the government, he added:

> However, as Mr. Urquhart is strictly opposed to the only party [the Chartists] prepared to overthrow the rotten Parliamentary basis on which the Coalition Government of the oligarchy rests, all his speeches are as much to the purpose as if they were addressed to the clouds.[77]

He told his readers that Urquhart was to be counted among the "utopian reactionaries"; the Scot held the "Quixotic idea" of supporting Prussia as a bulwark against Russia; his "Pythian oracle" style tended to be incomprehensible; he laid too much stress on "the power of secret designs [Palmerston's] over public history."[78] In June 1854 Marx explained in a letter to a friend that he was holding up reprints of his Palmerston articles in a publication which also carried Urquhart's writings, because

> I do not want to be counted among the followers of this gentlemen, with whom I have only one point in common, the viewpoint on Palmerston, but on all others I stand diametrically opposed, as was apparent right at our first meeting. He is a romantic reactionary—Turk, and would like to carry the whole West back to the Turkish standards and structure.[79]

Shortly before this, a problem had been created when a London paper, attacking Urquhart, asserted that many supporters had left him, including "Mr. Marx," and an Urquhartite reply had asserted that "Mr. Marx" was still an energetic supporter. Marx immediately wanted to disavow Urquhart; but there *was* a Mr. Marx who was a well-known Urquhartite—Francis Marx. The Urquhartites would respond to a disavowal by claiming they meant Francis all along. Marx gritted his teeth; he would have to bide his time: "The occasion will present itself to disavow Mr. Urquhart. I find the thing so much the more shameless since he knows, and I have stated to him, that I agree with him in *nothing*, outside of Palmerston...."[80] Then the episode blew over.

Marx's view of Urquhart's reactionary ideology can be followed in two other articles. One was partially quoted in *KMTR* 1: the Urquhartites were a "clique of 'wise men' emerging in England" who were opposed both to the revolutionary working class, as represented by the Chartists, and to the government and ruling classes. (That is, they were the third corner of the triangle.) Instead of extending the powers of Parliament "by elevating it to people's power," they were for breaking up "the representative system." Urquhart wanted to revert to the politico-legal system of "Anglo-Saxon times," or "better still, to the Oriental state."

> Highlander by birth, Circassian by adoption, and Turk by free choice, he is capable of condemning civilization with all its evils... David [Urquhart] is a prophet facing backwards, and he is enraptured in an antiquarian way by the picture of old England. He therefore has to think it normal for new England to pass him by and leave him standing still.... [81]

To help his friend Cluss in America, Marx sent him a note on Urquhart, which Cluss turned (with slight changes) into an article for publication. Urquhart (wrote Marx) was an "almost maniacal Russophobe," who "systematically rides a single fixed idea." For twenty years he had denounced Russian machinations, "and therefore naturally had to become half crazy, like everyone who has a single guaranteed-correct idea...." This born conservative proposed as remedy only the strengthening of the royal power or of local authority. He asserted that Russian agents have been the secret leaders of all revolutions since 1848. According to his subjective theory, history was the work of diplomacy. Then the note (or Cluss's article) ascribed a quote to a "critic" (presumably Marx) on Urquhart's character: "He is an old gentleman who is honest, obstinate, truth-loving, ardent, overworked by strong prejudices, and totally foreign to rationality." But (added the note, or Cluss) "since he has only a single task in life, the fight against Russia, which he carries on with monomaniacal acuteness and great knowledge of the subject, all this harms nothing."[82]

It should also be mentioned that Marx took Urquhart on also in his capacity as a political economist; he criticized Urquhart's economic theory in both his *Critique of Political Economy* and in *Capital*.[83]

• • •

Before we leave what may be called the Problem of the Third Corner of the Triangle, there are four or five minor considerations that should not be entirely neglected.

(1) Honesty in politics.

Urquhart could not be disposed of simply with epithets like 'crackpot' or 'reactionary,' though these labels were not unjustified. What also made an impression on Marx, as we have seen in passing, was this: Urquhart was a *rara avis* in public life as an honest opponent of government sins who was "not to be intimidated into silence, bribed into connivance, [or] charmed into suitorship" by those Palmerstonian seductions which had changed other "foes into fools."[84] Simple courage allied with honor was not very common.

Urquhart repeatedly performed the service of bringing this or that "discreditable piece of European diplomacy before the public"; he outraged "respectable" journalism because he was one of those "who have not sold themselves to any party"; he was "a champion of justice," and "an *incorruptible* interpreter" of international law; his agitation in the factory district to organize both labor and middle-class support put the spotlight on England's pro-Russian foreign policy; and no matter what his crotchets, he gave the public important *facts*.[85]

> He [Urquhart] is the only *official* personage in England who has the courage and honesty to affront public opinion. He's the only one of them who is incorruptible (whether by money or ambition). Finally, and strange to say, I have so far encountered *none but honest men* among his followers.... [86]

This was written in a letter; but on occasion Marx insisted on publicly giving Urquhart his due, as well as making clear his disagreements.

(2) What is the meaning of 'reactionary'?

If Urquhart could not be disposed of with the epithets 'crackpot' and 'crazy monomaniac,' neither could this be done with the label 'reactionary.' He was a "highly complex figure," thought Marx, and in hindsight we can see that part of the complexity lay in the ambiguity of the term 'reactionary.' Marx tried to explain this:

> He is, I grant you, subjectively reactionary (romantic) though not, indeed, in the sense of any *real* reactionary party but, as it were, metaphysically so; ...

It has already been explained that 'romantic' was used in German political circles not basically as a literary term but to designate a sociocultural tendency, one especially that looked backward to prebourgeois times and values. *Prebourgeois* enemies of bourgeois society typically lived on the third corner of the triangle, not on the left-right line of the class struggle under capitalism. On the left-right line, 'reactionary' implied antirevolutionary; but Marx ended the sentence just quoted in this way: "... this in no way precludes the movement in foreign policy, of which he is the head, from being *objectively revolutionary*."

That is, Marx was expressing the opinion that a movement like Urquhart's furthered revolutionary objectives, or some of them, despite the movement's subjective motivations. We would urge that this should not be considered primarily as a psychological pattern, but as a consequence of the triangular social struggle involved. The Urquhartite movement could play this role *because* it lay not along the left-right line but along one leg of a triangle.

In any case, Marx called attention to the ambiguity of the epithet 'reactionary.' Metaphysical dreams* about a return to Anglo-Saxon conditions were indubitably "reactionary," in the sense of "backward-looking," but this evaluation was not to be confused with the significance of the term in current politics. In an aside, Marx also remarked that Urquhart's " 'Anglo-Saxon' crotchets" [*Marotten*, fancies or whims] even constituted "a particular kind of distorted criticism" of modern society.[88]

(3) The "liberal" reactionary.

This "reactionary" Urquhart was certainly a very peculiar kind of reactionary, Marx noted. Backward-looking, yes, but—

> ... in spite of his fanatical hatred of the French Revolution and everything "universal," the Urquhartite romanticism is extremely liberal. The liberty of the individual, only in a very complicated way, is his last word. To bring it about, to be sure, he disguises the "individual" in all sorts of antique garb.

Plainly there are reactionaries *and* reactionaries: *these* "metaphysical" reactionaries were exponents of individual liberty because of the particular type of past they romanticized. Marx's conclusion in the letter being quoted sounds a little extreme: "Anyway, it goes without saying that in foreign policy nothing much is served by such phrases as 'reactionary' or 'revolutionary.' No *revolutionary* party exists at present in Germany generally speaking...."[89] It was a reminder that the Urquhartites were filling a vacuum.

---

*How metaphysical Urquhart could get was mentioned by Engels thirty years later. Again giving Urquhart his due posthumously, Engels summarized some of the material we have seen, and added: he "had to set himself up as a sort of Eastern prophet who taught, instead of simple historical facts, a secret esoteric doctrine in a mysterious hyper-diplomatic language, full of allusions to facts not generally known, but hardly ever plainly stated...."[87]

On the other hand, Marx was aware—and we cannot omit mentioning here—that Urquhart *did* take a position regarding the existent class struggle, and it was a reactionary position. The Urquhartite movement recruited actively among the Chartists as well as in liberal and conservative circles, and the Chartists had good reason to view him with hostility. In January 1856 the Prophet published his 1839-1841 correspondence with the government showing that he had abused the Chartists' trust and kept the government informed of their leaders' plans. Thus Urquhart (wrote Marx to Engels) "identifies himself as an English police agent, under the illusion that he played the role of Cicero against Catiline."[90] Indeed, "highly complex."

(4) Writing for nonrevolutionary periodicals.

The Urquhart question under this head should be seen as part of a wide-ranging problem, which constantly faced Marx and Engels as well as other radical writers with partisan connections. It would be interesting to survey the entire problem, but we cannot do this here. In any case, we have stressed that the Urquhart problem was *sui generis*, and here we set down only some aspects worth noting.

For Marx the question was whether he should continue writing articles for publication in the Urquhartite press, at the risk of being labeled an Urquhartite. Considering his frequent *public* repudiations of the Urquhartite ideology and movement, this would take a grim determination by a dedicated retailer of falsifiction, but there was no lack of such around even before Isaiah Berlin.[91] In the summer of 1856 the Urquhartite editor C. D. Collet—who was more radical-minded than his principal, and with whom Marx later became personally friendly[92]—proposed that he write for the new *Diplomatic Review* that Urquhart was planning.

Marx hedged, he told Engels. His line of thought was that everything depended on the character of the paper that Urquhart got out; he wanted to be "free to refuse—in case the conditions were too bad or the paper was too crazy."

> ... if Urquhart came out with his counterrevolutionary nonsense in such a way that I would be compromised by collaboration in the eyes of the revolutionaries here [in London], then °of course, hard as it would be under the present miserable [financial] circumstances°, I would have to give a refusal. However, *nous verrons*.[93]

At this point, the question merges into the united-front problem, which was detailed in *KMTR* 3, and the reader is referred to that discussion.[94]

8 | OF BOULANGISM: THE POLITICS OF THE THIRD WAY

In the late 1880s the French socialists confronted a political problem that augured the twentieth century; and Engels, who kept in touch with French affairs especially through Paul Lafargue and Laura Marx Lafargue, had to deal with the sticky problem.

It was this: France faced the threat of a reactionary dictatorship, a threat posed by General Georges Boulanger: the very model of the Man on Horseback appearing as Savior of Society in the midst of general discontent and disaffection, a social demagogue controlled by the reactionary right but appealing for mass support to the left as well. One aspect of the Boulanger situation (attitudes to dictatorship) was touched on in *KMTR* 3, but a fuller look is now needed.

It is not necessary to label General Boulanger a "fascist" to see that certain problems of revolutionary policy were heralded in 1888. For a time Boulanger did succeed in gaining a mass lower-class following, in addition to the support of the united Royalist reaction; indeed, a number of socialists of various hues either went over to his camp or leaned toward the policy that was later going to bear the strange device, "After So-and-So we come..."

It is not difficult to point out important differences between the Boulanger phenomenon and the fascism of Mussolini and Hitler; Boulangism was not a finished development, and it was an early flyer. But there was also a considerable area of overlapping, which raised the question of *how to fight reaction* in a way analogous to the later question called *how to fight fascism*. If one insists, the term 'protofascist' may be applied to the case. But in any case we must understand the problem that sent the French socialist movement of the day into a tailspin.

The trouble was that *sections of the socialist movement leaned toward support of the Boulangist movement*, looking to take a free ride into power on the coattails of the popular demagogue. This was true of a number of important unaffiliated socialists, and especially of a wing of the Blanquist group;

and it was also true of a relatively small number of the "Guesdist" (so-called "Marxist") socialist party in the country. The only leading figure of the Guesdists who leaned in this direction was—Paul Lafargue.

Engels was appalled as letters from Lafargue brought this out, and were supplemented by communication with Laura Marx Lafargue, who did *not* agree with her husband's view of Boulangism. In a correspondence extending over months of the Boulangist crisis, mainly 1888-1889, Engels sought to educate Lafargue on the mistake he was making.

Since the issues involved have an even keener interest for us nowadays than they had at the time, it is surprising to find that little attention from the marxological industry has been evoked by Engels' political position on the strategy of struggle against a protofascist dictator—even though the Engels-Lafargue correspondence was published over a quarter century ago.*

Let us first sketch the political situation in France out of which the Boulangist problem arose.

1. THE POLITICAL MATRIX OF BOULANGISM

The French political establishment, representing the comfortable bourgeoisie's contentment with the republic as the best guarantor of uninterrupted profit-making, was based on the center republican party commonly called the "Opportunists"—so called because this group was always in favor of doing all good things when the time was "opportune," namely, never. It was led by Jules Ferry, whose name led the list of politicians hated by the left as one of the "butchers of the Paris Commune."

To the left of the Opportunists was the Radical party led by Clemenceau, 'Radical' being the French translation of 'liberal.' It divided its energies between assuring the bourgeoisie it was a responsible defender of the social order (very true) and wooing the working-class and plebeian vote with invocations of its revolutionary past (very far past). The Radicals had a right, left, and center of their own: on the right, those liberals who

---

*The relevant letters appeared in 1956 in the second volume of the Engels-Lafargue *Correspondance* (French edition), and four years later in English. Since then there have been few mentions. Two are typical. (1) Lichtheim's *Marxism* offered a footnote with a caricatured version of the Guesdist party position, referring only to the existence of Engels' views; and (2) the Berlin-Moscow official biography of Engels by Gemkow made a general statement about this material which is contrary to fact in every respect.[1]

used the Opportunist rhetoric; on the left, those who used a socialistic vocabulary.

Right of center stood the traditional Royalist parties, with their traditional problem of how to achieve unity despite rival pretenders to the throne. Besides the Legitimists and the Orleanists, each with factions, there were two or three varieties of Bonapartists (in the literal sense of champions of the Bonaparte family).

Arching over the Royalist spectrum was a tendency of enlightened Royalists who wanted to sink all dynastic differences in a Conservative party (so named in order to claim it was not reactionary) which would subordinate its antirepublican soul to its antediluvian socioeconomic program. An encouraging start had been made in the 1885 elections toward packaging the various factions of Royalism under the Conservative party label, which won about a third of the seats. When Boulangism became a force, one of its by-products was the provision of a single corporate name under which all Royalists could operate.

The Royalist cause had suffered a historic defeat as recently as 1879, when the Orleanist chief of state MacMahon had been forced to step down, and for the first time the Third Republic fell into the hands of republicans. In 1880 the amnesty for Communards brought back to France, and into politics, a revived left force which mostly went to strengthening the Radicals but which also stimulated a revival of the socialist movement, divided into various factions. After the 1885 elections, with the Royalists stronger on the right and the Radicals stronger on the bourgeois left, the Opportunists could form a government only with Radical support. In this cabinet the minister of war was an ambitious general named Boulanger who at this point was a protégé of the Radicals.

Boulanger had many of the personal charismatic qualities that a would-be dictator needed; but (to anticipate) it was going to turn out that he had fatal defects. In particular he was at heart a cautious politician, more interested in womanizing than in ruling, and in addition rather stupid. The hindsight wisdom that Boulanger was personally no great danger is probably true, but not very relevant. What was dangerous was the Boulangist movement created around him, and these operators did not yet know that their Man on Horseback was a poor rider. The personal factor cut short the historical experiment of 1888-1889, but does not change its lessons.

Even before assuming the war ministry, and for two years afterward (1886-1887), Boulanger created a reputation for himself on two issues: modest military reforms of a mildly democratic character, and anti-German chauvinism. With regard to the second, Bismarck cooperated fully: the German chancellor needed some French saber-rattling in order to scare opposition at home into silence. Boulanger did this job, and built a following as "Général Revanche." In April 1887 an incident on the French-German border, called the Schnaebelé affair, benefited both parties by producing a great fear of war.

In a month Boulanger was forced out of the ministry by a more right-wing government, and his position as both a leftist and a patriot was enhanced. In July the popular general was "exiled" to the provinces; the following March he was released from active duty; and both measures produced a nationalist backlash, marked by great demonstrations of support. Boulanger became a national figure.

In the course, the Royalist right, sparked by its Bonapartist wing, recognized Boulanger as a tool it could buy up, and secretly began financing his political ambitions. He became their man. But the Boulangist popular movement that began forming was headed by a larger variety of dupes, political operators, and Jacobin radical adventurers who saw in him their *leftist* Man on Horseback. The right-left amalgam that was concocted in this movement has not yet been done justice in the literature.

In a series of by-elections in which Boulanger's name was entered as a symbol, the framework of a mass movement was created, first in the provinces. Then in a crucial by-election in Paris in January 1889, Boulanger showed that he had swept into his fold not only the reactionary right but also a substantial part of the working-class population.

There was no mystery about the reasons. The Royalist paymasters of this popular general were still secret; originally the creation of the Radicals, the Boulanger image was still that of some kind of leftist. Disgust with the government and its status quo was mounting to a peak. Scandals in high office, reaching to the president of the republic (who had to resign), convinced most people that the Opportunist-Radical political machine was a mess of corruption. The effects of the economic depression of the early 1880s were still felt, and the governing parties' big-bourgeois candidates hardly even made gestures about combating unemployment and distress. Boulanger did make gestures.

On the positive side, Boulanger's leading appeals were based on disgust with parliamentarism (concretized in proposals for constitutional revision) and on national chauvinism and anti-German hatreds. Against all this, the Opportunist and Radical republicans had no social program to counterpose, only panicky warnings against "dictatorship." As Engels said, the Radicals were "driving the masses into his [Boulanger's] arms almost forcibly."[2]

2. SOCIALISTS AND BOULANGER

The French ruling class had hoped to crush socialism forever by the bloodbath instituted after the fall of the Paris Commune; but with the passage of the 1880 amnesty and the return of key militants, the socialist movement revived, bigger than ever and on a more sophisticated political plane. Long before the decade was over, there were already three rival groups, with independents alongside.

'Socialism' was not a dirty word; even the Radicals adopted it whenever convenient, as in the 1885 elections.[3] The Radicals, wrote Engels, "were all 'Socialists' in the old sense of the word"[4]—that is, the sense in which it meant little more than concern for the Social Question. Enterprising reactionaries did not mind using it either—for example, the extreme chauvinist Maurice Barrès.[5] In his last days Boulanger himself came under the influence of an odd sort-of-socialist; and the distraught general, his career over, actually wrote letters recommending "revolutionary socialism" as the solution![6] (But we are running ahead.)

Even at the start, the Boulangist committees were peppered with people who were quite willing to adopt the socialist label, though they did not allow this eccentricity to incommode their political collaboration with the extreme right wing.[7] Two of the top leaders of the organized Boulangist movement, Alfred Naquet and C. A. Laisant, were militant Comtean Positivists—and both followed up their Boulangist adventure by becoming active anarchists. Naquet was the dominant theoretician of the Boulangist leadership, as well as the organizational head of its leading committees; already in 1890, in the midst of the affair, he published a book titled *Socialisme Collectiviste et Socialisme Libéral*, although he was ideologically *anti*socialist.[8]

The Boulangist groundswell sucked in unaffiliated odd-leftist types on every side. Just as Boulangism functioned as the umbrella organization of the divided Royalists, so too it provided a shelter for many of the homeless leftists who energetically kept away from the organized socialist movement. The very model of this type was Henri Rochefort, the influential editor of *L'Intransigeant*, who became the main leftist mouthpiece of Boulangism.

Inevitably this movement also appealed to the "socialism of fools," the then brand-new movement of political anti-Semitism led by Edouard Drumont—a movement widely regarded as a "social" mobilization, hence by usage "social-ist." Drumont's best-selling book *La France Juive* had, as it happened, appeared in 1886 coincident with Boulanger's rise. Drumont's support of Boulanger remained spotty, because of the prominence of Jews in the general's entourage (including Naquet) and because of the importance of rich Jewish contributors to the Boulangist movement (including Baron de Hirsch and the ex-Saint-Simonian Péreire brothers). But as the Boulangist movement began failing in 1889, key Boulangist leaders (including Laisant) themselves moved over to anti-Semitic agitation.[9]

So the organized Boulangist movement, through its committees, talked leftish and republican, while Boulanger explained in secret meetings with his Royalist backers that word-slingers had to be allowed leeway in order to garner the popular vote.[10] If the Boulangist "wave of the future" swept up a shoal of unaffiliated leftists of all sorts, it also posed a temptation to the organized socialist groups, in proportion to the latter's self-image of revolutionism, especially as Boulangism showed that it was capturing the support of working-class masses.

The Boulangist temptation was *not* great for the right-wing socialists, commonly called the "Possibilists," led by the ex-Bakuninist Paul Brousse, with Allemane and Joffrin. Politically this group functioned as Clemenceau's tail, that is, as a wing of the Radicals, looking to slipping in a dollop of socialism when it became "possible" (i.e., when it was acceptable to the powers that be). Their socialism was conceived in terms of the statification of *les services publics*.[11]

The perspective of this group was pure parliamentarism, in the immediate sense of the pursuit of parliamentary seats. Boulangism threatened directly the only political life it knew. In classic reformist fashion, the three leaders of the tendency issued a manifesto asking the workers to forget about socialism and their own interests in order to defend the status quo against the upsetting threat.

> We workers [they said] are ready to forget for the moment the sixteen years [since the crushing of the Commune] during which the bourgeoisie has betrayed the hopes of the people; we are ready to defend by any means the weak embryo of our republican institutions against any saber that would come along to threaten it.[12]

The Possibilists drew the political conclusion of this line by making a formal bloc with the Radicals and Opportunists, in a toothless save-the-republic front called the Society of the Rights of Man (not to be confused with similarly named societies in 1848 and later in the Dreyfus case). This front was commonly called the Cadettists, from its street of origin. Its main effect, a boon to the Boulangists, was to divide the Opportunists, many of whom shunned it.[13]

While the Possibilists were willing to abandon the interests of socialism and labor in order to defend the bourgeois republic, the workers in whose name they spoke were not. Boulanger seemed to offer *something*; in contrast, the whole status quo, including the Possibilists, admitted it had nothing positive to offer. Mere appeals to defend the status quo could not defend the republic against the swelling desire for fundamental change of some sort. While the Boulangist movement gained strength precisely because the status quo was so unappetizing, the reformists recommended clinging to the same status quo that was the recruiter of the general's popularity. In the Paris by-election of January 1889 that put Boulangism at the very peak of its popular power, tens of thousands of Possibilist socialist voters ignored their leaders' appeal and cast their ballots for the general who offered a change from the status quo.

The socialist group that was still usually called the Blanquists regarded itself as the very hearth of revolutionism; at the same time it had the strongest tradition of national chauvinism; and so naturally it was in this group that Boulangism made the heaviest inroads. In fact, in mid-1889 the group split along lines previously visible: Edouard Vaillant on one side; Ernest Granger on the other, as the leader of what came to be called the Boulangeo-Blanquists. The Granger faction was aided and abetted by Rochefort, who acted as a sort of fellow traveler of the Blanquist tendency.

The Boulangeo-Blanquist viewpoint was simple enough: Boulanger is smashing the status quo; we want to do so too; *vive Boulanger!* "It is the socialists alone," wrote Granger in 1888, "who must gather the fruits of the Boulangist work, a useful work in sum, a work of clearing away, of the disorganization of the bourgeois parties." One of his comrades wrote: "Boulanger has been elected by national discontent. Whether he likes it or not, the General is now committed to the irresistible movement which is carrying our modern society toward a more perfect and more just society."[14] Thus a sort of inevitability theory was joined to a myopic revolutionism to rationalize support for anything negative in society. This visceral attraction toward an anti-status-quo figure seen as a Winner was much easier than thinking out a political analysis.

The best-known leader of the Blanquist tendency, Vaillant, was somewhat acquainted with Marx's ideas (he could read German, for one thing), and had studied socialist problems with considerable intelligence. These deviations from Blanquist patterns were sufficient, not to make a "Marxeo-Blanquist" out of him, but to temper the natural mindlessness of Blanquist adventurism with knowledgeable caution. But Vaillant was much superior to the generality of his group.[15] It was Granger who represented the "old guard" Blanquists, or, as Lafargue put it, the "real Blanquists."[16] For the Grangerites, Boulanger's chauvinism and dictatorial aims were on the same rails as the left-Jacobin tradition.

In contrast, Vaillant knew in every fiber of his being that a working-class socialist could not support a reactionary-backed aspirant to dictatorship even if the latter had succeeded in duping a lot of workers. He told his followers: "We shall be neither Caesarians nor Cadettists, simply socialists; that is enough."[17] (It was not enough, to be sure, as we will see in the next section.)

Socialists were put to the test in the aforementioned crucial Paris by-election of January 1889, when the Cadettist bloc combined to oppose

Boulanger with a pallid Radical candidate, who stood up to the general like the proverbial lettuce leaf to the rabbit. Vaillant's Blanquists, supported by the Guesdists, opposed both of these candidates with a workers' candidate named Boulé, who received a small vote.[18] In the middle of the same year Granger ran for a seat as a Boulangist and was elected, along with another of his faction comrades. Encouraged by success, the Granger group made official the split from the Vaillant-Blanquists. These fiercely antiparliamentary revolution-mongers of old gloried in the possession of two parliamentary seats. (Looking ahead, we can add: by 1893, having failed not only to make the revolution but, worse, failed of re-election, with the Boulangist movement shipwrecked, Granger left the movement altogether, as his splinter group fell apart.)

Good riddance, wrote Engels in effect after the Blanquist split: "Granger is an imbecile chauvin[ist]," and his departure is a blessing.[19] But when the Boulangist movement was flourishing, Granger's course of riding on the aspirant-dictator's coattails looked like the acme of practicality and shrewdness. Then in 1890 Boulé himself ran as a Boulangist-supported candidate.[20] Why bother to overthrow the system yourself when a reactionary dictator is willing to do it for you?

Which brings us to the "impractical" and "dogmatic" socialists who refused to climb on to the Boulangist wagon *and also* rejected the Possibilist line of a "democratic people's front" against dictatorship (to use an anachronistic term). These were the Guesdists, who were already often called the "Marxists." (Engels called them the "so-called Marxists."[21]) The Blanquist group under Vaillant followed a similar policy.

But Engels, who denounced the policy of both the right-wingers and the Boulangeosocialists, did not hold with Guesde's line either.

3. THE GUESDIST LINE ON BOULANGISM

The Boulangist crisis produced *four* different lines of policy in the socialist movement. We have seen two of them.

1. The Possibilists (Right-wing Socialists)

What do you do when faced with a serious crisis of the system, so serious that substantial sectors of the ruling class turn toward scrapping the democratic (in France called "republican") institutions and toward setting up an anti-working-class dictatorship?

You *shelve* the socialist fight against capitalism for the duration of the emergency; you establish a front for the preservation of the status quo— a front which is necessarily dominated politically by its least common denominator, your bourgeois co-defenders against dictatorship; you declare a moratorium on class struggle in order not to alienate these allies or "force" them to go over to the side of the dictator. When the crisis of the system is past, you announce a return to advocating socialism. You advocate a socialist struggle *only* while the system is stable and secure, that is, while you cannot win.

It is customary for reformists to regard this odd policy as the zenith of common sense and practicality.

In addition, we have seen that the more the status quo alienates the masses of people, the more desperately you cling to it as your defense against the would-be dictator who is making hay on its basis.

2. *The Boulangeo-socialists*

Since you want to overthrow the status-quo, and since the aspirant-dictator claims the same goal, you craftily let the latter do your revolutionary work for you. "After [him], we come..."

Without repeating previous comments on this approach, the following point can be taken as basic. The Boulangeo-Blanquists and some other deep thinkers of 1888 saw the reactionary movement as an open framework, whose political character could be determined by the Left if it really gave support. These people, who thought they were being shrewd, were innocent babes taken in by the real operators of the Boulangist movement. State power was not a carousel bauble that could be grabbed by anyone who moved into position; there were ruling classes....

But to refute the pathetic notions of the Rocheforts and Grangers seems unnecessary after the experience of the twentieth century; on the contrary, one must understand their great attractiveness. For one thing, it was a shortcut in the class struggle. Why should Granger, who never claimed to be the theoretician of Freedom, be specially berated for seeing hope in a radical-looking general—when both of the Fathers of Anarchism, who looked to the Czar of All the Russias to make the revolution for them or at least to a lumpen-Bonaparte, are still touted by eminent authorities as the embodiment of Liberty?

3. *The Policy of Guesde*

Jules Guesde, the recognized leader in France of the "so-called Marxists"—or the so-called Guesdists, in fact called the French Workers' Party—

reacted to the Boulangist crisis on what seemed to be a straightforward class-struggle basis. The working class, he said, must not make common cause with its class enemies, either the parties of the bourgeoisie or the political instruments of the Reaction. With Vaillant, he rejected any support to either the Boulangists or the Cadettists. In the Guesdist ranks there were few advocates of a Possibilist-type policy.[22]

It must be said, to Guesde's honor, that it was only his and Vaillant's position in this affair that saved the honor of French socialism. Nor did the Guesdists have to wait long for history to pronounce the verdict: within a few years it was clear that both the Possibilists and the Granger-Blanquists had fatally discredited themselves.[23]

But the job of a revolutionary leadership is not merely to save the party's honor. The negativity of his plague-on-both-their-houses attitude was justified, but positively speaking, Guesde had no effectively revolutionary position to put forward.

Guesde came out with pronouncements like "Neither Boulangism nor Cadettism!" and "Neither Ferry nor Boulanger!" (Jules Ferry was the leading Republican among the Cadettists.) This was the strong side of Guesde's position; it stated what he was against. But what did he advocate as the positive socialist response?

The Guesdist leadership insisted that there was *nothing* to advocate positively. There was *nothing* that socialists could or should do. The concern of socialists was simply not to "get mixed up in this struggle" between "two factions of the enemy class." In its electoral manifesto for the August 1889 elections, the party proclaimed:

> Citizens, let us leave the various bourgeois parties to their contentions without our getting mixed up in this struggle except to strike blows at both of them. Let us remember that if the Opportunists, Radicals, Clericalists and Boulangists dispute today over who will rule over us and rob us, they made themselves *one* in 1871 to machine-gun our people, just as they will make themselves *one* to machine-gun us as soon as we attempt to break the capitalists' yoke.

The party declared "it was neither Boulangist nor anti-Boulangist"; it affirmed "it is socialist and nothing but socialist."[24]

This argument was essentially the classically sectarian line: we socialists are too pure to sully our hands by acting for anything but Revolution; the question of a republic and its democratic institutions versus a military dictatorship was merely a "family quarrel" within the bourgeoisie, in which we do not take sides. All other parties being bourgeois parties, their differences are only "tactical divisions" designed to deceive the people. And so on.[25]

This was why the party could even declare that it was *not anti-Boulanger*.

The hollow woodenness of this position was going to be spotlighted when, a few years later, Guesde and others took essentially the same hands-off attitude in the Dreyfus affair. And this fact shows that Guesde's line was not merely due to his lack of a party organ at this time, though this lack was certainly a difficulty.[26]

4. Engels' Position on the Boulangist Crisis

The view urged by Engels took off from an approach very different from Guesde's. The question was not *whether* but *how* to defend the Republic and its democratic institutions, in such a way as to win in the present and point to progress in the future. Whereas for Guesde the defense of the Republic was a bourgeois "family affair," for Engels the defense of the Republic was even more the concern of the working-class movement than it was of the alleged democrats.

The question as raised by Engels was this: *how to defend the Republic by working-class and revolutionary means.* Could the Republic be effectively defended by supporting the Cadettist front as society's bulwark against the appeal of Boulangism? No, because the main reason the people were moving to Boulanger was in order to repudiate precisely these discredited stewards of the discredited status quo. The status quo could not be shored up with the very beams whose rottenness was causing it to collapse.

Even the Cadettists dimly understood this: they told themselves occasionally they had to outbid Boulangism on social and political reform. But they could not rise above their social roots. The realities of class interests and class power could not be fuzzed over with elocution about Democracy Versus Dictatorship. The job of the socialists was to give the democracy/dictatorship choice a meaningful class basis, connected with the real life of the people.

This was the starting point of the political line embodied in Engels' letters on Boulangism to Paul Lafargue. It was an approach entirely alien to Guesde's rigid mentality.

Guesde's "family quarrel" view of the affair implied that the working class had no interests of its own involved in the institutions of the democratic republic. For example, he wrote, during the Boulanger crisis itself, that "the structure of power matters little; everything depends on the hand, the class, that exercises the power."[27] At that very time, the "structure of power" in Germany was such that the Social-Democratic Party was outlawed: did it make no difference to Guesde if the French party were illegalized too? After all, the ruling class would remain the same; the difference would be a mere juridical detail....

Such woodenheaded references to "ruling class" sound very Marxistical, no doubt, until one remembers that depreciation of the nature of the *state power* as a factor of revolution is a typical adjunct of reformist views, not of Marx's.

For Engels, the working class and its party had a socialist stake in the maintenance of the democratic republic as the arena of social change.²⁸ The difference between Engels and the Possibilists was not over *whether* to defend republican institutions but over *how* it could be successfully done: by extending the class struggle, or shelving it?

Guesde exhorted the party militants to ignore the bourgeois family quarrel and devote themselves exclusively to socialist propaganda.²⁹ This made a virtue out of ignoring the very issue that shook the working class out of political apathy. Instead of greeting the new opportunities to make "socialist propaganda" by clarifying the Boulangist phenomenon, it advised keeping socialist propaganda abstract, uncontaminated by the social struggle actually going on.

This sectarian rigidity was counterproductive. The Paris chairman of the Guesdist organization stated, in an announcement to the press after an important electoral victory by Boulanger:

> Considering that, in spite of the infamous means used, the votes cast for General Boulanger are a threatening expression of general discontent against a Republic that has been only the Republic of the capitalists...; considering that the anti-Boulangist agitation led by the Radicals and Opportunists, who are as thick as thieves, has no other purpose than to deceive the workers and turn them away from the pursuit of the social revolution, the local council of the [Paris Guesdist group] denounces to the French proletariat the trap which is set for it, and invites the militants to devote themselves exclusively to revolutionary propaganda, holding to the terrain of the class struggle.³⁰

So the militants were "invited" to—do nothing special about the crisis of the Republic, in fact act as if it did not exist. The clang was that of revolutionary intransigence; the reality was that the issue agitating everybody else could be dodged. The "family quarrel" theory made it unnecessary to *mobilize a movement* against Boulanger, a movement independent of the "bourgeois family" members.

A by-product of the Guesdist line was that it produced no collision with the pro-Boulanger elements. Indeed, was this a by-product or a motivation? The fact is this: there *was* a substantial pro-Boulangist current inside the Guesdist party itself. And even Guesde adapted himself to it—naturally, in order to moderate inner-organizational conflict. What seemed like a rigidly sectarian line was actually useful for fudging over differences.

The most active center of pro-Boulangism in the Guesdist party was the

Bordeaux organization. In this city the socialist and Boulangist electoral committees merged for the 1889 elections, and out of this arrangement two Guesdists, Jourde and Aimel,* won parliamentary seats.[31]

A Bordeaux party leader explained to Guesde that socialists' "rectitude" and "lack of craftiness" held down their influence on political life (not to speak of their enjoyment of parliamentary seats). He also explained, at a public banquet for the happy elected deputies, that while the means used by socialists and Boulangists differed, their principles were the same with regard to "the alleviation of the lot of the class of the poor." These Boulangeo-Guesdists were parliamentarians-in-a-hurry no less than the anti-Boulanger Possibilists. In Lyons, Guesdist candidates benefited from Boulangist support, but there was no formal bloc. In Paris, despite Guesde's opposition, about two-thirds of the party's delegates voted to support Boulanger if he ran in a city by-election.[32]

There was, then, an appreciable influence inside the Guesdist organization by pro-Boulangism of one sort or another. Guesde, while dominating the party's official pronouncements, does not seem to have conducted much of a struggle against this tendency. One can see, therefore, how convenient it was to exhort party members to devote themselves to abstract "socialist propaganda" instead of organizing an independent struggle against the Boulangists' aim of taking over the country. Behind the façade of rigid intransigence was a rotten compromise. It would be unreasonable to expect Guesde to conduct a real fight against Boulanger in the country if he was unwilling to conduct it inside his own party.

Now we are in a position to appreciate what Engels' special problem was in this situation. The problem was named Paul Lafargue.

4. PAUL LAFARGUE'S BOULANGEO-SOCIALISM

Within the central leadership of the Guesdist party, Paul Lafargue was the main figure leaning toward a Boulangeo-socialist position.

This was clear from his letters to Engels as well as letters from others, including Paul's wife, Laura Marx, who plainly did not agree with him on

---

*Aimel was an enthusiastic Positivist (Comtist), and during this very period was publishing a long series of articles exalting Comte and his doctrines: "La Politique Positive d'Auguste Comte," in several issues of Malon's *Revue Socialiste*, beginning April 1888. If we remember that at least two top leaders of the organized Boulangist movement were Comtists, Naquet and Laisant, we may wonder about the role of Comtean Positivism in this protofascist development. There is no adequate study of the Comtean movement to answer these questions.

the subject.[33] Incidentally, Bordeaux, the hotbed of Boulangeo-Guesdism, was a city in which Paul Lafargue had personal roots, both as a boy and as a socialist organizer there in 1870-1871.[34]

Lafargue's divagation was especially disconcerting for Engels, whose main French contact he was, together with Laura. Besides, as Marx's son-in-law Lafargue was sometimes regarded as a specially anointed representative of "Marxism" in France—not only a Marx-in-law but a Marxist-in-law. (It will not do to ask how Marx was supposed to be instructing Paul, since by this time the father-in-law had been dead for some years.) This was a cross that Marx had had to bear in his time.[35] Now Engels once again had to straighten out this spokesman for "Marxism" in France—a spokesman of sorts by virtue of his position in the party, despite the fact that, though a facile and useful propaganda writer, he was a lightweight in terms of theory.

A preliminary digression is necessary here to make clear that the Engels-Lafargue correspondence, which is the main source for the present subject, is plainly incomplete, and seriously so. In particular we obviously do not have all of Engels' letters to Paul Lafargue on the Boulangist affair. Gaps are most evident when Lafargue urgently asks Engels to express his views at certain points, yet there is no extant reply. It is almost out of the question that Engels failed to respond at precisely these times. There are certain basic aspects of the discussion that are covered only in Engels' letters to Laura Lafargue, or in letters that had already been collected, that is, letters that were *not part of the file of letters turned over to the Institute of Marxism-Leninism by the Longuet family in the 1950s.* In the crucial year 1888, after March 19, this file does not contain a single letter by Engels addressed to Paul Lafargue—precisely when Engels would be most strenuously anxious to argue him away from his disastrous course.

Instead of hinting, it is better to bluntly state a suspicion (naturally an unproved hypothesis). It is possible that somewhere along the line, as heirs of the Lafargue family held these letters, the file was purged of Engels' letters that were considered too prejudicial to Lafargue's memory; and that this was done by sensitive and pious-minded heirs who inherited the file down the road. The editor of the Engels-Lafargue correspondence writes circumspectly that "It must be supposed that some letters have been lost; others have probably not yet been disclosed to the public." (This is translated in the English edition as: "others have probably not yet been allowed to appear.")[36] It is not difficult to entertain the possibility of a bowdlerization when the same sort of pious purgation of the whole Marx-Engels correspondence was performed in its first edition by the work of Eduard Bernstein and Franz Mehring, when they suppressed publication of material derogatory of Wilhelm Liebknecht and Lassalle.

If this is so, then it follows that the missing letters, or parts of letters, may be among the *most* important for our subject, being the most outspoken. Engels' line of thought is sufficiently plain from what we already have; we would have to extend that line of thought into a rougher drubbing of Lafargue's pro-Boulangist ideas. This might well be accompanied by even more explicit statements of what Engels meant by the "third way."

• • •

From the correspondence, whether complete or no, we get an interesting picture of a type of politics that Marxism was often obliged to combat, although (and because) it was not infrequently offered in its name. Lafargue's approach was a mixture of revolutionism and opportunism, such as we meet in this chapter often enough.

Marx himself had repeatedly criticized Lafargue's propaganda articles for their "revolutionary" swaggering: "childish braggadocio about his future revolutionary atrocities"—competition in "horrifying, anarchistic-anti-police" language—making "big boners out of ignorance and childish endeavors 'to go as far as possible' "—"ultrarevolutionary phraseology" that was really empty, etc.—often in anxiety to outdo the anarchists' rhetoric.[37] Now (Engels felt) he had been swept away from all moorings by the swell of Boulangist sentiment in the country, plus his leftist animus against the Cadettist front.

We first find Lafargue reacting to the popular "Boulanger mania" by figuratively holding his head: "The French are mad," he lamented. He repeatedly asked Engels: "Have you ever witnessed anything like the madness of this enthusiasm for Boulanger?" he reported that "People are losing their heads over Boulanger," and that "All our people [the Guesdists] are in a blue funk" about him.[38] There was a powerful wind blowing in politics, and at bottom Lafargue, like the Granger-Blanquists, saw an opportunity to attach a weak socialist tail to a kite that had a chance of making the heights. There was no difficulty in seeing this tail-ending pattern in his letters.

More than once he wrote quite clearly that we must *not* swim against the current of mass sentiment: "To combat Boulangism, Boulanger should not be attacked...." The reason was pure funk: "There is no way of stemming the Boulangist tide; the country is demented. One ought to leave the general alone and go for the Radicals who are responsible for the present mess." He repeated that it was a "waste of time" to attack the popular general, meaning that he had no confidence in the power of his own politics. He insisted that "we" must not appear to be "anti-Boulangists," but he also protested indignantly at a comrade's charge of being pro-

Boulangist or flirting with Boulangism. That is, he wanted to don one mask before the "demented" masses, and another when he whispered his presumed anti-Boulanger sentiments in private. He argued that if we come forward as anti-Boulangists, we would be confused with the Cadettists; but plainly he had no fear of being confused with the aspiring dictator—on the contrary, *this* was the confusion he wanted to foster.[39]

5. ENGELS ON BOULANGISM

Engels put his finger first on the tail-ending pattern. To Laura he wrote: let us hope that Paul

> will brace himself up for the fight and no longer say despondingly: "There's no going against the current." Nobody asks of him *to stop* the current, but if we are not to go *against* the popular current of momentary tomfoolery, what in the name of the devil *is* our business?

If the Parisians are proving to be fools (as Paul claims), "that is no reason why we should be fools too."[40]

One way of rationalizing a refusal to fight against Boulanger was to claim that he was no real danger; and in fact Lafargue kept insisting (to Engels) that he believed this—up to the day he decided that, just the contrary, Boulanger's accession to power could not be stopped.[41] Thus he succeeded in being wrong on both sides of the question.

Engels, on his part, willingly agreed that Boulanger was not *personally* a dangerous figure, that he was an incompetent swashbuckler, a political ass, a ridiculous charlatan—most people agreed on this, especially after the general's personal collapse in the face of a mere threat of arrest. (In April 1889 he fled the country, and through 1889-1890 gradually attained complete discredit. On September 30, 1891, in Brussels, he went to the grave of his mistress, and there blew out his modicum of brains.)

But the Boulangist movement did not come to an abrupt halt. Engels insisted that Boulanger's personal incapacity did *not* mean that he was a mere cipher, and that the utilization of this adventurer by smarter people could give rise to a more serious danger.[42] In this case the man was not the movement. I would add at this point only the opinion that Engels was indubitably right about this.

Lafargue repeatedly admitted that the French were prone to "clamor for a savior, a personal government," and that there was fear of dictatorship, but apparently he argued that this was so standard in France that it meant little.[43] Engels, on the contrary, thought the admission was crucial:

> You say the people must personalize their aspirations: if this is true, in that case the French are therefore born Bonapartists, and in that case we might as well close up shop in Paris. But even if you believed this, is that to you a basis for taking this Bonapartism under protection?[44]

If the Parisians "embraced a barely disguised Bonapartism" out of anger with the corruption of status-quo politics, this is a *bad* symptom, indicating that "Paris has renounced its traditional revolutionary mission."[45] Even Boulanger's downfall and suicide in 1891 did not mean that Boulangism was dead: in 1892 Engels was writing that French reaction was trying to find "a second Boulanger," and that "if that ass Boulanger had not shot himself, he might now be master of the situation."[46]

Lafargue had to insist that Boulanger was not a real danger because he aimed to tail-end him. Since "we cannot do away with him," he craftily reasoned, "we can use him."[47] The tail was going to use the kite to go—somewhere. We will see that Lafargue (like the very revolutionary Boulangeo-Blanquists) meant: let us use the Boulangist appeal in order to gain parliamentary seats.[48]

Engels at first thought this was a bit of Lafargue's usual braggadocio-revolutionism, and pressed the realities of the situation on him. Use Boulangism—how? Fight the Radicals? Well and good, but only under our own flag:

> And as a *journée* [demonstration or mass action] is only possible—so long as the people are unarmed—with the help of the Radicals ... our people have only the ballot box to rely on for the present, and I do not see the advantage of having the voters' minds muddled by this plebiscitary Boulangism. Our business is not to complicate but to simplify and make clear the issues between the Radicals and ourselves.

The Boulanger threat, he continued, has brought the Radicals to power: good, but there is no more use to be got from it.[49] At this point he did not yet know that Lafargue was really thinking of socialists running for election *as Boulangists*.

In truth, Lafargue's view of Boulangism went beyond exaggeration of its "usefulness." Early on, Lafargue maintained that Boulangism "is a genuine popular movement, capable of taking on a socialist character if it is allowed to develop freely." In this same letter to Engels, he showed he thought of socialism and Boulangism as allies in the social struggle.[50]

Insofar as this was based on a train of thought, the theory went like this: Boulangism has mass support—"And when it's a matter of the people, there are the elements, not of a coup d'état, but of a revolution."[51] This sounds very "populist," full of Faith in the People, but it lacks real content; for Lafargue was not talking about a mass of people moving in independent struggle—the sine qua non of revolution—but of a mass flocking to the ballot box in response to a social demagogue, urged to put their faith in a savior from above. This was the opposite of Engels' view of proletarian revolution. Behind Lafargue's approach was a theory we have had to mention more than once: the enemy of our enemy is our friend.[52] Therefore if Boulangism was upsetting the Opportunist-Radical establishment it had to be "revolutionary."

Part of Engels' answer appeared in a letter to Laura (at least this letter is extant):

> °°It's all very well for Paul to repeat over and over again that they [the Parisians] are Boulangists out of pure opposition against the bourgeoisie—but so were those who voted for Louis Bonaparte [for president in December 1848], and what would our Parisians say if the German workmen, to spite Bismarck and the bourgeoisie, threw themselves blindfold in the arms of young [Kaiser] William? It is plainly cutting off your nose to spite your face....[53]

Lafargue's claim in a more attenuated form was that Boulangism was *leading* to revolution in some way: "General Boulanger," he wrote in an article in mid-1888, "is not yet dangerous, but for the ruling classes Boulangism is very dangerous: it is the forerunner of social revolution."[54] This was a version of the "usefulness" argument: "he is useful to us: he rouses public opinion, which was apathetic and no longer interested in anything," Lafargue told Engels.[55] He did not explain why socialists were obliged to give political support to anything that "rouses" the public—like corruption scandals, police brutality, or capitalism itself.

In a letter to Liebknecht, Lafargue put this argument in another form, the essential point being this: "The Boulanger election [victory] will throw government circles into confusion and contribute to the breakup of the parliamentary republic."[56] In this version the overthrow of the republic *by a reactionary general* became a positive good for its own sake—if the logic of the thought were carried through, as Lafargue was incapable of doing.

But a few months before, Lafargue had given Engels an entirely different version of the "rousing" argument, one in which Boulanger was useful because "his popularity will wake up the parliamentarians and force them into action."[57] There is quite a gulf between wanting the breakup of parliamentarism and merely wishing to rouse the parliamentarians themselves (presumably to defend parliamentary institutions, in this case democratic institutions). It seemed to be all the same to Lafargue as theoretician.

In contrast, Engels told the Lafargues that the inviolability of the republic was the great acquisition of recent years, so much so that the Opportunists would commit political suicide if they allied themselves with the Royalists, as they were under pressure to do. "The big step forward in

France's public opinion is this, that the republic is recognized to be the sole possible government form, that the monarchy is [recognized as] synonymous with civil war and foreign war." Within this republican framework, the discreditment of the Opportunists was driving the people to the left: "and if Boulanger unintentionally supports this movement—so much the better."[58] But all political conclusions to be drawn from *this* form of objective "usefulness" were the very reverse of Lafargue's.

In its most attenuated form, Lafargue's argument was reduced to symbolism: "We are approaching a revolutionary crisis," he huffed in a letter to Liebknecht, "and Boulangism is an advance sign of the debacle of parliamentarism."[59] The last statement was quite true, but (again) it did not mean that socialists had to give political support to "signs" of bourgeois breakdown (like war, dictatorship, famine, crime, etc.).

What Lafargue really had in mind was a different sort of symbolism. He wrote the following in a letter to Engels, a testament to political incompetence:

> Boulanger stands for the revolution in the eyes of a great many workers and petty-bourgeois; there is no denying the fact. We should not seek to destroy this sentiment by abuse, as do the Possibilist traitors.[60]

Well, "we" should not seek to destroy *anything* merely by "abuse." This wasn't saying much. What Lafargue was trying to say was that "we" should go along with the hurrahs for Boulanger as the leader of the Revolution, instead of standing out against the current confusions of the working class. For one thing, if "we" refused to attach ourselves to Boulanger's train, they would not elect us to parliamentary seats. We are back with the statement of pure tail-endism with which we began.

6. ENGELS' "THIRD WAY"

Lafargue was not primarily concerned with program or theory but with an opportunity, or what he saw as an opportunity. He could be turned around only by making him see another, and different, opportunity: a revolutionary opportunity. To be sure, Lafargue was unable to grasp the standpoint of revolutionary Marxist politics consistently, as he proved over and over in his career—for example, on the peasant question in France.[61] But Engels tried.

In at least one letter, probably more, Engels made an attempt to explain what the party could have done in the Boulanger affair, that is, in terms of presenting a positive alternative. We know this especially from a reply by Lafargue, which began: "You are mistaken about the role which the socialist party could have played in the Boulanger affair."[62] There is no use trying to reconstruct the content of Engels' missing letter from Lafargue's subsequent remarks, which go off on a tangent. Since we do not have these letters, we have to deduce Engels' general position from incomplete statements, and from Lafargue's muddled replies.*

Engels started where Guesde ended, that is, he started with the basic approach that Guesde had enunciated. Thus, when the crisis was over, Engels congratulated Guesde as follows: "I am very glad that the socialist workers' party, in accordance with your slogan 'Neither Ferry nor Boulanger,' has closed its doors in the Chamber [of Deputies] to the renegades and traitors of *both camps*."[64]

Neither Jules Ferry, representative of the antisocialist Opportunist party, nor Boulanger, representative of a reactionary dictatorship: this dual rejection was the starting point of an activist policy. Lafargue kept repeating that to oppose Boulanger meant to support the Cadettists; and Engels kept repeating that this was not the choice. In a letter to Laura, probably summarizing what he was then writing to Paul, Engels insisted that there was a *third way out*.

(There was a slight language problem here. Writing in English to Laura, Engels used the word *issue* with its French meaning of *outlet* or *way out*—which also happens to be the word's original meaning in English. In any case, the term "third issue" which occurs in this letter does not mean a third debate-subject or the like; it means a *third way* of meeting a situation.)

Here is how Engels handled this third way:

°°Why, if the French see no other issue than *either* personal government, *or* parliamentary government, they may as well give up. What I want our people to do is to show that there is a real *third* issue [way out] besides this pretended dilemma, which is a dilemma but for the vulgar philistine, and not to take the muddling philistine and *au fond* chauvinistic Boulangist movement for a really popular one.[65]

Paul Lafargue claimed that the Possibilists had sold out to the bourgeois establishment, but Engels replied sharply: "Do not forget that these gentlemen [the Possibilists] would answer that you have sold yourselves to the Boulangists." He dug the point in deeper:

You coquetted and flirted with the Boulangists, out of hatred for the Radicals, whereas you could easily have attacked both of them, and avoided any doubt about your independent attitude toward both par-

---

*For one element in an alternative approach, it may be mentioned that early in Boulanger's rise, in 1887, Engels raised the question of what he called "the only guarantee" against dictatorial aspirations by popular generals: socialists "ought to make our people demand again and again *l'armement du peuple*."[63]

ties. You were not compelled to choose between these two follies; you could pillory both alike. Instead of that, you handled the Boulangists with velvet gloves....[66]

"Attacked both of them"? This of course was exactly what Guesde refused to do. In this letter Engels tagged on the German equivalent of the Shakespearean "plague on both your houses," viz., the famous ending of Heine's poem "Disputation."*

> ...to throw oneself into the arms of Boulanger out of hatred of the Radicals is exactly the same as to throw oneself into the arms of the czar out of hatred of Bismarck. Is it then so hard to speak out and say that both of them stink, as Queen Blanca says in Heine?[67]

To this letter Lafargue replied that the "third way" policy has been tried and failed—with Boulanger's *horse*. The reader may think that Lafargue was joking when he referred to a jape that Guesde had pulled off several months before in a by-election in northern France:

> We have tried the tactic you suggested in your letter [wrote Lafargue, about an Engels letter that is not extant]. When Boulanger put up for the first time as the candidate in the Nord department, Guesde went there and started a campaign against both Boulanger and the Radical candidate; he told those who wanted neither the one nor the other to vote for Boulanger's horse. Leaflets were distributed, people laughed over it and barely a few hundred votes were cast [for the horse].[68]

This absurdity, which Lafargue (alas) meant quite seriously, was the high point of his consideration of the "third way" policy.

The episode also reflected on the emptiness of Guesde's position. For Guesde too, the content of the "Neither/nor" slogan was not a campaign for a third way, but merely—Boulanger's horse. To be sure, Laura Lafargue had a right to be glad that, like Guesde, "Vaillant attacks Boulanger on all occasions... and is as determined an anti-Boulangiste as he is anti-Cadettiste," as she wrote to Engels.[69] But neither Vaillant nor Guesde looked for a positive "third way" of action.

To Laura Lafargue, Engels wrote that socialists outside of France were sure to be put off by "the tender treatment the Boulangists undoubtedly have had from our side." He went on:

---

*Heine's poem describes a long theological debate between a friar and a rabbi, each spouting absudities. In the last stanza, the queen gives her verdict:

> "Which one is right I know not,
> But this is what I think:
> The rabbi and the friar—
> The both of them—they stink."

°°All I insisted on from the beginning, and all Paul declined to let me have, was a clear and unmistakable assurance that the Boulangists should be treated as bourgeois-enemies quite as much as the Cadettists....

I have never doubted the really anti-chauvinist character of the [French] Marxists but that was the very reason why I could not conceive how they could think of an alliance open or disguised with the party which lives upon chauvinism almost alone. I never asked more than the open acknowledgment that Cadettists and Boulangists *dass sie alle beiden stinken* [that both of them stink], surely such a self-understood thing I ought to have had long ago![70]

It must be noted that, in this correspondence, there was no question for a moment about supporting the Cadettist popular front against Boulanger; this was beyond debate.

The Boulangists, Engels stressed in a letter to Laura, made hay on the basis of the way the Cadettists posed the alternatives: *Boulangism or the status quo—choose!* This dilemma itself was what was keeping Boulangism alive, and anything was bad "which might prolong, at least, the apparent dilemma: either Boulanger or Ferry—a dilemma which alone gives vitality to either scoundrel."[71] The first step of wisdom was to drop this view of the alternatives. Fight Boulanger? Yes, and more than the Guesdists were doing; for example, in a recent article Lafargue had criticized the general's economic policy but he should have come down on it harder.[72] Fight the Radicals? Yes, but the Guesdists should do this "under their own flag," not under the flag of Boulangism.[73]

What would such an independent fight have entailed in practice? As mentioned, Engels' letters which might have taken this up are not extant; and it is difficult to project ourselves back into the tactical features of the situation. But suggestions are possible, for example in what the Possibilists *refused* to do in the course of the crisis on the ground of their "popular front" restraint. Brousse's biographer Stafford relates that, not for the first time, the Possibilist party

> found itself in the position of opposing or attempting to play down militant action on its Left. Thus the leadership opposed any attempt to generalize a strike of navvies in Paris in August 1888 . . . likewise in February 1889 the possibilists refused to join in nationwide demonstrations which had been voted for at the Bordeaux Congress of the Fédération des Chambres Syndicales in 1888 for the eight-hour working day and a minimum wage.

They justified this abandonment even of reform measures on the ground that actions of this sort could "end with demands for Boulanger," Stafford says. Their "instincts," we are credibly informed, warned them that to encourage popular demonstrations could only play into the hands of the Boulangists. (It was for this reason that early on in the Boulanger crisis the leadership had opposed the setting up of local anti-Boulangist action committees.)

This parenthetical information comes with a delayed impact. Local anti-Boulangist action committees had the potential of uniting both Possibilist and Guesdist workers with all other kinds of anti-Boulangists regardless of political doctrines. The Possibilists had to keep hands off this great weapon; they could not act to *get the workers themselves moving against Boulanger from below* because (to quote Stafford again) they were "in the politically unenviable position" of having to be "circumspect" in defending the republic.[74] That is, they had to be ineffective in order not to alienate their allies on the right, and they could not alienate the latter because without them they would be ineffective.

As for the hidebound Guesdists, we have seen why they could not contemplate such a way out either; for the action committees would necessarily be *anti*-Boulangist. Horrors! the Guesdist line said neither pro nor anti. And so Boulangism was able to flourish until it obligingly cut its own throat with little help from the revolutionaries.

For Engels the running of a "third way" socialist candidate in the Paris election of January 1889 was a beginning. He hailed the initial announcement as "at least one step in the right direction by proclaiming the necessity of an independent socialist candidature."[75] This was the policy that Marx had promoted: "For twenty years past," Engels told Lafargue, "we have been preaching the formation of a party separate from and opposed to all bourgeois parties...."[76]

At bottom, Engels thought, the crux was the old question, the basic one: the *independence* of the working-class struggle for self-emancipation.

7. THE INTERNATIONAL COMPLICATION

There was another factor, highly complicating, that hung in the background, especially of Engels' correspondence with the German party leaders (e.g., Bebel) about the Boulangist crisis. This complication was the contemporaneous preparations going on to re-establish the International (the Second International-to-be) through preparatory congresses. This complication was further complicated: there was a factional left-right struggle going on concerning the aegis under which the International was going to be founded. France was the focus for the international plans, for the target year of 1889 was the hundredth anniversary of the Great French Revolution.

The rival plans for preparatory congresses reflected the split in France between the left-wingers (Guesdists) and the right-wingers (Possibilists). The latter had their factional comrades, such as the Social Democratic Federation of Britain, working to set up the new International under the domination of Brousse and Hyndman.

Engels was much concerned that the influential German Social-Democratic Party should throw its weight in support of the Guesdists' plans. Of course, the Guesdists were closest to Marx and Engels politically, but besides, the Guesdist party's approach was based on all-inclusiveness, whereas the Possibilists, like the Hyndmanites, followed a more narrowminded factional exclusionary policy. Brousse's Possibilists and Hyndman's SDF were the very model of right-wing sects.

Unfortunately, the German leader who had the closest contacts with the French movement was Wilhelm Liebknecht; and, in Engels' eyes, for the nth time Liebknecht was demonstrating his congenital muddleheadedness, by waffling on the issues. Engels was afraid that Bebel, as a busy party leader beset by countless other problems, might simply depend on Liebknecht for guidance on the question.

Engels dealt with the problem in public debate and private letters. In collaboration with Bernstein he produced two polemical articles (for publication in the German central organ) replying to the Hyndman group's attacks in connection with the International congress of 1889. We are interested here in the Boulanger area of the question.

In this piece by Engels and Bernstein, the "third way" policy against Boulangism was turned against the Possibilist position. The Possibilists had just supported the bourgeois candidate put up by the Cadettists against Boulanger, instead of supporting the independent socialist candidate; and the Engels-Bernstein article denounced them for allying themselves with the most corrupt elements of bourgeois republicanism and accepting "the bourgeois chorus: 'No split inside the great republican party!'" The article argued:

> As if one did not fight Boulanger more effectively if one gave the workers the opportunity to vote for a representative of their own, instead of facing them with the alternative of voting either for Boulanger or for a representative of the very capitalists whose greedy desire to pocket France's wealth for themselves... was what made Boulanger into what he is.[77]

In a follow-up article, the argument was put strongly again:

> The Possibilists, with the excuse of fighting Boulanger, fraternized

even with the men whose sins in office alone brought about Boulanger's popularity and let hundreds and thousands of all classes say: "Better Boulanger, better the devil himself than this bloodsucking system of corruption!"[78]

This article was a classic statement of why the "lesser evil" policy had to be rejected by the International. The "lesser evil" concept was infiltrating the socialist movement from the right, claiming that the socialist struggle had to be abandoned in order to defend a moribund system against something worse.

It was in Engels' private correspondence with the German party leadership that he could most plainly be seen worrying about the International complication. This was evident from his letter to Bebel of January 5, 1889. This letter was a virtual brief on why the Social-Democratic Party had to support the Guesdists against the Possibilists. After a biting portrayal of the French reformists, especially of their narrow sectism and their vassalage to the government parties, Engels set out to show how different they were on Boulangism and on resistance to chauvinism in general. Keep in mind that Engels was trying to make the Guesdists look as good as possible in Bebel's eyes; this was no detached scientific evaluation.

Here was what he was able to write:

> The Marxists, who dominate the provinces, are the *sole* antichauvinist party in France; they have made themselves unpopular in Paris because they came out for the German workers' movement; and to send representatives to a congress in Paris hostile to them would be to strike a blow at them, a blow at your own selves. They also have the right method of fighting Boulanger, who represents the general discontent in France.

No doubt with fingers crossed behind his back, he appended an example he had found of a positive action by the Guesdist party:

> When B[oulanger] wanted to hold a banquet in Montluçon, our people took 300 tickets in order to present him with very categorical questions about his position on the workers' movement, etc., through Dormoy—a very staunch chap. When the worthy general heard of this, he had the whole banquet called off![79]

That was not much, but something, even if some hundreds of kilometers south of Paris.... In any case, Engels' main point, about the Guesdists' relative antichauvinism, was entirely true.

8. ANTIPARLIAMENTARISM AND OPPORTUNISM

Lafargue's Boulangeo-socialism and its rationalization offers an insight into another important question of the future: the cultivation of confusion over parliamentarism and antiparliamentarism, especially by would-be leftists.

This confusion was made explicit in an article Lafargue wrote in mid-1888 for a Russian socialist organ, reflecting and summarizing the views he was expressing at home. Entitled "Parliamentarism and Boulangism," it was a roundhouse attack on parliamentarism, and therefore very revolutionary-sounding. Behind the revolutionary *Klang* was a different reality.

In Lafargue's article, parliamentarism (which is one type of representative democracy) was never differentiated from representative democracy in general. Readers would have a right to assume that he was attacking representative democracy *per se*. He recognized no positive aspect of the democratic republic from the standpoint of the working class.

His attack simply said that parliamentarism had the purpose only of giving people the illusion of power; they really had no power; it was all a "trick." His revolutionary wisdom was characterized by gibes like this: "Parliamentary tricks are extremely numerous—the right to vote and to petition, which afford an innocent amusement to the electors...." The extension of the franchise does not "represent the slightest danger to the property owners...." It was all a matter of corruption.[80]

What Lafargue offered was only one side of a socialist critique of parliamentarism, reduced to leftist clichés until it was a caricature. The extreme narrowness of its view was perhaps accentuated by the fact that it was written for the Russian movement, which did not confront the problems of bourgeois democracy at all.

This would have been lightminded under any circumstances, but besides Lafargue was offering this sort of attack precisely at a time, and in a situation, where the reactionary Right was itself making an all-out assault on parliamentary institutions—in order to overthrow the republic and return to the good old days of monarchism, when Lafargue would no longer be bothered by bourgeois-democratic "tricks." (As was pointed out in *KMTR* 3, Lafargue chose to hint about socialist "dictatorship" just when the people were showing susceptibility to pro-dictatorship propaganda.)[81]

The Boulangist denunciation of parliamentary impotence and corruption was popular with the naive masses, who were disgusted with what the bourgeois republic had to offer. And the naive "so-called Marxists" chimed in, to translate this muddle into leftist rhetoric—without offering a distinctive, independent socialist interpretation of the disease or its cure. Lafargue did not attack bourgeois parliamentarism in order to counterpose an advance to genuine democracy; he hedged his critique within the same framework as the Boulangists. For he wanted to tail-end the mass popularity of Boulangism, instead of going against the current. How "realistic" and "practical" a course he thought it was!

In addition: behind this verbal leftism was a still more discreditable reality. The main result that Lafargue wanted out of this demagogic attack on parliamentarism was—a few more parliamentarians of his very own, that is, socialist deputies holding parliamentary seats.

His letters were clear enough on this point, though naturally he never made the connection. In October 1888 he wrote Engels with the assurance that "we can use him [Boulanger]" in the coming general election:

> ... we shall be obliged to form a coalition with them [the Boulangists] for the election period, if they do not ally themselves with the Bonapartists and Monarchists. Thanks to their cooperation we may perhaps be able to return several of our people to parliament.[82]

In another letter he referred to some deputies who, "had they been intelligent and vigorous socialists, would have captured some of the Boulangist infatuation for the benefit of the socialist party."[83] That is, they would have used the Boulangist befuddlement of the people to get socialists elected under its cover. In fact, it was only in electoral and parliamentary terms that he could think of party policy.

> If the socialist party had men like Vaillant and Guesde in parliament today [not to speak of P. Lafargue], that is the party which would succeed the Radicals and act as a counterweight to the Boulangist movement, which is nothing but an unconscious protest against what is going on in the political world.[84]

In short, if you want to oppose Boulangism (say, to pacify Engels), first you must *support* it, in order to get a few good socialists into the parliament, which by the way is bankrupt.... The only clear thing about this fatuity was that our red-hot antiparliamentarian was thirsting for a few seats in the Chamber of Deputies.

Engels wrote to Laura Lafargue about her husband's similars among the Blanquists:

> °°To believe as the Boulangeo-Blanquists do that by sustaining Boulanger they can get a few seats in Parliament is worthy of these ignorant *purs* [purists] who would burn down a village in order to fry a cotelette.[85]

When the results of the general election of October 1889 came in, there was a visible difference in evaluation between Engels and his French friends. To take a minor issue first, there was a difference on a marginal question about parliamentarism. Boulanger, who had fled the country by then, was elected on the first ballot in Montmartre, but the Interior Ministry annulled his election on the pretext he was now ineligible. Thus (*a*) the government defended the republic by gutting it a little; (*b*) it was the reactionary antiparliamentarians who insisted on the democratic formalities; and (c) Engels, no friend of parliamentarism, criticized the government's action, in a letter. The German party organ *Sozialdemokrat*, in part alerted by Engels, editorialized that the nullification was "a blow in the face of universal suffrage, which no socialist can approve, no matter how much he opposes Boulanger."[86]

More important: Engels disagreed with Paul Lafargue about the meaning of the results. "Because Paul and Guesde have not succeeded [in getting elected], they seem to despair of everything," Engels wrote to Laura Lafargue. He thought the results were a "relative success" for the party, and cited the figures.[87] Besides, the Boulangist danger was now scotched and the field was cleared for class struggle. Yet "Paul thinks the less said about these elections, the better!" wrote Engels in surprise. The truth was that Lafargue was a man in a hurry—and this is one of the ways of defining an opportunist. The man in a hurry thought that an election either gave you a parliamentary seat or else it was not worth mentioning: this was the defining characteristic of his politics.

There was a further question about electoral alliances. As we have seen, Engels had been scandalized by Lafargue's scheme to make an electoral alliance with the Boulangists; he charged Lafargue with handling the Boulangists "with velvet gloves"; and he added: "you even talked about putting up a common list at the next election."[88] He wrote:

°°If there has been an idea of getting some of our people into the Chamber by having them placed on the Boulangist list, that would be far worse than not getting them into the Chamber at all.[89]

Such acquisition of parliamentary seats, he thought, would mean discreditment. But we know that at least two Guesdists did get elected as Boulangists: Jourde and Aimel in Bordeaux; and in addition there were the Boulangeo-Blanquists of the Granger group. When the episode was over, what attitude should socialists take toward further collaboration with these discredited men?

Engels was for treating these Boulangeo-socialists as alien elements, making no alliance with them in electoral policy, and in general keeping at least the same distance from them as from the Possibilists. In short, he favored their effective excommunication, in the absence of repentance and atonement. The Guesdist leadership waffled.

On the one hand, after the October 1889 election the socialist parliamentary fraction (group of deputies in the Chamber) was formed without the hyphenated Boulangists. Engels wrote that "I am greatly relieved that the Boulangists—spurious or real—have been turned away from the party as well as the Possibilists."[90] On the other hand, the party solicited the support of some remaining Boulangists tacitly, if not formally.[91] Engels objected strenuously to any policy of reconciliation, particularly to quick rehabillitation of Jourde, and to continued alliance with the Grangerites. He summarized the reasons for this attitude, writing to Laura Lafargue:

> °°First of all, these men have shown they are absolutely unreliable when they passed over to Boulanger, and we can only expect being betrayed by them on the first occasion. Secondly, Paul says we must reap where Boulanger has sown. Exactly so, but *reap the masses* and *discard the leaders*, as the plan was with the Possibilists; but these leaders have no masses behind them, and are themselves highly undesirable bedfellows. Thirdly, they have crept into the Chambre *under false pretences* and are sure to be kicked out next election, so that it seems to me our friends are leaning upon an already broken reed. And as to *foreign policy*, fourthly, these men are pledged *Chauvinists*.... The passage to Boulanger of these fellows was an unpardonable treason.... [92]

If a worker (Engels argued in a follow-up letter) gets over his delusion about Boulanger and comes around to us, well and good. "But it appears to me, that it is a very different thing to accept...the leaders of that movement, and not as private individuals but at their own valuation and with the rank they held in the Boulangist crew."[93]

Paul Lafargue, unreconstructed, wanted to cover the Boulangeo-socialists with a protective amnesty—he was, after all, himself guilty—but Engels would hear only of individual rehabilitation. Lafargue was especially eager to hold on to Jourde: "perhaps," conceded Engels, "he can be made to slip in later on" if he turned out to be worth the trouble—"if he breaks off point-blank with the Boulangists," and in general "makes amends for it."[94]

Behind the question of reconciliation with the Boulangeo-socialists was determination of the party's future course. Lessons had to be drawn from the experience. Engels expressed this opinion:

> ...I do fail to see the slightest real advantage that can accrue to us from an alliance with the ex-Boulangist Radicals in the Chamber. Have we not, for the mere show of a group of some 25 men in Parliament, sacrificed very serious future chances?[95]

The technical term for this sacrifice is the one previously met: *opportunism*—the sacrifice of the future of the movement to short-range gains in the present.

9. WAR AND COUNTERREVOLUTION

Hovering over the internal French problem was a broader one: the relation of all this to the danger of world war. Among the auguries of the

Boulanger affair for the twentieth century was this: it cast a glaring light on the deep-lying national chauvinism that had historically developed among the French people, including the susceptibility of the mass of workers to be swept along by this chauvinism, and on the weakness of French socialism in resisting this current.

Engels emphasized this consideration over and over in his correspondence, though Lafargue remained obtuse. Engels often translated it into terms that the other could understand more easily: the international socialist movement, he threatened, would repudiate the French if the latter allied themselves with chauvinism.

°°There is nothing [Engels wrote Laura Lafargue] that has damaged the reputation of the French abroad so much as this infatuation with a new saviour of society [Boulanger], and such a one! And has it been the bourgeois alone—but the great mass of the working class too went down on their knees before this windbag![96]

Already in 1888 Engels had begun telling Paul Lafargue that a flirtation with *le Général Revanche*, who could live politically only by anti-German saber-rattling, would make the French socialists outcasts in the eyes of other parties.[97] To be sure, as we have already seen in Section 7 above, Engels also tried to play a mediating role: when writing to German party leaders he tried to moderate their displeasure at signs of French socialism waffling on Boulangism.[98] He did not want an explosion of anger from the German comrades while it was still possible to keep the French on the straight and narrow. The coming world war cast its shadow on the International, while Boulanger and Bismarck rattled sabers on the border.

Engels repeatedly told the French, via Lafargue, the following home-truths: *Boulanger is chauvinism. Boulanger means war. You French socialists are not reacting suitably against the chauvinism of this movement. Understand the task: it is not only a question of a chauvinistic bourgeoisie; the mass of people, especially the Parisians, are attainted by Boulangist chauvinism.* The fight against Boulanger was also a fight to turn the course of the French workers.

We have already encountered some incidental mentions of this theme in Engels' letters. Boulanger has grown strong, Engels warned, mainly because he embodies the French obsession with Alsace-Lorraine. His movement "is at bottom chauvinistic and nothing else," and plays into the hands of Bismarck, who is headed for war. Chauvinism is the reason why the Parisian workers are suffering from this "surfeit of Boulangism." Lafargue, on the other hand, specifically denied this—at least he did in a letter to Liebknecht.[99]

Although Lafargue had early written about the Boulangist "madness" that was sweeping the people, Engels at first gathered that it was not a really popular movement. He soon changed this estimate, at least as far as the Paris working class was concerned. Paris has given way to the "Bonapartist element" in its makeup, and "has, at least temporarily, abdicated as a revolutionary city."[100]

After all, it had happened twice before, with the two Napoleons:

°°Anyhow we must apparently come to the conclusion that the negative side of the Parisian revolutionary character—chauvinistic Bonapartism—is as essential to it as the positive side, and that after every great revolutionary effort, we may have a recrudescence of Bonapartism, of an appeal to a saviour who is to destroy the vile bourgeois....[101]

It meant that this "revolutionary city" was far less mature politically than it boasted to be:

But what an idea it gives you of the political maturity of the Paris public! To be humbugged—what do I say, to be stirred to a frenzy of enthusiasm—by this simple scoundrel...*Pfui Teufel!* Luckily the provinces are there to again make up for the stupidities of the Parisians. It is unbelievable![102]

We have sufficiently emphasized that what was worst, from Engels' standpoint, was that the Guesdist ("so-called Marxist") party itself failed to stand up totally against Boulanger's chauvinistic appeal. To be sure, the Guesdists were easily the *most* internationalist tendency in France, as Engels kept insisting; but in France that didn't say very much. In this regard too, Guesde's sectarian line of dodging was a convenience: *Don't attack Boulangism for its chauvinism, for we don't want to alienate support; just make socialist propaganda.*

Engels thought that the newly instituted May Day demonstrations might help, as an exercise in internationalism:

In France, May First *can* become a turning point, at least for Paris, if it helps to bring to their senses the big mass of workers who have gone over to Boulangism there. Our people [the Guesdists] have themselves to thank for this. They never had the courage to come out against the outcry against Germans as Germans, and now they are succumbing in Paris to chauvinism. Fortunately things are better in the provinces.[103]

The chauvinistic French attitude that the recovery of Alsace was the most important task in the history of the world "has been far too much bowed to by our friends in France, by everyone in fact, and this is the upshot." Again, Engels pointed to "the tender treatment the Boulangists undoubtedly have had from our side." It was to be expected from everyone else, to be sure: "Boulangism is the just and deserved punishment for the cowardice of all parties with respect to that bourgeois chauvinism which imagines it can stop the clock of world history till France has reconquered Alsace."[104]

Unfortunately, Engels pointed out, it was not the French alone that might suffer from this political blindness. The danger of war involved the world. This fear, which beset Engels' last years, especially haunted his letters on the Boulanger affair. If Boulanger came to power, he might resort to war as a way out of his predicament, or Bismarck might decide to take advantage of the situation for a quick war.[105]

Paul Lafargue denied that Boulanger wanted war, and Engels gave him a lesson in politics:

> Boulanger—so you say—doesn't want war. As if it is a question of what this poor man wants! He must do good or evil, whichever his situation demands of him. Once in power, he is the slave of his chauvinist program, the only one he has, apart from his program on how to win power. Before six weeks are up, Bismarck will have entangled him in a whole series of difficulties, provocations, border incidents, etc., whereupon Boulanger *must* declare war or else backwater; do you have any doubt how he will decide? Boulanger is war—that is about as good as certain.[106]

Perhaps this was overstated, but the political point did not depend thereon. Perhaps Bismarck would *not* want to push matters to the breaking point, but it was the danger that was decisive. The main point was that the danger of war did not depend on Boulanger's intentions—or even Bismarck's. And in this passage Engels proceeded to discuss what a world war would mean—one of several such passages in this period.

Paul Lafargue had an answer to this: it was simple revolutionary braggadocio. "We are advancing to a revolution ... [Soon] the situation will not be tenable by General Boulanger nor by God himself—it is bound to explode. The gallant general will have no time to dream about war, or else woe betide him! War today means the people in arms...."[107] This implied that the outbreak of war would be answered by immediate revolution (a very old myth by this time). In a later letter Lafargue fantasized in the same abstract way about war unleashing the revolution: "It is true that once he [Boulanger] is in power ... he will turn to thoughts of war; Russia will egg him on; but perhaps the declaration of war will usher in the revolutionary era."[108] Or perhaps it would destroy society: considering the context, the "perhaps" comes in with a limp.*

---

*Welcoming war to usher in revolution is a variant of the "worse the better" approach, one of the congenital cretinisms of socialist history. A "worse the better" approach was not new for Lafargue. When the Royalist reaction won a victory in the February 1871 election, Lafargue wrote to Marx with his usual lightminded impressionism:

To this fanfaronade, Engels had in advance given an answer that the lessons of history were going to confirm: far from the revolution breaking out to stop a threatening world war, the war would come in part in order to stop the slide into revolution. Boulanger knew that war was a sovereign remedy for revolution; Engels had read his statement in the press *"that France needs war as the sole means of killing the social revolution..."* If war came to France, its aim, or one of them, would be "to stem the victorious advance of the socialists."[110]

Confronted with Lafargue's bluster, Engels spelled this answer out in letters written in the spring of 1889. It was an answer to the thesis that would later be called "After Boulanger, we come."

No, Engels told him, the first thing Boulanger will do in power is "crush you," the French socialist movement. And a terrible world war of "unparalleled devastation" would mean that the German movement would be "overwhelmed," whereas continued peace would bring it to victory. Then the least threat of a revolution in France would throw France's inevitable ally Russia into a coalition with Bismarck. The advent of Boulanger would mean a "ferocious war" and terrible counterrevolution[111]—how far from Lafargue's fantasy!

In a pithy summary Engels described what the victory of Boulanger would mean. He would

> do away with parliamentarism, purge the judges under the pretext of corruption, establish a strong-fisted government and a mock parliament, and crush Marxists, Blanquists and Possibilists all together. And then, ma belle France—you'll have got what you asked for!†

Engels wrote this, like many of his most important analyses, in a letter to Laura Marx Lafargue. I have twice remarked, in other connections,

---

> ... I think that perhaps, for revolutionaries, the Orleans people would be preferable to the Jules Favres and the blue republicans, for the [Orleans] dynasty would have the whole turbulent part of the cities against it, and if the revolutionaries are intelligent enough not to compromise themselves and not to scare the republican party, they could organize and prepare seriously for a coming revolution that would not be long delayed."[109]

Note the typical combination with opportunism: this revolution would be fixed up so as not to "scare the republican party."

†This is my translation from Engel's macaronic-English. What he actually wrote was that Boulanger would

> do away with parliamentarism, epurate the judges under pretext of corruption, have a government a poigne and à Chambre pour rire, and crush Marxists, Blanquists and Possibilists all together. And then ma belle France—tu l'as voulu![112]

that she had the better political head in the Lafargue family,[113] and the correspondence on Boulanger is the best evidence.

To our ears, Engels' discussions regarding Boulanger have a bitter echo; they reverberate with many of the themes that crippled the socialist and Communist movements before Hitler's conquest of power. The political letters written by Engels on this now obscure episode in the life of the Third Republic—an episode dim in the history books, and letters which few have paid attention to—are more germane to the tragic history of socialism in our day than several tons of marxological works.

APPENDICES

SPECIAL NOTE A | **LASSALLE AND MARX: HISTORY OF A MYTH**
A note to Chapter 3, page 46

One of the myths firmly embedded in the literature of marxology is the thesis that Marx's hostility to Lassalle was present from the start, and was personal in origin: Marx disliked the man and therefore "quarreled" with him. This story has long been copied out of one book and into another, with suitable pseudo-Freudian explanations of varying degrees of vulgarity.

Not in question is the fact that Marx certainly became personally as well as politically hostile to Lassalle, and the Marx-Engels correspondence is peppered with virulently scornful references to him. However, the facts show that this hostility started only in 1856,* that it started with a definite episode, that it was then fostered by the unveiling of Lassalle's political character, and that it was Marx's political hostility that engendered the personal element—as was usually the case with Marx.

The claim about "personal quarrels" has been used for a long time to encourage the dismissal of Marx's anti-Lassallean criticism. In good part because of the disgraceful treatment of this question in Franz Mehring's prestigious biography of Marx—as discussed in Special Note C—the engendered confusion has been rife in all circles, Marxist and anti-Marxist.

The myth can be stated in a couple of concise undocumented sentences, and it usually is presented in this way; but the evidence against the myth is so massive that it takes a little more space to subject it to the test of facts.

---

*A correction: in one place in *KMTR* 3 (page 98), this date is misprinted as 1865, though accompanying information is obviously at variance with this erroneous figure.

1. LASSALLE'S CHARACTER AND PERSONALITY

Marx's *eventual* hostility to Lassalle is typically exhibited in marxological works as if it were so odd that it demands a deep explanation. But as soon as the focus is shifted from Marx to Lassalle himself, a different view appears. The problem becomes just the opposite: why Marx's hostility was so late in coming on, and why he so long resisted the general attitude toward Lassalle that dominated his friends and comrades.

Lassalle was a very easy man to dislike as well as to adulate. He tended to polarize people who knew him: in this, his flamboyant and strident personality was both a strength and a weakness. In current jargon, he was a charismatic character, and he worked hard at being so. When Marx's later hostility to this man is discussed as if it were unique, we have a common marxological pattern: only Marx is pixillated.[1]

We will first be concerned with the period from 1848 to 1856, that is, from the time when Lassalle and Marx first met to the time when Marx's hostility began.

Lassalle's base of operations was originally the Rhineland, around Düsseldorf. In the course of the 1850s particularly, Lassalle convinced many of his Rhenish comrades that he was an unscrupulous egoist and not to be trusted. We can no longer reconstruct all the experiences with Lassalle which must have affected the Rhenish radicals; but we have an advantage they lacked. The future leader's juvenile diary was published after his death. This amazing document offered Lassalle's self-revelations so vividly that we have a shortcut to viewing Lassalle close up, as his friends must have seen him. Indeed, most biographies begin here too, including the Bernstein/Engels critique. The essential Lassalle was in its pages.

The young man who wrote this diary was precociously aware of his intense egoism (in every connotation of that word), and he wholeheartedly accepted it. The future polarization between adulation and enmity was not his unconscious fate: he *sought* an entourage of sycophants, for whom he was the Hero on Horseback riding on to glory sword in hand, as the Master. He told himself as much before he was fifteen. Even more significantly, he also told his friends, the apprentice sycophants.

This side of Lassalle was quite extreme, and one must read the details in (say) David Footman's informative biography to get the whole impact. This would provide the context for the fact that one of the first exploits he entered in his diary was how he cheated a friend out of a sum of money, and collected a debt by blackmail threats.[2] In context, this was not ordinary juvenile delinquency; it was Nietzschean superman-egoism before Nietzsche.

He was just past fifteen when he told his diary, after seeing a play:

By God, this Count Lavagna is a great character! I don't know how it is, though I am as thorough a revolutionary democrat and republican as anyone can find, yet, if I had been in Count Lavagna's place I should have acted just as he did. I should not have been satisfied by being Genoa's first citizen but would have stretched out my hand for the crown. On consideration this boils down to the fact that I am an egoist. Had I been born a prince I would have been an aristocrat heart and soul. As it is, I am one of the middle classes, and therefore a democrat.[3]

This almost told the story of Lassalle's political life, down to the point where he stretched out his hand *to* (not for) the crown, after establishing himself as the dictatorial Prince of the myrmidons of labor. Still fifteen, he mused in his diary:

There are two extremes at war within me.... Shall I aim at cleverness or at virtue? Shall I take the line of least resistance, ingratiate myself with the eminent, win position and importance through subtle intrigues?... No, though I have all the talents for it I will not become a smirking cowardly courtier! I will proclaim freedom to the peoples....[4]

In fact, the Nietzschean egoist could do both—both the proclaiming and the ingratiating. He included everything in himself, like God. At his conversion to Hegelianism at eighteen, he wrote: "This second birth gave me everything, gave me clarity, self-assurance... made me self-containing Intellect, that is self-conscious God." The born-again Hegelian found this intimation of divinity so self-assuring that he was ready to take on the world. At the advanced age of twenty and quite sane, he wrote a "Manifesto of War Against the World," a long shriek of egoism unbridled, in which (not naively but divinely) he proclaimed the Jesuit ends-and-means formula in its classic form, and gloried in his readiness to use mere people as things, as tools:

Alike to me are all means; nothing is so sacred that I shunned it; and I have won the right of the tiger, the right to tear [others] to pieces.... Insofar as I have power over the mind of a person, I will abuse it without mercy....[5]

And he wrote: "From head to toe I am nothing but Will"—self-will.

This announcement of unscrupulousness about controlling people was not written as a private confession, but as a manifesto *to his friends*, that is, to the prospective tools. He had already acquired two willing sycophants, whom he was going to use (or abuse) for dirty tricks in the Hatzfeldt case. One of them helped steal a casket of papers for him, and was soon arrested out of sheer incompetence as a thief. In prison this wretched fellow wrote to Lassalle: "I will do whatever you tell me, because you are wiser than I.

I know that once you have gained your end you will throw me aside ... But all the same...."[6]

This sketch of Lassalle need not venture into the bogs of historical psychiatry. The point is that this is the picture of Lassalle which the man held of *himself*, quite consciously, and which he flaunted before others, quite openly. That fact is just as important as the character pattern itself.

2. THE HATZFELDT CASE AS CAREER

Lassalle's involvement in the Hatzfeldt case is important to this story *inter alia* because of the effect it had on Lassalle's friends.

The case is famous: how the beautiful Countess Hatzfeldt, refusing to bear her noble husband's abuse, sued for divorce and a generous financial settlement, aided only by the poor student to whom she had turned for help. To this cause, indubitably aiding women's rights, Lassalle devoted eight of the crucial years of his young life. As the years wore on, those whom he thought of as his "party" friends and comrades asked themselves questions about his involvement—especially this: How could an alleged revolutionary submerge himself, especially in revolutionary times, so totally in this sink of dirty dealings that the Hatzfeldt case more and more turned into?

There was a second question, about the means employed, as the facts came out into the open. It should not be thought that Lassalle carried on the case, and eventually won it, on the basis of his legal skills and eloquence (he was not a lawyer, anyway). The Hatzfeldt case began and ended with the lowest forms of skullduggery.

It began, in March 1846, with efforts on the Countess' behalf to intercept the Count's mail. "Old scandals [relates Footman] were raked up and embellished. Witnesses were bought, suborned, or terrorized. The struggle was conducted on both sides without mercy, inhibition or scruple." Lassalle mobilized his pitiful flunkies and friends to spy on the Count's women and to practice petty thefts of evidence. "No one who has not read the documents of the case can have any conception of the filth raked up," the Bernstein/Engels critique summarized. "And when Lassalle emerged from it he had been infected by the rottenness of the society with which he had had to deal." To make the story short, Lassalle finally won out by outright blackmail of the Count, not by a legal coup: so Footman makes clear.[7] The whole business unrolled as one of the dirtiest scandals of High Life that ever blessed a yellow press, with Lassalle gaining notoriety as one of the figures wallowing in the mire.

It was a far cry from Lassalle's dream of Leading the People to Freedom—but he convinced himself it was one of the great revolutionary campaigns of history; and in the midst of the revolution of 1848 he worked to involve Marx's *Neue Rheinische Zeitung* for propaganda on behalf of the Countess. When the revolution broke out, Lassalle was in prison, being held for trial in the casket theft. In August he was acquitted after his usual brilliant speech, in which he tied the Hatzfeldt divorce up with the revolution and the Spirit of the Age. In the eyes of the German Communists with whom he had contact in Düsseldorf and Cologne, the Spirit of the Age was not that much concerned about the Hatzfeldt case; they tended to look on Lassalle as a brilliant fellow with dirty hands.

This was what Marx pointed back to, on a later occasion, when a *Volksstaat* editor asked him about his hostility to Lassalle. Marx recalled the need in 1848 for a "struggle with the feudal-reactionary forces, in order to drive the revolutionary elements of the bourgeoisie forward as much as possible."

> Then along came Lassalle with his Hatzfeldt and thereupon their own personal affairs were mixed up with the revolutionary struggle in a most disagreeable way. "He did dirty things," said Marx grimly, "and we couldn't even disavow him." Marx was referring to the affair of the casket theft in the Hatzfeldt divorce fight and the lawsuits connected with it.

In 1860, writing to Engels, indignant that Lassalle was striking a moralistic pose at the expense of Liebknecht, Marx exclaimed: "[This is] the same fellow who used the most shameless means, and allied himself with the most shameless persons, in the service of the Countess von Hatzfeldt!" The Bernstein/Engels study also emphasized the cloud of dirt that hung around the Hatzfeldt case.[8]

There was a third question bothering Lassalle's Rhenish colleagues. When the case was over and won, and the Forces of Good behind the Countess had triumphed, it turned out that the lasting outcome was that Lassalle could live for the rest of his life as a rich man, on an annuity from the Countess, who had been awarded a fortune in the settlement (such was the power of blackmail, as Lassalle had verified as a boy).

Lassalle's whole mode of life changed accordingly, as he suited his status to his means. His Communist comrades in Düsseldorf—those who had not been driven into the penury of exile or put in jail—watched the onset of his High Life style of luxury, for he did not conceal it from these people whom he was leaving behind. There is no use dismissing their hostility as mere envy. For one thing, they had been given to understand that if the Countess won her battle for Justice and Freedom, there would be money coming to the *movement*; but now there was money flowing only to make

Lassalle a well-dressed dandy living the good life in the Countess' mansion. Lassalle was not ungenerous with handouts, you understand.

But as a rich man with prospects and with intellectual ambitions, his eyes turned to the fleshpots of Berlin, and away from the movement in Düsseldorf. His relations with the local Communist group grew strained, for more than one reason.

3. FRIENDSHIP: UP TO 1856

Does this explain why Marx developed that hostility to Lassalle? Not a bit. At this point Marx, who after all was in London and not in Düsseldorf, knew relatively little about Lassalle's personality, and he was one of Lassalle's few associates on the left who did *not* begin turning against him for "personal" reasons. This is a great difficulty for the myth.

There is hard evidence for this—an episode which virtually destroys much of the Marx-Lassalle myth in one go. In June 1850, Marx proposed to the Cologne committee of the Communist League (CL) that Lassalle should be accepted into membership. *The committee, backed by the branch, rejected Marx's proposal unanimously and repeatedly*—even though it came, sent (orally) through a Rhenish communist, C. W. Klein of Solingen, with all of Marx's prestige behind it.[9]

The committee's letter to Marx on the rejection of Lassalle, signed by Röser, dated June 18, 1850, is extant.[10] It explained, very briefly, that "we cannot comply with your proposal," because after close observation of the man we "have found that he still holds aristocratic principles, and is not so zealous as he should be about the general welfare of the workers." At Marx's end, this note would doubtless appear vague, and (Oh irony!) he might well have thought that the Cologne comrades acted out of personal hostility.

If it is needed, there is other evidence about this episode, namely, Cologne's rejection of Marx's proposal to admit Lassalle. Röser included a brief account of it in the statement he gave Prussian authorities while he was jailed in 1853-1854. He dated it to "the end of 1850 or the beginning of 1851," either because of faulty recollection (he was relying entirely on memory) or because he was remembering a later reiterated proposal by Marx, this time written down:

> ... Marx wrote me from London that I should get into contact with Lassalle and make the attempt to win him over for the League. I assured Marx that we had grounds for not accepting Lassalle into the League, without giving him these grounds. These grounds were: that

I trusted Lassalle as little as Bürgers and Pierre did; rather, I considered him to be egoistical, and believed that if the ruling power offered him benefits, he would renounce communism; in general, held the opinion that he was not sincere about the working-class movement [*Arbeiterpartei*].[11]

A few years later, when Marx mentioned this episode in a letter to Engels, he wrote that "although I wanted to admit him into the League, a unanimous decision of the Central Committee in Cologne rejected him on account of his ill-repute...."[12]

Lassalle was in prison from October 1, 1850 to the following April 1, serving out the long-delayed sentence on the 1848 charge for which Marx's *NRZ* had defended him. On his release, he invited friends to a celebration of his new freedom, but the Rhenish CL leaders stayed away. Röser declined the invitation on the pretext that he had to go away on a trip. Bürgers lectured Lassalle about the "self-will of the intelligentsia" and the "hankering for rule by big shots," and advised: "Above all ... you must win our people's confidence." (Bürgers knew Lassalle very well indeed, having been tutor to Countess Hatzfeldt's son; but the closer one came to Lassalle, the more likely to turn foe or flunky.)[13]

Dr. Roland Daniels, a leading Cologne Communist for whom Marx had high regard, wrote him that Lassalle was now "isolated," and that his efforts at "reconciliation" with the Communist group had been rejected. Daniels cautioned: "I think he will appeal to London, either to you or whomever—I don't know whom. But be careful." Marx replied with a letter (not extant) defending Lassalle. In the latter part of April 1851, Daniels once more chided him:

> Right after I spoke to you about the charlatanry of mesmerism, for which you always had a partiality [*faible*], I must in all seriousness call your attention to a charlatan, once again. The conflict between Lassalle and Bürgers is not a personal one, and I think you are deluded about Lassalle. Along with many people, I consider him a shallow *blagueur* [humbug] and a pure-and-simple-democratic charlatan, who will one day unmask himself like Tellering. Just let him run into any financial distress, let his Babylonian-style life come to an end, and I very much fear that this "hard Spartan" ... would be capable of Persian tricks.[14]

Apparently Lassalle's membership in the CL was again brought up in this period—perhaps because of Marx's continuing support—and again rejected by the branch.[15]

The irony grows thicker: it was still Marx who had to be persuaded that the hostility surrounding Lassalle was not "personal" in origin. This was the Marx-Lassalle myth standing on its head.

In short, in this period Marx was the *only* known associate of Lassalle who believed that Lassalle's membership would not besmirch the movement.[16] Of course, Marx, unlike Lassalle's associates inside Germany, had not had much to do with him personally. The two of them had had occasional personal contact only during a period of three months in 1848, in Düsseldorf and Cologne. If Marx's "personal" hostility dates all the way back, as the myth claims, then its source must be found in *that* period. The only trouble with this deduction is that (1) there is not a particle of evidence for it, and (2) there is a plethora of evidence against it. In fact, the real state of affairs was the reverse of the myth.

A flashback reveals the following picture.

As previously mentioned, in 1848 Lassalle was in jail during the decisive months of the revolution, on account of the casket theft affair. His acquittal in August was widely hailed in the press as a victory for the left, because of his defense strategy, and so he semiautomatically became a prominent figure in the revolutionary Democracy. From late August to late November, Lassalle acted as an effective orator and agitator for the Democratic movement; agitation was his forte. In the course, he occasionally met Marx, without actually collaborating in joint work, for Lassalle operated out of Düsseldorf as Marx did out of Cologne.

In November Lassalle was arrested, charged with advocating violent insurrection in a speech, and for the next several months Marx's *Neue Rheinische Zeitung* carried much material in defense of his case. (From February to May 1849 five articles written by Marx or Engels appeared in the *NRZ* titled "Lassalle.")[17] Lassalle had written to editor Marx of the *NRZ* asking for support, and this support came in abundance. In March 1849, Marx and Engels personally took part in a defend-Lassalle delegation to the Düsseldorf prosecutor.[18]

Biographer Footman writes as follows about the 1848 revolutionary period:

> Engels disliked Lassalle from the start. He disliked his glibness, ostentation and self-importance, and he disapproved of the trail of the Hatzfeldt scandal being dragged across the austere path of revolution.

If these statements about Engels are true (Footman indicates no source, and I have been unable to find any), it must be added that this was the general reaction to Lassalle among the Communists, not a special dislike by Engels. All the more interesting is it that Footman adds:

> Marx, though alive to all this, was more tolerant. His own Jewish blood may have given him more understanding of the young man's foibles. He liked him personally, and he appreciated the substantial contribution that his drive and his intellectual capacity might render to the cause.[19]

It is not clear how "Jewish blood" gives an understanding of foibles, nor why books on Lassalle have a tendency to maunder. One thing is clear, however: *Marx liked Lassalle personally.*

In fact Marx was going to say as much long afterward.[20] This may help explain why there was a gap, in 1850-1851, between Marx's estimation of Lassalle and that of the Communist League militants of the Rhineland, who knew their Lassalle from greater experience.

From 1849 on, for many years Marx's relations with Lassalle were epistolary only, and in this relationship not the slightest sign of hostility can be found—until 1856. On the contrary, we find only evidence that Marx *liked* Lassalle, as we have seen. On one occasion in 1849 Marx was nettled when Lassalle, having been asked for financial help, made a *public* appeal for funds; but in the very letter in which Marx expressed irritation over this gaffe, he said: "I know Lassalle's affection for me, I was far from foreseeing being compromised in this way." This was an incident in a correspondence which dealt mostly with the practical business of Lassalle's valuable help in getting literature distributed in Germany, collecting funds, and aiding generally. Here Lassalle was at his best. When there was a slip-up, Marx wrote reassuringly: "I know you are precise in sending replies..." It was Lassalle who was instrumental in getting Marx some work as a correspondent for the *Neue Oder-Zeitung*. Marx sent Lassalle economic statistics and analyses on request; he sent chatty political reports such as he supplied for close political friends. On request from Lassalle both Marx and Engels sent him criticisms of his Sickingen drama, without any tone of personal hostility.[21]

Indeed we know that in this period Marx did in fact consider Lassalle to be one of the best of the "party," that is, the small circle (unorganized) of political supporters around Marx. In 1853, writing to Engels, Marx expressed dissatisfaction with the competency of most of the others, but "Lassalle, in spite of many 'buts,' is hard and energetic." Engels agreed: "Next to Cluss, Lassalle is by far the most useful of all, especially from the time when Count Hatzfeldt's wealth will irrevocably become part of the public domain. He has his crotchets [*Mucken*, caprices, foibles], but he also has party spirit and ambition, and we are well enough acquainted with the little incidental hankerings and the personal affairs of his that he is always indulging in under pretense of public affairs."[22] No doubt Engels' *Mucken* meant the same as Marx's "buts"; from London's latitude Lassalle's faults were looked on as peccadilloes.

A little later Marx was concerned lest the literature distribution problems give Lassalle too much trouble: "Lassalle is still the only one who dares to correspond with London, and so care must be taken that he doesn't become sick of the business." This surely gave Lassalle a special place in Marx's regard. In 1855 Lassalle was visiting Paris, and Marx chided him for not crossing the Channel to visit him in London. He added: "If the gates of France were not hermetically sealed to me, I would surprise you in Paris."[23] Few others would have received such a letter from Marx.

Footman summarizes: "The correspondence of this period between Lassalle and Marx and his wife shows a real and warm friendship." In his letters to Marx, Lassalle spoke of himself as "the last of the Mohicans," holding the field for Communism in Germany. This was an offshoot of his strained relations with the Rhenish Communists: when the police seized the movement's papers to set up their frame-up trial of the Cologne Communists in 1851, they concluded that Lassalle was "not a Communist"; and this saved him from the subsequent witch-hunt. Hence, "the last of the Mohicans." But in connection with the trial of the Communists and its aftermath, Lassalle did what he could, staunchly enough. Marx, who was closely involved with the Cologne defense, must have known about this, and it no doubt strengthened his good opinion of Lassalle.[24]

This, then, is quite clear: for eight years of collaboration—during the revolution, and then during the post-revolution let-down—there was not the least sign in Marx of that obsessive "jealousy" and irrational prejudice which was supposed to have dominated his attitude toward Lassalle "from the beginning." Up to this point there is not the slightest shred of evidence for the myth. Exactly the contrary: if we look to the Communists among whom Lassalle sought to be accounted a comrade, Marx was the *only* one who liked the man, as far as anyone knows. If there was anything to the various psychiatric motivations and racial theories (about "Jewish blood" and so on) for Marx's later hostility to Lassalle, where were they up to 1856?

In 1856 something happened that led to Marx's taking the same dim view of Lassalle as did the rest of the Rhenish Communists who knew the man. No psychiatric theory is needed; the facts are on record.

4. GUSTAV LEWY'S MISSION

In early 1856 the Communists of Düsseldorf, Lassalle's immediate bailiwick, sent an emissary—Gustav Lewy[25]—to London to straighten Marx out on what Lassalle was really like, as they saw it.

By this time, we must recall, Lassalle had been living the part of the luxurious gentleman of wealth for most of two years. Even before this new phase, to be sure, the Düsseldorf and Cologne Communists had been opposed to admitting Lassalle to membership. Now it was not a question of membership—the Communist League had been smashed by the government witch-hunt—but the still-remaining Communists were convinced that the rich gentleman was going over completely to the bourgeois side, and that Marx should be made aware of this.

It does not settle matters to say, with hindsight, that after all Lassalle did *not* go over to the bourgeoisie, for we know the potentialities in Lassalle's mind. The same hindsight informs us that Lassalle made a public and determined effort to take over the leadership of the bourgeois liberals' movement, and was rejected by *them*, not by his Communist conscience. From the perspective of 1856 the Communists' fears about Lassalle were not fanciful. There may also have been a needling factor: it was galling that this man, out of all the Communists in the Rhineland, should be the close correspondent of the two London leaders.

This was not the first time that an attempt had been made to open Marx's eyes on Lassalle, from various quarters. An ineffective first attempt had been made in 1853. We have seen, in the preceding section, that Marx thought highly of Adolf Cluss, who had emigrated to America in 1849. It happened that a month before he had expressed this opinion (in a letter of March 10, 1853), Cluss had sent Marx a letter about Lassalle. Actually what he sent was a letter addressed to himself by one C. Wiss, charging that Lassalle was a "clever roué for whom no means are too bad, even betraying his friends, in order to tickle his palate, live in Lucullan luxury, and give himself airs." Such a man, said the Wiss letter, "is dangerous to every party; he will not be an ordinary traitor; but he will not refuse if a very high price is offered for his ambition and his luxurious style of life."[26]

Marx entirely ignored this letter. It offered no facts, and its source, Wiss, was no Communist but a petty-bourgeois Democrat in whom Marx had no confidence.

In 1856 Gustav Lewy was another matter altogether.

A Düsseldorf merchant, Lewy had for years been one of the leading activists of the Communist group. He had come to London once before as the emissary of the Düsseldorf comrades, in December 1853. The Düsseldorfers were then thinking (or dreaming) of a German uprising, and wanted Marx to prepare for a return to Germany; Marx naturally sought to cool down their tendency to putschism. At this time Lassalle apparently even regarded Lewy as his own emissary to Marx, at least in part.[27] Given this 1853 mission as precedent, Marx certainly had no reason to doubt that Lewy was in a position to speak for the Rhinelanders in 1856 (nor is there any reason to doubt this now). Marx had subsequent contacts with the Rhinelanders, and of course Lewy's role was confirmed.

There is another strong reason to accept Lewy's bona fides. Six years later, this same Lewy not only was converted into an enthusiastic supporter of Lassalle's propaganda work, but became an intimate collaborator of his in the administration of the then-new Lassallean movement. When Lassalle founded the General German Workers Association, Lewy became the organization's treasurer. Yet Lassalle knew that Lewy was the man who had "denounced" him to Marx in 1856; and in 1862 Lassalle would have given something to be able to bring Marx around to a favorable attitude. All he had to do was to have his new votary write Marx that he, Lewy, had (let us say) exaggerated a little when he ran down Lassalle in London. But no such thing happened. There is no indication that Lewy ever went back on his previous action, great as was his desire to promote the new cause. There was no reason to doubt Lewy's bona fides when he became a red-hot Lassallean, and there was no reason to doubt it before that happy transmogrification.

Before Lewy became his supporter, Lassalle himself made an attempt to discredit Lewy's motives. It was a poor attempt, discreditable only to Lassalle. It happened in 1860 when Marx put before Lassalle the charges made by Wiss and Lewy. Lassalle counterattacked: Lewy, he charged, "wanted the Countess [Hatzfeldt] to lend him 2000 thalers," and when refused, spread stories and presumably plotted to get even by going to London.[28] If we assume that Lewy really was refused a loan, the story was still far from proving his dishonesty and even farther from accounting for the rest of the Rhenish Communists. It is likely that by that time Lassalle had provided everyone who knew him with grounds for disgruntlement, but it did not follow that all disgruntled persons lied about him.

There is similar speculation by Lassalle biographers about possible "personal" motives held by Bürgers, who had been tutor to the Countess's son; but no facts have been attached to this speculation, any more than in Lewy's case. In addition to what has been said about that case, there is a dilemma for whitewashing biographers. If Lewy's bona fides of 1856 are successfully discredited, then he must have been a sinister sort of political gangster (for reasons known only to the whitewashers), and yet it was this vicious liar whom Lassalle made his right-hand man, knowing his offenses, as soon as said gangster came over to his own gang. I do not believe this picture, but one can't have it both ways.

Establishing Lewy's bona fides does not automatically confirm everything he said about Lassalle, but (1) his picture of Lassalle can today be substantiated with triplebound layers of evidence, to an extent that Marx did not even suspect; and (2) Lewy's bona fides *will* help to explain the deep impression he made on Marx, when previous criticisms of Lassalle had been shaken off.

5. LEWY'S EXPOSÉ OF LASSALLE

Lewy spent a whole week talking to Marx, leaving on February 28. He had two commissions from the Rhinelanders: the other was to give Marx information on the local situation, with an orientation toward a new uprising—which brought the same cautions from Marx that had been necessary in 1853. So only part of the week was spent on Lassalle.

Marx sent Engels a lengthy report after Lewy left.[30] The whole thing should be read to measure Lewy's impact on Marx, for Marx himself kept stressing that what shook him was Lewy's piling up detail on detail. But we will quote only the main conclusions.

The principal conclusion, indeed, came at the very beginning: "after a *very sharp* examination I think that *they are right*." (The "they" apparently refers to an antecedent "Düsseldorf workers.") Lewy had said:

> Lassalle [is] entirely transformed since the Countess received her 300,000 thalers: deliberately repulsing the workers; sybarite; flirting with the Blues [aristocracy]. Furthermore they tax him with continually exploiting the party for his *personal dirty affairs* and wanting to use even the workers *for personal crimes* in the interests of the [Hatzfeldt] lawsuit.

Marx's letter then summarized Lewy's account of just how the Hatzfeldt case was brought to its triumphant conclusion. Needless to say, it was a story of chicanery with blackmail *not* the only crime. "Thus," Lewy told Marx, "it was not his *legal* acuteness but an altogether sordid intrigue that brought about the sudden end of the lawsuit."* Marx listed some of the "mass of personal dirty tricks, which I cannot reproduce because I forget one after the other."

The next point concerns an element which can be conjectured to be a very strong motivation for the Rhenish Communists' disgruntlement with Lassalle. Lassalle had suborned Count Hatzfeldt's manager, Stockum, with an offer of 10,000 thalers for incriminating papers; but he had welshed on the payment,

> ... and the workers say with justice that such a breach of faith was to be forgiven only if he had handed the money over to the party instead of swindling it for the Countess.... Now when he has won, instead of letting the Countess pay him for his work and making himself

---

*This summary of how Lassalle won is accurate enough to be quoted by biographer Footman as his own book's history of the outcome; but Footman says that Marx wrote it and does not reveal that Marx was only retailing Lewy's account.[29] This very odd mistake is probably due to the fact that Footman seems to accept Lassalle's effort to discredit Lewy, though without examination or reasoning.

independent, he lives* disgracefully under her yoke as a kept man °without any pretext whatever°. He had always bragged about what he would do as soon as the lawsuit was won. Now he throws them [the Communists] aside as superfluous tools in a deliberately provocative way.

Marx's letter gave more items in Lewy's prosecutorial indictment:

> He [Lassalle] still attended one meeting (a private one), on New Year's Day, because a French colonel was present. To the general astonishment he spoke in front of 60 workers of nothing but the "struggle of civilization against barbarism," Western powers against Russia. His plan seems to have been to go to Berlin, play the great gentleman there, and open a salon. He promised the Countess in Lewy's presence to create "a court of literati for her" on his return from there. Likewise in Lewy's presence he constantly expressed his "hankering to be a dictator" (he seems to look on himself quite differently from how we look on him; he considers himself world-conquering because he was ruthless in a personal intrigue, as if a person of real significance would sacrifice ten years to such a trifle).

At the time, these were accusations, as the subjunctive verbs repeatedly showed. Now it reads as a very moderate account of Lassalle's life. The next accusation, reported Lewy, is still unconfirmed:

> Incidentally, as to how dangerous he seems to be: in order to smuggle a man of the workers' movement into the police as an apparent spy, he *gave one of my letters* to him, and the man was to say he had stolen it from Lassalle, in order to legitimate himself.

This charge was relatively mild compared with some of Lassalle's Hatzfeldt case operations, and altogether credible, even though it meant that Lassalle had handed over one of Marx's letters to the police for the sake of a personal ploy.

Lewy's account then raised the gravest accusation of all, today confirmed with no residue of doubt: "The workers say further: with his diplomatic ways he would not have come out against them so brusquely if he did not directly intend to go over to the bourgeois party." This was exactly what Lassalle attempted to do when he got to Berlin, as we will see. Lewy's account spoke of the *hatred* that had accumulated against Lassalle:

> Still he [Lassalle] is confident that he has enough influence to be able to talk them around when there is an uprising, if he climbs on a table and harangues the masses, etc. So great is the hatred against him, says

---

*Here and in the ensuing paraphrase of Lewy, the verbs are in the subjunctive, meaning that they are to be understood as reporting hearsay ("Lewy said that") and not as an assertion of the writer, Marx.

Lewy, that whatever we may decide the workers would massacre him if he were in Düsseldorf at the time of the action.

Well, the reader should remember that Lassalle succeeded in talking this same Lewy around, not in the context of an uprising but in the euphoria of founding a new socialist movement.

Marx wound up his letter to Engels with what he began, after apologizing for providing only patchy details:

> The *whole* has made a *definitive* impression on me and Freiligrath, however much I was predisposed in favor of Lassalle and however distrustful I am of workers' gossip.

With Lewy he was circumspect, expressed no opinion or conclusion, pointed out politely that he still had to get Lassalle's side, counseled against "any open rupture," and so on. We have seen that Marx was to be taken literally when he wrote at the end: "however much I was predisposed in favor of Lassalle." This was written to Engels, who could not have been fooled about Marx's attitude to Lassalle.

We have seen some evidence that Lewy's denunciation did not come out of the blue. Other indications can be cited to show that Marx must have been hearing things about Lassalle for years, brushing them aside like Wiss's letter. We know that around this period one of the Rhenish Communists whom Marx valued most, Roland Daniels, wrote him with a distrustful view of Lassalle.

Daniels' letter made clear that he had previously warned Marx against "the charlatanry of mesmerism, for which you have always had a weakness." For 'mesmerism' read *charisma* in today's jargon; Daniels was obviously referring to Marx's "weakness" for Lassalle, well known to his Rhenish friends. Daniels went on to say clearly: "I think you are mistaken in Lassalle. Along with many, I regard him as a superficial humbug and a Democratic charlatan...." We see again that Marx had been holding on to his "mistaken" view of Lassalle against repeated advice and pressure from the Rhinelanders who knew him. The biographer of Lassalle who quotes the Daniels letter, though leaning toward a whitewash, mentions "the distrust of Lassalle, which the Cologne Communists had so long striven in vain to infect Marx with."[31]

Now at long last Marx was beginning to see Lassalle as his Rhineland friends had long seen the man. As for the Marx-Lassalle myth about Marx's alleged "jealousy": at this juncture there was no reason to be jealous or envious about Lassalle *politically*; Lassalle was at a dead end. His immediate objective was to get permission from the Prussian government to move to Berlin. The Bernstein/Engels study has noted the "self-abnegation" of his petition to the government (polite language for its air of crawling before power). One of the loyalist arguments that Lassalle made in this petition was that the police would find it easier to watch him in Berlin.[32] In point of fact, the Berlin chief of police did decide to issue the order: *he* at least was convinced that Lassalle wanted to go over to the camp of the respectables; and if the Rhenish Communists were convinced too, it is not fair to charge them with unworthy motives.

6. WHO BROKE WITH WHOM?

From here on in the Marx-Lassalle story, politics takes over—first in its philosophical guise. For Lassalle first came forward as a philosopher.

In 1857 Lassalle published his scholarly work on Heraclitus. Marx could see clearly that Lassalle was thoroughly stuck in the old Hegelian idealist rut, as was true also of his last theoretical work, *The System of Acquired Rights* (1861).

> As a confirmed Hegelian of the old school [wrote Engels later, of the last-named work] Lassalle derived the provisions of the Roman law not from the social conditions of the Romans, but from the 'speculative conception' of the will, and thus arrived at this totally unhistoric assertion.[33]

Psychiatric biographers do not have to understand these issues: sufficient for them is the fact that Marx (privately) excoriated these works, and so no evidence is needed that Marx was "jealous." The fact that the philosophic content of these works was indubitably *old*-Hegelian idealism is, to them, only a technical detail of no interest. Marx, however, did not belong to this school of criticism.

When Lassalle published his verse drama on Franz von Sickingen in 1859, Marx—like anyone who actually read the stuff—could see the overtly elitist approach to revolution that it embodied. When Lassalle published his political pamphlet on the "Italian War" (Austria and Italy versus Prussia) of 1859, Marx could read, in plain German, that the author looked to Prussia to rule Germany's future. For analyses of these Lassalle writings indicating how Marx saw them, see the Bernstein/Engels critique.[34]

By 1862 Marx felt that they were poles apart, agreeing "on nothing except some far-distant ultimate ends."[35] This was the outcome of a rather slow development, as Lassalle unveiled his politics. It had been about six and a half years since Lewy's visit.

In 1862 when Lassalle visited London, the two men met for only the second time since 1848. As is well known, Marx's revulsion against Lassalle's character and personality, as well as his political views, came to a head as a result of this close encounter. But the personal antagonism itself had political elements, as well as being overshadowed by outright political differences.

On the personal side: there was the contrast between the rich gentleman, who could casually "lose 5000 thalers in a bad speculation" and spend over a pound daily on cabs and cigars—and the Marx household, beset by bills from the butcher and baker for necessities, and dogged by misery, so that Jenny Marx "had to take to the pawnshop everything that was not nailed down" in order to "maintain a certain exterior" for the visitor. Was it purely a personal characteristic? "This parvenu slapping his moneybags" had the effrontery to suggest a solution: let one of the Marx daughters come to serve the Countess as "companion"! All aristocrats knew this solution for the problems of poor relations and importunate peasants.

All this Marx reported to Engels as "amusing."[36] It is quite in order to make profound analyses of the bitter envy nurtured among the Marx family, amidst their misery, as the rich gentleman strutted before them—calling himself a communist. It is undoubtedly true, if not very profound, to deduce that Marx wanted to shout harsh insults at him. It is permissible to doubt the cheeriness with which they laughed at the posturing braggart, even as they reported his airs.

> He now takes himself to be not only the greatest scholar, deepest thinker, most brilliant researcher, etc., but in addition Don Juan and a revolutionary Cardinal Richelieu. Besides, there's the continual chatter in the sham-falsetto voice, the unesthetic demonstrative gestures, the didactic tone!

Lassalle told them the "deep secret" of how behind the scenes he was advising Garibaldi on how to carry on his campaigns and how "to set himself up as a dictator," and of his high-level relations with other movers and shakers. Lassalle (continued Marx's account) "presented himself to these people as 'representative of the revolutionary German working class,'" preventer of Prussia's intervention through his pamphlet on the Italian War, and in fact the presiding genius over "the history of the last three years."

> Lassalle was very furious at me and my wife because we made merry about his plans, chaffed him as an "enlightened Bonapartist," etc. He yelled, roared, jumped about, and finally was thoroughly convinced that I am too "abstract" to understand politics.
> As to America, it is, he says, quite uninteresting. The Yankees have no "ideas." "Individual liberty" is only a "negative idea," etc., and more of this old, decaying speculative rubbish.[37]

This is all "personal," but obviously also political. Jenny Marx drew a similar "personal" picture of Lassalle's 1862 visit to the Marx household, with a more impish sort of irony—this in a short autobiographical sketch:

> He was almost crushed under the weight of the fame he had achieved as a scholar, thinker, poet and politician.... There were still fields of science that he had not explored! Egyptology lay fallow: "Should I astonish the world as an Egyptologist or show my versatility as a man of action, as a politician, as a fighter, or as a soldier?" It was a splendid dilemma. He wavered between the thoughts and sentiments of his heart and often expressed that struggle in really stentorian accents. As on the wings of the wind he swept through our rooms, perorating so loudly, gesticulating and raising his voice to such a pitch that our neighbors were scared by the terrible shouting and asked us what was the matter. It was the inner struggle of the "great" man bursting forth in shrill discords.[38]

That this description was no exaggeration was shown by Lassalle's youthful diary.

This was also how Lassalle operated in "his" workers' movement, except less restrainedly. In London, as Jenny remarked, he had with him "his faithful companion Lothar Bucher, who... performed for him the duties of messenger, informer, errand boy and entertainer." In Berlin he had a larger entourage of followers, to whom he was the enlightened Bonaparte; the very constitution of his General German Workers Association (GGWA) made it a personal dictatorship. It was very difficult not to get "personal" about Ferdinand Lassalle. A Lothar Bucher enjoyed groveling before him—Bucher did the same flunky service for Bismarck—but Marx was another matter. As McLellan writes, mildly: "It must indeed have been difficult for Marx to tolerate long the company of a man who could, with complete self-assurance, begin a speech with the words: 'Working men! Before I leave for the Spas of Switzerland...' "[39]

There is a revelatory anecdote about Lassalle as he went on an 1863 speaking tour, told by Paul Lindau, the friend who later edited Lassalle's juvenile diary. Note that it typically begins: "He did not disguise the fact that..."

> He did not disguise the fact that his political campaign had its disagreeable side for him. "Believe me," he said, "a man of my way of life and my social inclinations... speaking to packed houses in an unbreathable atmosphere.... I have a real horror of workers' deputations where I always hear the same speeches and have to shake hard, hot and moist hands. I hate to be touched. But there it is. One must go through with it. But I think that in the not too distant future I shall be able to devote myself to the direction of the movement, without the need for taking the field in person...."[40]

Lindau remarked that for these occasions he wore suits so elegant that

Lindau had never seen their like except on the stage. The idea was to put hoi polloi in their place. It would be invidious to bring this up, perhaps, except that people who were understandably repelled by this Lassalle persona are often slandered as "jealous" wretches.

There was a sequel to the story of Lassalle's 1862 visit to Marx. There was some correspondence on a money matter, for Marx was in great financial distress and took amiss Lassalle's hedging about making a loan. In any case, on November 7 Marx wrote him a remarkable letter, reading in every line as a letter of apology after a contretemps, with the aim of getting back to friendly relations. He even said flatly that he had been wrong, though he chided Lassalle for reacting as a lawyer or prosecutor "when I was in the state of mind where I wanted to put a bullet through my head." He added: "I hope, therefore, that our old relationship will continue unspoiled 'in spite of all.' "[41]

It was an amazing letter. The only other person who ever received a letter like this from Marx was Friedrich Engels. Footman's estimation is entirely valid:

> Coming from a man as proud, bitter and unhappy as Marx was then, it was a generous letter. But for Lassalle, smarting under his real and imagined slights, it was not enough. He did not answer; and the break with his former friend and leader was now final and complete.[42]

Lassalle did not answer!

It was he, not Marx, who definitively broke off all personal relations for the future. Why? Besides the obvious explanations of Lassalle's character, there was a political motive at hand. For by this time Lassalle must have been quite cured of the illusion that he could enlist Marx as house theoretician for the coming Lassalle political empire in Germany.

There was not much time to repair the situation. By August 1864 Lassalle was dead, killed in a stupid duel over a woman. All of the oratory that has been lavished on Lassalle's historic accomplishment in launching the GGWA refers to a period of about two years. There are few "historic accomplishments" that have been bought from history so cheaply.

7. THE MYTH OF THE CREATOR

We must take special note of the most persistent of the myths around Lassalle. It was based on Lassalle's campaign work of about one year, from the spring of 1862 when he issued his "Open Reply" to the spring of 1863 when the General German Workers Association was founded.

A typical statement of the myth was the one issued in 1913 by Franz

Mehring: Lassalle's "flaming word kindled the revolutionary workers' movement in Germany." A modern historian has turned myth into bombast: the GGWA "was created by Ferdinand Lassalle, almost out of thin air. . . ."[43] The Spirit of Ferdinand moved upon the face of the waters, and said, Let there be a movement.

Marx conceded an attenuated form of the myth, in order to make his *political* critique of Lassalleanism: "After fifteen years of slumber, Lassalle—and this remains his immortal service—reawakened the workers' movement in Germany."[44] So wrote Marx to Schweitzer to introduce his critique of Lassalle's views. But the statement was not true.

It was not true that Lassalle had called a movement into being (or "kindled" or "reawakened" it). He did something else to it. There is no question about the factual side today, though it is hard to say how much of it was known to Marx at the time. The facts are commonly ignored or reduced to background curiosa, because of historians' mind sets that glorify leaders and downplay workers' movements from below.

The German workers' movement started stirring from its fifteen years of slumber in the early 1860s.[45] Leipzig was in the van; in February 1861 a Workers' Educational Association was founded there, linked with bourgeois reform circles and the Progressive Party of bourgeois liberalism; it had a strong interest in cooperatives and insurance, trade-unionism being illegal. This was a common pattern elsewhere.

In 1862 the Progressives sent twelve of "their" workers to the London International Exhibition. Just as this British event acted as a center of infection which familiarized the French workers with British trade-unionism and cooperatives and soon led in stages to the founding of the International, so too the German worker-delegates were contaminated by British ideas and examples of independent workers' organization. On their return, these workers gave reports to meetings and spread their impressions of the new reality they had seen in Britain. In contrast, that same year a guildsmen's congress had met in Weimar and had alienated more modernized workers by its reactionary backward-looking demands for medieval privileges. In August Berlin workers came together to hear a report on the brave new London world, and there were other meetings.

In October a committee of twenty-five was set up to prepare for a workers' congress (as distinct from the guildsmen's congress). The Leipzig workers' societies were organizing on the same road; they elected a Central Committee of workers' organizations to prepare the congress. The Berliners and Leipzigers joined in calling for a workers' congress to be held in Leipzig. An organ, the *Arbeiter-Zeitung*, was already being issued from Leipzig, and its very name was a call for modernism.

In January 1863 a deputation of the Leipzig workers' Central Committee—comprising two workers, F. W. Fritzsche (soon to be a leading trade-union organizer) and Julius Vahlteich (soon to be the secretary of the Lassallean party) plus a writer, Dr. Otto Dammer—went to Berlin to make a last attempt to organize cooperation with the Progressives. In vain; they received the classic answer that the workers should consider themselves "honorary members" of the bourgeois organization, that is, non-voting "members." At this point they were ready to go on their own. A young liberal named Löwe directed their attention to Lassalle, and they entered into communication with him.

Lassalle's career was at a turning point.[46] While the workers' movement was thus being "kindled" and "reawakened," the man of the Flaming Word had just finished his efforts to go over to the bourgeois progressives, as his Rhenish comrades had foreseen. But he was no ordinary turncoat—not by a long shot. He would enter that camp as its Leader, or nothing. He had been looking for some way to insert himself into the political arena as the shining knight of Progress, and he had found that the Progressives were too timorous to accept him as leader. In an address ("What Now?") in December, he had made a sweeping proposal to the Progressives: that they fight the government by refusing to cooperate in the Reichstag; the government would be forced to yield, "the hand at the throat, the knee on the breast." This was his bid for a common front with the Progressives against the absolutist government, if they accepted his leadership. But militant leadership was not what the Progressives were looking for; this was no revolutionary bourgeoisie.

So Lassalle's bid for the leadership of the main bourgeois party was crumbling when the Leipzig workers were casting about for a mouthpiece. Lassalle arranged with the Leipzigers to present him with a public query on the mission of the workers' movement. This they did: in an "Appeal to the German Workers" on February 10, they declared for a workers' congress, and under date February 11 they sent a letter to Lassalle requesting him to express his views. (This whole *comédie* testifies to the workers' lack of class-conscious self-confidence, but that is another history.)

Lassalle's response was his "Open Reply" of March 1, 1863, which Social-Democracy later celebrated as the inauguration of the movement. It was the inauguration of Lassalle's socialistic agitation. From this point Lassalle took over the burgeoning movement completely, as its *Führer*, and put it into his own livery.

Since these facts are not controversial, the question is whether they mean that Lassalle's "flaming word kindled" etc., or even that he "reawakened" the movement (let alone the theory of the "thin air"). Here are two propositions:

(1) The movement was already quite reawakened when Lassalle got his

hands on it. *It was this reawakened movement that got in touch with Lassalle, not the other way round.* And it got in touch with him because it was *already* orienting toward workers' organization. The accomplishment by Lassalle was to steer this burgeoning movement into his own service and into the blind alley of his own political crotchets, that is, into Lassalleanism—for a whole period.

This interpretation was stated flatly in the Bernstein/Engels study. Its last paragraph said: "Lassalle no more created German Social Democracy than any other man. We have seen how great were the stir and ferment among the advanced German workers, when Lassalle placed himself at the head of the movement." It went on to give Lassalle due credit for services as an agitator and elementary educator of this movement[47]—a dubious boon. The myth of the Creation came a few years later, after Engels' death and Bernstein's emergence as the theoretician of Revisionism.*

(2) What if there had been no Lassalle? Such "iffy" questions are usually unanswerable; not so in this case. A new leadership was already emerging, especially in Leipzig, and in fact it was this new cadre that made the movement an organizational reality while Lassalle made the flaming speeches. The man who became the GGWA secretary, Julius Vahlteich, came from this new cadre. Among the Leipzig workers was a young turner named August Bebel. These new militants were shortly going to organize a movement *against* the Lassalleans, leading to the so-called Eisenacher party.

Besides, there was the old cadre of Communists, who contributed another experienced element to the new GGWA. At its founding congress in Leipzig on May 23, 1863, the delegates from ten cities were not people who had been called into being by Lassalle's flaming word. This was the point that Engels made in an article published in 1869:

> It has been customary in Germany to see Ferdinand Lassalle as the founder of the German workers' movement. And yet there is nothing more erroneous. If six or seven years ago the proletariat in mass flocked to him in all the factory districts, in all the big cities, the centers of working-class population; if his tours were triumphal processions that reigning princes could envy: was not the soil already

---

*Bernstein's first retreat from his 1928 study appeared in a 1902 article.[48] Then in 1904 appeared the scholarly biography of Lassalle by Hermann Oncken, a nonsocialist, celebrating Lassalle as the real founder of Social-Democracy. Also in 1904 Bernstein came out with his new line in a work titled *Ferdinand Lassalle und seine Bedeutung für die Arbeiterklasse*. In 1911 his brochure *Von der Sekte zur Partei* pushed his new view even more brashly. In 1919 he published a rewritten version of his 1928 study under the title *Ferdinand Lassalle, Eine Würdigung* (. . . An Appreciation). In these four stages, the Revisionist revised himself.

fertilized on the quiet, that the fruit it bore sprouted so quickly?* If the workers applauded his teachings with cheers, did this happen because these teachings were new to them or because they had already been more or less familiar long ago to the thinking people among them?

The present generation lives fast and forgets fast. The movement of the 1840s, which culminated in the revolution of 1848 and came to its end in the reaction of 1849-1852, is already forgotten along with its political and socialist literature. It must therefore be recalled that before and during the revolution of 1848, among the workers particularly of western Germany there existed a well-organized socialist party. To be sure, it collapsed after the Cologne Communist trial, but individual members continued quietly to prepare the ground which subsequently Lassalle took over.[49]

There *was* a reawakening of these ex-Communist League elements. They supplied a significant part of the cadre that formed the GGWA and got it working.[50] These elements had indeed been in suspended animation; a reborn workers' movement such as the Leipzigers were getting under way, with or without Lassalle, would have called them back to life.

Then in a year there was still another rallying center coming into existence: the International. But when the International did get going and started reaching out to Germany, *the German field had already been pre-empted by Lassalleanism.* This was a fateful fact for the history of German socialism.[51]

The fact that Lassalle put his imprint on the new movement meant that it was cradled in the swaddling clothes of a bureaucratic dictatorship, nurtured on state-cultist politics, and educated in the spirit of the Cult of the Individual Leader. *That* was the flame that Lassalle kindled. Naturally all this was already in the air, in bourgeois politics even more than in socialist; Lassalle did not invent it; but that is not our question, and we need not make Lassalle out to be a devil in order to prove he was not the Creator. It is the Lassalle myth that is in question.

The Lassallean pre-emption of the burgeoning movement did not mean the gift of independent organization from a shining knight but rather the injection of a toxin.

8. ENGELS' CAMPAIGN AGAINST THE LASSALLE MYTH

In 1891, when the German party was getting ready to adopt a new program at its Erfurt congress, Engels precipitated something of a party crisis

---

*This picture of Lassalle's mass influence is much exaggerated, no doubt absorbed by Engels from Lassallean claims. If anything, Engels gives Lassalle too much credit.

by publishing a suppressed document: Marx's 1875 letter to the party leadership known as his "Critique of the Gotha Program." There were two bombshells in this document: there was its revolutionary content (typified by its use of the disconcerting expression "revolutionary dictatorship of the proletariat"), and there was its revelation of Marx's attitude toward Lassalle's politics.

The party leadership, especially Liebknecht, tried—once again and still—to suppress its publication, and might well have succeeded if Engels had not been alive to defy them. He got it published, in the party press to boot, with some applied pressure on Kautsky's jugular. On its appearance, the whole pack of cards flew up in the air. The "old Lassalleans" yelled with fury at this desecration of their idol; the party bureaucrats held their heads at all this boat-rocking. A party deputy made sure to repudiate Marx's document on the floor of the Reichstag, so that all the right people might hear. For a while the party leaders, including Bebel, broke off all relations with Engels; he was sent to Coventry for breaking the conspiracy to conceal Marx's views.

It is often assumed that the party leaders were put out mainly because of the revolutionary reference to the "dictatorship of the proletariat," but while this certainly worsened the offense, it was not what produced the deep-lying animus against Engels. This can be seen, among other evidence, from the letter written by Engels to Kautsky, who had to be bucked up. It was almost all about the Lassalle myth—the historical record had to be set straight:

> Lassalle has belonged to history for twenty-six years. While under the Anti-Socialist Law historical criticism of him was left in abeyance, the time is at last at hand when it must have its say and Lassalle's position in relation to Marx be made plain. The legend that conceals and glorifies the true image of Lassalle can surely not become an article of faith of the party.

He disabused Kautsky of the "shining knight" fable:

> However highly one may estimate Lassalle's services to the movement, his historical role in it remains an equivocal one. Lassalle the socialist is dogged at every step by Lassalle the demagogue. Everywhere Lassalle the conductor of the Hatzfeldt lawsuit shows through Lassalle the agitator and organizer: the same cynicism in the choice of means, the same preference for surrounding himself with shady and corrupt people who can be used as mere tools and discarded.

He put a finger on the reality of Lassalle's politics:

> Until 1862 a specifically Prussian vulgar democrat in practice,* with

---

*That is, since getting into Berlin politics after moving from the Rhineland.

strong Bonapartist leanings (I have just looked through his letters to Marx), he suddenly switched round for purely personal reasons and began his agitation; and before two years had gone by, he was demanding that the workers should take the part of the monarchy against the bourgeoisie, and intriguing with Bismarck, akin to him in character, in a way that would certainly have led to the actual betrayal of the movement, if fortunately for him he had not been shot in time.

And he went on to declare war on the myth, with a further threat:

> It was my duty finally to settle accounts between Marx and Lassalle. That has been done. For the time being I can content myself with that. Moreover, I myself have other things to do now. And the published ruthless judgment of Marx on Lassalle will have its effect by itself and give others courage. But should I be forced to it, there would be no choice for me: I should have to make a clean sweep of the Lassalle legend once and for all.[52]

To Bebel, who was worrying about party unity, Engels emphasized the line of *Here I stand, I can do no other*, pointing out that he had kept silent about "the Lassalle cult inside the party" as long as the Anti-Socialist Law made party discussion difficult (i.e., till 1890).

> An end had to be put to it [the cult], and this I promoted. I will no longer permit Lassalle's false glory to be maintained and preached anew *at Marx's expense*. The people who knew Lassalle personally and adulated him are thinly sown; in the case of all others the Lassalle cult is *purely fabricated*, fabricated by our silent sufferance against our better knowledge, and therefore does not even have the justification of being due to personal devotion.

It was wrong to promote a lie for the alleged good of the party: "But in general I cannot concede that in such matters historical truth must be pushed aside—after fifteen years of meek patience—to suit the convenience of the party and the possibility of giving offense inside it."

The cry that Marx was merely "jealous" of Lassalle's glory had been raised immediately, virtually as a reflex action of the Lassalle cultists; it was not invented by marxologists. Engels simply dismissed it with contempt: "And if it is said that Marx was jealous of Lassalle... this bothers me less than a flea bite."[53]

Engels could see the Lassalle myth being "fabricated" not only in Germany but before his very eyes in England, and he noted one of the driving reasons: "the bourgeois-tinged socialists in this country [England]," he wrote, "are also trying to make Lassalle a legend as against Marx."[54] The reformists needed a figure to rally around *as against Marx*. Lassalle provided such an alternative, or at least the myth did.

For one thing, the Lassalle image played this role especially for those who wanted a patriotic-nationalist-German kind of radical to counterpose to the internationalist Marx. "The enemy press *lives* on the opposition of the *national* Lassalle to the *fatherlandless* Social-Democrats," wrote Engels in the letter just quoted.[55] In an article in the *Neue Zeit* the still-unrevised Bernstein had made a similar point: the Lassalle legend "is cultivated nowadays, to be sure, less by socialist supporters of Lassalle than by hysterical bourgeois littérateurs."[56] One of the most prominent enemies of the Social-Democratic Party had made such a notable attack on the party a few years before, and indeed Engels and Bernstein may have well had him in mind. This glorifier of the good nationalist Lassalle against the bad internationalist Marx was Franz Mehring, who was not yet under the impression he was a Marxist.

The whole process of leaching Marxism out of the German Social-Democratic tradition, and replacing its bones with Lassallean fossils, may be better seen in historical perspective if we mention now the end-result, the terminal point, of this process. This came in 1959 at the Bad Godesberg congress of the Social-Democratic Party, which is best known for its complete elimination of any socialistic plank from the new party program. At the same time this party made a symbolic change: for the first time it formally threw Marx's name out of the place of honor in its program, and replaced it with the name of Lassalle. The fact that at this late date the party bothered to perform the symbolic rite at all—like switching statuettes in a church niche—shows its significance: "Lassalle" was simply a way of repudiating Marx. That had been true since 1875, when this allegedly "Marxist party" first suppressed Marx's critique of Lassalle.

9. THE BERNSTEIN/ENGELS CRITIQUE OF LASSALLE

Let us now explain more fully why Bernstein's book on Lassalle is here called the "Bernstein/Engels" study or critique, without questioning its authorship by Bernstein.

In his letter to Kautsky of February 1891, quoted above, Engels had threatened to take time off from his pressing work "if forced to it ... to make a clean sweep of the Lassalle legend once and for all."[57] Whether forced or not, he saw an opportunity for the clean sweep: the German Social-Democratic Party had decided to publish an edition of Lassalle's writings, and Bernstein was to edit it with an introduction. Bernstein was in London, working in close collaboration with Engels.

In March Engels wrote to Sorge in America: "*Bernstein* will take care of it *(among ourselves!)*."[58] Since the new edition itself was no secret, the semiconspiratorial caution expressed here must have referred to Engels' plan for the edition. In short, he was going to try to involve Bernstein in making the "clean sweep," that is, settle political accounts with Lassalle. Engels had previously pressed Bernstein to write other material against deleterious (rightist) trends in the party.[59]

The Engels household put its friends to work in arranging Lassalle's letters to Marx for publication. The major-domo, Louise Kautsky, worked at putting Marx's correspondence files in order. Eleanor Marx helped make clear copies of the letters. Besides the use of the letters for the Lassalle edition, Engels also planned to publish all the letters with accompanying notes; while "all party censorship is excluded," his preface (he thought) would be "written diplomatically."[60] (In fact, Engels never accomplished this task, and the letters were not published until 1902—bowdlerized by Bernstein and Mehring to suppress Marx's views on Lassalle.)

There was one major outcome of the publication plan. Bernstein wrote the introduction to the edition of Lassalle. Engels wrote frankly to one of the few persons abroad he trusted implicitly, Marx's daughter Laura:

°°Lassalle's [letters to Marx] will be published in Germany; Bernstein is now using them for an introduction to Lassalle's works to be published by the party. The Lassalleans will not like it, but since Liebknecht has taken Lassalle's party [*read:* part] so much in the *Vorwärts*, I am determined to have it out, and to use their own Lassalle-veneration as the peg whereupon to hang a criticism of the man.[61]

"*I am determined,*" wrote Engels about the essay that *Bernstein* was writing; and this is an indicator of the situation, since there could be no question of giving or taking orders. Even without such indications, we could have little doubt about the close attention that Engels would insist on giving to the idol-breaking enterprise that Bernstein was engaged in.

Bernstein's introduction had to pass the censorship of the party Executive's representatives in Berlin, and so it too had to be "written diplomatically." In June Engels wrote Kautsky:

I would almost wish that the Berliners [the Executive] reject Ede's [Bernstein's] introduction to Lassalle so that he can work the thing up more completely and freely in the *Neue Zeit*. How little the people in Germany know the *real* Lassalle I saw precisely in Ede. Lassalle's letters to Marx, harmless as they seem to many, and the need to view the man as a total phenomenon, have given him, Ede, a wholly new light on it all. But the Berliners want *peace* in the party above all, and this is difficult to reconcile with free criticism.[62]

Ede's "wholly new light" on Lassalle was stated publicly by Bernstein in a *Neue Zeit* article.[63] We see that Engels was engaged in educating the educator, Bernstein himself. "Well, it will work itself out all right," Engels' letter concluded.

The publication of Bernstein's introduction in the new edition, whose first volume appeared in 1892, sent the pack of cards flying into the air again. The Lassalle-cultists and glorifiers of anyone-but-Marx were entirely unable to deal with the content of the essay, but were able to take deadly aim at the trivial. Their anger was concentrated on a two-word footnote by Bernstein, identifying Lassalle's chronic illness: "Probably syphilis." The trouble was not its truth but its undiplomatic frankness. The Berliners' censorship had overlooked this note, to their discomfiture, but Bebel tore his hair again, and Engels actually had to remind him that it was unjust to condemn the whole work over "one lousy footnote," for which the center was equally responsible.[64]

The real commotion, of course, was over the smashing theoretical and political analysis of Lassalleanism and the exposure of the idol's character; but here the cultists had no serviceable arguments or facts. The to-do, Engels felt sure, affected mainly a few elements on top. When an old-line Lassallean named Tölcke (famed for cheering the Kaiser) stated in a public speech that he protested against Bernstein's critique, the response of the Berlin party audience was so feeble, reported Kautsky, that it showed there was less adoration of Lassalle than was thought.[65]

But Bernstein was not as tough-skinned as his mentor: he fell ill, with what may have been a *crise de nerfs* brought on by the sometimes brutally hostile reaction he had evoked. I offer this theory free of charge. Engels advised Bernstein to treat the hostility with "a velvet glove on an iron fist," but Bernstein was not the man to take this advice. There is a symbol: in the same letter in which Engels mentioned Bernstein's illness, he also first mentioned his "enthusiasm over the Fabians."[66] There was naturally no evidence of a causal relationship. If at this time Bernstein's political fiber was beginning to weaken in the gut, he would have been ill equipped to respond to hostility by revolutionary staunchness. During the writing of the Lassalle critique, Engels' spirit had held him up, and I suspect that now he went a bit limp as the full realization of what he had done hit home.

Eleanor Marx was made of different metal. She must have started translating the Bernstein/Engels critique immediately, for in October 1891 Engels was already writing about the arrangements for its publication, though it did not actually appear until 1893.[67]

There is no information on how much, or what, Engels contributed to the content of the essay. My best guess would see evidence of his aid only through the impact of discussion and critical review, not in actual writing. On its publication Engels' overall judgment was that it "is really very good and made me very glad." He predicted that opponents would "take care not to take up a book in which the legend of the national[ist] Lassalle is so thoroughly smashed."[68] In fact, its opponents preferred not to attack it but to shove it out of sight as much as possible.

This book was one of the most acute Marxist analyses ever published. The facts give us good reason to treat it as the Anti-Lassalle produced by "Bernstein/Engels," even though it was undoubtedly Bernstein who wrote down every sentence.

SPECIAL NOTE B | BAKUNIN AND THE INTERNATIONAL: A "LIBERTARIAN" FABLE
A Note to Chapter 6

KMTR has taken up the Bakunin myth in sections, as particular questions have arisen. Three sections of *KMTR* 2 are concerned with issues about the class basis of Bakuninism: its perspective on "riding the peasantry," on the key revolutionary role assigned to brigands and other lumpen-elements, and on the dictatorship of the intelligentsia. *KMTR* 3 summarized the facts on Bakunin's plan of "secret (or invisible) dictatorship," firstly on the 1848 period, and secondly on his later career as an anarchist.[1] And in the present volume, Chapter 6 has sketched the basic politics of anarchism, as analyzed by Marx.

What remains is a subject that must be taken up only because of the massive bulk of anti-Marx literature claiming that Marx's "authoritarianism" was evidenced by his reprehensible treatment of the "libertarian" Bakunin, who only wanted to introduce Freedom into the International. This commonplace of marxological writings is a tissue of falsifictions, none of which holds up before documentary scrutiny.

1. PRELIMINARY CONSIDERATIONS

Bakunin's drive to take over the International through a conspiratorial bore-from-within operation was the first of its kind. It was hard for the International's militants to grasp its nature; it was hard for Marx himself, who was duped sufficiently to let Bakunin's Alliance into the International when its master lyingly agreed to dissolve its parallel structure and join only as just another Geneva section. It was hard to document the charge when it first came up.

The situation is different today; the mass of documentation that is now available is very large. But even by the time of the Hague Congress in 1872, a considerable body of documentation had been assembled, and this documentation has recently become available in English.[2]

One of the few original thoughts for which Bakunin could take credit was the idea of a conspiracy *within* the socialist movement. For the victims of this conspiracy, the difficulty was especially great because the perpetrators naturally sought to systematically conceal the traces of their real activities, methods and aims. They did not have to defend what they were doing before the bar of the movement—because they routinely denied they were doing it. The acolytes of this movement took this attitude not only in the face of the police (who were only sporadically interested) but especially in the face of other socialists, the rivals who were to be gulled by the conspiracy.

Bakunin's was the first leftist movement to apply its conspiratorial patterns of subversion not to assail society at large or to defend itself against the police, but to destroy other socialists' organization. Its rationale was its own theory that these rivals were part and parcel of the Authoritarian Enemy, or maybe worse (compare the similar rationale, sixty-five years later, of the Stalinized Communist International with the adoption of the theory of social-fascism).

The Bakuninists took this attitude not only in the face of their rival socialists but also in the face of history. It is known that Bakunin's friends repeatedly combed through his posthumous papers in order to destroy compromising documentation, especially correspondence.[3] Destroyed on sight was any paper confirming the existence of the conspiracy inside the International for which Bakunin was expelled. What we have left in written documents is the tip of the iceberg; what the International had available in 1872 was the tip of the tip—but it was still plenty.

For example, all copies of the now notorious letter of June 2, 1870, sent by Bakunin to Nechayev were supposed to be destroyed; only Natalie Herzen failed to obey orders, but even so her copy was not found until 1966—that is, not found by anyone who was willing to reveal it. It survived apparently because Natalie Herzen, at that time acting as archivist of Bakunin's intimate circle of four or five insiders, was partially disaffected, being especially hostile to Bakunin's partnership with Nechayev. In his introduction to the *Archives Bakounine*, Volume 4, Lehning has expressed some wonder that she kept it in her files while never mentioning its existence to researchers she cooperated with. It sounds as if she walked a middle way between two tugs of responsibility.

It was discovered in 1966 among her papers in the Bibliothèque Nationale by Professor Michael Confino, who immediately published it (with other materials) in an academic journal and a book. Was he the first to find it? How many researchers sympathetic to anarchism saw it there before Confino—and kept the secret of the conspiracy against history? Five years after publication, Lehning mentioned in the aforementioned introduction that *he* had seen this material in the library some years before Confino. He did not explain why he remained silent.[4]

Bakunin apologists have made maximum use of this conspiracy against history, for over a century, in order to maintain the cloak of secrecy that the anarchist band sought to throw over their rule-or-ruin drive in the International. One remarkable argument, common in the apologetic literature, is based on the well-known fact that most of the plans Bakunin made during his lifelong hobby of inventing conspiratorial organizations were, in fact, sheer fantasies. (Or, to be blunter, in some cases a tissue of lies.) The apologetic argument then goes that Marx and the International were "unfair" in reacting as if Bakunin's claims (for example, of an immense membership) were real.

There are two answers. The less important answer is this: the apology seems to assume that Marx and the defenders of the International should have known that Bakunin was merely a fantasizing buffoon (which is the attitude essentially taken by Carr's biography). Carr, for example, likes to emphasize Bakunin's usual impotence, but neither Marx nor the Hague delegates had the advantage of being able to read Carr's work. One aim of the typical Bakunin conspiracy was to conceal its own emptiness; it wanted to convince enemies that the titanic forces of Anarchy were as fearsome as advertised, a goal in which the right-wing press industriously cooperated.

In any case the International had the right to protect itself from those who were *planning* to smash it, without waiting to make sure that they had succeeded in doing so or that the plan was being carried out successfully. In part the Hague Congress explicitly expelled Bakunin for what he and his agents boasted of doing; its resolution openly expressed some uncertainty on what he had actually accomplished in the way of establishing his organization-smashing machine.

The more important answer is that the apologetic argument rests on a factual evasion. It was precisely in his International operation, and only there, that Bakunin succeeded in putting flesh on his schemes for Anarchic Pan-Destruction. The trouble is in part that Carr, with the bonhomie of an English gentleman, implicitly looks on Bakunin basically as an entertaining eccentric, a lovable Crazy Russian (though with cultured politeness he does not let his amused smirk be seen). And we should not fault him for believing that the wrecking of the "Marxist" International by this buffoonery was no historical disaster; he is entitled to his politics. But surely one cannot criticize the people who built the International for lacking Carr's detached sense of humor about the wrecking crew.

Anyway, the historical controversy over the figure of Bakunin is not primarily over what he succeeded in actually doing—never anarchism's long suit—but over what he stood for. We have dealt with this in large part, but there is an aspect so far unmentioned. We have dwelt, for example in *KMTR* 3, on Bakunin's aspirations for a "secret dictatorship" in the working-class movement; but it remains to be said that he did not hold the narrow view that dictatorship was wielded only through a mass movement.

All his life, Bakunin sought a shortcut to effective power: by convincing a suitable czar, emperor, king, or other autocrat to declare the People's Revolution from above, and impose the Rule of Anarchy (or Whatever) through the convenience of an already established despotism.

This, we already know, was the delusion of the "Social Monarchy," which goes back a long way in socialist history. Lassalle took one flyer in that direction: his appeal through Bismarck for a Hohenzollern utopia.[5] The Father of Anarchism who preceded Bakunin, namely Proudhon, was less selective: at one time or another he looked to the imposition of a social-despotism from above by a series of monarchical powers—Louis Philippe, the Russian czar, General Cavaignac (the dictator of the 1848 June Days), and no less than three Bonapartes (Napoleon I, Louis Bonaparte, and the adventurer Prince Jerome).[6] There were not many other possible contenders for the honor.

There was, then, good anarchist precedent for Bakunin. We have seen that in his "Confession" he appealed to Czar Nicholas I to put himself at the head of a revolutionary Pan-Slavist movement as the "savior" of Europe, and that the czar reasonably replied "No, thank you."[7]

A few years later, while Bakunin was exiled in Siberia, he hobnobbed with the Governor-General, who happened to be his cousin and boyhood friend—an old imperialist happy to chat about reforms. Bakunin decided that General Nicholas Muraviev was a fit instrument of the liberatory mission previously assigned to the royal Nicholas. The good general would have no truck with constitutions or parliaments; he would establish an "iron dictatorship," a "rational dictatorship" to save Russia. Bakunin wrote this down in a public defense of his Siberian jailer-dictator when Herzen's organ *Kolokol* attacked the notorious imperialist in its columns.[8]

Bakunin's next appeal of this sort was published broadside in 1862 in a brochure titled *The People's Cause: Romanov, Pugachev, or Pestel?* The czar was now Alexander II: won't he please carry out a bloodless revolution for the people? That was the "Romanov" alternative. The other two alternatives indicated by the title were: a peasant rebellion or a revolt of the intelligentsia.

> We should most gladly of all follow Romanov, if Romanov could and would transform himself from a Petersburg Emperor into a National Tsar. We should gladly enroll under his standard.... We would follow him because he *alone* could carry out and complete a great, peaceful revolution without shedding one drop of Russian or Slav blood.[9]

It is not recorded that Alexander bothered to reply "No, thank you."

In the same year Bakunin also made an attempt at a political flirtation with a Bonaparte—with the same Prince Jerome who had been the object of sheep's-eyes by Proudhon. The following year in Stockholm (as we related in Chapter 6), Bakunin, having been paid some flattering attention by King Charles XV himself, made the public rapprochement to the monarchy that astonished his friends.[10] This gets us very close to Bakunin's formal assumption of the mantle of anarchism about 1866.

In the ensuing years, this type of appeal was muted. In the period 1869-1870, in association with Nechayev, Bakunin either collaborated on or approved an "Appeal to the Russian Nobility" to establish a revolutionary monarchy on the throne in place of Alexander. Near the end of his life, he confessed that he had become "to a certain extent a Bismarckian"—"half seriously," says biographer Carr.[11] But by this time he was a burnt-out hulk and no more than half serious about anything.

These are the facts that have to be added to the material previously adduced in order to understand the mentality that decided in 1868 to take over the International.

2. BAKUNIN'S FIRST TAKEOVER OPERATION

Contrary to one of the myths about Marx's relations with Bakunin, there is *no* evidence of any special hostility by Marx against the Russian—before the International period. This myth is usually based on an incident that took place in 1848 in connection with the *Neue Rheinische Zeitung*; but the facts of this case are enough to throw it out of court.[11a]

As related in Chapter 6, soon after the founding of the International Marx took the initiative in approaching Bakunin about helping to build the new movement, especially in Italy whither the Russian was bound; and Bakunin promised that henceforth he would "take part only in the socialist movement."[12] That was November 1864. In fact, Bakunin proceeded to pay no attention whatever to either socialism or the International. He spent the next period in Italy, playing with outlines of one conspiratorial scheme or another of his usual type.

On leaving Marx and London, Bakunin first went to Florence, where he founded an Italian "Brotherhood" with a few cronies. As far as biographer Carr can make out, "the ideas of Bakunin seemed limited to the childish game of inventing each week a new cypher," and to squeezing the gullible for contributions to the Revolution, which went through his own pocket. In October 1865 he moved to Naples, where he struck it rich: Princess Obolensky, a blue-blooded eccentric, adopted him as her revolutionary pet and kept him in high style along with a large entourage at her luxurious villa.

Here Bakunin invented an "International Brotherhood," with no more warm bodies in it than before, but with a program which is commonly hailed as the first one enunciating an anarchist viewpoint and including some harsh words about capitalism. He was now a "revolutionary anarchist." It was the summer of 1866; he was 52; after a quarter century of revolution-making, let no one think that his conceptions about revolution changed a whit after he adopted anarchist rhetoric and concepts.

In the spring of 1867 the Princess and her moneybags moved to a Swiss villa on Lake Geneva, and in August Bakunin found a reason to move into the same vicinity. A committee of internationally prominent liberals had announced that a congress would be held in Geneva in September to establish a Peace League. Bakunin gathered his friends for the project of capturing world liberalism for the Revolution by talking at its leaders in Geneva.

The liberal Peace Congress duly met, and Bakunin, as a live "Russian revolutionist" in person, was a smash hit. After making a gratifying splash as a very important person, he was elected to the Executive. His address made no mention of the International, which was still struggling along.

During the following year it became evident that the leaders of world liberalism were resisting the Bakunin charisma, while on the other hand the International was growing. Bakunin conceived the "bold plan" of capturing both movements by fusing them into one, with himself as the champion of unity in both—thus to become "co-equal with Marx" at one bound, says his biographer.[13]

In pursuance of the bold plan, in mid-1868 he enrolled in the Geneva section of the International, and then had an invitation sent to the General Council of the International to send delegates to the Peace League's second congress in Bern, where he, Bakunin, would naturally appear as the leader of the United Left. The clever scheme fell apart when the General Council flatly rejected the invitation to participate officially in the liberal International.

When the Peace League congress opened in September 1868, Bakunin was set to denounce the General Council for its "insolence," but he found that his hopes in the League liberals had been misplaced. The liberals somehow remained liberals, even though Bakunin made an eloquent speech attacking communism (in favor of something he called collectivism). Our anarchist then split out of the congress with a handful of followers.

Having failed to capture the liberals' International, Bakunin turned his attention to the other International targeted by the "bold plan." This time he took the precaution of furbishing his organizational tool to capture the movement. He baptized his followers the "International Alliance of Socialist Democracy," and wrote statutes establishing his approximately eighteen cronies as an international framework of sections and congresses, etc., *parallel to the International's structure.* He then applied for admission to the workers' International as a dual International within it, with dual structural organizations right down the line and up to parallel congresses—all on the basis of its own special (sect) program. We have discussed the special Bakuninist planks of this program.

The General Council rejected this breathtaking proposal. Bakunin thereupon informed the General Council that the "International Alliance" had been dissolved and would it kindly accept the "Alliance of the Socialist Democracy" as a mere section in Geneva. Marx fell for this simple lie as naively as a rube at a carnival, and recommended acceptance to the General Council. Bakunin's Trojan Horse was inside the walls.

3. FIRST ROUND AT BASEL

At first Bakunin and his Alliance operation were absorbed in a local battle in Geneva, where they aroused considerable opposition in the International membership as the latter came to know them firsthand. The International loyalists consolidated themselves, especially under the leadership of a Russian Narodnik émigré named Nicholas Utin, who *inter alia* had the advantage of being able to read what Bakunin had been publishing in Russian. The result was this: when Bakunin attended his first and only International congress, the 1869 congress in Basel, he was afraid of being tossed out by the Swiss, not by the General Council. This explains what some think was strange in Bakunin's conduct.

As mentioned in Chapter 6, Bakunin entirely refrained from bringing up any anarchist ideas at the congress, though he was now secretly recruiting to his little private army on the basis of his newly hatched ideology.

The anarchist Truth was for the elite insiders; at the congress he talked out of the other side of his mouth. He not only refrained from proposing anarchist ideas, he put forward proposals and views that were incompatible with anarchism. This applied to four interventions from the floor.

1. Powers of the General Council

The GC had requested that the congress grant it power, subject to congress veto, to exclude a section acting contrary to International principles, in order to defend the movement against alien elements. Bakunin not only became the most enthusiastic proponent of this proposal, but went further: *he proposed substantially greater powers for the leading body*, powers that the GC had not requested. These proposals were carried through, perhaps largely because of his advocacy.

The contemporaneous press report through which we know of this episode summarized the facts as follows:

> Bakunin proposes to give the General Council the right to veto the entrance of new sections into the International until the following Congress, and the right to suspend existing sections; as for National [i.e., Federal] Committees, he wants to grant them the right to expel sections from the International.... Hins [Belgian delegate] asks that the right of suspension belong only to the Federal Committees and not to the General Council ... Bakunin [speaking again] puts emphasis on the international character of the Association; it is necessary for this reason that the General Council not be without authority. He points out that, if the national organizations [Federal Committees] had the right of suspension, it could happen that sections animated by the true spirit of the International might be expelled by a majority unfaithful to the principles.[14]

What this meant—as Bakunin later admitted when he beat his breast and wailed *Mea culpa*[15]—was that he was afraid the Swiss Federal Committee might expel his Alliance, and so he looked to the General Council to protect his rights. That is, he was ready to jettison anarchist rhetoric about federalism and anti-authority as soon as his own local power base was threatened.

Besides, as Carr points out, "Bakunin's ambition at this stage was to capture the General Council, not to destroy it."[16] A Bakunin-run General Council would be a power; the function of anarchy was to disorganize your enemies, not your own power base. Hence it was only toward the end that Bakunin demanded the abolition of all central bodies. If you can't capture, destroy.

2. The Resolution on Land Collectivization

At this congress the long-standing effort to commit the International to land collectivization (the first socialistic proposal adopted by the movement) finally overwhelmed the Proudhonist opposition.[17] Bakunin voted with the large majority.

But among this majority were five different positions put forward on the *form* in which to implement collectivization. Here was an opportunity for an educational anarchist point of view! One of the five positions was a clearly anarchist proposal made on behalf of Lyons by Albert Richard, who had been close to Bakunin for a year.

Instead of supporting his own disciple's principled position, Bakunin took the floor to argue for the commission's majority report by Rittinghausen, a proposal which (as one would expect) plainly presupposed that a *state* was doing the collectivization.[18]

In the discussion Bakunin performed an awkward straddle. His speech talked about "the destruction of all national and territorial states," but proposed "on their ruins, the construction of the international state of millions of workers, a state which it will be the role of the International to constitute."[19] In short, he put forward the "workers' state" idea which was the nemesis of anarchism.

When his first lieutenant Guillaume asked him privately how "he, the enemy of the state," could make this proposal, Bakunin explained that it was a sly-foxy trick of language.[20] This account has to be read to understand how Bakunin's mentality worked, about principles and about the exigencies of grabbing power in a takeover operation.

3. Direct Legislation

A delegate made a to-do about adding his favorite political nostrum to the agenda: the system of initiative and recall, so-called "direct legislation" by the people. There was little support, but it was the subject of Bakunin's first intervention at the congress.

Far from using the occasion to expose and oppose "politics" in general, as anarchist principle demanded, Bakunin pitched his opposition on the ground that the movement must be internationalist in its politics. The minutes do not clearly show what sense this made in the debate, but there could be no doubt that our anarchist emphasized that "political and social questions are closely linked," and so on.[21]

There was not a hint of anarchism about it. Later Bakunin invented the lie out of the whole cloth that the direct-legislation proposal had been secretly inspired by Marx; for this meant that he, Bakunin, had administered a defeat to the Authoritarian Enemy. What this meant in his scheme we will see in the next point.

4. Abolition of the Right of Inheritance

As we saw in Chapter 6, this was one of the reform planks on which Bakunin had rested his operation in the liberal Peace League.[22] Not only was there nothing anarchistic about it, it was not even socialistic in content—as Marx had argued.

Though this programmatic proposal failed of adoption by falling short of a majority, it did get more votes than the GC resolution drawn up by Marx. To be sure, the voting lineup had little to do with the Bakunin operation, for any reformists could and did vote for it, especially if they were unable to follow the GC's argumentation. Only Bakunin's speech on the issue introduced glancing references to ideas which might be claimed to be anarchoid, but these undoubtedly passed over the delegates' heads like the GC's economic arguments.

Still, this inconclusive vote on a side issue was the only talking point Bakunin got out of the congress. So he puffed it up into an epochal event: Marx had been "defeated," on the issue of the century! It did not matter that Marx had been "defeated" at International congresses before this; but from here on, it became a dogma of the Bakunin clique that Marx had been thrown into such heart-rending despair that the Pan-German Dictator in London in a red-eyed frenzy had vowed then and there to expel the Paladin of Freedom from the International.

This rubbish is echoed in a number of marxological works, solely on the claim of the two self-proclaimed liars at the head of the Bakunin clique, despite the evidence in Marx's correspondence and papers that nothing of the sort happened.

It is true that a battle to tear the International apart was starting. But not in London, as we will see in the section after next.

4. BAKUNIN'S DESTRUCT-O-CLIQUE: THE SECRET ALLIANCE

First we must review the engine designed by Bakunin to accomplish what he always maintained was the primary task of his movement: destruction. We have seen that Bakunin's plan on entering the International was to take it over by nucleating it with one of his standard conspiratorial constructions. He had been operating this way for a quarter century. It is remarkable that any historian swallows the claim that Bakunin, at the polite request of the General Council, changed the whole nature of his lifelong activity and mode of thought. He merely took his normal steps to conceal the real state of affairs from the eyes of Authority.

To be sure, the secrecy of Bakunin's operations was as watertight as a colander, and Bakunin himself was a blabbermouth. It must be understood that Bakunin's type of operation was concerned about what could be *proved*, not so much about what might be known. In the course of the conspiracy, there were many people who had been touched by Bakuninist recruiting, and emerged to talk about it, even if they could not offer the kind of documentation that turns up in libraries a century later. When (for example) any one of Bakunin's short-lived recruits told others of what he was doing, a working certainty spread in rippling circles.

Carr mentions one case that got written down. Charles Perron, who was Bakunin's hope for a while, left "an extraordinary record of a conversation" that took place around the time of the Basel Congress. It affords a glimpse:

> Bakunin assured him that the International was an excellent institution in itself, but that there was something better which Perron should also join—the Alliance. Perron agreed. Then Bakunin said that, even in the Alliance, there might be some who were not genuine revolutionaries, and who were a drag on its activities, and it would therefore be a good thing to have at the back of the Alliance a group of "International Brothers." Perron again agreed. When next they met a few days later, Bakunin told him that the "International Brothers" were too wide an organization, and that behind them there must be a Directorate or Bureau of three—of whom he, Perron, should be one. Perron laughed, and once more agreed.[24]

The name of the conspiracy kept changing in Bakunin's mind, but it was always the same organ of secret domination whatever the current name. The existence of the "*Secret* Alliance" alongside the public Alliance—or rather, denial of its existence—was the crux of the Bakuninist defense campaign and still is the crux of much of the marxological attack on Marx for mistreating that paladin of Freedom, Bakunin. On this we focus in the present section.

After the Hague Congress split, now out in the open, Bakunin openly recounted how he had used his Alliance* as a splitting tool in the Peace

---

*The name Alliance of the Socialist Democracy was not adopted until *after* the split from the Peace Congress. In the Peace Congress operation the conspiracy was mainly called the "International Brotherhood." By 1873 Bakunin was entitling it

Congress operation that preceded the takeover drive in the International. In the book he published in 1873, he frankly celebrated "the split which was for the first time consummated at this [Peace] Congress" between the liberals and his own revolutionaries. He wrote further: "The question [of equality of classes] which served apparently as pretext for this rupture, which had become inevitable beforehand, was posed by the 'Alliancists' in clear and distinct terms." And then he even played with the question of what might have happened if the majority had accepted his proposal about equality:

> If the bourgeois Congress had behaved in this way, the situation of the "Alliancists" would have been incomparably more difficult; between the [Peace] League and them would have been joined the same battle as the one that takes place today [1873] between them and Marx.[25]

We see that, in his own thinking, his split operation in the Peace League was properly equated in his own mind with his split operation in the International.

Ensconced in the International, Bakunin at first maintained his "International Brotherhood" as the conspiratorial nucleus for recruiting future co-dictators, as Perron's account indicated. During 1868 these apprentice Dictators of the World apparently consisted of about a dozen cronies—a figure, we know, that Bakunin considered quite ample for the nonce.[26]

But even this grouplet blew up after a meeting in January 1869 in Geneva, with about ten Brothers present. Carr relates that "it seems to have developed into a meeting of protest against the dictatorial methods of Bakunin, who treated the Brotherhood as his own personal domain and kept every decision regarding it in his own hands." This particular group soon dissolved formally, though this detail did not stop Bakunin from using its name when convenient.[27] At about the same time Bakunin pretended to accept the General Council's condition that the "International Alliance" format be dissolved, and settled for a Geneva section which would call itself the Alliance.

With the refractory "International Brotherhood" dissolved, Bakunin immediately proceeded to form a new conspiratorial organization to fill the same role. This crucial fact was flatly stated by the chief organizer of the conspiracy, James Guillaume, not in his fabuliferous "history" of the International but in his last book, *Karl Marx, Pangermaniste* (1915). After mentioning that the International Brotherhood was dissolved in 1869 because of internal conflict, Guillaume wrote: "A new secret organization

---

the "Alliance of Revolutionary Socialists." And so he wrote as if this were the name of the group even in the International fight.

was immediately reconstituted by the first founders, Bakunin, Fanelli and Friscia," and he revealed that he, Guillaume, had joined as well—despite all the lies on that score he had told orally and literarily. He gave a list of eight men who joined "during 1869," and lo, leading this list are his own name and that of Schwitzguebel (who was the third man on trial at the Hague Congress).[28]

This statement, by itself, is enough to end the historical controversy, confirming the verdict of the Hague Congress. Guillaume's book, *Karl Marx, Pangermaniste*, by the way, was as filled with anti-Semitic and racist anti-German ranting as Bakunin's writing.*

This "new secret organization," whatever name it might be given at any given time, was what Bakunin always thought of as the *secret* Alliance, in distinction from the "public Alliance." The "public Alliance" was the front that was employed to dupe Evil Authority. Bakunin may have reverted back to the name "International Alliance of the Socialist Democracy," as Albert Richard later reported.[30] No matter; the "Alliance" became the generic name for the Bakuninist operation in the International, in Italy and Spain as well as Switzerland.

The Geneva "Alliance" acted as a center to give instructions and advice to, or at least coordinate factional work with, the Italian and Spanish Alliancists.[31] Fanelli and Friscia (who, as we have seen, were co-founders of the secret Alliance) were respectively from the Italian and Spanish groups. Albert Richard, then a Bakunin disciple operating as the "Brother" in Lyons, later wrote about the comings and goings of Bakuninist agents weaving connections among the secret Alliance groups, telling how the Alliance mediated "complete accord" between Bakunin and the Brothers at the time of the Basel Congress. Richard's account simply took it for granted that the Bakuninist "Spanish groups," the "Swiss from the [Jura] mountains," and the "badly organized Italian International" were all part of the "Alliance." Incidentally, Richard confirmed that Guillaume *was* a member of the secret Alliance.[32]

The more sophisticated apologists for the Bakunin operation do not deny that *secret* Bakuninist groups were indeed organized in the International in (say) Spain. Thus A. Lehning has admitted:

> It was Farga-Pellicer who, after spending several weeks of 1869 in close relations with Bakunin, established the main lines of a secret

---

*There is an interesting aspect of this fact. Guillaume, as editor of the *Bulletin de la Fédération Jurassienne*, chief house organ of the conspiracy, had carried virulently anti-Semitic garbage in its columns,[29] but when he composed his four-volume snow-job *L'Internationale* he had carefully muted this aspect of Bakuninism. It is no exaggeration to say that it was written for the purpose of befuddling marxologists and gullible historians.

organization attached to the International in Spain. In spring 1870, before the first Federal Congress in Barcelona, he founded the Alianza de la Democratia Socialista.[33]

Lehning merely argues, in effect, that the documents do not exist to prove in a court of law that this Spanish branch named Alliance of the Socialist Democracy was really a part of the same Alliance that operated in Switzerland under Bakunin. One is apparently expected to believe that this spread of a secret organized faction in the International, extending through at least four countries, was a coincidence.

Guillaume, in his cover-up work *L'Internationale*, even claimed that "The existence of the Alianza, an exclusively Spanish organization, remained unknown to us" in Switzerland! Yet Lehning has stated clearly enough that the Spanish conspirators consulted Bakunin regularly "on all sorts of questions."[34] Of course it is theoretically possible that Bakunin kept even his chief organizational lieutenant, Guillaume, in ignorance of his dealings (for this was what all his associates and dupes often complained about), but he could hardly keep Guillaume unaware of a whole section of the organization in Spain. The alternative is to conclude that Guillaume was simply lying as usual. This is hardly a startling conclusion: it was Guillaume who explained to the Hague Congress commission that he refused to answer their questions because it was silly to pose questions to conspirators who are duty-bound by their conspiracy not to reveal the truth.[35]

The existence of the secret Alliance has, in recent times, also been proved by the contents of Bakunin's letter to Nechayev of June 2, 1870 (the one discovered by Confino, which we mention more than once in this work). Bakunin wrote in passing:

> Having founded the secret International Revolutionary Alliance some years ago, I cannot and will not abandon it in order to devote myself entirely to the Russian cause.[36]

Alongside such direct references to the secret Alliance, one should note Bakunin's references to the "public Alliance," since such references naturally imply the existence of a secret one.

Thus, in a letter of May 1870 to intimate collaborators in which great secrecy was enjoined, Bakunin referred to a fellow Russian in Geneva who was not to be trusted with secret work, but "On the other hand we have established with him close and rather sincere ties as far as concerns the questions of the International and the public section of the Alliance."[37] The charge that there was both a secret and a public Alliance was exactly the basis of the Hague Congress action. As Venturi has written, Bakunin "had never surrendered to pressure from the General Council to dissolve his countless Brotherhoods, Alliances, etc."[38] This is a very odd statement, for it was not a question of "pressure": the dissolution had been the condition for admission into the International, and Venturi took this obscure way of saying that Bakunin lied his way into the International.

There are few less dubious propositions in history than the conclusion that Bakunin was doing in the International no more and no less than what he had been doing for decades, and what he believed on principle in doing to any broad movement he was infiltrating.

But at this point we are only beginning the story and only touching on the evidence. It was in the last stage, in the months of 1872 before the Hague Congress, that the full character of the Bakunin operation exposed itself.

5. BAKUNIN DECLARES WAR

As early as the spring of 1870, Bakunin began spurring his followers to launch the "final conflict" in the International. The date is important because the later cover-story claimed that it was the Evil Authoritarian Dictators of the General Council, led by Marx, who brought the struggle to a head by deciding to expel the doughty champions of Freedom.

This date is put beyond doubt by a letter sent by Bakunin to his Lyons lieutenant, dated April 1, 1870—two and a half years before the Hague Congress. (Later we will see even earlier documentation, but not as detailed.)

The recipient was Albert Richard, who still thought he was one of the World Dictators. When Bakunin wrote this letter, the Swiss federation was preparing a congress at La Chaux-de-Fonds, and the Bakuninists expected to have a fight on their hands with their *Swiss* opponents. Bakunin sought to broaden Richard's perspective:

> Besides its local importance, the battle which is going to be joined at La Chaux-de-Fonds will have an immense universal interest. It will be the forerunner and precursor of the one that we have to launch at the next general congress of the International.

The battle "we have to launch at the next general congress of the International": nothing could be clearer. The next congress was going to be the Hague Congress. And just what would this battle be waged *for*? Defense of the Freedom-lovers against the sinister Authoritarians in London? Not a bit. The *casus belli* was simply the imposition of the anarchist ideology and program on the International.

In making clear the motivation, there was not a word about any threat from the General Council. It was, Bakunin declared, a choice between "the great politics [*sic*] of universal socialism or the petty politics of the radical bourgeois." It was a fight for "the universal, socialist and single state" after the abolition of "political states" (we refrain from comment on this slippery use of 'state'). These, he announced, are the questions for the next congress. Several countries will be on our side; on Marx's side will be the "German leaders who are in large part Jews, that is, exploiters and bourgeois." (We will see much more of this garbage further on.) So—"Let us close our ranks and prepare for combat. For at stake is the triumph of the International and the Revolution."[39]

This was Bakunin's secret declaration of the secret war, by his secret conspiracy.

It was a portent of what was to come in many ways. All our enemies, wrote Bakunin, are Jews: "I have started a series of letters in reply to all these Jewish and German barking dogs. I want to have done with them."[40] When you read these letters (below), remember that their inception dates back at least to the spring of 1870.

Bakunin's yearning for a showdown battle was interrupted, first by the Franco-Prussian War, then by the Paris Commune. In the aftermath of the Commune, *with the International under attack by every government of Europe by 1872*, Bakunin went in for the kill.

Early in 1872 he was rallying his secret troops to establish organized nuclei in the International's ranks where they had not yet done so. Writing to a top henchman in the Italian federation, in March, Bakunin gave his expert conspiratorial advice. Firstly: in the face of government persecution the Italians might have to dissolve the public organization of the International and set up a secret one. But secondly: there was an important task given "the existence of your public sections." This was to organize secret nuclei alongside the public sections.

> I think you will sooner or later come to understand the necessity of founding, inside of them [the public sections], *nuclei* composed of the surest, most devoted, most intelligent and most energetic members, in short, the closest ones. These nuclei, closely linked among themselves and with similar nuclei which are organized or will organize in other regions of Italy or abroad, will have a double mission: to begin with, they will form the inspiriting and vivifying soul of that immense body called the International Working Men's Association in Italy as elsewhere, and next, they will take up questions *that it is impossible to treat publicly*.... For men as intelligent as you and your friends, I think I have said enough.... Naturally this secret alliance would accept into its ranks only a very small number of individuals....

This "secret alliance" would be led by a secret General Staff, in accordance with Bakunin's standard doctrine, while the "army" of manipulated people did their work outside.[41]

In the course of this preparation for war, the secret General Staff made a fateful strategic decision.

6. BAKUNIN'S SPLIT DRIVE

Up to around the middle of 1872, probably, Bakunin was still looking toward a successful takeover of the International. Around July he made the strategic decision to head for a split instead.

The reason may have been an accumulation of setbacks or disappointments, but certainly in June he met a setback that had a considerable impact on him. The General Council rejected the Alliancist proposal to hold the coming congress in Switzerland, that is, in Bakunin's own bailiwick; it accepted the Belgian and Dutch proposal to hold the congress in the Hague. There was more than one good reason for the Hague, from the standpoint of the GC. It was only from the conspirators' standpoint that this decision was a make-or-break matter.

Why Bakunin *did* make this decision his touchstone for a split perspective is puzzling only because the case against the Hague site was so weak, indeed virtually nonexistent. The alternative explanation is that Bakunin was simply in a hurry to establish his very own anarchist International without further hassling, and paid little attention to pretexts.

The history of the question shows this weakness plainly. Two other cities, even farther from Switzerland, had been selected for this same congress before, without trouble—that is, before the disruption of the war, the Commune and its aftermath. The last congress at Basel in 1869 had picked Paris; in December 1870 the General Council announced it would be Mainz, whose branch was anxious to host the congress. When the GC took the question up on June 18, 1872, it knew that in 1869 and 1870 the Belgians had proposed the Hague (Netherlands) and now the same proposal was before them from the Dutch themselves, reported by the French Blanquist leader Cournet, who moreover added his own voice to the push.

When the GC Sub-Committee, on GC instructions, met the next day to settle the matter, it was told that besides the Swiss and the Italians, the *Germans* were against the Hague location. In the minutes of this meeting taken down by Cournet, it appeared that Engels thought the Hague a good location because of the number of GC members who wanted to attend; at least, this is all that the minutes recorded. Serraillier thought the Hague location would result in more international attention to the congress. And Marx!

Marx nonetheless points out the dangers that the city of the Hague presents.

Whatever this means (it was the sum total of Marx's contribution to the discussion according to the minutes), he did not sound very enthusiastic about the choice![42]

In answer to the protests from the Swiss Bakuninists, the GC pointed out a salient fact: of the four congresses so far held by the International, *three* had been held in Switzerland already. In effect, the Swiss seemed to argue that their happy country should have a monopoly on congresses. The Bakuninists argued further that the Hague was not in a "central" location, and, since this was obviously ridiculous, they added another jolting argument. A letter from the GC had pointed out that Switzerland was one "focal point" of the dispute at issue. Guillaume's Bakuninist *Bulletin* of the Jurassians had an answer to that one: by choosing the Hague *you* have chosen the worst kind of city—"*un milieu germanique*"! (Long afterwards Guillaume apologized for being so ignorant about Switzerland's neighbor down the Rhine; but it makes one wonder about aspirants to World Dictatorship.) The ethnic character of the Dutch was not the only thing that was not known to Guillaume, who by the way was easily the cleverest of the Bakuninist leaders. The major charge made by the clique was that the GC had selected the Hague "to assure a ready-made majority"; but in fact the delegates of the Dutch Federation voted *against* the GC at the Hague.[43]

The obvious extreme weakness of the Bakuninists' objection to the Hague site did not help their faction, and may have shaken Bakunin's confidence. In any case, in mid-July Bakunin held a council of war with his Swiss lieutenants to cogitate grand strategy. It is clear that he felt that a successful takeover was looking dimmer; in any case the question of split became only the question of just how to bring it off.

The Bakuninist council decided: first a last attempt would be made to pressure the GC into rescinding the decision on the Hague; but if the GC stood pat, the Jura Federation would refuse to send delegates, would coordinate the same decision by the Italians and the Spanish, and would convene a rival congress. In the next few days Bakunin communicated this decision to Italian agents, presumably also to Spanish agents, to turn them toward a split course as well.*

---

*The account here will follow the facts as summarized by A. Lehning, in his edition of Bakunin's works[44]—plus the Bakunin documents themselves. As a Bakunin apologist, Lehning can scarcely be suspected of favoring Marx. But we follow only Lehning's facts. While he describes the split drive, he never uses the bad word 'split,' and seems to write as if such a splitting operation was as normal an activity as any other. I have had to add references to relevant documents; Lehning's summary does not usually give them.

There is an extant letter by Bakunin spelling his split line out to an Italian lieutenant, on July 16. If the GC persisted in designating the Hague,

> the Italians and the Spanish will be invited to do what the Jurassians will do, that is, to send no delegates to this [Hague] Congress but to send them instead to the Conference of the dissident and free sections in Switzerland, to affirm and preserve their independence and to organize their close Federation, the Federation of the autonomous sections and federations in the International.[45]

The organization to be formed by the splitters at this conference would be represented as being the International.

However, on or about July 19 James Guillaume changed Bakunin's mind on the tactical aspect of this course: how to bring about the split while throwing the onus on the General Council. The new tactic, worked out by Guillaume, was to go to the Hague Congress long enough to operate the split *there*, in order to pick off delegates in the confusion of the breakup.

But the Italians refused to go along with the change, insisting on an immediate split, honestly performed, instead of the Guillaume flimflam. At their Rimini Congress opening August 4, the Italian Bakuninists declared their open split with the General Council, and called for a splitters' congress at Neuchtel (Switzerland) on September 2, the same day as the Hague Congress. But the Spanish Alliancists, as well as the Jurassians, agreed to follow Guillaume's new scheme: go to the Hague and split *there*.

At the Jura Federation congress on August 18, the new split line was spelled out. First, a "principle of autonomy" (autonomy of federations and sections) was adopted which *inter alia* called for the abolition of any General Council. Then an "imperative mandate" (binding instruction) was imposed on the delegates to regulate what to do when the Marxist Authoritarians refused to abolish the General Council. The Bakuninist delegates were instructed to walk out; also to walk out if Bakuninist delegates were refused admission. Bakunin personally helped to draft this line at the Jura congress.*

The imperative mandate to split was kept a secret: it was not published in Guillaume's Jura *Bulletin* along with other congress material. But, apparently by mistake, a Bakuninist organ in Italy published it on August 27.

In this same period Bakunin made another secret move that would have proclaimed split if made public. In July and August he helped found a Slavic Section of the International in Zurich (a center for Russian students

---

*The text of this Imperative Mandate is in *Archives Bakounine*, 2:129. This set of instructions binding on *every* delegate was, of course, adopted by a majority vote. In any case, its anti-anarchist "authoritarian" character is obvious; but for a classic exposition of its incompatibility with democratic functioning, see Engels' post-congress article on "Imperative Mandates at the Hague Congress."

and émigrés). The new section applied for affiliation to the Jura Federation, not to the General Council, from which it was kept secret. Moreover, on August 14 Bakunin drafted a program for it that assumed the split was consummated. The program not only stated explicitly that it was "anarchist" (which was as illegal as calling itself "communist"), but it also implied that the International had to be made an anarchist organization. This program included various anarchoid nostrums—such as abolition of the family and atheism—which the GC would naturally have refused to recognize. And there was an even plainer provocation: it stated openly that the section accepted the existence of no "power" within the International and no programmatic positions "imposed either by the General Council or even by the general congresses."[46]

When the secretary of the new section sent this raucous document to Guillaume for publication in his *Bulletin,* the wily Guillaume suppressed it.[47] This was just before the Hague Congress, and it would have provided proof of exactly what the splitters were going to deny with idealistic indignation. It is possible that in Bakunin's mind the Zurich program was not intended to be an open provocation: in the longitude of Zurich he was already living in an anarchist International of his own, if not in his own universe. Guillaume was a more slippery trickster, as we will see again.

Back home, Bakunin criticized the Italians for making "a very serious mistake." This paladin of Freedom, who was engaged in demanding total release from all control in the International in the name of principle, censured his followers for breaking his own discipline: "You have forgotten," he scolded them, "that in our affairs no individual has the right to *fare da se* [act by oneself] and to take arbitrary steps."[48] So much for anarchist anti-authoritarianism. In point of fact, the Italians had had no say in the adoption of the new Guillaume-Bakunin split strategy, though Bakunin expected them to obey it blindly.

But since Bakunin had not yet established his mighty Invisible Dictatorship, he had to make the best of the Italians' intransigent insistence on an honest Instant Split (as instant as the abolition of the state). On August 31 Bakunin wrote to his Italian agent Gambuzzi with a clear account of the split line. First he deplored the Italians' course:

> The Italians should have acted in concert with the Spanish and Jurassians, both of these having decided to send their delegates to the Hague, but with *imperative mandates,* clearly set forth, ordering them to walk out of the Congress in solidarity, as soon as the majority has declared itself in the Marxian direction, on any question whatever.

Split... on any question whatever: this was not exactly the wording of the plan, but it represented Bakunin's understanding of the real line.

But how (continued Bakunin) can the "disastrous effects" of the Italians' course be lessened? First, the Italian Bakuninist leader Cafiero has already gone to the Hague, to attend the Congress, "precisely with this intention." What is the already-declared splitter from Italy going to do at the Hague? Bakunin explained:

> He went there not as a delegate, but as adviser to our Jurassian and Spanish friends, of whom the latter in particular find themselves in a rather delicate position vis-à-vis their own sections—not demoralized, it is true, but confused by the intrigues of Marx and his son-in-law M. Lafargue.... He [Cafiero] will add a very powerful element of courage to the revolutionary firmness of our friends of the Jura and Spain.

So the chief splitter from Italy would be personally present at the Hague to ride herd on any Bakuninist delegate who might weaken in the resolve to split ("on any question") as a result of being "confused" by hearing the other side at the congress for the first time. From the Italians' standpoint, Cafiero's assignment was insurance that the split plan would be carried out on schedule, and that they, as premature splitters, would not be left in the lurch.

Finally, Bakunin's letter even estimated the exact session at which the walkout would be "loudly" staged, and fixed the follow-up splitters' congress to set up a rival simulacrum of the International.

> We hope that the big battle, the decisive battle will be joined in the second session of the Congress and that then the Spanish and Jurassians will walk out of the Congress protesting loudly, in the name of the autonomy and liberty of their respective federations, against all the subsequent decisions of the Congress, but at the same time proclaiming and solemnly affirming the individual solidarity of these federations with the International, with the proletariat of the entire world.

We see the picture: under all this draconic discipline and "imperative" control by the commanders of the secret splitters' plot, all these paladins of Freedom were to carry out the conspiracy to smash the International while "protesting loudly" all about Autonomy and Liberty....

> After that [continued Bakunin's letter], we will come to *Saint-Imier*... to hold, on September 10-12, the Congress of the free federations and set up a closer alliance of these federations, not outside of but in the International.
> *Such is the plan.*[49]

Well, after all that planning, the revised split strategy was *not* going to be carried out unmodified by the Bakuninist floor leader Guillaume. He added a twist. The plan as so far described called for what splitters' jargon tagged a "cold split." Guillaume, to be sure, had persuaded Bakunin not to split in advance of the Hague; now, at the Hague itself, he evidently saw, with the same cunning, that a "cold" walkout by his delegates might not be productive and would certainly be revelatory.

What is certain is this: at the congress, the Jura delegates Guillaume and Schwitzguebel simply ignored the imperative mandate under which they had been elected. They likewise abandoned the strategy agreed on with Bakunin. Instead of a cold split, Guillaume persuaded the Bakuninist faction to *stay in the congress in order to force the majority to take action against them.* The splitters would then be able to yell that the "Marxists" were imposing their horrendous dictatorship.

This third version of the split strategy worked brilliantly—with marxologists and historians. The Swiss schoolmaster from the Jura Mountains has not been given the credit he deserves as the strategist of the big lie.[50]

7. RACISM AND THE SPLITTERS' CAMPAIGN

As has been mentioned, the ideological drive that Bakunin conducted in the period leading to the Hague Congress was *not* focused on "Marxism versus Anarchism," despite the standard myth. Bakunin's focus was on anti-Semitism and racist anti-Germanism, these two being freely presented as more or less the same thing.

It was explained in *KMTR* 1 that the contemporary (post-Hitler) habit of treating all manifestations of anti-Jewish sentiment as one and the same thing is unhistorical, and masks the specific meaning of *racist* anti-Semitism. Anti-Jewish prejudice on a racial ("blood") basis is relatively modern as an important movement. The stereotype of the "economic Jew" was virtually universal, to be sure, but racist anti-Semitism became a movement in Germany only in the late 1870s and 1880s.[51]

The political and social anti-Jewish feeling (which can also be called anti-Semitism) that was rife before that time was often similar in essential type to xenophobic prejudices of other sorts, whether directed against Limeys and Yanks, Spicks and Dagoes, or gypsies, redskins, and Micks: and so on *ad nauseam*. One key indicator was the treatment of converted Jews: when they assumed Christianity (like Heinrich Marx or Heinrich Heine) their juridical situation definitely changed. But in racist anti-Semitism it is "blood" that counts. This is a different political and social phenomenon especially from the standpoint of its historical role.

The racist anti-Semitism that was launched by Stoecker and the Christian Social movement in Germany, or the racist Drumont movement in France a little later, is the anti-Semitism that was brought to a high pitch by Hitlerism. If Hitlerism stands at the end of its evolution, a number of pioneers stand at its beginnings. One of these pioneers was Michael Bakunin, the great paladin of Freedom.

Bakunin's ideology, indeed his mentality, was impregnated with racism from his earliest period of activism. It first took the form of Pan-Slavist racism; for example, Bakunin's "Confession" of 1851 was as filled with exaltation of the Slavic destiny as with the dirtiest racist ranting against Germans. We must emphasize that it was not simple anti-Germanism—in the sense of that simple anti-Americanism which is met in many parts of the world today. *This* anti-Germanism was an overt interpretation of a world struggle of races in terms of "blood." In those years as well as in 1872, Bakunin's theory of history revolved around "blood" racism just as closely as Marx's did around the class structure of society. In fact, one of the best examples of Bakunin's racist theory of history at large was one of his 1872 denunciations of Marx. While Bakunin was usually exercised about Slavic, Teutonic, and Latin "blood," he did not neglect to raise a racist scare against the Yellow Peril that threatened Mother Russia from the Chinese hordes.[52]

Thus this anarchist with a race-saturated mentality became one of the first people (perhaps *the* first) to launch a political campaign around "blood" anti-Semitism—well in advance of the Stoeckers and Drumonts who are better known for it. In Bakunin's preanarchist life, anti-Jewish hatred cropped up only sporadically (as far as we know), perhaps no more than with other scions of the Russian nobility.[53] It burgeoned and flowered in his strategy when he saw it was a weapon against his opponents in the International. That does not mean his anti-Semitism was solely demagogic: he gave free rein to its fetor when it coincided with his Freedom-loving operation.

This pattern first came to bloom in the autumn of 1869, that is, about the same time that Bakunin started speeding up his takeover drive in the International. Immediately after the Basel Congress, Moses Hess published in the French press a strong attack on Bakunin as the representative of barbarism, despotism, and violence. It was thoroughly political in content. Bakunin immediately began writing a reply that began with a lengthy anti-Semitic tirade, entitled "Study on the German Jews."

There is no point in taking space to quote long anti-Semitic vituperations which, unfamiliar then, are well enough known today. Bakunin was quite aware of his pioneering in this field, and boasted of it in a passage which also shadowed forth the typical "Elders of Zion" fable about the Jewish Conspiracy to Control the World—an idea which no doubt appealed to him since he thought of himself as head of a rival conspiracy with the same objective. This passage is worth quoting:

I know that in speaking out my intimate thoughts on the Jews with such frankness I expose myself to immense dangers. Many people share these thoughts, but very few dare to express them publicly, for the Jewish sect, which is much more formidable than that of the Catholic and Protestant Jesuits, today constitutes a veritable power in Europe. It reigns despotically in commerce and banking, and it has invaded three-quarters of German journalism and a very considerable part of the journalism of other countries. Then woe to him who makes the mistake of displeasing it![54]

This was an early anti-Semitic flight; later he did not protest that he was not "the enemy or detractor of Jews," and anyway he proceeded to ladle out pages of empty-minded slurs on Jews in general: "Devoid of all moral sense and all personal dignity, they seek their spirit in the mud, and have made a daily amusement and pastime out of calumny"—this sort of thing, on and on and on.[55]

Likewise, in *this* work Bakunin specifically exempted five Jews from his strictures: Jesus, St. Paul, Spinoza, and two socialists, Marx and Lassalle."[56] Bakunin asked Herzen to publish this diatribe, but the liberal Herzen refused: "Why talk about races, about Jews?" he wanted to know. More important, Herzen asked Bakunin why he had unleashed his fury against an unimportant figure like Hess, while going easy on his real enemy Marx.[57] Bakunin's reply brings us back to the main point. With his usual elephantine cunning, our anarchist explained that it was all an exercise in tactical hypocrisy.

I know, Bakunin told Herzen, that Marx is really behind Hess's slander. (On the contrary, everyone knew that Hess had nothing to do with Marx by this time; but no matter.) Why then, Bakunin continued, did I praise Marx? For two reasons. First, there are his real merits. Second, as a calculated tactic. You, Herzen, think that "I lack calculation" in the movement, but you are wrong. "My attitude toward Marx ... will prove it to you."[58]

Bakunin then revealed his plan to start the fight in the International; *the calculated tactic was to lull Marx with fulsome praise.*

... it could happen, even in a short time, that I will begin a battle with him, not for the personal offense [Hess's attack], of course, but for a question of principle, apropos of state communism.... Then it will be a struggle to the death. But there is a time for everything, and the hour for the struggle has not yet sounded.

Note that this plan to "begin a battle ... to the death" was taking shape on the very morrow of the Basel Congress, without any pretense that it was needed to defend against alleged injustices by the General Council. On the contrary, Bakunin was concerned to stress that the aim was a straight-out political takeover, "for a question of principle," that is, anarchist principles.

Bakunin continued, with smug appreciation of his own cunning:

> I have therefore spared my opponents by a tactical calculation. Don't you see that all these gentlemen who are our enemies form a phalanx which it is essential to disunite and split in order to be able to rout them more easily?

Split and destroy ("rout"). Writing privately, Bakunin throws cant away: it is, he actually explains, "the principle *Divide et impera*." Further:

> If at the present moment I had undertaken an open war against Marx himself, three-quarters of the members of the International would turn against me and I would be at a disadvantage; I would lose the terrain on which I have to stand. But by launching myself into this war by an attack against the riffraff surrounding him, I will have the majority on my side.

Bakunin then explained another trick he had up the same sleeve: if Marx defends his friends against me, "then it is he who will openly declare war: in this case I will also take the field, *and I will have the good-guy role*."[59] (That triumphant emphasis was Bakunin's; it has not been added here.)

Before we go on to see what Bakunin actually intended by the strategy of attacking the "riffraff" around Marx, let us make sure that we understand Bakunin's conscious use of systematic hypocrisy. Bakunin's letter to Herzen, explaining the pretense of praising Marx, casts a backlight on an incident of the previous year—an incident which has been naively quoted by Bakunin apologists and gullible marxologists.

In December 1868, when the Bakuninist Alliance first sent in its proposal to affiliate to the International as a parallel international body, Marx was half amused at the *chutzpah* of the scheme. He wrote to Engels: "*Herr Bakunin*—who is in back of this business—is condescending enough to be willing to take the workers' movement under *Russian* leadership." The French members of the GC, he reported, were in a fury over the proposal; Marx had hoped that the scheme would fade away, but now a public rejection was necessary.[60] But first he tried to find out what Bakunin was up to.

He wrote to a Russian acquaintance in Geneva, asking what friend Bakunin was doing, and adding parenthetically: "I don't know if he still is [my friend]."[61] The acquaintance showed this to Bakunin, who wrote Marx a fulsome letter of praise. He assured Marx he *was* his friend, "more than ever"; praised his revolutionary course; and ended, "You see then, dear friend, that I am your disciple and I am proud of being it."[62]

This is the butter that was laid on, in accordance with a thought-out scheme, by the man who was organizing his myrmidons as a secret body of conspirators to take over the International. Yet this transparent sham has been quoted a hundred times to show that the warm and sincere homage by the paladin of Freedom could not penetrate the hard heart of that monster Marx.

8. BAKUNIN'S POLITICAL POGROM OF 1872

We return to the "riffraff" around Marx who were targeted by Bakunin. It turned out that this meant first of all the Jews: not Marx's friends, but the whole "race."

Because of the aforementioned purge of Bakunin's posthumous papers by his protective friends, it is hard to say how much our libertarian had pursued his anti-Semitic line in the period ending with 1871, that is, before the start of the 1872 campaign. We saw how he went at it in his 1870 letters to Albert Richard,[63] and there is no reason to think this was an aberration. In any case, it was in his campaign of 1872 preceding the Hague Congress that Bakunin revved his anti-Semitic drive into high gear.

His main agit-prop channel was a series of circular letters addressed to the main centers of the Alliance as guides to their work. Extant are a handful of these letters, for they were distributed as widely as possible to Bakunin's supporters and naturally could not all be expunged from history by his friends. They were long and rambling, like all of Bakunin's productions.

The first thing that can be ascertained about them, now that they have returned to the world in the *Archives Bakounine*, is that anarchist argumentation was a small part of the wordage. *The major front on which he sought to whip up hatred of the "Marxists" was purely racist agitation: long anti-Semitic harangues, with special stress on the Jewish conspiracy to dominate the world, interwoven with anti-German tirades of an equally racist type.*

We cannot here do justice to their length and verbose repetitiveness without boring readers to death, and so we will quote only passages of special interest.

Bakunin apologists who have allowed themselves to mention this ordure have emphasized, in extenuation, that anyway he depicts "the Jews" as very intelligent and capable. But racist anti-Semitism was founded with this theory of the all-dominating brainpower of the Jews, beginning with the first popular brochure of agitational anti-Semitism to rock Germany, by the man who invented the term 'anti-Semitism,' Wilhelm Marr. In fact, the theory of anti-Semitism that filled Bakunin's circular letters was remarkably like Marr's famous work—but Bakunin *preceded* Marr by a year.[64]

What was distinctive about Bakunin's anti-Semitic production, historically speaking, was its early Jewish Conspiracy theory. After all, the *Protocols of the Elders of Zion* was fabricated only in 1895-1900 and published in 1905. However, it is possible that there was a direct link between Bakunin and certain shady predecessors of the *Protocols* forgery, so that the *Protocols* on the one hand and Bakunin's output on the other constituted separate developments from a similar source.*

Bakunin went well beyond the traditional anti-Semitic pattern of merely derogating Jews; the conspiracy to rule the world embraced *all* Jews-by-blood, and extended over all countries and classes. Rothschild and Marx were both conscious participants in this conspiracy. This is unadulterated *Elders of Zion* garbage and should not be stuffed into the same rubbish can as ordinary anti-Jewish diatribes.

In one of his first circular letters, sent out in December 1871 to the Bologna section of the International, there was the usual lengthy insistence on the all-compassing power of the Jews in Germany and elsewhere. They control business, politics, journalism, high finance, and "in recent years" they have begun to take over socialism.

> Well now, this whole Jewish world which constitutes a single exploiting sect, a sort of bloodsucker people, a collective parasite, voracious, organized in itself, not only across the frontiers of states but even across all the differences of political opinion—this world is presently, at least in great part, at the disposal of Marx on the one hand and of the Rothschilds on the other. I know that the Rothschilds, reactionaries as they are and should be, highly appreciate the merits of the communist Marx; and that in his turn the communist Marx feels irresistibly drawn, by instinctive attraction and respectful admiration, to the financial genius of Rothschild. Jewish solidarity, that powerful solidarity that has maintained itself through all history, united them.

"That must seem strange," Bakunin admitted, but the bond was this: "Marx's communism" wants a centralized state; a centralized state requires a central State Bank; such a bank nurtures the Jews. You see? So the Jews who run the German socialist party are working to win over "the Jews of Austria"; Switzerland too is being taken over. In 1869 "the General Council, which had long meditated plans for universal monarchy born in Marx's intelligent brain," made the first attempt to realize it at the Basel Congress. That was why all those Jews fell on me, Bakunin, with their "calumny and intrigue."[66]

Multiply this manyfold, for pages of rubbish. In a similar circular dedi-

---

*The immediate ancestor of the *Protocols*, Jacob Brafman's *Book of the Kahal*, was concocted in the mid-1860s and sponsored by the Russian governor of Vilna, Michael Muraviev. It was circulated to czarist government officials, especially the political police.[65] Bakunin could have known this work. It may be that the conspiracy theory had a history before Brafman; I do not know.

cated to the education of the Jura section, Bakunin continued his revelation that what happened at the Basel Congress was "a dire conspiracy of German and Russian Jews against me." The Jews were now "sovereign masters" in finance, had a "monopoly in literature," and had installed a Jewish editor at every German newspaper. There was a vitriolic smear attack on the Jewish religion: Jehovah was a "homicidal god"; Moses ordered Jewry "to massacre all people in order to establish its own power"; fortunately the Jews were conquered and dispersed, but as a result formed "a vast commercial association" to exploit all other nations.[67]

Then Bakunin's circular letter virtually came out for a pogrom—as indeed Russian populist-anarchists did later, and as the other father of anarchism Proudhon had done earlier:

> Therefore in all countries the people detest the Jews. They detest them so much that every popular revolution is accompanied by a massacre of Jews: a natural consequence, but one which is not such as to make the Jews partisans of popular social revolution.

This was followed by another version of the all-class capitalist-communist conspiracy theory. The Jews, being born bourgeois exploiters, hate revolution. "At bottom, the Jews of every country are really friends only with the Jews of all countries, independently of all differences existing in their social positions, degree of education, political opinions, and religious worship." A baptized Jew "remains no less a Jew," whether reactionary, liberal, or socialist.

> Above all, they are Jews, and that establishes among all the individuals of this singular race, across all religions, political and social differences that separate them, a union and solidarity that is mutually indissoluble. It is a powerful chain, broadly cosmopolitan and narrowly national at the same time, in the racial sense, interconnecting the kings of finance, the Rothschilds, or the most scientifically exalted intelligences, with the ignorant and superstitious Jews of Lithuania, Hungary, Roumania, Africa, and Asia. I do not think there exists a single Jew in the world today who does not tremble with hope and pride when he hears the sacred name of Rothschild.

This time Bakunin wants to make no exceptions. "Every Jew" is an authoritarian; "it is the heritage of the race."

With this thesis Bakunin worked his way through Rothschild, through the liberal German leader Johann Jacoby, to "the eminent socialist writer Charles Marx." Alongside these "illustrious Jews" were a host of "little Jews, bankers, usurers ... journalists ... socialists," and what not. They served their masters, and pullulated in the German socialist party; individually they were wretches. "But they are a legion, and, what is worse, a very well disciplined legion, awaiting only a sign from the master [Marx] to pour all their venomous slime over the individuals pointed out to their fury...."[68]

This man knew all about "venomous slime." Throughout his tedious pages of rubbish against "the" Jews, Bakunin always directed his point into the channel of a political pogrom in the International, against Marx and the "Hebrew-German sect" that controlled the International just as Rothschild controlled the banks.[69] There was a difference after the Hague Congress: in Bakunin's book *Statism and Anarchy*, his anti-Semitic sewerage was no longer a torrent but only an occasional gurgle in the rambling anarchist stream. The hatchet job had been done.[70]

9. THE GREAT SMEAR CAMPAIGN

In the split drive of 1872, Bakunin paralleled or supplemented his anti-Semitic agitation with just as lengthy tirades of racist anti-Germanism, in which Germans and Jews could not always be distinguished. We will be concerned not with this form of racism *per se* but with the political campaign for which it was the vehicle.

Suffice to say that (1) for Bakunin this was not merely a matter of a smear against a whole people, but was formulated to discredit precisely those Germans who were most courageously fighting *against* the Bismarck regime and German imperial power; and (2) it was not a question of German or Prussian society or state, but of German "blood."[71]

He had at least two objectives in doing this.

(1) One was to whitewash Russian society in comparison, though he usually remembered to interject protestations of hostility to the czarist state, as to all states. There were a number of passages in which he got at a backhanded exaltation of the Russian or Slavic world by contrasting it with a caricature of Teutonic evil. In the back of his mind was a lesser-evil acceptance of the Russian imperium, and on at least one occasion it came off his pen—thus:

> German conquest would pan-Germanize the world; Russian or Slavic conquest would end sooner or later in the absorption of the conquerors in the civilization of the conquered peoples. Both are detestable; but if it would be absolutely necessary to choose between them, I would advise Europe to sooner accept Slavic or Russian conquest.[72]

This was intertwined in his mind with an apocalyptic vision of a war of races for the conquest of the world, in which the "Latin race" and the

"Slavic race" would be allied to crush the "German race"—"on the day of the ultimate and ineluctable combat of the Slavs against the Germans."[73]

We have mentioned that Bakunin habitually saw history in racist terms; and his view of the race struggle for the world was transferred holus-bolus to the International. Invoking the support of the French, Spanish, Belgian, and Italian sections, he cried: "It is the Latin world that federalizes, organizes, and rises in the name of liberty, against the dictatorship of the pan-Germanists of London." And as he denounced Marx's "dictatorship," he gave the watchword: "To this monstrous pretension of pan-Germanism, we must counterpose the alliance of the Latin race and the Slavic race...."[74] These were constantly repeated ideas. The last word of this "anarchism" for the world was bloody race war.

(2) This indicated the second of his objectives: smearing Marx and the "Marxists" in control of the International. They were not only part of the Rothschild-Jewish conspiracy but also agents of the Teutonic Peril. Thus, in one of the circular letters expounding the Jewish Conspiracy theory, he revealed that Marx and the General Council, who were "fanatically devoted to their dictator-messiah Marx," were really Bismarckians: "this thinking is inspired in them by a sentiment of race. It is pan-Germanism... the thinking of the pan-German state subjecting more or less all Europe to the domination of the German race which they believe is called on to regenerate the world...."[75]

(To anticipate a point. How did Bakunin *know* this was how the "Marxists" thought? Because that was how a Bakunin thought. Marx had to think the same way; you just change the names.)

Bakunin did not merely claim that Marx thought *like* Bismarck. He charged, over and over, that Marx's *conscious* objective was to use the International to expand the Bismarckian German Empire, like a good German patriot. Marx puffed up the danger from czarist Russia only "in order to turn the attention of the good public away from the ambitious plans of his own fatherland, and in order to bring about the acceptance of Germany's conquests." (If that were Marx's motive, there was no need to answer Marx's attacks on Holy Russia.) According to this systematic liar, Marx's "patriotic goal" was to make the European proletariat sympathetic to German power over the world. "Mr. Marx has shown himself to be ... not an international socialist revolutionary but an ardent patriot of the great Bismarckian fatherland." Marx's "fundamental" belief was that "the Germanic race alone" can exist and rule as "the legitimate representative of humanity." In fact, Marx was really working for Bismarck (consciously), for "all the actions" of the German socialists were inspired by the desire to "extend the *borders of the [German] Empire as far as possible*." Bismarck only pretended to be an enemy of the German socialists, because they were propagandizing for "the German concept of the state" and not for socialism. "To spread this concept is today the main concern of Mr. Marx...."[76]

This campaign of uninhibited hooligan-like slander has precedents today, and perhaps even worse has been seen. But it was an innovation for 1872, and for the socialist movement.

Alongside the anti-Semitic and anti-German diatribes in Bakunin's campaign was a third element, likewise represented by constantly repeated harangues. This was a torrent of systematic *personal* slander against Marx. There was more to it than meets the eye.

In passage after passage Bakunin fed the prejudices of his dupes with a description of Marx as a veritable monster. Some of the more briefly quotable pleasantries were: "vain to the point of dirtiness and folly" ... fanatically "vainglorious and ambitious" ... cowardly ... "given to intrigue like the real Jew he is" ... "if anyone refuses to bend his neck before him, he begins to detest him" ... and so on and on, without restraint.[77] There was no question of evidence; the lack of this detail was made up by the sheer bulk of the dirt.

Out of these mephitic fumes, a certain suspicion may be born ...

10. THE PALADIN OF LIES

The suspicion may be furthered by another series of unbridled smears. Over and over, Bakunin repeated that this Marx-monster was devoted to systematic lying; he spread the "dirtiest calumnies" against anyone for any reason; he was "vindictive to the point of insanity"; he was convinced that "all infamies" and any "horrors" were permissible against an enemy; he sought "occult and real power" in the movement; he aspired to govern the International by "discipline," under a "dictatorial government."[78]

Whose portrait is this?

It was not a mere invention; it was recognizably the picture of a real person. He was describing himself, with touches borrowed from Nechayev. He wanted to describe a ruthless aspirant to total control over society; he knew his enemy *must* be so because it was the only way to run a conspiracy to dominate the globe.

It was noted in *KMTR* 2 that "It was Bakunin's regular pattern to accuse Marx in public of exactly what he, Bakunin, was planning in secret." Look back to this passage.[79]

This pattern extended to his concocted Marx-anecdotes. Let us contemplate a passage drafted by Bakunin for a piece entitled "Personal Relations with Marx," a compendium of personal smears and anti-Semitic abuse that contained no references to any real relations with Marx. In this laboratory specimen of Bakunin's methodology, we find him swearing on his personal knowledge that the following occurred in 1848:

> And then, in the middle of a half-jocular half-serious conversation, Marx told me: "You know, I am now at the head of a communist secret society, so well disciplined that if I told one of its members, 'Go kill Bakunin,' he would kill you."[80]

It may be thought that Bakunin's vicious mendacity was simply running wild. Not so; this story had a factual basis. When he wrote this around the end of 1871 or beginning of 1872, Bakunin had gone through a political-organizational partnership with a real monster named Nechayev, *who, he knew, not only believed in functioning exactly that way but had in fact ordered the murder of a refractory comrade in similar terms.*

Without going here into the details of Bakunin's well-known partnership with this archetype of the "revolutionary" gangster, we remind the reader that when Bakunin put these words into the mouth of a dummy named "Marx," he *knew* that in December 1869 his protégé Nechayev, while organizing a conspiratorial group in a Russian town, had decided that a member of the group had to be liquidated, and had given orders for his assassination. *Go kill Ivanovich*, he had told his anarchist zombies, and they killed him. The case had been tried a few months ago in Russia, and had made Continental headlines to the discreditment of the socialist movement everywhere. Bakunin's admiration of Nechayev as a revolutionary hero was unbounded.

Now look at the very terms of Bakunin's smear of Marx: who was it that really made a conscious system out of lying and slander against any enemy? out of vindictiveness, as a revolutionary virtue? out of infamies and horrors up to murder to intimidate opposition? The answer was, in the first place, that this was a portrait of Nechayevism, and the whole pattern was specifically endorsed by Bakunin in his own name.* As for the distinction between "occult power" and dictatorship, etc., we have seen that these were commonplaces of Bakunin's secret doctrine.

In short: the long tirades of slander against the fictional character named "Marx" were not simply the random vituperations of a vicious liar foaming at the mouth. This was a self-portrait (a little Nechayevized, as mentioned). It was Bakunin's conception of how a would-be world dictator could be

---

*Not covered here is also an account of the affair of Nechayev's "Lyubavin letter," a gangsterish threat against the publisher of a planned Russian translation of *Capital*, an affair which figured in Bakunin's expulsion at the Hague Congress. It is a complicated plot, and would take more space at this point than it is worth. I hope to cover this tale between other covers, but anyway the main facts are accessible today.[81]

expected to act, while pretending to the gullible masses that he was a libertarian saint.

The second line of defense for the Bakunin myth has it that Nechayev pulled the wool over the veteran's eyes. This apologia was always thin enough to see through; but with the aforementioned discovery of new documents, it evaporated.

Bakunin sat down to write his long letter of June 2, 1870 to "Boy" (Nechayev) *after* he had finally accepted the truth about his partner's mode of gangsterism in general and the murder of Ivanovich in particular. But this letter was not a repudiation of Nechayevism: it was a *reaffirmation* of the revolutionary merit of the little murderous punk, and a proposal for continued partnership—with a proviso. *The proviso: if Nechayev confined his gangster methods to opponents and did not apply them to Bakunin himself, as he had started to do.*

In this letter to Nechayev, with the facts out in the open, with everything known and admitted, Bakunin more than once stated his complete agreement with Nechayev's ideology and modes of operation. Our programs are "identical," he repeated. (This applied also to the brochures and other documents which, even when drafted by Nechayev, represented their joint ideas.) Bakunin assured Nechayev that he too understood the need for "cunning and deceit," for "Jesuit methods," *but* only against rivals and opponents, not among ourselves.

> Thus this simple law must be the basis of our activity: truth, honesty, mutual trust between all Brothers and toward any man who is capable of becoming and whom you would wish to become a Brother;—lies, cunning, entanglement, and, if necessary, violence toward enemies.

The "simple law" of lies, cunning, swindling, and violence was what they both stood for—inside the opponents' movement which was to be destroyed from within. You, Nechayev (wrote the older swindler), have perpetrated "many dirty tricks," but it was all for the cause. After all, "whoever is frightened of horrors or dirt should turn away from this world and this revolution." But—he kept repeating this since it was the main burden of the letter—you must confine the use of "police and Jesuitical systems" to enemies, to "inimical parties."[82]

He left no ambiguity about the targets of the "dirty tricks" and "Jesuitical methods." *All this was being written down in the midst of his drive to take over the International.* In case there is a retarded child somewhere who cannot deduce that he was writing about what he was then actually doing— doing in and to the International—he also wrote the following down in so many words:

> Societies whose aims are near to ours must be forced to merge

with our Society or, at least, must be subordinated to it without their knowledge, while harmful people must be removed from them. Societies which are inimical or positively harmful must be dissolved, and finally the government must be destroyed. All this cannot be achieved only by propagating the truth; cunning, diplomacy, deceit are necessary. Jesuit methods or even entanglement [*Another translation:* mystification] can be used for this....[83]

This was the blueprint for the immediately ensuing campaign of racist calumny, anti-Semitic filth, and personal slander.

From the standpoint of this campaign, there was a last edifying vignette to be mentioned. For another month after writing the cited letter to Nechayev, Bakunin continued to make efforts to re-cement relations with "Boy." In early July, Bakunin journeyed to Geneva for a face-to-face effort; and there he finally decided after some weeks that Nechayev was hopeless.

He thereupon gave the young gangster a lesson in what an old one could do. Leaving the last talk with Nechayev with the usual amenities and a good-bye kiss, he sat down to write confidential letters behind the assassin's back, warning friends against further relations. One friend was mobilized to steal back the compromising letters that Nechayev had stolen from him, Bakunin. Another friend was asked to cooperate in a second little scheme. *This was to help spread the belief that it was not Bakunin who was sending around these warnings against Nechayev but—the General Council in London.*[84]

Nechayev quickly learned what was going on. He wrote Bakunin: you gave me a "Judas kiss" at our last meeting, now these letters are the "vilest acts of a dirty hatred." He added: "So you want... to roll in the mud. Well, go ahead and roll!"[85]

This was the last word in Nechayev-Bakunin relations. It is still echoing.

"Roll in the mud" is also an appropriate summary for the career of the paladin of Freedom. With the possible exception of Nechayev, there is no dirtier personage in the history of the leftist movements of the nineteenth century; there is no more evil aspirant to oligarchic dictatorship; there is no more "authoritarian" mentality than his; there is no more systematic exponent of virulent racism and slander, of lies and "revolutionary" swindling.

It is time that even marxologists stopping exalting this sinister figure for the sake of "getting" Marx.

• • •

NOTE ON A. LEHNING

My incidental references to Arthur Lehning, editor of the *Archives Bakounine*, who is usually regarded as an eminent scholar, may raise questions in the reader's mind. Since an adequate comment on Lehning would be digressive here, such a reader is referred to the extraordinary pages devoted to Lehning in Aileen Kelly's *Mikhail Bakunin* (Oxford, 1982), pages 238-241, which I saw only after this Note was written. Kelly's outspoken verdict on Lehning took courage and integrity, and deserves a salute.

SPECIAL NOTE C | **THE STRANGE CASE OF FRANZ MEHRING**
A Whistle-Blowing Note to Chapter 3

The Lassalle-Marx myth discussed in Special Note A received its definitive enrootment, if not its initial impetus, from the pen of Franz Mehring.

There is a myth about Mehring too, especially in this connection. It is a peculiar sort of myth, for it is not so much the propagation of a fals*ifiction*, a false story, as a suppression of half the true story. In the case of the Mehring problem (and I know no other such case), we must confront the usual portrayal of Mehring not by distinguishing between what is true and what is false, but between what is true and what is *suppressed*.

Most people who know anything at all about Mehring know him mainly, if not only, as the author of a biography of Marx that has often been called the "standard" biography. Of Mehring's career they probably know only, or mainly, what they read about him in the Translator's Preface, by Edward Fitzgerald, to the English translation of the biography.[1] Current German reference sources are not appreciably more enlightening than this account.[2]

In all these sketches, and in passages in numerous books where he is only a minor figure, the picture one gets of Mehring can be put briefly: here was a brilliant intellectual figure, historian and literary critic, who opposed Marxism most of his life but at the ripe age of 44-45, not only joined the social-democratic movement, but became one of the most effective Marxist champions; moreover a *revolutionary* Marxist, a virulent enemy of the revisionist current, an opponent of World War I from the beginning, and finally, together with Rosa Luxemburg and Karl Liebknecht, one of the founders of the German Communist Party—shortly before his death in early 1919.

All this was true. If we say no more about this side of Mehring, it is because it has been adequately celebrated in numerous books and articles. But it was only one side of the human amalgam that was Mehring; and practical considerations force us to bend the helm in this short note by emphasizing what constituted the other side.

1. MEHRING'S CIRCUITOUS ROAD TO MARXISM

The main fact about Mehring that is usually suppressed is the peculiarity of his political career: he adopted socialistic views long before he joined the Social-Democratic Party (SDP) in 1891, and apparently held them alongside left- and right-liberal views, even when collaborating with conservative publicists. The point of mentioning this complicated thought-life is not to indict him for political light-mindedness (though this was done in his time by the revisionist right wing). The point is that these socialistic views were derived from his permanent admiration for Lassalle. Insofar as he wavered in and out of socialistic ideas in the 1870s and 1880s, he began as a Lassallean—and he remained a Lassallean.

When the socialist unity of 1875 was achieved at Gotha, Mehring praised the Lassalleans and reviled the Eisenachers. In his once-notorious history of the German Social-Democratic Party published in 1877-79 (in various and numerous editions), he subjected most of the party leaders, particularly also Marx and Engels, to contemptuous and contemptible slanders and vilifications of an uninhibited sort unusual even for the *Sozialistenfresser* (or *Sozialistentöter*) of the day. But at the same time he praised Lassalle as a far-seeing statesman; he wrote as an admirer of the good nationalist Lassalle against the bad internationalist Marx.

Let us say at once that only one scholar has made a study of Mehring's first half-life, his political development up to 1891 when he joined the SDP. This was Thomas Höhle, an East German authority on Mehring who in 1956 published his work *Franz Mehring: Sein Weg zum Marxismus 1869-1891*.[3] (West German reviewers opined that its publication had become possible only with the notable 1956 thaw.) The present note, insofar as it refers to this period, is based on Höhle. But let it not be imagined that Höhle writes as a breaker of idols; he bends over backward to put everything in the kindest light possible. It is my impression that Höhle kept reminding himself that his responsibility to science demanded presentation of the whole truth, but it did not require him to grind the idol underfoot. For example, of the rather shameful contents of that 1879 history of German socialism, Höhle has a duly horrified sentence summary, followed by one specimen, which he finds so revolting that he cries "Enough!" and brings down the curtain over it. There are pages where Höhle devotes a paragraph to stating, heart-heavy, what Mehring said or did, and then devotes the rest of the page to sanitizing it. Only a scholar who has repeated Höhle's work—and there are none such either in the past or in sight—can confirm that he has given us all the necessary facts; but I am willing to accept Höhle's work on its face value, on the ground that its apologetics can be separated on sight from its scholarship.

At any rate, there is nothing else.

We have said that Mehring adopted socialist views long before joining the SDP in 1891. The question is: What kind of socialist politics did Mehring adopt? The answer is unabashed Lassallean reformism.

Mehring greeted the unity of two socialist groups in 1875 at the Gotha congress with enthusiasm. In a letter to Wilhelm Liebknecht he expressed his desire to aid the new party by offering it the opportunity to publish in pamphlet form a series of articles he had written for the democratic newspaper *Die Wage*. These articles were a reply to the attack by Heinrich von Treitschke of the National Liberal Party (that is, the principal procapitalist party) on the SDP *and* the Katheder-Sozialisten. The Katheder-Sozialist, Gustav Schmoller, entered into a polemic with Treitschke and Mehring's contribution took the form of a defense of the SDP *and* the Katheder-Sozialisten against the defender of a "pure and simple" capitalist politics.

As Höhle remarks, "It is characteristic of the 'Anti-Treitschke' that the conservative party, the Junkers and especially the German Empire are not attacked even indirectly. At one point Mehring even speaks reverently of the 'Crown, the highest authority in the land'. His critical edge is directed against Liberalism."[4] Mehring defended Lassalle, and by implication the SDP, from Treitschke's attack by denying that Lassalle's agitation was meant to stir up the working class. "Lassalle has never appealed, as you charge, to unleashed passions, and the 'wild appetite' of the masses; the great basic idea of his agitation was that only science [Wissenschaft] could elevate the workers to the height of cultivation and welfare that befit it. . . ."[5] The worker, according to Mehring, resented Treitschcke's assertion that the class struggle was unbridgeable.[6] Mehring pointed to the Katheder-Sozialist Schmoller as an example of the man of "head and heart" who rejected "Manchesterdom" and unbridled capitalism and did bridge the gap between workers and men of education. Schmoller is strongly recommended to the working-class audience. Indeed, the whole pamphlet is based on the Lassallean notion of socialism as the alliance of men of education (Wissenschaft) and the worker in support of the "modern" ideology of state intervention.

"Down with liberal corruption" is the battle cry of the anti-Treitschke.

2. THE SONNEMAN AFFAIR

It is characteristic of Mehring's political development that his break with the SDP came as a result of a combination of personal and political factors. In May of 1876, Mehring after some months of unemployment accepted a position with the Berlin *Staatsbürger Zeitung*, which he himself had earlier attacked as a scandal sheet. In his new job he shortly became involved in a literary and legal quarrel with one of the most distinguished liberal newspapers in Germany, the *Frankfurter Zeitung*, published by Leopold Sonneman. Sonneman was a Reichstag deputy of the *Progressive* party and a leader of its liberal wing. (The left wing was, in fact, referred to as the "Sonneman liberals.") The paper was widely read abroad and its foreign policy coverage was highly thought of. More importantly, it was generally sympathetic to the working class movement and the SDP.[7]

Mehring charged in an article of May 21, 1876, shortly after joining the staff of the rival newspaper, that Sonneman had used the *Frankfurter Zeitung* to promote certain business enterprises for personal gain. Whether the charge was true or not is difficult to determine. The matter came to court twice. In one instance the ruling was in favor of Sonneman; in the other, the case was decided in Mehring's favor. Fair is fair.

From the standpoint of the SDP, however, the scandal embarrassed an ally. In particular, the Berlin SDP paper, the *Berliner Freie Presse*, which was a rival of the *Staatsbürger Zeitung*, came down on Sonneman's side.

The congress of the recently united party, held in Gotha in 1876, was forced to take up the issue. Liebknecht, the editor of *Vorwärts*, who had previously remained silent on the issue, defended Sonneman as "a bulwark of democracy." Liebknecht chose to ignore the content of the charges against Sonneman.

Mehring was pushed by this relatively unimportant fight in the direction of the *National Liberals*, the pro-Bismarck party which was also the party of most of the *Katheder-Sozialisten*. The 1876 Gotha Congress lasted from August 19 to August 23. Mehring began work on an anti-SDP polemic in the *Magdeburgischer Zeitung* on September 1. The result, titled *Zur Geschichte der Deutsche Sozial-Demokratie*, was published as a Reichstag election campaign pamphlet in January 1877. It was revised and published by the *Weser Zeitung* as *Die Deutsche Sozial Demokratie, Ihre Geschichte und ihre Lehre; eine historisch-kritische Darstellung*. It was again revised and expanded in 1878. There was still a third edition in 1879. A serial popularization appeared in *Die Gartenlaube* "Zur Geschichte der Sozialdemokratie." This last was even more hostile personally to leaders of the movement.[8]

The whole work was permeated with the hero worship of great, or at least powerfully willed, men who made history. Lassalle was the prime example. "The German Social-Democracy was... stamped out of the ground by the forceful will of an autocratic man."

But these were not only powerful men. They were dangerous. Mehring's former (and future) friend Liebknecht was "an apostle of subversion" who "almost together with his mother's milk... seems to have absorbed the insatiable drive to instill people's heart with hate, envy and wrath."[9] Marx and Engels were "sybarites of the spirit, who, as if in disgust with the limitations and finiteness of all earthly existence, carry on propaganda for subversion as a kind of Mephistophelian sport."

Internationalism was the great sin. "This decade long dispute... in the main was the product of a protracted battle of the internationalist communist Marx against, and his final victory over, the tradition of the national Socialist Lassalle."[10]

The present leadership of the SDP was only following in a long tradition. "The instinctive hatred against education and knowledge, which is so prominently evidenced by present-day communism, came out already in the earliest beginnings of the movement." For Mehring there is no distinction between hostility to the educated *classes* and hatred of learning as such. Schweitzer was treated as a victim of this "anti-intellectualism." His flirtation with Bismarck (as well as Lassalle's) was treated favorably. Mehring's own earlier criticisms, as a liberal journalist, of Bismarck went by the board.

In general, Mehring, in a frenzy over his slight by the SDP over the Sonneman affair, abandoned a good deal of his own earlier politics. The year of revolution, 1848, became "the crazy year"; "hatred of Prussia" was denounced as "the most insipid of passions." A real low point was reached when Mehring was forced, in the middle of this period, to confront the witch hunt against the socialist movement. In 1878 the Bismarck government pushed through the Reichstag legislation that severely restricted the activity of the socialist movement. This was in the aftermath of the half-witted assassination attempts on the Kaiser by Karl Nobiling and Max Hödel. Mehring endorsed the government justification of this antisocialist law. Social-Democracy was, of course, not *directly* responsible for the attacks, but it contributed to the *spiritual confusion* which led to these attacks. Mehring attacked the "unfathomable immorality" of socialist agitation.[11]

This antisocialist polemic, in its several editions, was a big commercial success. Kautsky says that in those years Mehring was the bourgeois writer most despised by the SDP.

3. THE MORNING AFTER

From 1879 on Mehring began to drift politically and economically. The picture is of a man sobering up after a serious binge. From 1878 to 1884 he was most closely associated with the *Weser Zeitung* which was pro-Bismarck but which also supported free trade and was nervous about Bismarck's protectionism. Besides, some of the personalities in the SDP most hostile to him in the Sonneman affair had left the party or been expelled. Johann Most and Hasselman of *Berliner Zeitung* were among them.

Mehring became more and more disillusioned with Bismarck. He wrote a series of articles attacking the Accident Insurance Law, one of the government's social welfare measures which was meant to demonstrate the possibilities for reform by a "social monarchy," as a mere palliative.

A glimpse into Mehring's confused politics in this period is given by his response to the rise of the antisemitic demagogue Adolf Stöcker. Stöcker was a Protestant preacher whose antisemitic sentiments won him favor with the imperial court and he enjoyed a brief period of electoral success in the 1880s. Mehring, in an article on the Berlin vote in 1881, compared Stöcker's supporters—"a motley crowd of fools"—to the "determined, serious, often gray-haired workers" who supported the Social-Democrats. One "experiences a deep feeling of shame at how much more sympathetic the enemies of contemporary society appear than those who unabashedly present themselves as its professional saviors."

Then followed a curious article in which Mehring attacked the antisocialist law for its inconsistency: it was applied to one set of demagogues but not another.

> If this law is directed not at the socialist *goal*, which can still be legally advocated in respectable, academic forms, but only at the demagogic *methods* of the Social-Democracy, then it makes no sense if campaigns for very different goals but using very similar methods are allowed to use the German Empire for a parade ground. This, however, is obviously the case because the campaigns of the antisemites and the Social-Christians are as much like those of the Social-Democrats as one rotten egg is like another.[12]

It is unclear whether Mehring is arguing in this passage for the repeal of the antisocialist law or for its application to all the "demagogues." This may have just been an attempt to score a debater's point. Mehring, however, consistently opposed the Social-Democrats' emphasis on class conflict right up until the day he joined the party. Over the next ten years he was to base his increasingly bitter opposition to the antisocialist law on its ineffectiveness. It did not lessen class hostility; it increased it. Its main consequence was to drive the working class to the left. As we shall see, it finally ended up driving Mehring to the left.

4. 1882—A YEAR OF CHANGE

Over the next year Mehring moved personally and intellectually to the left in this same zig-zag pattern. In terms of party politics he moved closer to the Progressive Party, and in March of 1882 became associated with the *Politische Wochenschaft*, a liberal paper.

By the end of 1882 he came out against the antisocialist law while continuing to bemoan "the poisonous and uncontrolled demagogy of the party [which] planted the idea of assassination in the minds of useless types like Hödel and Nobiling."[13] The point was that the antisocialist law encouraged this kind of demagogy. Mehring, for example, denounced the stupidity of banning the legal party newspaper the *Süddeutshen Post*, a relatively moderate local paper, and, as a consequence, leaving the party rank-and-file with nothing to read but the radical *Sozialdemokrat* published illegally in Zürich.[14]

Examples of this kind of political schizophrenia could be multiplied indefinitely. The detail is not necessary to draw a political portrait of Mehring. Here was a man won over by the *growing strength* of social-democracy. A *frontal attack* on "Marxism" (i.e., the militant anti-Junker *and* anticapitalist politics that was so attractive to the rank and file) could only isolate the attacker from the ranks of SDP. Parenthetically, this also explains Mehring's subsequent wavering in the 1900s. A long period of legal activity brought elements into the party who hesitated at joining an illegal party. Electoral and trade union success seemed to offer at least the possibility of indefinite progress. Reformism became a far more realistic prospect for the party.

None of this is meant to imply that Mehring was a hypocritical place seeker. If he had been, the road that led him to social-democracy would not have been as long and tortured. He was changing his mind because he was "realistically" taking account of changing circumstances. Mehring, the skilled materialist historian, would have understood the process if he had been explaining the political evolution of some historical personage.

5. LAST STOP

Mehring's last stop on the road to social-democracy was Die Demokratishe Partei—a fusion of the Progressives and a splinter faction of the Liberals. Its newspaper, the *Demokrätischen Blätter*, was edited from 1885 to 1887 by Georg Ledebour, the later left-wing leader of the Social-Democratic Party. In the 1887 Reichstag election the party was unable to win even one seat. The paper ceased publication. As Höhle puts it, "The last attempt in the nineteenth century in Germany to call into life a radical petty-bourgeois party failed."

Mehring was the most important literary collaborator of the *Demokrätische Blätter* in 1884-85. In an article called *"Über die Gründbedingungen sozialer Reformen"* he reviewed the history of attempts at reform from above (a la Bismarck-Lassalle). He came to a negative verdict.[15] For him "social reform from below" was the only *alternative* to revolution.

Mehring in this period became more and more openly sympathetic to Marx. He wrote numerous articles in the paper popularizing Marx and Engels' historical studies. It was at this point (1885) that he approached Engels for material on a projected Marx biography. Engels was cool to the idea.[16] (Bebel, to whom Engels confided his doubts about Mehring, was even more cool toward Mehring.[17]) Nevertheless, in July, Engels expressed admiration for Mehring's literary talent and he expressed the hope that this would be kept in mind "if he comes over to us again, as he surely will, as soon as the times change."[18]

Beginning in 1884 Mehring began work with the Berlin *Volks-Zeitung*. It was this newspaper that was to be his mouthpiece for the next few years until he was driven out of bourgeois journalism and into the Social-Democratic Party. The *Volks-Zeitung* was sympathetic to social-democracy even before Mehring became its most prominent writer. In its columns Mehring was free to express his growing interest in the party. To take one example, he closely followed the internal politics of the party in the dispute over the Steamship subsidy and made clear his support for the right wing.[19] That is, Mehring was beginning to think of himself as a social-democratic sympathizer or fellow-traveler, but as a sympathizer or fellow-traveller of the right wing.

In early 1885 a Bismarckian newspaper denounced the "socialism" of the *Volks-Zeitung*.[20] There was some justification in the charge. Mehring became more anti-Bismarck as the room for opposition shrank. No quarter year went by without an issue of the *Volks-Zeitung* being banned. Yet Mehring remained pro-monarchist! On Kaiser Wilhelm I's ninetieth birthday Mehring enthused over the embodiment of "the unity of the Fatherland." "The gray figure of the restorer of the German Empire stands high over all these struggles."[21] In an article of April 13, 1888 he denounced those who agitated against the monarchy as "traitors."

Two years later it was Mehring whose career as a bourgeois journalist was ended as a result of a conflict with the monarchy. The brief reign of the "liberal" Friedrich III was followed in 1889 by the accession to the throne of the new Kaiser Wilhelm II. Mehring mistrusted the man in part because of Wilhelm II's notorious political sympathy for Stöcker's antisemitic alternative to socialism.

Mehring's attack on the Speech from the Throne of November 1888 was, according to Höhle, unheard of.[22] The final crisis, however, came in 1889. On March 9, Mehring published a lead article on the anniversary of the old kaiser's death. The man Mehring had shortly before praised as "the restorer of German Empire" was attacked as the representative of narrow dynastic and military interests. He had no interest in the social problems of the German people.

This open break with the Bismarck-Lassalle politics of the social monarchy lead to Mehring's ouster. Although even the antisocialist law provided no legal basis for action against Mehring, the personal outrage of the kaiser and the president of police made it necessary for the authorities to act. The issue of the paper which contained this outrageous attack on the "restorer of the German Empire" (No. 58) was seized despite the Public Prosecutor's finding that there was no legal pretext for the action. Mehring's office and home were searched and manuscripts were seized.

On March 17, Mehring published an article celebrating the March 18 anniversary of the 1848 insurrection. The same day, Police President von Richthofen banned all further issues of the *Volks-Zeitung*. This is the only occasion on which a bourgeois paper was banned under the antisocialist law, according to Höhle. The Reichskommission, which oversaw the application of the antisocialist law, lifted the ban on April 12. Nevertheless, Mehring's steady drift to the left and the SDP was given new impetus.

Mehring's actual break with the *Volks-Zeitung*, however, was something of an anticlimax. Shortly after this political episode he became embroiled in a literary quarrel with a prominent critic who, if Höhle's account is accurate, had arranged a boycott of his former lover who was an actress. Ordinarily, a literary campaign over such a scandal would only boost circulation. Mehring, however, developed the series of articles into a muckraking pamphlet which attacked the general corruption of the press and the theater.[23] This particular injustice was only a symptom. The cause was the turning of the press and theater into money-making machines and the consequent growth of toadying and nepotism. Since the *Volks-Zeitung* itself had recently been bought out by just the kind of capitalist entrepreneur Mehring was denouncing, the campaign led to a purge of the staff including Mehring and Ledebour.

In 1890 the antisocialist law had been allowed to expire. The social-democratic press was now easily available to workers and leftists who had previously depended on papers like the *Volks-Zeitung* as the only *legal* press sympathetic to social-democracy and the workers' movement. The owners of the *Volks-Zeitung*, therefore, had less to lose by getting rid of their leftish staff. They would probably be unable to compete for that audience anyway. Mehring was effectively boycotted by the liberal press which, moreover, carried on a campaign of slander against him. The SDP press was practically his only outlet.

From June 1, 1891, Mehring's correspondence from Berlin appeared in the SDP theoretical organ, *Neue Zeit*, the leading international theoretical journal of "Marxism," practically as the lead article. Mehring was not yet even a member of the party. He had never had the least connection with the labor movement or with workers in any way. Up to virtually the day before yesterday, he had been arguing that Germany needed a radical democratic party in order to prevent the triumph of social-democracy. Höhle's comment is: "We are justified in seeing in Mehring and his development a typical example of the development of the best German intellectuals."

6. MEHRING AS A LEFT-WINGER

Mehring's reputation as a left winger, prior to World War I, derives from his opponents. Within a few years of his joining the movement the inner party conflict over Bernsteinism broke out. Bernstein, like Mehring, drifted throughout his political career between two poles. Both were attracted by class instinct to radical democratic reform politics. Both were repelled in the direction of socialism by the inhospitable political climate of Bismarckian Germany. No mass base for a radical reform politics existed in Germany before World War I. (For that matter, there wasn't much of a base for such politics between the wars.) In the 1890s, Mehring and Bernstein were moving in opposite directions even if they were moving in the same force field.

Mehring supported the anti-Bernstein position. He became a favorite target of the right wing of the party because of an obvious weak point. He had, for almost twenty years, been notorious as a vicious public opponent of the party. Bernstein's modest proposal to revise Marxism out of existence paled alongside Mehring's direct and widely publicized attacks. The Bernsteinians at the 1903 Dresden Party Congress opened up with a full-scale attack on Mehring going back to the Sonneman affair twenty-five years before. He was forced to resign his posts as writer for the *Neue Zeit* and as editor of the *Leipziger Volkszeitung* until the party executive committee investigated the charges. The pamphlet he wrote in his defense, *Meine Rechtfertigung*, was, however, a smashing polemical success and he was completely vindicated. The party executive issued a public statement inviting him to resume his party work.

Mehring's opposition to Bernsteinism made perfectly good sense from a personal point of view. He had fairly recently been driven from the very radical democratic milieu Bernstein was reaching out to. What is more important, Mehring's Lassallean version of reformism was not directly involved in the revisionist fight. Lassalle's good reputation was still widespread in the party and his particular nostrum—state-sponsored cooperatives as a reward for a pro-monarchy political program—was no longer relevant enough to be a target of political attack.

7. MEHRING'S BIOGRAPHY OF MARX AND THE 1913 DISPUTE WITH KAUTSKY

Mehring's role in the dispute with Bernstein has drawn attention away from his own reformist past. As a consequence, the political bias of his pro-Lassallean biography of Marx has rarely been recognized for what it is.

This stems from the larger problem. In general, Mehring's lead has been followed by most historians, all of whom minimize the political differences between Marx and Lassalle. For example, the Bernstein-Engels anti-Lassallean tract which I have used so heavily in the third chapter of this volume is mentioned by neither Höhle nor Josef Schleifstein, Mehring's other East German biographer.[24] However, the issue of Mehring's distortion of the dispute in his biography was raised at the time the book was being written. The exchange between Karl Kautsky and Mehring in *Neue Zeit* in 1913 has been buried even deeper than the Bernstein-Engels book.

Mehring's stance in his biography is that of a man who reveres Marx as a "great man" but who is willing to critically examine his subject with no holds barred. What is concealed by this pose is that what Marx is criticized *for* is his hostility to Lassalle. That is, Mehring fairmindedly criticizes his hero, Marx, for disagreeing with Mehring.

Marx's political differences with Lassalle, however, had to be minimized. Not only would that give the game away, it would reawaken the old conflict over the party's political stance vis-a-vis the Prussian state. It was not an issue that social-democracy wanted to face in 1913. This was the conflict, basically, that was to split the party over the next few years. The personal antagonisms which accompanied political disputes, then as now, had to be elevated to causes of the dispute at least equal in importance to the political differences.

Marx and Engels' public break with von Schweitzer, to take one example, is treated as petty factionalism. Mehring goes so far as to state that "it is impossible to find anything in the columns of [the paper] which savors of an 'alliance' with the government against the Progressives."[25] Yet, a page later Mehring himself mentions the five articles by von Schweitzer, "drawing a masterly parallel between the Greater Prussia policy and the proletarian revolutionary policy in the question of German unity." Given Mehring's own political support for Lassalleanism for over a decade, primarily because of his own attraction to the German Empire, this is playing fast and loose with the reader. In fact, even in the biography itself, Mehring's politics on this issue remain the same. Mehring dismisses Marx and Engels' hostility to Prussia as mere provincialism. "As Rhinelanders Marx and Engels were inclined to regard everything East Elbian too contemptuously and they therefore underestimated the importance of the Prussian state...."[26]

Throughout, Mehring presents the disputes between Marx and Lassalle as "outlived." One issue which *Mehring* chose to emphasize, however, was to turn out to have considerable contemporary significance within less than a year.* That was the issue of the Prussian state's war policy and social-democracy's attitude toward it. For over forty years the defiance flung in the face of the Prussian state during the Franco-Prussian war of 1870 by the Social-Democratic Reichstag deputies August Bebel and Wilhelm Liebknecht had been honored as one of the shining moments in the party's history. Marx and Engels had always pointed to Bebel and Liebknecht's refusal to vote for war credits in that instance with pride. Mehring rakes them over the coals, especially Liebknecht: "the abstention of Liebknecht and Bebel was not practical politics, but a moral protest which, irrespective of how justified it might be in itself, was not in accord with the exigencies of the situation."[27] That is, Mehring not only justifies the support of the war by the Lassallean deputies in 1870 but does so in the language that was to be shortly used to justify the collapse of the SDP in 1914 and at a time when everyone's attention was focused on the coming war. Mehring buttresses his argument with selected quotes from Marx (and especially Engels) which indicated some uneasiness *at the time* with the behavior of Liebknecht and Bebel.† The well-documented historical fact that Marx and Engels subsequently always pointed to this act with pride disappears down the Memory Hole.[28]

---

*Mehring's biography of Marx was completed in 1913. It was not actually published until 1918. The Prussian state that Lassalle and Mehring had so admired considered it part of its progressive mission to suppress the book. It was published in 1918 after the victory of that proletarian revolution which Mehring had hoped to avert.

†This is a somewhat complicated issue which cannot be discussed in detail here. The evidence indicates that Engels, and only Engels, briefly questioned Liebknecht's position. That was not unusual because neither Marx nor Engels trusted Liebknecht's political judgment. Mehring has no quotes from Marx criticizing the refusal to vote war credits. He has to be content with laboriously reinterpreting a statement by Marx *praising* Liebknecht's stand.

Mehring's biography was not published until after the revolutionary earthquake that followed World War I had altered the political landscape. By the time Mehring died in 1919 shortly after helping to found the Communist Party, the prewar disputes had faded into the background. But in 1913 Mehring himself provoked a debate in *Neue Zeit* over the Lassalle-Marx issue which laid bare the politics underlying the book he was finishing.

In February 1913 Mehring published an article on "A Party Jubilee," celebrating the fiftieth anniversary of Lassalle's "Open Reply." In this dithyrambic piece Mehring wrote one of the most hagiographic testimonials the magazine had ever carried on Lassalle, "whose flaming word kindled the revolutionary workers' movement in Germany." He took the occasion to attack Marx's failure to appreciate Lassalle. He wound up his lament against Marx's "harsh and often so unjust criticism" with a call to arms against the "Marx-Priesthood" in the party. There was not a word about the political differences between Marx and Lassalle. The only specific charge against Marx was that he "shoved aside with a contemptuous wave of the hand the 'Open Reply' and the other pamphlets which stirred the German working class so mightily as sixth-grade ideas which they would not waste their time reading."

Karl Kautsky at first reacted with only a short editorial note which sounded as if he wanted to gloss the provocation over and followed in May with a longer article which seemed to be anxious to concede as much as possible to Mehring. But the short note was enough to elicit a blast from Mehring, sent in before the May article appeared.

Mehring's article, "On the Antagonism Between Lassalle and Marx," will come as a surprise to someone who does not know Mehring's reputation as one of the noted polemical brawlers of the day. Some highlights: (1) The "couple of lines" in the Jubilee article were, he claimed, a come-on to provoke Kautsky into giving a corrected estimate of Marx's mistakes on Lassalle. (2) It is Kautsky's fault, nevertheless, that the Lassalle-Marx antagonism had become a matter of dispute *because Kautsky had failed to suppress Marx's critique of the Gotha program.* (3) The substantive issues which divided Marx and Lassalle—on statism, trade union independence, and so on, are explicitly tossed out of the discussion because they were now passé.

Kautsky was forced to take up the challenge in a major article, "Lassalle and Marx." He began with the single factual point that Mehring had made that was subject to verification: the charge that Marx was so filled with antipathy that he refused to read Lassalle's productions. Kautsky read into the record the (still unpublished) letter that Mehring was misquoting and demonstrated that Mehring's account was a pure fabrication. He went on to defend the publication of the critique of the Gotha program against the reprehensible demand that it should have been suppressed.

In conclusion, Kautsky carried the attack home to Mehring in a section headed "The Rebirth of Lassalleanism." He showed that Mehring, in glorifying Lassalle's practical wisdom in not going beyond the state of consciousness of the workers, was only repeating the revisionists' main argument. He lamented Mehring's new phase, especially Mehring's jubilation over the beclouding of the "sun of Marx" and the coming dimming of the "Marx idol," and his nasty remarks about "Marx-piety" and "Marx-Priests." It was Mehring's way of avoiding a discussion of the political issues involved.

In July 1913, Mehring replied with an article that avoided all the substantive issues and presented himself as a victim of "intellectual terrorism" at the hands of the "stalwart defenders of Zion in the Marxist ranks." They attacked him simply because he refused to make the "traditional kow-tow to the official party legend." The legend of Lassalle, which Mehring had celebrated in his original article, however, was one he continued to defend.

Mehring did not have to reply to Kautsky's substantive criticisms of Lassalle in *Neue Zeit* because in his book he had the floor *in permanenz* and did not even have to take note of his critics. Ironically, when the biography was published in 1918 Mehring was on the road to minor "Marxist" sainthood himself. His biography has therefore always been accepted as a critical, but sympathetic, "Marxist" production rather than as the Lassallean hatchet job it is.

REFERENCE NOTES

Titles may be given in abbreviated form; full titles and publication data are provided in the Bibliography. In the case of writings by M/E, book and article titles are not distinguished in form and are not italicized; book titles by others *are* italicized. Where only the author's name is given, there is only a single entry under that name in the Bibliography. Page numbers apply to the edition cited in the Bibliography. Volume and page are usually separated by a colon: for example, 4:328 means Volume 4, page 328.

A Marx/Engels source is sometimes followed by a bracketed reference. In this case, the first source given is the one actually used; the bracketed reference may cite an extant translation if the first one is to the original, or vice versa.

To identify abbreviations and initials, see the Index. Some frequently used abbreviations are:

DBZ = Deutsche-Brüsseler-Zeitung (Brussels)
E = Engels
ed = editor, editorial
GCFI = General Council of the First International
IISH = International Institute for Social History (Amsterdam)
IML = Institute of Marxism-Leninism
IRSH = International Review of Social History (Amsterdam)
KMTR = Karl Marx's Theory of Revolution
ltr = letter
M = Marx
ME = Marx and Engels
M/E = Marx or Engels
MECW = ME:Collected Works
MEGA = ME:Gesamtausgabe [old edition]
MESW = ME:Selected Works in Three Volumes
MEW = ME:Werke
New Mega = ME:Gesamtausgabe [new edition]
NOZ = Neue Oder-Zeitung (Breslau)

NRZ = Neue Rheinische Zeitung (Cologne, 1848-1849)
NRZ Revue = Neue Rheinische Zeitung, politisch-ökonomische Revue (London, 1850)
NYDT = New York Daily Tribune
rev. after = revised after [original text]
rev. from = revised from [extant translation]
qu. = quoted, quotation
tr. = translation, translated in

FOREWORD

1. In *KMTR* 3, the passage here indicated in Special Note C refers back to p. 121 for the basic quote from *The Holy Family*. (Indeed, this latter passage had already been presented in *KMTR* 2:594.) For other material in the first two volumes concerning the French Revolution, of interest in this connection, see especially *KMTR* 1:45 and *KMTR* 2:89, 184, 203, 593-95.
2. See *KMTR* 3:365.
3. Ltr, E to Adler, Dec. 4, 1889, in MEW 37:318.
4. Ltr, E to Mehring, end of Apr. 1895, in MEW 39:474.
5. Köppen, "Noch ein Wort..." in *Deutsche Jahrbücher* (Leipzig), 1842, p. 515; quoted in Walter Schmidt's article, p. 19. (For data on both articles, see Biblio.)
6. This interpretation is stated in *KMTR* 3:361 (including the footnote); it is based on the evidence given by the Special Note as a whole.
7. The original French version of Furet's book (for which see Biblio.) was published in 1986.
8. This is stated in Furet's one-page Preface (in the original, *Avertissement*).
9. These pearls are from Furet's "Introduction" (which is the title of his essay); they are to be found scattered from its first page to pages 26-28, 32 (in the French, pages 13, 38, 40f, 45).
10. René Revol, "François Furet, historien ou idéologue?" in *Cahiers Leon Trotsky* (Grenoble), June 1989. For Furet's main books on the French Revolution, see the Bibliography.
11. Furet, 41 (French, 58f).
12. Ltr, M to Sorge, June 21, 1872, in MEW 33:491. There is a similar translation in *The Hague Congress* [&c], Vol. [2], Reports and Letters, p. 352.
13. Ltr, M to Kugelmann, July 29, 1872, in MEW 33:505; cf. *The Hague Congress* [&c], loc. cit., 408.
14. For example, see the letters by correspondents in *The Hague Congress* &c; R&L, 445, 450, 491.
15. Ltrs, E to Liebknecht, Jan. 2, 1872, in MEW 33:367; the warning was repeated, MEW 33:452; E to Liebknecht, May 15-22, 1872, in MEW 33:467. E to Cuno, Jan. 24, 1872, in MEW 33:392, 393. E to J. P. Becker, Aug. 5, 1872, in MEW 33:513f.
16. In the source cited in n.14 above, see pages 324, 327, 332, 334, 360, 417, 455, 488, 508, for some of these cases.

1. OF UTOPIAN SOCIALISM

1. Cole: *History of Socialist Thought*, 1:4.
2. J. A. Blanqui: *Histoire de l'Economie Politique*, 2:322 (for "économistes utopistes"); 174, 333 (for the use of "socialiste"); "utopiste" and various cognates appear several times with general connotations, e.g., 164 (Godwin), 314, 331, 340.— For the English translation, the corresponding pages, in order, are: 508, 408, 516, 402, 502, 514, 520.
3. Qu. in Müller: *Ursprung u. Gesch. des Wortes Soz.*, 138.
4. ME: Communist Manifesto, in MECW 6:516, rev. after MEW 4:490f.
5. ME: German Ideology, in MECW 5:505, 510; cf. also 512 (on Fourier).
6. Ibid., 462.
7. ME: Communist Manifesto, in MECW 6:516.
8. E: Peasant War in Germany, Pref. (Supplem.), in MESW 2:169.
9. E: Socialism Utopian and Scientific, in MESW 3:115.
10. For the role of criticism (critique) in Marx, see KMTR 1:55f.
11. E: Socialism Utopian and Scientific, in MESW 3:119f.
12. Ibid., 120-25.
13. For example, M: Ltrs from D.F.J., in MECW 3:143; M: Economic and Philosophic Manuscripts of 1844, in MECW 3:297; ME: Holy Family, in MECW 4:131; ME: Communist Manifesto, in MECW 6:516; also see E: Köln. Ztg. on Eng. Cond., in MECW 7:298. For some background, see KMTR 1:97-105 passim.
14. Re respect for Cabet as a practical organizer, see ltr, M to Schweitzer, Jan. 24, 1865, in MESW 2:28, and Engels' subsequent comment in ltr, E to Lafargue, Mar. 11, 1884, in E/Lafargues: Corr. 1:183 (the word 'loyalty' here is a poor translation).
15. See ME: German Ideology, in MECW 5:226f.
16. Ibid., 461, edited after MEW 3:448f.
17. E: Socialism Utopian and Scientific, in MESW 3:126.
18. E: Anti-Dühring, in MECW 25:252-54.
19. These phrases occur in Manuel's intro to his *French Utopias*, 1, and in Daniel Bell's article "Socialism" in *Intl. Encyc. of Soc. Sci.*, 14:507. See also Mannheim's article "Utopia" in the (old) *Encyc. of Soc. Sci.*, 15:201; Mumford's *Story of Utopia*, 5; E. Fischoff's intro to Buber's *Paths in Utopia*, xii; but examples are legion.
20. M: Note on Poverty of Phil., in M: Lettres et Doc., 204f. (Written in the third person, the note reads "Marx" rather than "I.")
21. M: Economic and Philosophic Manuscripts of 1844, in MECW 3:294; ME: German Ideology, in MECW 5:504-09.
22. M: Capital, 3:591, including footnote [MEW 25:618f, 619 fn]. For an early comment by Marx on the Saint-Simonians along these lines, see M: On F. List's Book, in MECW 4:283 [not in MEW].
23. On these operations, see KMTR 1:440, 442-50 passim.
24. For ex., see the implication in ltr, E to Tönnies, Jan. 24, 1895, in MEW 39:395.
25. Williams: *Keywords*, 234f.
26. The dictionary quoted here is the Wildhagen German-Eng. dictionary, the best desk dictionary of this type.
27. See KMTR 1:594.
28. E: Peasant War in Germany, Pref. '75, in MESW 2:170 [MEW 18:517].
29. Girardin quoted in *Larousse du XIXe Siècle*, "Socialisme," 14:799.
30. So according to Mönke: *Über Mitarbeit. Hess*, 316. For the "scientific" pretensions of True Socialists, see e.g. ME: German Ideology, in MECW 5:482f. The

so-called Ricardian socialists have also been nominated, not without justice; cf. E: Lawyers' Socialism, in MEW 21:502.
31. For Buchez, see Cuvillier: *Hommes et Idéologies*, 44-47; for *Phalanx*, see Sams, ed.: *Autobiog. of Brook Farm*, 51; Feuer: *M. & Intellectuals*, 190, claims *Phalanx* as the first, apparently because he has no idea of how common the idea was.
32. Re the Saint-Simonians, see Iggers: *Cult of Authority*, 159f.—Re F. Wright, see the latest biography, Eckhardt: *F.W.*, 271.
33. Stein: *Der Soc. und Com. des heut. Frankr.*, 203, 211 (note this refers to the 2d ed., dated 1848, which appeared in 1847).
34. Stein: *Hist. of the Social Movement in Fr.*, 278; cf. also 279, 283; Mengelberg's intro, 27.
35. See above, p. 320, ref. n. 3.
36. E: Peasant War in Germany, Pref. '75, in MESW 2:169.
37. M: Conspectus of Bak., in MEW 18:636; the whole passage was quoted and discussed in KMTR 2:564.
38. For example, see KMTR 1:16f.
39. M: Vienna Revolution & K.Z., in MEW 5:451 [MECW 7:496].
40. Ltr, E to Bernstein, May 23, 1884, in MEW 36:151.
41. For example, M: Pauperism & Free Trade, Nov. 1, 1852, in MECW 11:359; and M: Parliament [&c], Dec. 28, 1852, in MECW 464 [MEW 8:369, 477].
42. M: Thiers' Speech [&c], in MECW 7:467; cf. also 468 [MEW 5:423f].
43. Ltr, M to Ruge, Nov. 30, 1842, in MECW 1:394 [MEW 27:412].
44. See KMTR 1:100-03.
45. M: Ltrs from D.F.J., in MEW 1:344 [MECW 3:142].
46. Ibid., MEW 1:344f [MECW 3:142-44].
47. Ibid., MEW 1:346 [MECW 3:144].
48. Hegel: *Philo. of Right*, 10-11 esp., also 12-13.
49. E: Description of Com. Colonies, in MECW 4:214 or MEW 2:521; ltr, E to M, Feb. 22 to Mar. 7, 1845, in MEW 27:20 [MECW 38:23]. On the basis of no evidence whatever, but with his customary eagerness to put down the devil, Feuer: *M. & Intellectuals*, 181, 195, erroneously asserts Marx's agreement with E on this point.
50. See ltr, E to M, Feb. 22 to Mar. 7, 1845, in MEW 27:22f [MECW 38:25]; ltr, E to M, Mar. 17, 1845, MEW 27:24f [MECW 38:27]; for M's list, see MEGA I, 5:549 [MECW 4:667]. Engels announced the project in E: Fragment of Fourier, in MEW 2:609f [MECW 4:644]. For other info, see MECW 4:719, n. 242; for a later reference, see ltr, E to Bebel, Oct. 25, 1888, in MEW 37:118.
51. E: Fragment of Fourier, in MECW 4:614f [MEW 2:605].
52. M: Moralizing Crit., in MECW 6:337 [MEW 4:357].
53. M: Page from the Rough Draft [of ME: Communist Manifesto], in MECW 6:578 [MEW 4:610].
54. M: Poverty of Philosophy, in MECW 6:177f, rev. after the French original, M: Misère de la Phil., 133f.
55. E: Fragment of Fourier, in MECW 4:642 [MEW 2:608]; the entire passage is worth reading in this connection.
56. M: Poverty of Philosophy, in MECW 6:210.
57. Ibid., 178, rev. after the original, M: Misère [&c], 134. For Marx on the petty-bourgeois mind, see KMTR 2, Chap. 11.
58. Proudhon's mutual-credit utopia, with himself as boss, was most frankly set down in his *Carnets*; for a summary of his plan, see Draper: *Note on the Father of Anarchism*.

59. M: Poverty of Philosophy, in MECW 6:138; see also ltr, M to Kugelmann, Oct. 9, 1866, in MECW 42:326 [MEW 31:530].
60. E: Pref. to M's Poverty of Philosophy, in M: Poverty of Philosophy (FLPH ed.), 23 [MEW 21:187]; the preceding exposition is from p. 13-23 [MEW 21:179-87]. See also ltr, E to Kautsky, Aug. 1, 1884, in MEW 36:190, on Rodbertus.
61. On Hist. of C.L., in MESW 3:179 [MEW 21:212].
62. M: Herr Vogt, in MEW 14:439 [MECW 17:79].
63. M: Civil War in France, First Draft, in ME: Writings on the Par. Com., checked with MECW 22:499f.
64. See Lehning: *Discussions à Londres*, esp. 94-104; and *Bund der Kom.*, 1:170f, 1013-15.
65. [Schapper]: "Auswanderungsplan," in the trial issue of the *Kommunistische Zeitschrift*, ibid., 509f; perhaps written with Engels' help but this is purely speculative.
66. ME: Communist Manifesto, in MECW 6:515, rev. after MEW 4:490; the Moore-Engels translation inserted the word 'new' into this statement.
67. Ibid.
68. Ibid., 515f.
69. E: Socialism Utopian and Scientific, in MESW 3:119 [MEW 19:194].
70. Ibid., 126 [MEW 19:200].
71. Ibid., 132 [MEW 19:208].
72. E: Lawyers' Socialism, in MEW 21:493.
73. M: Débat Social, in MECW 6:538f [MEW 4:512f].
74. For the Höchberg group, see KMTR 2, esp. 516f, 522.
75. Ltr, M to Sorge, Oct. 19, 1877, in MEW 34:303.
76. Ltr, M to Kugelmann, Oct. 9, 1866, in MEW 31:530 [MECW 42:326]; the comparison here was with Proudhon as a "petty-bourgeois utopian."

2. OF SENTIMENTAL SOCIALISM

1. Ltr, E to Lafargue, Feb. 16, 1886, in E/Lafargues: Corr. 1:338; this reference was to the socialistic phrases hanging on in the French Radical party.
2. Ltr, M to Annenkov, Dec. 28, 1846, in ME: Corr. (Fr.), 1:457f [MECW 38:104].
3. Proudhon's fantastically woman-hating (not merely antifeminist) views are found in some bulk in his posthumous work *La Pornocratie*; also in his *De la Justice dans la Révolution*, Vol. 4; his *Système des Contradictions Economiques*, Chap. 11; and scattered through his *Carnets*. The extremeness of his viciously anti-woman ideology has been generally glossed over in books about him, mostly apologias.
4. E: Debate on Poland in Frankf., in MECW 7:376 [MEW 5:358].
5. E: Democratic Pan-Slavism, in MECW 8:363 [MEW 6:270f].
6. Ltr, E to Lavrov, Nov. 12-17, 1875, MESW 3:477f [MEW 34:170].
7. See KMTR 2:518f.
8. M: Debates on Freed. of Press, in MEW 1:68 [MECW 1:172]; for the whole passage and context, see KMTR 1:40.
9. Re "True Socialism," see Lewis: *Life & Teachings of K.M.*, 66-68; Hook: *From Hegel to M.*, 205-19; Cornu: *K.M. und F.E.*, 2:53 sqq (or in French ed., 3:36 sqq). In M/E the most compact discussion (apart from the Manifesto) is in ME: German Ideology, in MECW 5:455-57 [MEW 3:441-43]. Engels' unfinished

booklet, E: Status Quo in Ger. (see Bibliog.), is focused on the politics of the tendency, for which see KMTR 2:180-83, 197f. See also KMTR 1:216f, 285.
10. ME: Communist Manifesto, in MECW 6:511 [MEW 4:486].
11. Ibid., 512, 504, 499 [MEW 4:487, 480, 476]. On the economic meaning of 'freedom,' see KMTR 1:270-74.
12. E: Status Quo in Ger., in MECW 6:76 [MEW 4:41].
13. Ltr, M to E, Aug. 1, 1877, in MEW 34:66.
14. Ltr, M to Sorge, Oct. 19, 1877, in MEW 34:303.
15. ME: Circular Ltr to Bebel et al., Sept. 17-18, 1879, in MEW 34:406 [MESW 3:92].
16. E: Democratic Pan-Slavism, in MECW 8:365 [MEW 6:273].
17. M: Capital, 1:84-85 fn (with French terms translated).
18. Re Lassalle, see ltr, E to M, Dec. 2, 1861, in MEW 30:203, about his "superstition" of "absolute law" [*Recht*, law, justice].
19. See Marx's comment on Harney's slogan, in ltr, M to E, Feb. 4, 1852, in MEW 28:18f [MECW 39:30].
20. For a good example of a longish attack by Marx and Engels on hollow abstractions, see their discussion of an elocutionary manifesto issued by a committee of liberals; in ME: Review, May to Oct. 1850, in MECW 10:530-32 [MEW 7:460-63].
21. Ltr, Eccarius to Marx, Oct. 12, 1864, in *GCFI* 1:375f.
22. Ltr, M to E, Nov. 4, 1864, in MEW 31:15 [MECW 42:18]. For a narrative account, see Collins & Abramsky, 41-43, or McLellan: *K.M.*, 363f.
23. This text follows the 1864 "Provisional Rules" as given in *GCFI* 1:289. (The text in MESW 2:19f is that of 1871.) English was the original language. The last sentence, about rights and duties, was later italicized.
24. Villetard: *History of International*, 67.
25. M: Inaugural Address, in MECW 20:13 or MESW 2:19f.
26. GC meeting of Nov. 8, 1864, in *GCFI* '64-66, 1:45.
27. M: Fourth Annual Report of the GC . . ., dated Sept. 1, 1868; in *GCFI* 2:326.
28. M: Report of the GC to the Hague Congress, 1872, in *GCFI* 5:457.
29. GC meeting of Feb. 28, 1871, in *GCFI* 4:138. For Marx's complaints about minutes and reports, see ibid., 133f.
30. For a short survey of Marx's views in this field, there is a useful essay by John Lewis, "Marxism and Ethics," in his *Marxism and the Open Mind*.
31. M: Civil War in France, First Draft, in ME: Writings on the Par. Com., 169, or MECW 22:505.
32. E: Anti-Dühring, in MECW 25:140 [MEW 20:141].
33. M: Moralizing Crit., in MECW 6:325 [MEW 4:344f].
34. E: Housing Question, in MECW 23:341 or MESW 2:327 [MEW 18:236f].
35. E: Anti-Dühring, in MECW 25:138 [MEW 20:139]; this analysis is continued on 144-46 [MEW 20:145-47].
36. See KMTR 1:196-98.
37. E: Anti-Dühring, in MECW 25:146 [MEW 20:146f].
38. This and the previous extract are from M: State of British Manufactures, *NYDT*, Mar. 15, 1859; in MECW 16:191.
40. E: Ludwig Feuerbach, in MESW 3:353 [MEW 21:282].
41. M: Economic and Philosophic Manuscripts of 1844, in MECW 3:232 [MEW Eb.1:468]; for more on this, 295f [MEW Eb.1:535].
42. ME: Holy Family, in MECW 4:7, 125 (italics removed) [MEW 2:7, 132].
43. Ibid., 130f [MEW 2:138].

44. ME: German Ideology, in MECW 5:466, 468, 469; cf. also 492, 512 [MEW 3:454, 455, 457; also 479f, 500f].
45. M: Moralizing Crit., in MEW 4:353, 349 [MECW 6:334, 330]; the italicized words were set off by Marx with quote marks, not italics. (The second passage is quoted at greater length in KMTR 2:507.)
46. ME: Great Men of the Emig., in MEW 8:278 [MECW 11:270].
47. See McLellan: *Young Heg. & K.M.*, 159; Hook: *From Hegel to M.*, 251-53.
48. Hess: *Phil. Soz. Schrift.*, 366.
49. Venable: *Human Nature*, 163.
50. E: Ludwig Feuerbach, in MESW 3:359 [MEW 21:289].
51. Ibid., 359f [MEW 21:289].
52. E: Origin of the Family, in MESW 3:333 [MEW 21:172].
53. E: Ludwig Feuerbach, in MESW 3:360 [MEW 21:289f].
54. Ibid., 344 [MEW 21:272].
55. Qu. in Wittke: *Utopian Com.*, 76.
56. E: On History of the C.L., in MESW 3:181, rev. after MEW 21:214.
57. Qu. in Lehning: *International Association*, 213f.
58. Ltr, E to Lavrov, Nov. 12-17, 1875, in MESW 3:477f [MEW 34:170].
59. See KMTR 2:419-21, also 154.
60. E: On History of the C.L., in MESW 3:180, rev. after MEW 21:213.
61. ME: Circular Ag. Kriege, in MEW 4:7 [MECW 6:36-41]; the previous citations come from MEW 4:4-6 [MECW 6:36-40].
62. Ibid., MEW 4:13f [MECW 6:47]. Here and elsewhere in quotes from Kriege, the italicization was probably added by Marx.
63. Ibid., MEW 4:14 [MECW 6:47].
64. Ibid., MEW 4:15 [MECW 6:49]. For Marx on "the social principles of Christianity," see KMTR 2:150-52.
65. See KMTR 1, Chap. 10, and KMTR 2, Chap. 6.
66. These phrases are from ME: Circular Ag. Kriege, in MEW 4:3, 11, 12 [MECW 6:35, 44f, 45].
67. Ibid., MEW 4:17 [MECW 6:50].
68. Ibid., MEW 4:14 [MECW 6:48].

3. OF STATE-SOCIALISM: LASALLEAN MODEL

1. Stein: *Hist. of the Social Movement*, 389. This English ed. translates Stein's 1850 work (see Biblio.); the statement does not appear in the earlier ed. of Stein's work.
2. See Blanc's intro to the 1848 ed. of his *Organisation du Travail*, in Fried & Sanders, 232-36; Loubère: *L. Blanc*, 26f, 38; also Cole: *Hist. Soc. Thought*, 1:169f. (Cole denies that Blanc was a state-socialist but gives no definition.)
3. Ltr, M to Schweitzer, Oct. 13, 1868, in MEW 32:569 [MECW 43:133]. See also ltr, M to E, Sep. 19, 1868, in MEW 32:155 [MECW 43:105]; ltr, M to Ludlow, Apr. 10, 1869, in MECW 43:260; ltr, E to Bebel, Mar. 18-28, 1875, in MESW 3:33 or MECW 34:127, and M: Critique of the Gotha Program, in MESW 3:25 [MEW 34:27]. In E: Socialism in Ger., in MEW 22:248 (1891), Engels seemed to say that the movement to which the Buchez-type program was counterposed in the 1840s was Blanc's.

4. Ltr, M to Ludlow, Apr. 10, 1869, in MECW 43:260. For early critical comment on Buchez, see ME: German Ideology, in MECW 5:226f [MEW 3:207-09].
5. Cuvillier: *Hommes et Idéol.*, 51, 63, 65.
6. Blanc: "Socialism," in *Friend of the People*, July 12, 1851, p. 263.
7. ME: Pref. to Blanqui's Toast, in MEW 7:568 [MECW 10:537].
8. E: Reform Movement in Fr.—Banquet, in MECW 6:398f; reiterated, ibid., 410f. See also ltr, E to Bebel, Mar. 18, 1886, in MEW 36:465, for the reference to "national-French socialism."
9. M: untitled article, *NYDT*, Mar. 24, 1854; in MECW 13:50 as "Opening of the Labor Parliament [&c]."
10. Blanc, "Socialism," op. cit. (n. 6 above), 263.
11. Blanc: *Organization of Work*, 53.
12. See KMTR 2:24; also all of Chap. 1, Sec. 3.
13. See KMTR 1, Chap. 3.
14. Mayo: *Intro to Marxist Theory*, 270; Rossiter: *Marxism*, 172.
15. GC minutes of June 6, 1871, in *GCFI* 4:207.
16. See KMTR 1:441 to end of Chap. 18.
17. See KMTR 1:97-99.
18. M: Grundrisse, 845 [Nicolaus tr., 885].
19. E: Housing Question, in MESW 2:339f [MEW 18:249f].
20. Ltr, E to Zasulich, Mar. 6, 1884, in MEW 36:119, checked against the French original, which has been published in a German edition of the correspondence.
21. Bernstein: *F. Lassalle as Soc. Reformer*, 29f. (All quotes from the Bernstein/Engels critique are from this translation by Eleanor Marx.)
22. Ibid., 122.
23. Qu. in Lidtke: *Outlawed Party*, 140.
24. Bernstein: *F. Lassalle as Soc. Ref.*, 104.
25. Ibid.
26. Ibid., 105.
27. Ibid., 106.
28. See KMTR 1, Chap. 16 and Chap. 20.
29. Vahlteich: *F. Lassalle und die Anfänge ... [&c]*, qu. in Huhn: *Etatismus*, 164. Noyes: *Organization and Rev.*, Chap. 7-8, discusses some similar demands in 1848.
30. E: Socialism in Germany, in MEW 22:248.
31. Bernstein: *F. Lassalle as Soc. Ref.*, 123f.
32. Ibid., 145.
33. Ltr, Lassalle to Rodbertus, Apr. 28, 1863, in Lassalle: *Nachgel. Br. u. Schr.*, 6:329.
34. For the attack, see ME: Circular Ltr to Bebel et al., Sep. 17-18, 1879, in MESW 3:88-94 [MEW 34:401-08]. See KMTR 2:516f, 522.
35. [Höchberg et al.]: "Rückblicke [&c]," 78; the idea is repeated on 79.
36. Bernstein: *F. Lassalle as Soc. Ref.*, 147.
37. Ibid., 125f.
38. Ibid., 125; this exposition refers to Lassalle's "Open Reply."
39. Ltr, Lassalle to Bismarck, June 8, 1863, in Mayer: *Bismarck und Lassalle*, 60-61. This passage was cited, in a different context, in KMTR 3:99.
40. Bernstein: *F. Lassalle as Soc. Ref.*, 172.
41. Ibid., 178.
42. Ibid., 178f.
43. Ibid., 179f.
44. Ibid., 176.
45. H.: "Karl Marx / Interview," 17 [MEW 34:513]. The exact words should be considered to be the interviewer's, but the point was clearly Marx's.

46. Both of these citations are given in Mayer: *Lassalleana*, III (V. A. Huber &c), 191-92, 196; the first is from ltr, Lassalle to Huber, Feb. 24, 1864 (also cited in Mayer: *Zum Verständnis*, 100), and the second is from Frese's article "Zur Frage von der Staatshilfe" (also cited in Mayer: *Aus der Welt d. Soz.*, 43).
47. See Special Note A, Section 5.
48. Ltr, M to E, Aug. 7, 1862, in MEW 30:270 [MECW 41:400].
49. Ltr, M to E, Apr. 9, 1863, in MEW 30:357f [MECW 41:467].
50. Ltr, E to M, June 11, 1863, in MEW 30:354 [MECW 41:478].
51. Ltr, M to E, June 12, 1863, in MEW 30:357f [MECW 41:481].
52. Ltr, Liebknecht to M, June 12, 1864, in Liebknecht: *Briefwechsel mit M und E*, 37f.
53. Footman: *F. Lassalle*, 175.
54. Landauer: *Europ. Socialism*, 1:269.
55. Ltr, E to Lafargue, Dec. 29, 1887, in E/Lafargues: *Corr.* 2:84 (French ed., 2:92).
56. Ltr, M to E, Nov. 4, 1864, in MEW 31:10 [MECW 42:12].
57. Ltr, M to E, Jan. 25, 1865, in MEW 31:43 [MECW 42:66]. For more on the Sickingen analogy, see KMTR 2:528f.
58. Ltr, E to M, Jan. 27, 1865, in MEW 31:45f [MECW 42:69].
59. Ltr, M to E, Jan. 30, 1865, in MEW 31:47f [MECW 42:71].
60. Ltr, E to M, Feb. 13, 1865, in MEW 31:69 [MECW 42:88].
61. See Special Note A, Section 7.
62. See KMTR 2:278-83.
63. Ltr, E to M, Feb. 5, 1865, in MEW 31:55 [MECW 42:77]; quoted in another context in KMTR 2:384. For the Lassallean line, see Rosenberg: *Democracy & Socialism*, 159.
64. Ltr, M to E, Feb. 10, 1865, in MEW 31:64 [MECW 42:84].
65. Dawson: *German Socialism*, 221f; Kampffmeyer: *Changes in Theory & Tactics*, 50-52.
66. Ltr, M to E, Feb. 3, 1865, in MEW 31:52f [MECW 42:75f].
67. Ltr, M to E, Feb. 13, 1865, in MEW 31:71 [MECW 42:90].
68. This passage was quoted in KMTR 2:98.
69. Ltr, M to Schweitzer, Feb. 13, 1865, as contained (cited) in ltr, M to E, Feb. 18, 1865, in MECW 42:96 [MEW 31:76f].
70. Ltr, M to E, Feb. 18, 1865, in MECW 42:96 [MEW 31:77].
71. ME: Statement to Ed. Bd. *Sozialdemocrat*, d. Feb. 23, 1865, in MEW 31:77f (or 16:79) [MECW 42:97].
72. About this article, see KMTR 2:182f.
73. E: Pref. to Marx's *Poverty of Phil.*, in MEW 21:175.
74. E: Review of *Capital* for *Beobachter*, in MEW 16:227f [MECW 20:224]. Marx's draft for this passage is in ltr, M to E, Dec. 7, 1867, in MEW 31:404f [MECW 42:494].
75. Ltr, M to Kugelmann, Feb. 23, 1865, in MEW 31:453f [MECW 42:104].
76. For this pamphlet, see KMTR 2:180f. About "Feudal Socialism," see the *Communist Manifesto*, Section III, first subsection; it is discussed at large below, in Chapter 7, Section 2.
77. This question was discussed in KMTR 1, esp. Chapters 19-20.
78. Ltr, M to Kugelmann, Feb. 23, 1865, in MEW 31:452 [MECW 42:103]. Marx has quotes around "revolutionary," apparently as a sort of emphasis.
79. Ibid, 453 [MECW 42:103].
80. Ibid., 454 [MECW 42:104+].
81. Ltr, M to Schweitzer, Oct. 13, 1868, in MECW 43:133 [MEW 32:569]. Cf. the

approach on this point attempted by Liebknecht in an 1865 report to the International, in *GCFI* 1:256f.
82. Lassalle: *Nachgel. Briefe u. Schr.*, 6:339.
83. E: Housing Question, in MESW 2:349 [MEW 18:260]. Concerning Bismarck as a Bonapartist, see KMTR 1, Chap. 16.
84. E: Role of Force, in MESW 3:418f [MEW 21:452].
85. Ltr, M to Bracke, May 5, 1875, in MESW 3:11 [MEW 34:137].
86. M: Critique of the Gotha Program, in MESW 3:28 [MEW 19:31].
87. Ibid., 15, 21 [MEW 19:17, 23]. About the "one reactionary mass" formula, see KMTR 2:308-16.
88. Ltr, E to Bebel, Mar. 18-28, 1875, in MESW 3:31 [MEW 34:125f].
89. For the term, see ltr, M to Sorge, June 20, 1881, in MEW 35:199. The Manifesto's ten-point program is in MECW 6:505 [MEW 4:481].
90. Ltr, E to Bebel, Oct. 12, 1875, in MEW 34:158.
91. For present purposes, on this point the reader may refer to the following letters, E to Bebel: Dec. 30, 1884, in MEW 26:260-62; Apr. 4, 1885, in MEW 36:292; Nov. 17, 1885, in MEW 36:390; Jan. 20-23, 1886, in MEW 36:425f.
92. E: Pref. to Internat. aus d. Volksst., in MEW 22:417.
93. M: Critique of the Gotha Program, in MESW 3:25 [MEW 19:27].
94. H.: "Karl Marx / Interview," 11f [MEW 34:510].
95. M: Critique of the Gotha Program, in MESW 3:24 [MEW 19:26f].
96. Ibid., 25 [MEW 19:27].
97. Cole: *Hist. Soc. Thought*, 2:244; Miller: *Problem der Freiheit*, 74.
98. See Special Note A, Section 7.
99. Morgan: *German Social Democracy*, 250f.

4. OF STATE-SOCIALISM: BISMARCKIAN MODEL

1. Lidtke: *Outlawed Party*, 157.
2. Ibid., 156.
3. Ibid., 163.
4. Ltr, E to Bebel, Nov. 6, 1892, in MEW 38:511.
5. Cf. Engels' comments in E: Socialism of Herr Bismarck, first paragraph [MEW 19:167].—Note that a similar "Social Monarchy" program had been proposed to the Crown by Minister von Radowitz in the revolutionary days of March 1848 (see Noyes: *Organization and Revolution*, 82f).
6. For a Bismarck anecdote of this sort, see Laveleye: *Socialism of Today*, 274 fn.
7. Laveleye: *Socialism of Today*, 89-92.
8. Keeble: *Industrial Day-Dreams*, 133.
9. Lidtke: *Outlawed Party*, 156.
10. For the origin and forerunners of the term 'Kathedersozialismus,' see Ladendorff: *Hist. Schlagwörterbuch*, 164f.
11. Ely: *French & Ger. Socialism*, 237.
12. Ibid., 242f; for the preceding statements, 236, 241f.
13. Laveleye: *Socialism of Today*, 276f.
14. Ibid., 83.
15. Engels discussed the Rodbertus claim especially in two prefaces: E: Pref. to Marx's Poverty of Phil. (1884), in MEW 21:175-87; and E: Pref. to Marx's Capital, Vol. 2, in MEW 24:13-26 (for both, see also editions of the main work). Cf.

also ltr, E to Kautsky, Sep. 20, 1884, in MEW 36:209f. For references to this anti-Rodbertus campaign, see ltr, E to Zasulich, Mar. 6, 1884, in MEW 36:119, and, after its successful conclusion, E to L. Lafargue, Nov. 24, 1886, in E/Lafargues: Corr. 1:394, and E to Kautsky, Mar. 30, 1892, in MEW 38:310.

16. See M: Theories of Surplus Value, 2:15-113, 127-29, 149-60 [MEW 26.2:7-106, 120-22, 145-57]; also M: Capital, 3:137f, 759 fn [MEW 25:148f, 786 fn]; and M: Notes on A. Wagner, in MEW 19:373-76; and cf. ltr, M to Lassalle, June 16, 1862, in MEW 30:627.
17. For Rodbertus' early approach to surplus value, see ltr, E to Bernstein, Feb. 8, 1883, in MEW 35:428; E to Kautsky, Aug. 1, 1884, in MEW 36:190; and E to Bebel, Dec. 22, 1882, in MEW 35:416. For the rest, see ltr, E to Kautsky, May 23, 1884, in MEW 36:149.
18. Ltr, E to Bebel, Dec. 22, 1882, in MEW 35:416; E: Pref. to Marx's Poverty of Phil., in MEW 21:177, 182, 185.
19. Ltr, E to Kautsky, May 23, 1883, in MEW 36:149.
20. Ltr, E to Danielson, Nov. 13, 1885, English original in ME: Sel. Corr./1966, 388 [MEW 36:384].
21. For the "Manifesto of the Three Zurichers," see KMTR 2:516f, 522, 532f.
22. Ltr, Kautsky to E, Feb. 14, 1884, qu. in Lidtke, 173.
23. Ltr, E to Bernstein, Aug. 22, 1884, in MEW 36:204.
24. Lidtke: *Outlawed Party*, 171-75; for the 1884 *Sozialdemokrat*, see Bartel: *M und E im Kampf*, 141.
25. Dawson: *Bismarck and State-Socialism*, 8.
26. See above, this chapter, Section 1 (ref. n. 7).
27. Ltr, E to Bernstein, Feb. 27 to Mar. 1, 1883, in MEW 35:444.
28. On Schäffle, see Lidtke: *Outlawed Party*, 63-65.
29. For many examples, see Lidtke, 139, 141, 147, 157-60, 165-67, 170.
30. Ltr, M to Fleckles, Jan. 21, 1877, in MEW 34:243.
31. M: Notes on A. Wagner, in MEW 19:326.
32. Ltr, E to Kautsky, Feb. 1, 1881, in MEW 35:150.
33. Ltr, E to Bernstein, Mar. 12, 1881, in MEW 35:170; repeated in ltr, E to Stegemann, Mar. 26, 1885 (where the sentiment was ascribed to Marx), in MEW 36:289.—Further on Schäffle: see Engels' similar remark about an earlier book, in ltr, E to M, Sep. 12, 1870, in MEW 33:62; and Marx's reference to Johann Most's "groveling article" on Schäffle, in ltr, M to Sorge, Sep. 19, 1879, in MEW 34:413.
34. M: Economic and Philosophic Manuscripts of 1844, in MECW 3:295 [MEW Eb.1:535].
35. ME: Address to the Communist League (Mar.), in MECW 10:280.
36. M: untitled article, NYDT, Dec. 22, 1857, in MECW 15:405 ["The Financial Crisis in Europe"].
37. For ex., in M: Capital, 2:97 [MEW 24:101].
38. M: Notes on A. Wagner, in MEW 19:370. Cf. also Marx's criticism of a Kathedersocialist in ltr, M to E, July 25, 1877, in MEW 34:60f.
39. E: Anti-Dühring, Pref., 2nd ed. (1885), in MECW 25:9 [MEW 20:9]. About the Engels-vs.-Marx myth, see KMTR 1:23-26; the considerations raised here are not repeated in the present volume.
40. Lafargue, in the collection *Reminisc. M. E.*, 83f, or in Lafargue & Liebknecht: *K. Marx*, 23.
41. Eleanor Marx, in *Reminisc. M. E.*, 186.
42. Ltr, Jenny Marx (daughter) to Mrs. Kugelmann, Apr. 18, 1871, in *Labour Monthly*, Mar. 1956.

43. E: Anti-Dühring, in MECW 25:264 [MEW 20:258f]; or E: Socialism Utopian and Scientific, in MESW 3:142f [MEW 19:219f].—Note: for comparisons between *Anti-Dühring and Socialism Utopian and Scientific*, a convenient English edition (not used here) is that published in 1959 (2nd ed.) by the F.L.P.H., Moscow; at all points it shows the relationship of the two texts.
44. E: Socialism Utopian and Scientific, in MESW 3:143f [MEW 19:220f].
45. E: Anti-Dühring, in MECW 25:265, rev after MEW 20:259; or E: Socialism Utopian and Scientific, in MESW 3:144, rev. after MEW 19:220f.—Note that the phrase "At a further stage" was in the original text of *Anti-Dühring*, but was edited out of *Socialism Utopian and Scientific* when the preceding insertion was connected up.
46. For the addition of the word 'ultimately' *(schliesslich)*, compare MEW 20:259 with MEW 19:221.
47. E: Anti-Dühring, in MECW 25:265 [MEW 20:259]; or E: Socialism Utopian and Scientific, in MESW 3:144 [MEW 19:221]; in both cases, revised as per footnote on p.96. The reference at the end to brothel statification was added in *Socialism Utopian and Scientific*.
48. E: Anti-Dühring, in MECW 25:265 [MEW 20:259]; or E: Socialism Utopian and Scientific, in MESW 3:145 [MEW 19:221].
49. E: Anti-Dühring, in MEW 20:260, rev. from MECW 25:266; or E: Socialism Utopian and Scientific, in MEW 19:222, rev. from MESW 3:145.
50. Ibid.
51. E: Anti-Dühring, in MECW 25:267 [MEW 20:261]; or E: Socialism Utopian and Scientific, in MESW 3:146 [MEW 19:223].
52. Ltr, E to Bracke, Apr. 30, 1878, in MEW 34:328.
53. Ltr, E to Bernstein, Mar. 12, 1881, in MEW 35:170, 169. Engels intended to make this point also in the last part of his unfinished *Role of Force in History*; see his outline, in MEW 21:464.
54. Re the "two new armies," ltr, E to Bracke, Apr. 30, 1878, in MEW 334:328.— Re "state = socialism," ltr, E to Bernstein, Mar. 12, 1881, in MEW 35:170.— Re tobacco workers, ltr, E to Bracke, Apr. 30, 1878, in MEW 34:328f.
55. Ltr, E to Bracke, Apr. 30, 1878, in MEW 34:328.
56. Ltr, E to Bebel, May 16, 1882, in MEW 35:324.
57. E: Socialism of Herr Bismarck, Part II, here trans. from the original French of *L'Egalité* [MEW 19:173, 175].
58. Ltr, E to Bebel, May 16, 1882, in MEW 35:324.
59. ME: Circular Letter to Bebel et al., Sep. 17-18, 1879, in MEW 34:399. The last sentence refers to ltr, E to Bebel, Nov. 14, 1879, in MEW 334:418f.
60. Ltr, E to Bracke, Apr. 30, 1878, in MEW 34:328. This passage begins from the one referenced by note 55 above.
61. Ltr, E to Bernstein, Aug. 17, 1881, in MEW 35:215.
62. [Bernstein]: "Es fehlt uns..." [article] in *Sozialdemokrat*, July 28,, 1881.
63. Ltr, E to Bebel, May 16, 1882, in MEW 35:323.
64. Ibid., 324.
65. Ltr, E to Bernstein, Mar. 12, 1881, in MEW 35:170.
66. Ltr, E to Bracke, Apr. 30, 1878, in MEW 34:329.
67. Ltr, E to Bernstein, Mar. 12, 1881, in MEW 35:170.
68. Ltr, E to Oppenheim, Mar. 24, 1891, in MEW 38:64f.
69. Ltr, E to Bernstein, Nov. 30, 1881, in MEW 35:238.
70. Ltr, E to Bernstein, Sep. 13, 1882, in MEW 35:359f.
71. Ltr, E to Bernstein, Feb. 8, 1883, in MEW 35:427.
72. Ltr, E to Bernstein, Feb. 27 to Mar. 1, 1883, in MEW 35:444. The description

"this little man" is from E: On the Death of K.M. (2nd art.), in MEW 19:346, which also contains Engels' indignant letter to Loria, end of Apr. 1883 (the Italian text of which is in ME: Corr. con Ital., 296f). Further on Loria, see E: Pref. to Capital, Vol. 3, in MEW 25:25f [M: Capital, 3:16-18], and ltr, E to L. Lafargue, Nov. 23, 1884, in E/Lafargues: Corr. 1:248.

73. Ltr, P. Lafargue to E, June 24, 1884, in E/Lafargues: Corr. 1:210f.—Ltr, E to L. Lafargue, Aug. 9, 1887, in E/Lafargues: Corr. 2:58.—Paul Lafargue's article "Les Services Publics" appeared in *Le Socialiste*, Aug. 6, 1887.
74. Ltr, E to Vollmar, Aug. 13, 1884, in MEW 36:199.
75. Ltr, E to Bebel, Jan. 20-23, 1886, in MEW 36:427.
76. Ltr, E to L. Lafargue, Jan. 17, 1886, in E/Lafargues: Corr. 1:331f; this passage was quoted in KMTR 2:513f.
77. E: To the German Workers 1893, in MEW 22:400.
78. E: Role of Force, outline of 4th chap., in MEW 21:465.
79. Miller: *Das Problem der Freiheit im Sozialismus*, 193 (for the first extract), 203 fn (re the Erfurt Program).
80. Ltr, E to P. Lafargue, Mar. 6, 1894, in E/Lafargues: Corr. 3:325.
81. Ltr, Bernstein to E, Sep.. 1, 1882, qu. in Lidtke, 166.
82. E: On Social Rel. in Russia, Afterword, in MEW 22:433; the trans in MESW 2:408 is defective.
83. Ibid., 425 [MESW 2:400].
84. See KMTR 1:559; the discussion summarized after this will be found on p.558-60.
85. Re Bellamy, see his *Looking Backward*, Chap. 6-7; also Lipow: *Authoritarian Socialism in America*, Chap. 8. Re Blatchford, see Semmel: *Imperialism & Soc. Reform*, 222-33.
86. Money: *Java*, 1:43, 48, 125, 137f.
87. For "peasant of genius," as well as some background of the French discussion, see KMTR 2:448f; for Engels on Jaurès, see ltr, E to P. Lafargue, Mar. 6, 1894, in E/Lafargues: Corr. 3:325.
88. Ltr, E to P. Lafargue, Mar. 6, 1894, in E/Lafargues: Corr. (Fr.) 3:353f, rev. from the English ed., 3:324f.
89. So described in ltr, E to Adler, July 17, 1894, in MEW 39:272.
90. Ltr, E to L. Lafargue, Apr. 11, 1894, in E/Lafargues: Corr. 3:329.
91. Ltr, E to P. Lafargue, Mar. 6, 1894, ibid., 3:325.
92. So, for ex., said the deputy G. Schumacher, as qu. in MEW 36:806, note 509; or see Lidtke: *Outlawed Party*, 198, for a similar statement by Auer.
93. This was covered in KMTR 2, Chap. 17, also Chap. 18, esp. its last section.
94. For Engels' emphasis on the international reaction, see the following letters: E to Bebel, Dec. 30, 1884, in MEW 36:261f; E to Becker, Apr. 2, 1885, ibid., 291; E to Bebel, Apr. 4, 1885, ibid., 292.
95. Engels' thought is explained most clearly in two letters to Bebel a little over a year apart: Dec. 30, 1884, in MEW 36:260-62, and Jan. 20-23, 1886, in MEW 36:425f.
96. This incomprehension also characterizes an otherwise excellent work (required reading for background) which is much used in the present chapter, viz., Lidtke's *Outlawed Party*, 193-203.
97. To the American correspondent: ltr, E to Sorge, Dec. 31, 1884, in MEW 36:623; similarly, E to Becker, Apr. 2, 1885, ibid., 291.—To Bebel: ltr of Apr. 4, 1885, ibid., 292.—In subsequent years: ltr, E to Sorge, Mar. 3, 1887, in MEW 36:623; E: Reply to Ed. Bd. *SAZ* (Draft), in MEW 22:67 (this passage not in the final

text); E: Farewell Letter to Readers, in MEW 22:77f; ltr, E to Bebel, Oct. 7, 1892, in MEW 38:489f, followed up by ltr, E to Bebel, Nov. 6, 1892, ibid., 510.
98. On "blowup of the Fraction," see ltr, E to Bebel, Dec. 30, 1884, in MEW 36:261. For the rest: ltr, E to L. Lafargue, Apr. 16-17, 1885, ibid., 299; and E to P. Lafargue, May 19, 1885, ibid., 317 (both letters retrans. from German).
99. Ltr, E to Becker, June 15, 1885, ibid., 328; and ltr, E to Sorge, June 3, 1885, ibid., 323f.

5. OF ANARCHISM: PROUDHONIST MODEL

1. Cf. KMTR 1:179 fn.
2. M: Class Struggles in France, in MECW 10:118 or MESW 1:273.
3. Cf. KMTR 1:322, 510.
4. Cf. KMTR 1, Chap. 4, Sec. 3, esp. p. 105, 179 fn.
5. Re Foigny: see Berneri: *Journey Through Utopia*, 7, 188, 197f, and cf. page X. For the edition of Foigny that I used, see the Bibliography. Re Weitling: see KMTR 3:39f, 53-55, 147f. For the anarchist utopia by Pataud & Pouget, see the Bibliography.
6. M: Indifference to Politics, in ME: Scritti Italiani, 100.
7. Ibid., 101f, 104.
8. Cf. KMTR 1:170 fn, 650.
9. Ltr, E to Cafiero, July 1, 1871, in ME: Corr. con Ital., 21.
10. Ltr, E to Hildebrand, Oct. 22, 1889, in MEW 37:293.
11. E: Cond. Eng./18th Cent., in MECW 3:486 [MEW 1:567].
12. E: Condition of the Working Class in England, in MECW 4:528 [MEW 2:455]; ME: German Ideology, in MECW 5:412 [MEW 3:397]. M: Plan of Library, in MECW 4:667; re this plan, see this volume, Chap. 1, Sec. 3.
13. Ltr, E to M, Mar. 17, 1845, in MEW 27:25 [MECW 38:27]. Later references to Godwin in the M-E correspondence are inconsequential.
14. On the "Free," see KMTR 1:60 and, on the Bauer brothers vs. the masses, 222-26. On the protoanarchism and "egoism" of the "Free," see Cornu: *K.M. und F.E.*, 1:313f, 359f (in the French ed., 2:60f, 112f); see also McLellan: *Young Hegel. & K.M.*, 38f. For the quote from Edgar Bauer, see Cornu: *K.M. und F.E.*, 1:313.
15. Cornu: *K.M. und F.E.*, 1:313, 359f.
16. M: Attitude of Herwegh & Ruge, in MECW 1:287 [New Mega I, 1:371].
17. Ltr, M to Ruge, Nov. 30, 1842, in MECW 1:393-95 [MEW 27:411-13].
18. Cf. KMTR 1:270-74.
19. M: Debates on Freed. Press, in MEW 1:64 [MECW 1:168]; this passage is given in context in KMTR 1:44.
20. Apropos of Plekhanov's *Anarchism and Soc.*, 38f, the French historian Maitron in his *Mouve. Anarch. en Fr.*, 1:41 fn, made this underestimation. Cf. Carr: *M. Bakunin*, 451; Pyziur: *Doctr. of Anarch.*, 41.
21. See, for ex., the remarks on this by McLellan: *Young Hegel. & K.M.*, 131.
22. ME: German Ideology, in MECW 5:212, 380 [MEW 3:193, 364].
23. Stirner: *Ego and His Own*, 125.
24. Brazill: *Young Heg.*, 221.—Re *Idiotismus*, see KMTR 2:344f.
25. Cf. KMTR 1:322, 510.
26. Ltr, E to M, Nov. 19, 1844, in MEW 27:11f [MECW 38:11f].
27. Hess's articles "Sozialismus und Kommunismus" and "Philosophie der Tat"

were published in the collection ed. by Herwegh, *Einundzwanzig Bogen* (see Biblio.); reprinted in Hess: *Phil. Soz. Schrift.*, 197, 210. For the anarchoid element, see Silberner: *M. Hess*, 133, 137.
28. Hess's article "Deutschland und Frankreich in Bezug auf die Centralisationsfrage," May 17, 1842, was reprinted in Hess: *Phil. Soz. Schrift.*, 175.
29. M: Centralilzation Question, in MECW 1:183 [MEW Eb.1:380].
30. Cornu: *K.M. und F.E.*, 1:373-77 (French ed., 2:136-42).—M: Economic and Philos. Mss., in MECW 3:232 [MEW Eb.1:468].
31. Carr: *M. Bakunin*, Chap. 6 (pp. 113-17) and Chap. 11.
32. *Reminisc. M. E.* (Voden), 332. We met Voden in KMTR 3:323f.
33. Cf. KMTR 1:216f, 309 fn.
34. E: Cond. of Eng./18th Cent., in MECW 3:476, 485f [MEW 1:557, 566].
35. Cf. KMTR 1:216f, 309 fn.—E: An Evening, in MECW 2:107f [MEW Eb.2:89f]; similarly in several other poems of this period.—Re publisher for Shelley: ltr, E to W. Graeber, July 30, 1839, in MECW 2:467 [MEW Eb.2:414]; and E to Schücking, June 18 & July 2, 1840, in MECW 2:494f, 497 [MEW Eb.2:444f, 447f].
36. Shelley: "The Masque of Anarchy."
37. M: Crit. Heg. Phil. Rt./Ms., in MEW 1:232 [MECW 3:30]. This point was set forth in KMTR 1:90. By the "modern French" Marx certainly was referring to Proudhon, and perhaps also to Saint-Simon and/or Fourier.
38. M: Crit. Notes King of Pruss., in MEW 1:409 [MECW 3:206]; this passage was discussed in more detail in KMTR 1:178-81.
39. M: Draft Plan for Work on the Modern State, in MEW 3:537 [MECW 4:666]; Marx's entire outline was given in KMTR 1:187 fn.
40. ME: Holy Family, in MECW 4:121 [MEW 2:128].
41. ME: German Ideology, in MEW 3:364 [MECW 5:380].
42. See esp. KMTR 1, Chap. 8, Sec. 8.
43. Cf. the estimation given in Woodcock: *P. J. Proudhon*, 99.
44. M: Poverty of Philosophy, in MECW 6:212 [M: Misère, 178f].
45. ME: Communist Manifesto, in MECW 6:505f [MEW 4:482].
46. For a typical example, see M: 18th Brumaire, in MESW 1:476 or MECW 11:184 [MEW 8:196].
47. ME: [Review of] Le Socialisme et l'Imp., in MEW 7:285f [MECW 10:330f].
48. Ibid., 288 [MECW 10:333].
49. Ibid., 288f [MECW 10:333f].
50. M: Conspectus on Bakunin, in MEW 18:610; the quote from Bakunin is given as it appears in Marx's notes, mostly trans. into German; emphasis by Marx.—Kropotkin: *The State*, in his *Selected Writ.*, 212.
51. E: On Slogan of Abol. of State, in MEW 7:417f [MECW 10:486f].
52. This background is offered in ed. notes in MEW 7:615 (n.279-80) or MECW 10:694 (n.346-47).
53. E: On Slogan of Abol. of State, in MEW 7:418 [MECW 10:487].
54. Ibid., 420 [MECW 10:489].
55. Ltr, M to E, Aug. 8, 1851, in MEW 27:297-304 [MECW 38:409-16].
56. Ltr, E to M, Aug. 21, 1851, in MEW 27:318 [MECW 38:435].
57. M: Grundrisse, 326 [Nic. tr., 424].
58. Proudhon may have come to view anarchy as an ideal goal centuries away, simply out of pessimism; this is not merely speculative: cf. Woodcock: *P. J. Proudhon*, 249.
59. E: Critical Notes on Proudhon's Book, in MECW 11:556-58.—Ltr, M to E, Aug. 8, 1851, in MEW 27:299, 304 [MECW 38:411, 416]. Engels also made the

connection with Stirner, in ltrs, E to M, ca. Aug. 11, 1851, in MEW 27:311 [MECW 38:422], and ca. Aug. 27, 1851, ibid., 328 [MECW 38:444].
60. Ltr, E to M, Aug. 21, 1851, in MEW 27:318 [MECW 38:435].
61. The article was cast in the form of a letter to the editor of *Sozialdemocrat*, d. Jan. 24, 1865; in MEW 16:25+ [MECW 20:26+].—Cf. Marx on Proudhonian "indifference to politics" (pub. end of 1874), for which see KMTR 3:295+.
62. Ltr, E to Bernstein, Jan. 28, 1884, in MEW 36:92; the context of this passage will come up below, in Chap. 6, Sec. 12.
63. So according to Maitron: *Mouve. Anarch. en Fr.*, 1:34 fn.
64. S. Bernstein: *First Intl. in America*, 182.
65. Ltr, E to M, ca. Aug. 10, 1851, in MEW 27:306 [MECW 38:418].
66. Ltr, E to M, ca. Aug. 11, 1851, in MEW 27:308, 310 [MECW 38:420, 421].
67. For Proudhon's *Carnets*, see the Biblio. The development of his ideas on the Mutual Credit utopia can be followed through the thematic index in the published volumes. For the biographical side, see Woodcock: *P. J. Proudhon*, 143f, 146f, keeping in mind that this biography is generally a roseate whitewash. For brief information on Proudhon's yearning for "mastery," see KMTR 3:58f, also 239f; for more information from the *Carnets*, see Draper: "Note on the Father of Anarchism" (see Biblio.).

6. OF ANARCHISM: BAKUNIN MODEL

1. See KMTR 3:93 and the following pages.
2. For ex., see the editorial remarks by L. S. Feuer in his compilation of the Marx-Engels *Basic Writings*, 481.
3. Godwin: *Political Justice*, Book 8, Chap. 8, Appendix, p. 760 (for "evil," 758). This is the same section that Engels pointed to in the letter quoted above in Chap. 5 (ref. n. 13).
4. M: Capital, 3:376 [MEW 25:397].
5. Ibid., 380 [MEW 25:401].
6. M: Critique of Heg. Phil. of Right/Ms., in MEW 1:249 [poor trans. in MECW 3:47].
7. See KMTR 1:316.
8. Perret's letter is quoted in ltr, M to De Paepe, Jan. 24, 1870, in ME: Corr. (Fr.) 10:267 [MECW 43:413].— Marx's comment: ibid., 269 [MECW 43:415].—E: Imperative Mandates, in MECW 23:280 (original in Spanish).—E: The GC to All the Members [&c], in GCFI 5:440.
9. Ltr, E to P. Lafargue, Dec. 30, 1871, in E/Lafargues: Corr. 1:34f.
10. Ltr, E to Cuno, Jan. 24, 1872, in MEW 33:389.
11. E: On Authority, in MESW 2:376 [ME: Scritti Ital., 94].
12. Ibid., 377 [ME: Scritti Ital., 95].
13. M: Capital, 1:331f; see also 356, 402, 435f ("autocracy"), 640, 645 [MEW 23:351, also 377, 424, 459, 669, 674]. See the discussion of the term 'despotism' in KMTR 3:77-79, and cf. also 68f.
14. E: On Authority, in MESW 2:377f [ME: Scritti Ital., 96].
15. Ibid., 378 [ME: Scritti Ital., 96f].
16. See Carr: *M. Bakunin*, Chap. 29.—The six times: first in ltr, M to Beesly, Oct. 19, 1870, the English original pub'd in various letter collections [MEW 33:158]; then ltr, E to Cafiero, July 1, 1871, in ME: Corr. con Ital., 20; in ME: Alleged

Divisions, 17 [MESW 2:258]; and three times in ME: Alliance of S.D. &c., 12, 13, 21 [in the collection *Hague Congress &c*, 517, 518, 527]. In addition, Marx gave an oral report of the affair at the Oct. 11, 1870 meeting of the General Council, in *GCFI* 4:68.
17. ME: Alliance of S.D. &c., 21 [*Hague Congress &c.*, 527]. Actually, Bakunin sneaked out of town to Marseilles.
18. Aeschylus: *Prometheus Bound*, in Oates & Oneal: *Complete Greek Drama*, 1:128.
19. As mentioned before, the prime example was the story by Pataud & Pouget (see Biblio.).
20. ME: Alliance of S.D. &c., 12 [*Hague Congress &c.*, 517].
21. Pyziur: *Doctrine of Anarch.*, 108f.
22. ME: Alleged Divisions, 17 [MESW 2:258].
23. Ltr, E to Terzaghi, ca. Jan. 14-15, 1872, in ME: Corr. con Ital., 127f.
24. E: From the Intl., in MEW 18:475.—Minutes of the Hague Congress, in Gerth, ed.: *First International*, 218f.
25. E: On Authority, in MESW 2:379 [ME: Scritti Ital., 97].
26. Minutes of the Hague Congress, in Gerth, ed.: *First International*, 218f.
27. See KMTR 3:55-57, 93-98.
28. Mendel: *M. Bakunin*, 306; and cf. 305-15.
29. ME: Alliance of S.D. &c., in *Hague Congress &c.*, 519 [original, 14].
30. Ibid. (Emphasis added by the International pamphlet.)
31. Cf. KMTR 1:557, 662.
32. E: For. Pol. of Russ. Cz., in MEW 22:21.
33. The quote: from ME: Alliance of S.D. &c., in *Hague Congress &c.*, 520 [original, 15]. For the smaller number: see KMTR 3:95.
34. Ibid.
35. For Marx's basic views on the primacy of class organization over ideological program, see KMTR 2:24-28.
36. Ltr, E to Cafiero, June 14, 1872, in ME: Corr. con Ital., 227f.
37. ME: Alliance of D.D. &c., in *Hague Congress &c.*, 507, also 575f [original, 3, 67f].
38. Ltr, E to Bernstein, Oct. 20, 1882, in MEW 35:374.
39. ME: Alleged Divisions, in MESW 2:285 [original, 49f].
40. Ibid., 285f [original, 50].
41. Ltr, E to Terzaghi, ca. Jan. 14-15, 1872, in ME: Corr. con Ital., 127.
42. This was touched on in KMTR 2:555-57, esp. the footnote on 556.
43. M: Revelations of the Dip. Hist., in MECW 15:28.
44. Ltr, E to Terzaghi, same as in n.41 above. Along the same lines, see also ltr, E to Cuno, Jan. 24, 1872, in MEW 33:389; and the article, E: Congress of Sonvillier, in MEW 17:477f.
45. Ltr, M to Bolte, Nov. 23, 1871, in MEW 33:329 [MESW 2:423].—For Engels, see E: Housing Question, in MESW 2:354 [MEW 18:265]; E: Ludwig Feuerbach, in MESW 3:360 [MEW 21:291]; ltr, E to Hildebrand, Oct. 22, 1889, in MEW 37:293.
46. This was M: Conspectus on Bakunin (see Biblio.).
47. This is the subject of KMTR 1, Chap. 23.
48. Ltr, E to Cuno, Jan. 24, 1872, in MESW 2:424f [MEW 33:388].
49. Ltr, E to Van Patten, Apr. 18, 1883, in ME: Sel. Corr. ('65), 362.
50. Ltr, M to Lafargue, Apr. 19, 1870, in MECW 43:490f; this continues the passage quoted in KMTR 2:145.
51. Ltr, M to E, June 20, 1866, in MECW 42:287 (bit rev. after MEW 31:228f).
52. Ltr, E to Cafiero, July 1-3, 1871, in ME: Corr. con Ital., 20. See also ltr, E to Pio, Mar. 7, 1872, in MEW 33:415.

53. Ltr, E to Cuno, Jan. 24, 1872, in MESW 2:425 [MEW 33:388f]; this passage follows immediately on the one in n.48 above.
54. E: In Italy, in MEW 19:92.
55. M: Indifference to Politics, in ME: Scritti Ital., 100, 99f [MECW 23:394, 393].
56. E: Workingmen of Europe in 1877 (published Mar. 1878) took up the anarchists in Sec. II and III; this work has not been reprinted in its original English (not reached by MECW as yet).
57. In KMTR 3, see esp. Chap. 10, particularly p. 127, 275.
58. Ltr, M to Sorge, Sep. 19, 1879, in MEW 34:411.
59. Ltr, M to Kugelmann, Oct. 9, 1866, in MECW 42:326 [MEW 31:529f].
60. ME: Great Men, in MECW 11:307 [MEW 8:314]; for a mention of Faucher, see above, Chap. 4, Sec. 4.
61. M: Revel. on Com. Trial in Cologne, in MECW 11:419.
62. Venturi: *Roots of Revolution*, 52; Carr: *M. Bakunin*, 153f; Somerhausen: *Humanisme Agiss.*, 197; Annenkov: *Extraord. Decade*, 183. For Bakunin's previous peripheral connection with the *Deutsch-Französische Jahrbücher*, see McLellan: *K. Marx*, 78.
63. Carr: *M. Bakunin*, 321.
64. This is related in ltr, M to E, Nov. 4, 1864, in MEW 31:16.
65. Ltr, M to Bolte, Nov. 23, 1871, in MEW 33:329.
66. Re the "shameless ignorance" &c., ltr, M to Lafargue, Apr. 19, 1870, in MECW 43:490 (English orig.).—Bakunin's letter to M of Dec. 22, 1868 is found, in English trans., in Padover's collection, M: On the First Intl., 460. The motivation of this letter is discussed in Special Note B.—Bakunin: *Statism and Anarchy*, in *Archives Bak.*, 3:353.
67. Ltr, M to Lafargue, Apr. 19, 1870, in MECW 43:490.
68. Carr: *M. Bakunin*, 303, 305f.
69. Ltr, M to De Paepe, Sep. 14, 1870, in ME: Corr. (Fr.) 11:108f [MEW 33:147].
70. The text of the Bakuninist manifesto is given in Guillaume: *L'Internationale*, 2:83f; the quotes that follow are cited from these pages.
71. M: Second Address on the War, MECW 22:268f or MESW 2:200. For a summary of this activity, see esp. Collins & Abramsky, 181-88.
72. E: Bakuninists at Work, in MECW 23:596-98 [MEW 18:491-93]. See also Engels' summary in ltr, E to Sorge, July 26, 1873, in MEW 33:598.
73. See KMTR 2:356 (peasantry); 2:459n, 466f (brigands, &c.); 2:520, 564-69 (intelligentsia).
74. Re the hundred, see above, this chapter, Sec. 5, page [159] (ref. n. 33). The quote is from ME: Alliance of S.D. &c, in *Hague Congress &c*, 520 [original, 15].
75. M: Conspectus of Reichstag Debate, in MEW 34:497f.
76. Ltr, E to Becker, Dec. 16, 1882, in MEW 35:411.
77. E: GC to All the Members [&c], in GCFI 5:440f.
78. Ibid., 445.
79. Re the "wire-pullers": E: In Italy, in MEW 19:94.—Re *La Plebe:* ltr, E to M, Mar. 6, 1877, in MEW 34:37f. Cf. the similar passage in E: In Italy, in MEW 19:93f.
80. Nechayev's "The Fundamental Principles of the Future Social Order," quoted in the International's pamphlet, ME: Alliance of S.D. [&c], in *Hague Congress &c.*, 596f [original, 87f].
81. ME: same pamphlet, ibid., 597 [original, 88f].
82. Ibid., 598, 609f [original, 89, 102f].
83. Re the Jesuit operation in Paraguay: see, for ex., Cunninghame Graham's *A Vanished Arcadia*, and his intro to W. H. Koebel's *In Jesuit Land*; also Hyndman: *Historical Basis of Soc.*, 435. For the historical background, see Baudin: *Une Théocratie Socialiste*; Koch: *Quelques Expériences Collectivistes.*—Re Bakunin on the

Jesuit system: see, for ex., Bakunin: "To the Officers of the Russian Army," in *Archives Bak.*, 4:175; ltr, Bakunin to Richard, Feb. 7, 1870, in Richard: *Bakunin et l'Intle.*, 127; and Bakunin: "Letter to Nechayev of June 2, 1870," Pt. 1, p. 87, and Pt. 2, p. 88; other loci may be by Nechayev in collaboration with Bakunin.
84. Ltr, E to Becker, Jan. 30, 1879, in MEW 34:367.
85. For Bakunin's disintegration from 1873 on, see Carr: *M. Bakunin*, 476-506. For Bakunin's advice to Guillaume, see Guillaume: *L'Internationale*, 3:186.
86. Ltr, E to Becker, Dec. 16, 1882, in MEW 35:411.
87. Ltr, M to daughter Laura (Lafargue), Dec. 14, 1882, in MEW 35:408.
88. Ibid. (This was word play on the Greek sense of *idiotes*.)
89. Ltr, E to Iglesias, Mar. 26, 1894, in MEW 39:229 (retrans.).
90. Plekhanov: *Anarchism and Soc.*, 145f.
91. See above, this chapter, Sec. 6, pp. 150f, ref. n. 39.
92. See above, Chap. 5, Sec. 1.
93. Quoted above, Chap. 4, p. 104 (ref. n. 9).
94. See M: Civil War in France, in MECW 22:334, 338 (for workers' government or equivalent), 339, 350 (for people's government or equivalent); there are other passages referring to the Commune as a *government* explicitly or implicitly.—For the governmental institutions of the Commune, see KMTR 3:269-74.
95. Ibid., 332f.
96. M: Civil War in Fr./Draft 1, in MECW 22:486.—Same, Draft 2, ibid., 537.
97. Ltr, E to Bernstein, Jan. 28, 1884, in MEW 36:92; for the background, see ibid., 756f, note 120; previously cited in Chap. 5, Sec. 5 (ref. n. 62).
98. Quoted, with source, by Gay: *Dilemma of Dem. Soc.*, 249.
99. Kelsen: *Sozialismus und Staat*, 50; see also his essay "Marx oder Lassalle."—Pranger: *M & Political Theory*, 191; the next two pages are likewise amusing.

7. OF THE REACTIONARY ANTICAPITALISMS

1. Draper: "Neo-Stalinist Type," 25.
2. E: Principles of Communism (Ques. 24), in MECW 6:355f [MEW 4:377f]. For Engels on the Democracy (as a class bloc), see KMTR 2:186-92.
3. ME: Communist Manifesto, in MECW 6:494 [MEW 4:472].—E: Principles of Communism, in MECW 6:355 [MEW 4:378].
4. See KMTR 1:104; the source is M: Ltrs from D.F.J., MEW 1:344 [MECW 3:143].
5. See the related point made in KMTR 1:639.
6. For the Marx-Lassalle discussion on Sickingen, see KMTR 2:160f, 383f, 528f.
7. Ltr, M to Lassalle, Apr. 19, 1859, in MEW 29:591 [MECW 40:420].
8. Cf. ltr, E to Zasulich, Mar. 6, 1884, in MEW 36:119 (checked against French original).
9. ME: Communist Manifesto, in MECW 6:507 [MEW 4:483].
10. Ibid., 508 [MEW 4:483].
11. Re the retrogressive swing: see, for ex., Hauser: *Social Hist. of Art*, 2:653, 672f; Hook: *From Hegel to M.*, 132-35.—Re King F.W. IV: this passage is given in KMTR 1:208 fn.—Re Engels on Young England: see below, this chapter, Sec. 3 [ref. n. 37].—Other ME usages: for ex., M: Comments Latest Pruss. Cens., in MECW 1:125 [MEW 1:19f]; E: Cond. Eng./Past & Pres., in MECW 3:461 [MEW 1:542]; ltr, M to E, Mar. 25, 1868, in MECW 42:557 [MEW 32:51]; ltr, E to

Mehring, Sep. 28, 1892, in MEW 38:480.—As a cross-check, note the same frequent usage in Heinrich Heine's journalism and poetry.
12. M: Grundrisse, 113 [Nic. tr., 199].
13. See KMTR 1:174-77.
14. M: Crit. Notes King of Pruss., in MECW 3:190 [MEW 1:393].
15. On the triangular class struggle as a whole, see KMTR 2, Chap. 7 to 10. Re Feudal Socialism, see KMTR 2:179-83.
16. E: Status Quo [or Constit. Question] in Ger., in MECW 6:77 [MEW 4:42f].
17. For this problem, see KMTR 2:180 fn.
18. ME: Communist Manifesto, in MECW 6:508, and cf. MEW 4:484 and its notes.
19. On Lamennais, E in 1843: see E: Progress Soc. Reform,, in MECW 3:399; about this article, see KMTR 1:156.—Invitation to *DFJ*: see M (with Ruge): Ltr to Dém. Pac., Dec. 10, 1843, in MECW 3:132 [MEW Eb.1:437].—"Far behind": see ME: Circular Ag. Kriege, in MECW 6:41 [MEW 4:7].—Re June uprising: see E: Köln. Ztg. & June Rev., in MECW 7:155 [MEW 5:144].
20. ME: Communist Manifesto, in MECW 6:508 [MEW 4:484].
21. Ibid., 487 [MEW 4:483].
22. Ibid., 508 [MEW 4:483]. For the immediately preceding words, see ref. n. 9 above.
23. M: Communism of Rh. Beo., in MECW 6:220 [MEW 4:191]; for the background of this article, see KMTR 2:182f.
24. Re the Lassalleans: ME: Statement to Ed. Bd. Soc.-Dem., in MECW 20:80 [MEW 16:79 or 31:77]; and see above, Chap. 3, Sec. 7, p. 63.—Re 1847: quoted above, this chapter, Sec. 2, ref. n. 16.
25. Qu. by Ryazanov in a note, in ME: Com. Manifesto/Ryazanov, 200.
26. ME: Holy Family, in MECW 4:205 [MEW 2:217]; for Marx's analysis of Sue's hero, see KMTR 1:228-32.
27. E: Condition of the Working Class in England, in MECW 4:578 fn [MEW 2:502 fn].
28. E: Eng. Ten Hour Bill, in MEW 7:234f [MECW 10:292].
29. Ibid., 236 [MECW 10:293].
30. E: Condition of the Working Class in England, in MECW 4:578 fn [MEW 2:502 fn].
31. Symons: *T. Carlyle*, 200; see also Wilson: *T. Carlyle*, 3:200f.
32. For the "herald of fascism" thesis, see Schapiro: *Lib. & Chall. of Fasc.*, Chap. 15; for the recurrent discovery of Carlyle's radicalism, see for ex. Rosenberg: *Seventh Hero*.
33. M: Capital, I, in MEW 23:270 [M: Cap. 1:255 fn].
34. For the reception of *Latter-Day Pamphlets*, see Symons: *T. Carlyle*, 225f; Wilson: *T. Carlyle*, 4:215, 249.
35. For this phase of young Engels, see KMTR 1:216f, 309 fn; and 3:43. In the present volume, see Chap. 5, Sec. 2, p.[[172f]].
36. See KMTR 1:217.
37. "National talkshop": Engels quoted this phrase of Carlyle's in an early article of 1843: E: Letters from London, I, in MECW 3:379 [MEW 1:468].—For the rest (not in order), see E: Cond. Eng./Past & Pres., in MECW 3:444f, 455f [MEW 1:525f, 537f].
38. See KMTR 1:158f.
39. E: Cond. Eng./Past & Pres., in MECW 3:447 [MEW 1:528].
40. The quote is from ibid., 460f [MEW 1:542f]. The preceding paragraph is based on ibid., 467 [MEW 1:549].
41. Ibid., 466, 467.

42. The hope: ibid., 467 [MEW 1:547f].—Re the book, see E: Condition of the Working Class in England, in MECW 4:389f, 414, 560, 562f, 578f [MEW 2:320f, 345f, 484, 486f, 502].—Other references to Carlyle before 1850 are only incidental; see MECW 3:476, 4:14, 6:416 [MEW 1:557, 2:14, 6:536].—Reception of Engels' review: see ltr, E to M, Oct. 1844, in MECW 38:4 or MEW 27:6.
43. E: Condition of the Working Class in England, in MECW 4:579 fn [MEW 2:502 fn].
44. ME: Review/Latter-Day Pam., in MEW 7:255f [MECW 10:301f]. The last sentence was later quoted (approximately) in *Capital*, in MEW 23:270 fn [M: Cap. 1:255 fn].
45. For Macfarlane's acquaintance with Marx and Engels, see KMTR 2:632. Her article on Carlyle appeared in *Democratic Review* for April, May and June, 1850; her translation of the Manifesto, in June. The M-E review appeared about mid-May.
46. See ltr, E to F. Graeber, Dec. 9, 1839 to Feb. 5, 1840, in MECW 2:489 [MEW Eb.2:438f].
47. ME: Review/Latter-Day Pam., in MEW 7:261 [MECW 10:306f].
48. Ibid., 262.
49. Ibid., 264. For later comments on Carlyle's "Captains of Industry," see E: Cotton & Iron, 42; and M: Palmerston, in NYDT, Oct. 19, 1853, in MECW 12:347 fn.
50. Ibid., 265. Also about Carlyle on prisons, see M: Political Movements, in NYDT, Sep. 30, 1853, in MECW 12:303.
51. Ibid., 265.
52. See KMTR 1:232-34.
53. See above, this chapter, Sec. 5, p. 189, ref. n. 44.
54. See KMTR 2:422-24.
55. ME: Review/May to Oct. [1850], in MEW 7:445 [MECW 10:314f]; the continuation of this passage was given in KMTR 2:301f.
56. See KMTR 2:300-302.
57. Ltr, E to Ehrenfreund, Apr. 19, 1890, in MEW 22:49f; for the whole passage, see KMTR 2:301f.
58. M: Civil War in Fr./Draft 1, in MECW 22:504 (checked against reading in New Mega I, 22:73).
59. Ltr, M to E, July 7, 1866, in MEW 31:234 [MECW 42:292].
60. Re "ignorance": ltr, M to E, Mar. 20, 1869, in MEW 32:284 [MECW 43:244], and M: Civil War in Fr./Draft 1, in ME: Writings on Par. Com., 168. "Arrogance": ltr, M to daughter Jenny, June 10, 1869, in MEW 32:614 [MECW 43:293]. "Crotchets": same letter; also M to Kugelmann, Dec. 13, 1870, in MEW 33:162. "Sectarian": M: Civil War in Fr./Draft 1, in ME: Writings on Par. Com., 161.—By Engels: ltr, E to M, Mar. 21, 1869, in MEW 32:286 [MECW 43:246, different trans.]. Re Rappoport, see *Mohr und Gen.*, 578. See also ltr, E to M, Apr. 14, 1869, in MEW 32:301 [MECW 43:261].
61. Ltr, E to Tönnies, Jan. 24, 1895, in MEW 39:394f.
62. Landor: "Curtain Raised," in MECW 22:605.
63. M: Civil War in France, in MESW 2:224 or MECW 22:336.
64. M: Civil War in France/Draft 1, in MECW 22:504; previously referred to above, see ref. n. 58.—M: Cap. 1:332 fn [MEW 23:352 fn].
65. M: Civil War in France/Draft 1, in MECW 22:498.
66. For the English Comtists and the Commune, see Harrison, ed.: *English Def. of Commune*.—Re the draft, see the preceding note.
67. To a friend: ltr, M to Kugelmann, Dec. 13, 1870, in MEW 33:162.—To Beesly:

June 12, 1871, in MEW 33:228; the English original is not extant. But cf. Marx's earlier and less complimentary comment on Beesly's ability, in ltr, M to E, Mar. 20, 1869, in MEW 32:284 [MECW 43:244]; apparently provoked by a particular incident.

68. Ltr, E to Tönnies, Jan. 24, 1895, in MEW 39:395f.
69. For a section on Marx's united-front problem with Urquhart, see KMTR 3:141-43.
70. Ltr, M to E, Apr. 22, 1854, in MEW 28:348; for Marx's announcement of his conclusion, see ltr, M to E, Nov. 2, 1853, in MEW 28:306. For Marx's unenthusiastic opinion of Urquhart's anti-Palmerston material, see, for ex., ltr, M to E, July 27, 1854, in MEW 28:381; and ltr, M to E, Apr. 9, 1859 (re Anstey), in MEW 29:415.—"Poles apart": for this distinction, see also the emphasis in Marx's *cursus vitae* in ltr, M to lawyer Weber, Mar. 3, 1860, in MEW 30:510f.—Re M on Palmerston in general, see remarks in KMTR 3:86-88.
70a. For the "softer evaluation," see Fedoseyev et al.: *K. Marx*; for the "attenuated interpretation" by Engels, see the article E: Marx, Heinrich Karl, in MEW 22:345.
71. Ltr, E to M, Mar. 10, 1853, in MECW 39:284f [MEW 28:218f, dated Mar. 9].—E: Turkish Ques., in NYDT, Apr. 19, 1853, in MECW 12:26.
72. Ltr, M to Cluss, mid-Nov. 1853, in MEW 28:599 [MECW 39:398]; ltr, M to E, Jan. 10, 1854, ibid., 318 [MECW 39:407].
73. Ltr, M to E, Feb. 9, 1854, in MEW 28:324 [MECW 39:413].
74. These pleasantries may be found at MEW 29:505 (cracked); MEW 30:378 (nonsense), also 30:406, 408; MEW 31:142, 115; MEW 28:306 (monomaniac), 356; MEW 32:82 [in the same order: MECW 40:523; 41:497, 536, 537; 42:183, 154; 39:395, 448; 43:31]. For other acid comments on Urquhart, see MEW 29:457; 30:81, 433; 31:354; 32:203, 211 [in order: MECW 40:468; 41:175, 562; 42:434; 43:159, 166].
75. For ex., ltr, M to E, Feb. 13, 1855, in MEW 28:435 [MECW 39:523], re Chartism; on which see also ltr, M to E, Sep. 12, 1863, in MEW 30:372 [MECW 41:491f]; also see, re Mazzini, MEW 29:473 [MECW 40:482]; re Polish uprising, MEW 30:325 [MECW 41:454]; re Flerovsky, MEW 32:447 [MECW 43:433]; re a negative example, MEW 32:362F [MECW 43:345F]. Also, at the General Council, cf. M: Wages, Price & Profit, in MESW 2:40 or MECW 20:112.
76. For ex., in untitled articles in NYDT of the following dates: Jan. 28,, 1854 [MECW 12:562f]; Feb. 21, 1854 [MECW 12:607]; Feb. 27, 1854 [MECW 12:615]. Earlier, there had been hostile references in untitled articles of Oct. 4, 1853 [MECW 12:312], and Oct. 7, 1853 [MECW 12:326].
77. M: untitled article, NYDT, June 24, 1854 [MECW 13:228].
78. M: untitled articles, NYDT, Aug. 9, 1854 [MECW 13:325], and Aug. 25, 1854 [MECW 13:359]; also M: Eng. Press on Dead Czar, in MEW 11:109 [MECW 14:68], and M: Parl. Affairs, in MEW 11:270 [MECW 14:245].
79. Ltr, M to Lassalle, June 1, 1854, in MEW 28:608 [MECW 39:455].
80. Ltr, M to E, Apr. 22, 1854, in MEW 28:347f [MECW 39:439f].
81. M: Assoc. for Admin. Ref., in MEW 11:269 [MECW 14:243f]; the first part was quoted in KMTR 1:284 fn.
82. Marx's note on Urquhart, sent to Cluss in America, was in turn quoted by Cluss in a letter to Weydemeyer; this text, which is naturally in German, is given in MEW 28:734f (n. 586), and my citations are translated directly from it. Cluss turned this note, with slight changes, into an article for the

American publication *Die Reform*; a translation of this article is given as an article *by Marx*, titled "David Urquhart," in MECW 12:477f.
83. M: Contrib. to Crit. Pol. Eco., in MECW 29:313 fn [MEW 13:58 fn]; M: Cap., 1:100 fn, 363, 505 fn [MEW 23:115 fn, 385, 528 fn]. In this connection, see also M: Grundrisse, 680f, 730, 747, 846 [Nic. tr., 795f, 847, 864, 886], and also see 856, 861 (index to notebooks).
84. M: Lord Palmerston, in MECW 12:390; the sixth section of this article series had other material on Urquhart vs. Palmerston.
85. For these sentiments (in short ref. form), besides the preceding note, see in articles: MECW 13:489, 590; 14:394; 19:108f; and in letters: MEW 31:280; 32:603; 34:213.
86. Ltr, M to Lassalle, ca. June 2, 1860, in MECW 41:153 [MEW 30:548].
87. E: Foreign Pol. Czar. Russ./Time, in *Time*, Apr. 1890 [cf. MEW 22:13 fn].
88. Ltr, M to Lassalle, ca. June 2, 1860, in MEW 30:547 [MECW 41:153].
89. Ibid., MEW 30:549 [MECW 41:154f].
90. Ltr, M to E, Jan. 18, 1856, in MEW 29:6f [MECW 40:4f].
91. Re Prof. Berlin, see KMTR 3:143 fn.
92. Fedoseyev: *K. Marx*, 296. On Collet, see ltr, M to E, Nov. 14, 1868, in MEW 32:203 [MECW 43:159].
93. Ltr, M to E, Aug. 1, 1856, in MEW 29:67 [MECW 40:62].
94. See KMTR 3:141-44.K4-N8

8. OF BOULANGISM: THE POLITICS OF THE THIRD WAY

1. Lichtheim: *Marxism*, 229 fn; the page references here given by Lichtheim are incompetent. Gemkow et al.: *F. Engels* (English ed.), 440. Stepanova: *F. Engels*, 230, does mention Engels' warnings but not the position against which they were directed.
2. Ltr, E to Sorge, Oct. 10, 1888, in MEW 37:104f. Cf. also ltr, E to Kautsky, Jan. 28, 1889, in MEW 37:144.
3. Seager: *Boulanger Affair*, 15f.
4. Ltr, E to P. Lafargue, Feb. 16, 1886, in E/Lafargues: Corr. 1:338.
5. Droz, ed.: *Histoire Gén. du Soc.*, 2:161f.
6. Dansette: *Boulangisme*, 357. 'Revolutionary socialism' was then a label mostly used by the Blanquists, among whom "Boulangeo-socialism" was strongest.
7. Cf. the general statement in Willard: *Les Guesdistes*, 36 fn.
8. Re the future anarchists, see Pisani-Ferry: *Gén. Boulanger*, 13, and Seager, 249; for their activity in the anarchist movement, see Maitron: *Mouve. Anarch. en Fr.*, 1:392, 475, and 2:15. Re Naquet, see Seager, 75, 99f, 105, 135f, 142, 176; his antisocialism, 74; his book, 267. Re Laisant, ibid., 72, 101.
9. Seager, 178-81.
10. See Dansette, 229, for a crude occasion.
11. See the reference to the Brousse position in Chap. 4, Sec. 8 (ref. n. 78).—Allemane later split from Brousse to form his own (Allemanist) sect.
12. Pisani-Ferry, 128; and Stafford, 210, where the passage differs somewhat but not materially.
13. Seager, 162; cf. also Stafford, 212. Benoît Malon and his *Revue Socialiste* took essentially a Possibilist position; cf. Malon's magazine, issues of May and Oct. 1888. (Seager, 173, is wrong about this.)

14. Qu. in Pisani-Ferry, 129; Seager, 169.
15. On this point, cf. ltr, L. Lafargue to E, Dec. 21, 1888, in E/Lafargues: Corr. 2:176f; and ltr, P. Lafargue to E, Aug. 4, 1889, ibid., 300.
16. Droz, ed.: *Histoire Gén. du Soc.*, 2:152, 158; ltr, P. Lafargue to E, Oct. 23, 1890, in E/Lafargues: Corr. (Fr.) 2:434 (defective trans. in Eng. ed., 2:413).
17. Seager, 170.
18. For Vaillant's sentiments in this contest, see Pisani-Ferry, 163.
19. Ltr, E to L. Lafargue, Oct. 29, 1889, in E/Lafargues: Corr. 2:333.
20. Seager, 244.
21. For this labeling pattern, see the information in KMTR 2:11 fn.
22. Willard: *Les Guesdistes*, 36 fn, mentions one member in the Paris organization.
23. Even by 1890: cf. ltr, E to Sorge, Nov. 26, 1890, in MEW 37:505; ltr, E to Vaillant, Dec. 5, 1890, in E/Lafargues: Corr. 2:425.
24. These party statements were chosen to represent the position by the party-patriotic Guesdist, Vérecque, for his entry on "Boulangisme" in his *Dictionnaire du Socialisme*, 43.
25. Willard: *Les Guesdistes*, 36-38; Zévaès: *Histoire de la Trois. Rép.*, 297f.
26. Cf. ltr, L. Lafargue to E, Dec. 27, 1888, in E/Lafargues: Corr. 2:178.
27. Willard: *Les Guesdistes*, 36.
28. For Engels on defense of the democratic republic, see esp. his disgust in 1877 with the "nonsense" (by German socialists) of taking a negative attitude toward defense of the republic in France; see for ex. MEW 34:54, 57, 281f, 315f.
29. Willard, 37.
30. Qu. in Pisani-Ferry, 128f.
31. Willard, 306 (footnote 6); Seager, 173, says three won seats, apparently erroneously.
32. Re Bordeaux and Lyons: Willard, 38. Re Paris: Seager, 174; but while he quotes documents in the French National Archives, he does not make clear where these "delegates" were voting, or on what.
33. Ltr, L. Lafargue to E, Dec. 27, 1888, in E/Lafargues: Corr. 2:177; and note Engels' reply of Jan. 2, 1889, ibid., 181; also ltr, Liebknecht to E, Oct. 26, 1889, in Liebknecht: *Briefwechsel M&E*, 349. As for Laura's superiority: I have noted this in KMTR 2:303 and 3:308 fn.
34. Stolz: *P. Lafargue*, 5, 9; and see Bottigelli's intro in E/Lafargues: Corr. 3:497f.
35. For the bizarre assumption by certain later historians that Marx spoke oracularly through sons-in-law, see KMTR 3:139 fn. We should recall that Marx's noted "I am no Marxist" quip had been directed in the first place to Lafargue and his French comrades; see KMTR 2:5-8. For Marx on Lafargue, see note 37 below.
36. Bottigelli's intro in E/Lafargues: Corr. (Fr.) 1:viii; in the English ed., 3:490.
37. All are letters by Marx in 1882: to E, Nov. 11, in MEW 35:109; to daughter Jenny Longuet, May 26, ibid., 326 (retrans.); to Laura Lafargue, Dec. 14, ibid., 407. Also cf. ltrs, M to E, Nov. 20 and Nov. 27, ibid., 111, 120.
38. Various letters, P. Lafargue to E, Mar. 18 to Apr. 27, 1888, in E/Lafargues: Corr. 2:104, 116, 118, 109.
39. Ltrs, P. Lafargue to E, Apr. 13, 1888 to Nov. 4, 1889, ibid., 2:168, 134, 172, 114, 119, 186, 334, 335.
40. Ltr, E to L. Lafargue, Feb. 4, 1889, ibid., 2:194f.
41. "No danger": ltrs, P. Lafargue to E, ibid., 2:109, 112, 119, 129, 133, 147. The contrary: ltrs, P. Lafargue to E, Mar. 23, 1889, ibid., 208.
42. See esp. ltr, E to P. Lafargue, Mar. 19, 1888, ibid., 2:107, and ltr, E to Sorge, Oct. 10, 1888, in MEW 37:105. On Boulanger's incompetence: ltr, E to P. La-

Notes to Pages 219–229   343

fargue, Oct. 25, 1886, in E/Lafargues, Corr. 1:389 (which became an article), and E to L. Lafargue, July 15, 1888, ibid., 2:142; also letters in MEW 37:47, 52. As for Paul's evaluations, see for ex. his letters in E/Lafargues: Corr. 2:105, 117.
43. Cf. ltr, P. Lafargue to E, Mar. 21, 1888, in E/Lafargues: Corr. 2:110; Apr. 8, 1888, ibid., 111; and qu. in ltr, E to Laura Lafargue, June 3, 1888, ibid., 131.
44. Ltr, E to P. Lafargue, Dec. 4, 1888, in MEW 37:123 (retrans.). Cf. also similar statement in ltr, E to Laura Lafargue, June 3, 1888, in E/Lafargues: Corr. 2:131.
45. Ltr, E to Kautsky, Jan. 28, 1889, in MEW 37:144.
46. Ltr, E to Bebel, Dec. 22, 1892, in MEW 38:554f (cf. also 537); and E to Sorge, Dec. 31, 1892, ibid., 564.
47. Ltr, P. Lafargue to E, Oct. 15, 1888, in E/Lafargues: Corr. 2:160; cf. also 2:112, 119.
48. Besides the material that follows in the text, see ltr, P. Lafargue to E, Nov. 27, 1888, ibid., 168 (re Basly and Numa Gilly).
49. Ltr, E to L. Lafargue, July 15, 1888, ibid., 2:142f.
50. Ltr, P. Lafargue to E, May 27, 1888, ibid., 2:129, 128.
51. Ltr, P. Lafargue to E, Apr. 24, 1888, ibid., 117.
52. On this, see KMTR 1:390, 2:180f.
53. Ltr, E to L. Lafargue, Apr. 16, 1890, in E/Lafargues: Corr. 2:370.
54. Lafargue: *Parliamentarianism and Boul.* (see Biblio.), 377.
55. Ltr, P. Lafargue to E, in E/Lafargues: Corr. 2:109. Cf. also Laura's comment about the Boulangeo-Blanquists in ltr, L. Lafargue to E, Dec. 21, 1888, ibid., 176.
56. Ltr, Lafargue to Liebknecht, Jan. 16, 1889, in Liebknecht: *Briefwechsel M&E*, 476.
57. Ltr, P. Lafargue to E, Apr. 8, 1888, in E/Lafargues: Corr. 2:112.
58. Ltr, E to L. Lafargue, Apr. 10-11, 1888, in MEW 37:47 (retrans.).
59. Ltr, Lafargue to Liebknecht, Feb. 2, 1889, in Liebknecht: *Briefwechsel M&E*, 476.
60. Ltr, P. Lafargue to E, Jan. 3, 1889, in E/Lafargues: Corr. 2:186.
61. On Lafargue and the peasant question, see KMTR 2:436-39.
62. Ltr, P. Lafargue to E, Nov. 27, 1888, in E/Lafargues: Corr. (Fr.) 2:183 [English ed., 2:168].
63. Ltr, E to L. Lafargue, July 15, 1887, in E/Lafargues: Corr. 2:50.
64. Ltr, E to Guesde, Nov. 20, 1889, in MEW 37:315 (retrans.).
65. Ltr, E to L. Lafargue, June 3, 1888, in E/Lafargues: Corr. 2:131f.
66. Ltr, E. to P. Lafargue, Dec. 4, 1888, in MEW 37:122 (retrans.).
67. Ibid., 123.
68. Ltr, P. Lafargue to E, Dec. 6, 1888, in E/Lafargues: Corr. 2:171f.
69. Ltr, L. Lafargue to E, Dec. 21, 1888, ibid., 2:176.
70. Ltr, E to L. Lafargue, Jan. 2, 1889, ibid., 2:181f.
71. Ltr, E to L. Lafargue, Aug. 27, 1889, ibid., 2:302.
72. Ltr, E to L. Lafargue, Feb. 11, 1889, ibid., 2:196; and see also the passages quoted above in ref. notes 66, 70.
73. Ltr, E to L. Lafargue, July 15, 1888, ibid., 2:142.
74. The citations are from Stafford, 213f.
75. Ltr, E to L. Lafargue, Jan. 2, 1889, in E/Lafargues: Corr. 2:181.
76. Ltr, E to P. Lafargue, Nov. 16, 1889, ibid., 2:340.
77. E (with Bernstein): Intl. Workers Cong. of 1889, in MEW 21:521.
78. Same, Article II, ibid., 530.
79. Ltr, E to Bebel, Jan. 5, 1889, in MEW 37:131.
80. Lafargue: "Parliamentarianism and Boulangism" (see Biblio.), esp. p. 376. (The form 'parliamentarianism' is used in the cited trans.)

81. See KMTR 3:307-09, where the question is discussed at greater length.
82. Ltr, P. Lafargue to E, Oct. 15, 1888, in E/Lafargues: Corr. 2:160.
83. Ltr, P. Lafargue to E, Nov. 27, 1888, ibid., 2:168.
84. Ltr, P. Lafargue to E, Nov. 24, 1888, ibid., 2:167.
85. Ltr, E to L. Lafargue, Aug. 27, 1889, ibid., 2:303.
86. Ltr, E to Liebknecht, Oct. 3, 1889, in MEW 37:282; and Liebknecht: *Briefwechsel M&E*, 348 (ed. note).
87. Ltr, E to L. Lafargue, Oct. 8, 1889, in E/Lafargues: Corr. 2:324f; see also ltr, Oct. 29, 1889, ibid., 2:333.
88. Ltr, E to P. Lafargue, Dec. 4, 1888, in MEW 37:122 (retrans.).
89. Ltr, E to L. Lafargue, Jan. 2, 1889, in E/Lafargues: Corr. 2:182. Cf. also ltr, E to Liebknecht, Oct. 29, 1889, in MEW 37:299, re Jourde.
90. Ltr, E to P. Lafargue, Nov. 16, 1889, in E/Lafargues: Corr. 2:340. And see the letter to Guesde, Nov. 20, 1889, cited in Sec. 6 above.
91. Willard: *Les Guesdistes*, 38, 88f.
92. Ltr, E to L. Lafargue, Mar. 14, 1892, in E/Lafargues: Corr. 3:164f.
93. Ltr, E to L. Lafargue, Apr. 19, 1892, ibid., 3:168.
94. Ltr, P. Lafargue to E, Nov. 4, 1889, ibid., 2:335. Ltr, E to L. Lafargue, Oct. 29, 1889, ibid., 2:333; and ltr, E to Liebknecht, same day, in MEW 37:299.
95. Ltr, E to L. Lafargue, Apr. 19, 1892, in E/Lafargues: Corr. 3:169.
96. Same letter, ibid., 3:168.
97. Ltr, E to P. Lafargue, Dec. 4, 1888, in MEW 37:122; ltr, E to L. Lafargue, Oct. 29, 1889, in E/Lafargues: Corr. 2:333, and in this connection cf. ltr, Liebknecht to E, Oct. 26, 1889, in Liebknecht: *Briefwechsel M&E*, 350; also ltr, E to P. Lafargue, Nov. 16, 1889, in E/Lafargues: Corr. 2:340; and ltr, E to L. Lafargue, Apr. 16, 1890, ibid., 2:371.
98. For ex., see ltr, E to Bebel, Jan. 5, 1889, in MEW 37:131, and ltr, E to Liebknecht, Oct. 29, 1889, ibid., 299.
99. Ltr, E to L. Lafargue, June 3, 1888, in E/Lafargues: Corr. 2:132; and ltr, ditto, Apr. 16, 1890, ibid., 2:370. Along the same lines, see ltr, ditto, Feb. 4, 1889, ibid., 2:193; and ltr, P. Lafargue to Liebknecht, Feb. 2, 1889, qu. in Liebknecht: *Briefwechsel M&E*, 476.
100. Re the Boulangist "madness": see Section 4 above (ref. n. 38). Re E's first estimate: ltr, E to L. Lafargue, July 15, 1888, in E/Lafargues: Corr. 2:142. Re changed estimate, about the provinces: see ltr, E to Kautsky, Jan. 28, 1889, in MEW 37:144, and see note 101. Re Paris Bonapartism there is a great deal of attention: ltr, E to L. Lafargue, Feb. 4, 1889, in E/Lafargues: Corr. 2:193; cf. "Bonapartist vein" in ltr, E to L. Lafargue, Aug. 27, 1889, ibid., 2:302; about renouncing revolutionary mission, ltr, E to Kautsky, Jan. 28, 1889, in MEW 37:144. See also ltr, E to Bebel, Nov. 15, 1889, ibid., 37:302; ltr, ditto, Feb. 17, 1890, ibid., 37:358; and ltr, E to P. Lafargue, Nov. 16, 1889, in E/Lafargues: Corr. 2:3340.
101. Ltr, E to L. Lafargue, Apr. 16, 1890, in E/Lafargues: Corr. 2:371; cf. a related passage on 370.
102. Ltr, E to P. Lafargue, Sep. 19, 1890, in MEW 37:459 (retrans.).
103. Ltr, E to Sorge, Apr. 19, 1890, in MEW 37:395; and ltr, E to L. Lafargue, same day, in E/Lafargues: Corr. 2:370.
104. Re Alsace: ltr, E to L. Lafargue, June 3, 1888, in E/Lafargues: Corr. 2:132. Re "tender treatment": ltr, E to L. Lafargue, Jan. 2, 1889, ibid., 2:181; and see also the "velvet gloves" cited above, ref. n. 66. Re last citation: ltr, E to L. Lafargue, Apr. 10-11, 1888, in MEW 37:46f (retrans.).
105. Haunted letters: for examples, see E's letters in E/Lafargues: Corr. 2:165, 193f,

and in MEW 37:57, 144f.—Danger of war: ltr, E to Sorge, Oct. 10, 1888, in MEW 37:105, and ditto, Feb. 23, 1889, ibid., 161.
106. Ltr, E to P. Lafargue, Dec. 4, 1888, in MEW 37:123 (retrans.).

SPECIAL NOTE A:
LASSALLE AND MARX

1. For the 'pixillated' analogy, see KMTR 1:591.
2. Footman: *F. Lassalle*, 13.
3. Ibid., 19f.
4. Ibid., 21.
5. Ibid., 35 (re "This second birth..."). On Lassalle's egoism in general, see also Bernstein: *F. Lassalle as Soc. Ref.*, 30-33.—The extract quote: Lassalle: *Nachgel. Br. & Schr.*, 1:227, 230. Footman: *F. Lassalle*, 45, also quotes from this manifesto.
6. Footman: *F. Lassalle*, 55.
7. The quotes from Footman are on p. 54f, 76; from Bernstein: *F. Lassalle as Soc. Ref.*, on p.22.
8. For the *Volksstaat* editor, see Wilhelm Blos: "Karl Marx in Leipzig," in *Mohr und Gen.*, 351.—Ltr, M to E, Feb. 9, 1860, in MEW 30:31 [MECW 41:35].—Bernstein: *F. Lassalle as Soc. Ref.*, 22f.
9. Re unanimity: see Footman: *F. Lassalle*, 70f, and quote from Marx (ref. n. 12 below). "Repeatedly": see Dowe: *Aktion und Org.*, 267; see also Na'aman: *Zur Gesch. d. Bundes*, 76.
10. The letter is reproduced in facsimile in Mehring: *K. Marx*, 232 (in the 1962 reprint, 205), though Mehring's text does not mention it; the date is clearly visible. But when Mehring published the text of the letter in the *Neue Zeit* (Mehring: "Bund d. Komm.," 68), the date was printed as 1851. This inaccurate date was also given, no doubt following Mehring, by Gustav Mayer in his intro to Lassalle: *Nachgel. Br. & Schr.*, 2:8 fn. The 1850 date is confirmed by Ramm: *Lassalle und M*, 190 fn; in a MEW ed. note (MEW 30:707 n.59); the date and the text of the letter are now confirmed in New Mega III, 3:565 (*Apparat*, 1305), and in *Bund d. Komm.* 2:212f.
11. Peter Röser: "Aus den Aussagen von Peter Gerhard Roeser" [selections], in New Mega III, 3:740; note that this paragraph is not included in the selections from the same document ("From Peter Röser's Evidence") included in MECW 38:550-54.—Re Röser's document, see KMTR 3:165 incl. fn.—Both Pierre (first name not known) and Heinrich Bürgers were leaders of the Cologne branch of the Communist League.
12. Ltr, M to E, Feb. 9, 1860, in MEW 30:31 [MECW 41:35].
13. Ltr, Röser to Lassalle, Mar. 31, 1851, in *Bund der Kom.* 2:400f; ltr, Bürgers to Lassalle: Apr. 1, 1851, in Lassalle: *Nachgel. Br. & Schr.* 2:47; and cf. Footman: *F. Lassalle*, 71. See ed note, *Bund der Kom.*, 2:749 n.583.
14. Ltr, Daniels to M, Apr. 12, 1851, in *Bund der Kom.* 2:419f.—Re M's letter, see *K.M. Chronik*, 106.—Ltr, Daniels to M, Apr. 24, 1851, in *Bund der Kom.* 2:423.
15. *Bund der Kom.* 2:639 n.443; *K.M. Chronik*, 105 (and see its references); but Daniels' letter of Apr. 12 (see preceding note), as printed (*"gekürzt"*) in *Bund der Kom.*, does not clearly refer to membership.
16. Bernstein made a contrary assertion as soon as he started reversing himself

Notes to Pages 248–256

on Lassalle, but without adducing a single fact in support; see Bernstein: *Über das Verhältnis*, 159.

17. See, in Bibliography, M: Lassalle, and E: Lassalle; also M: Drigalski, in MEW 6:58, 60 [MECW 8:77, 79], and M: Tax Refusal Trial, in MEW 6:259 [MECW 8:341]; in addition there was material in the *NRZ* by other writers.
18. See the ed note, in MEW 6:636f (n. 262) or MECW 8:576 (n. 299).
19. Footman: *F. Lassalle*, 64.
20. Ltr, M to Hatzfeldt, Oct. 16, 1864, in MEW 31:419 [MECW 42:5]. See also Marx's statement, quoted below in this Special Note about "being predisposed to Lassalle," in ltr, M to E, Mar. 5, 1856.
21. "Lassalle's affection": ltr, M to Freiligrath, July 31, 1849, in MEW 27:503 [MECW 38:204]; cf. also ltr, M to Freiligrath, Sep. 5, 1949, in MEW 27:512 [MECW 38:216f].—Business help: not all this business correspondence is extant; see ltr, M to Lassalle, Feb. 23, 1852, in MEW 28:495 [MECW 39:46]. There are many references in the M-E correspondence to Lassalle's help: see (short ref. form) in MEW 28:48, 57, 254, 256, 270, 275, 327f, 329, 331, 391 [MECW 39:76, 88, 334f, 339, 350, 354, 414, 418, 419, 481.] See also Jenny M to E, in MEW 28:654 [MECW 39:588], and M to Elsner, ibid., 620 [MECW 39:550].— "Precise in sending replies": ltr, M to Lassalle, Feb. 23, 1852, in MEW 28:495 [MECW 39:46].—Re *NOZ*: Ltr, M to E, Dec. 2, 1854, in MEW 28:415f [MECW 39:501].—What M sent Lassalle: Ltrs, M to Lassalle, in MEW 28:604-09, 612-15 [MECW 39:430+, 454+, 511+]; also see ltr, E to M, Mar. 223, 1854, and M to E, Mar. 29, 1854, in MEW 28:331f, 333 [MECW 39:419f, 421]. Re political reports: e.g., ltr, M to Lassalle, Feb. 23, 1852 and Nov. 8, 1855, in MEW 28:495, 624f [MECW 39:43+, 556f].
22. Ltr, M to E, Mar. 10, 1853, in MEW 28:224 [MECW 39:290].—Ltr, E to M, Mar. 11, 1853, in MEW 28:226 [MECW 39:293].
23. Ltr, M to E, July 18, 1853, in MEW 28:224 [MECW 39:354].—Ltr, M to Lassalle, July 28, 1855, in MEW 28:617 [MECW 39:543].
24. The summary by Footman: *F. Lassalle*, 69.—"Last of the Mohicans": ltr, Lassalle to M, June 13, 1853, in Lassalle: *Nachgel. Br. & Schr.*, 3:60.—Re trial: Footman, 72.
25. Marx's letters spell the name Levy, and so do MEW and MECW throughout, with no explanation. All other sources I have seen use the spelling Lewy.
26. Lassalle: *Nachgel. Br. & Schr.*, 3:256f; cf. Footman: *F. Lassalle*, 83, and Ramm: *Lassalle und M*, 191f.
27. Re the 1853 visit: see ed note, MEW 29:664, n.39 [MECW 40:584, n.36].—Re the Lassalle connection: Na'aman: *Zur Gesch. d. Bundes*, 76 & fn; also Na'aman: *Lassalle*, 209; and see Lassalle's reference in ltr, Lassalle to M & E, Feb. 1860, in his *Nachgel. Br. & Schr.* 3:268.
28. Ltr, Lassalle to M & E, Feb. 1860, in Lassalle: *Nachgel. Br. & Schr.* 3:268.— Footman: *F. Lassalle*, 112, seems to swallow Lassalle's claim without examination, perhaps following G. Mayer, who is equally trusting in his intro to Lassalle's *Nachgel. Br. & Schr.* 5:28.
29. Footman: *F. Lassalle*, 76.
30. Ltr, M to E, Mar. 5, 1856, in MEW 29:26-28 [MECW 40:23f]. Incidentally, Marx gets to the Lewy visit only after four book pages of chat on other topics.
31. The Daniels letter is quoted in Na'aman: *Lassalle*, 204, without date or source; note that Daniels died at the end of summer 1855.—For the biographer's comment: ibid., 207.
32. Bernstein: *F. Lassalle as Soc. Ref.*, 27f.—Footman: *Lassalle*, 93.
34. See Bernstein: *F. Lassalle as Soc. Ref.*, 29-31 (Heraclitus), 33-43 (Sickingen), 44-

63 (Italian War), 73-90 (Sys. of Acqu. Rights). Also re Sickingen, cf. KMTR 2:160f, 383f, 528f.
35. Ltr, M to E, Aug. 7, 1862, in MEW 30:270 [MECW 41:400]. For the context of this statement, see Chap. 3, Sec. 5.
36. Ltr, M to E, July 30, 1862, in MEW 30:257f [MECW 41:389].
37. Ibid., 258 [MECW 41:390].
38. Jenny Marx: *Short Sketch*, 234.
39. McLellan: *K. Marx*, 322.
40. Qu. in Footman: *F. Lassalle*, 183.
41. Ltr, M to Lassalle, Nov. 7, 1862, in MEW 30:636f [MECW 41:425].
42. Footman: *F. Lassalle*, 144.
43. Mehring: "Ein Parteijubiläum," 793f.—Gay: *Dilemma of Dem. Soc.*, 29.
44. Ltr, M to Schweitzer, Oct. 13, 1868, in MECW 43:132 [MEW 32:568].
45. The historical sketch that follows is mainly based on Mehring: *Gesch. d. deut. S.D.*, 2:7-33. (Mehring knew, or had once known, the facts.)
46. The passage that follows is mainly based on Bernstein: *F. Lassalle as Soc. Ref.*, 114-21.
47. Ibid., 192.
48. Bernstein: "Über d. Verhältnis," 158.
49. E: Karl Marx [1869 article], in MEW 16:361 [MECW 21:59]; this is *not* the biographical article by E that is usually reprinted.
50. For details, see Hümmler: *Oppos. gegen Lassalle*, 24-30.
51. For this aspect, Roger Morgan: *German Soc.-Dem. & First Intl.* provides valuable information, throughout its pages.
52. Ltr, E to Kautsky, Feb. 23, 1891, in MESW 3:39f, slightly rev. from MEW 38:40f. A different opinion about the possible "actual betrayal" was expressed in Bernstein: *F. Lassalle as Soc. Ref.*, 185f.
53. Ltr, E to Bebel, May 1-2, 1891, in MEW 38:93f. Also cf. ltr, E to Bebel, Oct. 6, 1891, in MEW 38:170.
54. Ltr, E to Kautsky, Dec. 3, 1891, in MEW 38:235.
55. Ibid., 234.
56. Bernstein: "Selbst-Anzeige" (1891), 560.
57. See above, ref. n. 52.
58. Ltr, E to Sorge, Mar. 4, 1891, in MEW 38:46.
59. G. Mayer: *F. Engels*, 2:393f.
60. The household: ltr, E to L. Lafargue, June 13, 1891, in E/Lafargues: Corr. 3:78; ltr, E to Bebel, Oct. 18-21, 1893, in MEW 39:154.—E's plan: ltr, E to Kautsky, June 29, 1891, in MEW 38:125; ltr, E to L. Lafargue, Dec. 17, 1894, in E/ Lafargues: Corr. 3:347.
61. Ltr, E to L. Lafargue, June 13, 1891, in E/Lafargues: Corr. 3:78.
62. Ltr, E to Kautsky, June 16, 1891, in MEW 38:119.
63. Bernstein: "Selbst-Anzeige," 559.
64. The "lousy footnote" is in Bernstein: *F. Lassalle as Soc. Ref.*, 66. For the to-do, see ltr, E to Bebel, Sep. 29-Oct. 1, 1891, in MEW 38:163; same, Oct. 6, 1891, ibid., 170; and ltr, E to Kautsky, Dec. 3, 1891, ibid., 234.
65. Qu. in ed note, MEW 38:619, n. 305.
66. Ltr, E to Bebel, Aug. 20, 1892, in MEW 38:433.
67. Ltr, E to Kautsky, Oct. 25, 1891, in MEW 38:290; and cf. also ltr, E to Schmidt, Nov. 1, 1891, ibid., 205.
68. Ltr, E to Kautsky, Dec. 3, 1891, in MEW 38:235, 234.

SPECIAL NOTE B:
BAKUNIN AND THE INTERNATIONAL: A "LIBERTARIAN" FABLE

1. In KMTR 2, see resp. Chap. 12, Sec. 11; Chap. 15, Sec. 4; Chap. 18, Sec. 6. In KMTR 3, see resp. Chap. 3, Sec. 5; Chap. 7, Sec. 1-2.
2. This documentation is now available in the two volumes of *The Hague Congress &c.* (see Biblio.).
3. Three such purges are noted by Lehning in his introduction to the *Archives Bakounine*, 2:LVIII fn.
4. Lehning's intro, *Archives Bakounine*, 4:LIX fn.
5. See this volume, Chap. 3, Sec. 4.
6. See the summary reference to this in Draper: Note on the Father of Anarchism, 83. The most important case, that of Bonaparte, is well covered in Schapiro, 335, 354-57, 367.
7. Bakunin: *Confession*, 90f. See KMTR 3:56f.
8. Carr: *M. Bakunin*, 240-42; Kaminski: *M. Bakounine*, 179f.
9. Carr: *M. Bakunin*, 278; for the background, 277-79. The expression "National Tsar" is Carr's translation; for the version in the International's pamphlet, see KMTR 2:356 incl. fn.
10. Re Jerome: Carr: *M. Bakunin*, 261.—Re Charles: see this volume, Chap. 6, Sec. 9, pp. 161-62.
11. Re the Appeal: see Carr: *M. Bakunin*, 394. But there is some confusion with another appeal to the nobility in 1870, which may have been drafted by Nechayev; see intro to *Archives Bakounine*, 4:XXV; text on 305-08.—"Bismarckian": see Carr: *M. Bakunin*, 497.
11a. A handy summary of the facts of the case is provided by an editorial note in MECW 7:630, n.210. It is accurate, and sufficient for present purposes.
12. See Chap. 6, Sec. 8, p. 159. In general, the account in this section follows Carr's standard biography, though not always with Carr's coloration.
13. The two quoted phrases are from Carr: *M. Bakunin*, 352.
14. Report in the *Vorbote* (Geneva), qu. in Guillaume: *L'Internationale*, 1:207f.
15. Bakunin: Lettre aux Int. de la Romagne, in *Archives Bakounine*, 1.2: 214.
16. Carr: *M. Bakunin*, 380.
17. See KMTR 2:407.
18. Freymond, ed.: *Prem. Intle.*, 2:61-92; for Richard's proposal, 76-79.
19. Ibid., 67.
20. Guillaume: *L'Internationale*, 1:198. For Bakunin's later rationalization, see *Archives Bakounine*, 1.2: 212.
21. Freymond, ed.: *Prem. Intle.*, 2:17.
22. See Chap. 6, Sec. 8, p. 160.
23. Freymond, ed.: *Prem. Intle.*, 2:92-96; for Bakunin's remarks, 94f.
24. Carr: *M. Bakunin*, 363.
25. Bakunin: *Statism and Anarchy*, in *Archives Bakounine*, 3:354; for the preceding citations, 353.
26. Ltr, Bakunin to Nechayev, June 2, 1870 (Pt. 2, p. 86), for which see Biblio.; here Bakunin considered as few as ten to be enough.
27. Carr: *M. Bakunin*, 367.
28. Guillaume: *K. Marx, Pangermaniste*, 55f.
29. Silberner: *Soz. zur Jud.*, 276.
30. Richard: *Bakounine & l'Intle.*, 121..

31. *Prem. Intle. (Colloque)*, 432, article by M. Molnar, who uses the word "instructions."
32. Richard: *Bakounine & l'Intle.*, 121-25, 142.
33. Lehning's intro, in *Archives Bakounine*, 2:XX. ("Democratia" is so spelled here.)
34. Guillaume: *L'Internationale*, 2:273; it is also quoted in Lehrning's intro to *Archives Bakounine*, 2:XXII.—Lehning's intro, in *Archives Bakounine*, 2:XX.
35. Guillaume: *L'Internationale*, 2:344.
36. Ltr, Bakunin to Nechayev, June 2, 1870, Pt. 1, p. 86; but this translation from the Russian says "Revolutionary Union" instead of "Revolutionary Alliance."
37. Ltr, Bakunin to Mroczkowski &c., May 31, 1870, in *Archives Bakounine*, 4:212.
38. Venturi: *Roots of Revolution*, 437; see also the statement on 462.
39. Ltr, Bakunin to A. Richard, Apr. 1, 1870, in Richard: *Bakounine & l'Intle.*, 128.
40. Ibid., 129.
41. Ltr, Bakunin to C. Ceretti, Mar. 13-27, 1872, in *Archives Bakounine*, 2:251f.
42. All this information on the GC's handling of the question is found in the GC minutes for the dates given, in *GCFI* 5:230, 310 [Eng., 485], 313 [Eng., 488]; also 437f.
43. For the GC position, besides the references preceding, see esp. the formal letter sent to the Swiss, in *GCFI* 5:437f. For the Bakuninists' position, including Guillaume's gaffe, see Guillaume: *L'Internationale*, 2:301-02.
44. Lehning's intro, in *Archives Bakounine*, 2: XXXV-XXXVII.
45. Ltr, Bakunin to C. Gambuzzi, July 16, 1872, in *Archives Bakounine*, 2:134.
46. Bakunin: "Programme de la Section Slave de Zurich," in *Archives Bakounine*, 3:185f. The version of this program published by Bakunin in 1873 (not materially different) is at 3:379f.
47. Lehning intro, in *Archives Bakounine*, 3:XVIII, XIX.
48. Ltr, Bakunin to C. Ceretti, Aug. 25, 1872, in *Archives Bakounine*, 2:134.
49. Ltr, Bakunin to C. Gambuzzi, August 31, 1872, in *Archives Bakounine*, 2:135.
50. Even Engels opined that Bakunin was slicker than Guillaume (see ltr, E to M, Mar. 6, 1877, in MEW 34:38); but Engels could not know how much Guillaume did behind the scenes.
51. See KMTR 1, Special Note A and its references, on this subject. Also consult the works by Massing and Pulzer (see Biblio.).
52. His 1872 denunciation: Bakunin: Lettre à *La Liberté*, in *Archives Bakounine*, 2:163.—Yellow peril: Bakunin: *Statism & Anarchy*, in *Archives Bak.* 3:282f.
53. Silberner: *Soz. zur Jud.*, 270f; Carr: *M. Bakunin*, 152; Bakunin: *Confession*, 98.
54. Bakunin: Etude sur les Juifs Allemands, in his *Oeuvres*, 5:243f.
55. Ibid., 243, 245, for these quotes.
56. Ibid., 244.
57. Ed intro by Guillaume in Bakunin: *Oeuvres*, 5:230f. About Herzen, see also Carr: *M. Bakunin*, 384f.
58. Ltr, Bakunin to Herzen, Oct. 28, 1869, qu. in Guillaume intro, ibid., 230, 232, 233f.
59. Ibid., 234f.
60. Ltr, M to E, Dec. 15, 1868, in MEW 32:234 [MECW 43:190].
61. Qu. in ltr, M to E, Jan. 13, 1869, in MEW 32:243 [MECW 43:202].
62. Ltr, Bakunin to M, Dec. 22, 1868, in Guillaume: *L'Intrnationale*, 1:103.
63. See above, this Special Note, Sec. 5, p. 284.
64. On Marr and his brochure, see Massing: *Rehearsal for Destruction*, 6-10. There is a possibility that Bakunin was familiar with Marr's earlier work, about which see ibid., 6.
65. Parkes: *Enemy of the People*, 27f.

66. Bakunin: Lettre aux Int. de Bologne, in *Archives Bakounine*, 1.2:109 (for the extract and more), also 110, 111, 115f.
67. Bakunin: Aux Compagnons... du Jura, in *Archives Bakounine*, 2:3f.
68. Ibid., 5, 6, 7, 7-9. (This applies to all the citations since the preceding note number 63.)
69. Ltr, Bakunin to C. Ceretti, Mar. 13-27, 1872, in *Archives Bakounine*, 1.2:255.
70. Some incidental bursts of anti-Semitism in 1872 by the Bakuninists were cited in another connection in KMTR 2:10.
71. The "blood" formula was explicit, for example, in Bakunin: *Statism & Anarchy*, in *Archives Bakounine*, 3:237.
72. Bakunin: Aux Compagnons... du Jura, in *Archives Bakounine*, 2:29.
73. Bakunin: *Statism & Anarchy*, in *Archives Bakounine*, 3:286.
74. Ltr, Bakunin to C. Ceretti, Dec. 15, 1871, in *Archives Bakounine*, 1.2:135; and Bakunin: Lettre aux Int. de Bologne, ibid., 106.
75. Bakunin: Lettre aux Int. de Bologne, in *Archives Bakounine*, 1.2:106.
76. M's "patriotic goal": Bakunin: Aux Compagnons... du Jura, in *Archives Bakounine*, 2:56.—"Ardent patriot": Bakunin: Écrit Contre Marx, ibid., 2:172.—Only "legitimate representative": Bakunin: L'Allemagne et le Communisme d'Etat, ibid., 2:108.—Last three sentences: Bakunin: *Statism & Anarchy*, ibid., 3:359f; also the whole passage 359-62.
77. The particular phrases quoted here are to be found in *Archives Bakounine*, 1.2:106, 123, 217, 218; and 3:316; but they are not so much outstanding as brief.
78. These turds, among many similar ones, are found in *Archives Bakounine*, 1.2: 106, 108, 122-27, 217-22; and 3:316.
79. See KMTR 2:565 fn.
80. Bakunin: Rapports Personnel avec Marx, in *Archives Bakounine*, 1.2:127.
81. See Carr: *M. Bakunin*, Chap. 28; but a necessary supplement, now, is Confino's intro to his *Violence dans la Violence*, 13-93.
82. All these citations are to ltr, Bakunin to Nechayev, June 2, 1870.—"Identical" programs: Pt. 1, p. 82 (twice), 84, 87.—The extract: Pt. 2, p. 88; and it offers much more of the same. See also Pt. 1, p. 81, 85, 89 for similar assurances.—"Many dirty tricks": Pt. 2, p. 92.—"Horrors or dirt": Pt. 1, p. 89.—"Police and Jesuitical systems": Pt. 2, p. 92.
83. Ibid., Pt. 2, p. 88.
84. Ltr, Bakunin to Talandier, July 24, 1870, in Confino: *Violence dans la Violence*, 193; for the background, see Confino's intro, 83-92.
85. Ltr, Nechayev to Bakunin, end of July 1870, in Confino, 195.

SPECIAL NOTE C:
THE STRANGE CASE OF FRANZ MEHRING

1. Mehring: *Karl Marx* (1935), vii-xi.
2. E.g.: for the West German Social-Democratic standpoint, see the article on Mehring in Osterroth, *Biographisches Lexikon des Sozialismus*; for the East German official view, see its *Philosophenlexikon* (1983), where the article is by the same Schleifstein discussed below.
3. Höhle: *Franz Mehring: Sein Weg zur Marxismus* (Berlin: Rütten & Loenig, 1958). This is the semiofficial biography published in East Germany, the most exten-

sive treatment available; it is entirely written within the bounds of the official line, and tries to combine a viewpoint treating Mehring as a great Marxist while admitting his Lassallean "deviations." In its own way it is Janus-faced, like its subject, but with a different set of faces.
4. Höhle: *Franz Mehring*, p. 100.
5. Ibid., p. 94.
6. Ibid., p. 95.
7. Ibid., p.108
8. See Höhle, p. 123 for a summary of this publication history.
9. Ibid., p. 125.
10. Ibid., p.127.
11. Ibid., p. 130.
12. Ibid., pp. 146-47.
13. Ibid., p. 154. There is no evidence, by the way, that either of the two would-be assassins had *anything* to do with social-democracy.
14. Ibid., p. 162.
15. Ibid., p. 174.
16. MEW 36:273.
17. Ibid., 36:787
18. Ibid., 36:348.
19. Höhle: *Franz Mehring*, p. 192.
20. Ibid., p.200.
21. Ibid., p. 207. Is the "gray figure" a reference to the kaiser's age or his military uniform?
22. Ibid., p. 210. He means, of course, that it was unheard of in the respectable, bourgeois press.
23. Ibid., p. 271.
24. Josef Schleifstein: *Franz Mehring: Sein Marxistisches Schaffen 1891-1919*. Schriftenreihe des Instituts für Deutsche Geschichte an der Karl-Marx-Universität, Leipzig. Hrsg. von Prof. Dr. Ernest Engelberg. Band 5 (Berlin: Rutten & Loenig, 1959). First Edition.
25. Franz Mehring: *Karl Marx: The Story of His Life*. Trans. Edward Fitzgerald (New York: Covici, Friede, 1935), p. 357.
26. Ibid., p. 358.
27. Ibid., p. 462.
28. Ibid., pp. 460-66.

BIBLIOGRAPHY

Abbreviations
FLPH = Foreign Languages Publishing House
GCFI = General Council of the First International
IML = Institute of Marxism-Leninism
IRSH = International Review of Social History (Amsterdam)
KMTR = Karl Marx's Theory of Revolution
MECW = ME: Collected Works
MEGA = ME: Gesamtausgabe [the old edition]
MESW = ME: Selected Works in Three Volumes
MEW = ME: Werke
New Mega = ME: Gesamtausgabe [new edition]
NRZ Revue = Neue Rheinische Zeitung, politisch-ökonomishe Revue (London, 1850)
NYDT = New York Daily Tribune

WRITINGS BY MARX AND ENGELS

Address to the Communist League, March 1850, in MECW 10:280.
Circular Kriege, April-May 1846, in MEW 4:7 [MECW 6:36-41].
Circular Ltr to Bebel et al., Sept. 17-18, 1879, in MEW 34:406 [MESW 3:92].
Against The Communist Manifesto, 1848, in MECW 6:516, rev. after MEW 4:490f.
The German Ideology, in MECW 5:466.
Great Men of the Emigration, in MEW 8:278 [MECW 11:270].
The Holy Family, 1844 in MECW 4:131.
LA CORRISPONDENZA DI MARX E ENGELS CON ITALIANI 1848-1895.
   A cura di G. Del Bo. (Instituto G. Feltrinelli. Testi e Documenti di Storia Moderna e Contemporanea, 11) Milan: Feltrinelli, 1964.
Review of *Latter-Day Pamphlets* [Carlyle], in MEW 7:255f [MECW 10:301f].
[Review of] *Le Socialisme et l'Imperialisme*, in MEW 7:285f [MECW 10:330f].
SCRITTI ITALIANI.
   A cura di G. Bosio. (Saggie e Documentazioni, 1) Milan/Rome: Ed. Avanti, 1955.

353

WRITINGS BY MARX

Basic Writings on Politics and Philosophy [by] Karl Marx and Friedrich Engels. Edited by Lewis S. Feuer. 1st ed. Garden City, N.Y., Doubleday, 1959.
The Class Struggles in France, 1848-1850, in MECW 10:118 or MESW 1:273.
Conspectus of Bakunin's Book, *Statism and Anarchy.*
    Konspectus von Bakunins Buch "Staatlichkeit und Anarchie." (W) 1874 to beginning of 1875, as notes. (S) MEW 18:597.
Critical Notes on the King of Prussia, August 1844 in MECW 3:190 [MEW 1:393].
Critique of the Gotha Program, 1875, in MESW 3:28 [MEW 19:31].
Debat Social, in MECW 6:538f [MEW 4:512f].
Debates on Freedom of Press, 1842, in MEW 1:68 [MECW 1:172].
Economic and Philosophic Manuscripts of 1844, in MECW 3:232 [MEW Eb.1:468].
["The Financial Crisis in Europe"] untitled article, NYDT, Dec. 22, 1857, in MECW 15:405 .
Grundrisse. Foundations of the Critique of Political Economy. Translated with a foreword by Martin Nicolaus. New York, Vintage Books [1973].
Herr Vogt, 1860, in MEW 14:439 [MECW 17:79].
LETTRES ET DOCUMENTS DE KARL MARX 1856-1883. Instituto G. Feltrinelli (Milan) Annali, Anno I.
Misère de la philosophie, en réponse a la philosophie de la misère de M. Proudhon. Preface by Fr. Engels. Annotations by Proudhon. Paris, Costes, 1950.
Moralizing Criticism and Critical Morality, 1874 in MECW 6:325 [MEW 4:344f].
Notes on Adolph Wagner, 1879-80, in MEW 19:373-76.
On Freidrich List's Book, 1845, in MECW 4:283 [not in MEW].
"Palmerston," in NYDT, Oct. 19, 1853, in MECW 12:347 fn.
Parliament [&c], Dec. 28, 1852, in MECW 464 [MEW 8:369,
Pauperism & Free Trade, NYDT, Nov. 1, 1852, in MECW 11:359.
"Political Movements," in NYDT, Sep. 30, 1853, in MECW 12:303.
Revelations of the Dip. Hist., in MECW 15:28.
Second Address on the Franco-Prussian War, 1870, MECW 22:268f or MESW 2:200.
State of British Manufactures, NYDT, Mar. 15, 1859; in MECW 16:191.
Theories of Surplus Value [MEW 26.2:7].
Thiers' Speech [&c], in MECW 7:467; cf. also 468 [MEW 5:423f].
Vienna Revolution & Kölnische Zeitung, in MEW 5:451 [MECW 7:496].
Writings on the Paris Commune [by] Karl Marx and Friedrich Engels. Edited by Hal Draper. New York, Monthly Review Press, 1971.

WRITINGS BY ENGELS

Anti-Dühring, 1878 in MECW 25:140 [MEW 20:141].
The Condition of England: 1. The Eighteenth Century. Die lage Englands: 1. Das achtzehnte Jahrhundert. (W) 1844: Feb. (P) Aug. 31 to Sept.11 in *Vorwärts* (Paris), in 7 installs.
Condition of the Working Class in England, in MECW 4:528 [MEW 2:455].
CORRESPONDANCE / FRIEDRICH ENGELS, PAUL ET LAURA LAFARGUE.
    Annotated by Emile Bottigelli. Translated by Paul Meier. Paris, Editions sociales, 1956-1959.
Debate on Poland in Frankfurt, 1848 in MECW 7:376 [MEW 5:358].

Democratic Pan-Slavism, in MECW 8:363 [MEW 6:270f].
Description of Commmunist Colonies, in MECW 4:214 or MEW 2:521.
The Foreign Policy of Russian Czarism, 1889-90 in *Time,* Apr. 1890 [cf. MEW 22:13 fn].
Fragment of Fourier, in MEW 2:609f [MECW 4:644].
The Housing Question, 1872-73, in MECW 23:341 or MESW 2:327 [MEW 18:236f].
Lawyers' Socialism, 1886-87, in MEW 21:502.75, in MESW 2:170 [MEW 18:517].
Ludwig Feuerbach and the End of Classsical German Philosophy, 1886, in MESW 3:353 [MEW 21:282].
On English Conditions, *Kölnische Zeitung* in MECW 7:298.
On History of the Communist League, 1855, in MESW 3:181, rev. after MEW 21:214.
The Slogan of The Abolition of The State, Oct. 1850, in MEW 7:417f [MECW 10:486f].
On Social Relations in Russia, Afterword, in MEW 22:433; the trans. in MESW 2:408 is defective.
The Origin of the Family, in MESW 3:333 [MEW 21:172].
The Peasant War in Germany, Preface, 1875, in MESW 2:169.
Preface to Marx's Poverty of Philosophy, in *Poverty of Philosophy* (FLPH ed.), 1885, 23 [MEW 21:187].
Principles of Communism, 1847, in MECW 6:350 [MEW 4:370].
Review of *Capital* for *Beobachter,* in MEW 16:227f [MECW 20:224].
The Role of Force in History, 1888, in MESW 3:418f [MEW 21:452].
Socialism in Germany, 1891-92, in MEW 22:248.
Socialism Utopian and Scientific, 1880, in MESW 3:115.
The Status Quo in Germany (Draft of unfinished pamphlet),1847, in MECW 6:76 [MEW 4:41].
The Turkish Question, in NYDT, Apr. 19, 1853, in MECW 12:26.

WRITINGS BY OTHERS

Annenkov, P. V.
  The Extraordinary Decade: Literary Memoirs. Edited by Arthur P. Mendel. Translated by Irwin R. Titunik. Ann Arbor, University of Michigan Press [1968].
Bakunin, Michael.
  Archives Bakounine/Bakunin-Archiv. Published for the International Institute for Social History, Amsterdam, by A. Lehning, A.J.C. Rüter, P. Scheiert. Leiden: Brill, 1963-(in progress). Tome 111: *Etatisme et Anarchie/1873.* Ed. A. Lehning, 1967 (orig. Russian + French tr.).
Bakunin, Mikhail Aleksandrovich.
  Oeuvres . . . Paris, P.-V. Stock, 1895-1913. 6 v. 19 cm. Series: Bibliotheque sociologique. Vol. 1 was published without volume number. Vol. 2-6 edited by James Guillaume.
Bakunin, Mikhail Aleksandrovich.
  Oeuvres completes de Bakounine. Paris, Editions Champ Libre, 1973-<1982> First published under the title *Archives Bakounine.* E. J. Brill, Leiden. Some vols. in French and Russian.
Baudin, Louis.
  Une theocratie socialiste: l'Etat jesuite du Paraguay. Paris, M.-T.Genin [1962].

Bellamy, Edward.
  Looking Backward. With an introduction by Joseph Schiffman. New York, Harper [1959].
Berneri, Marie Louise.
  Journey through Utopia. Freeport, N.Y., Books for Libraries Press [1969].
Bernstein, Eduard.
  Ferdinand Lassalle as a Social Reformer. London, S. Sonnenschein & Co., 1893. Translated by Eleanor Marx-Aveling.

———.
  Von der Sekte zur partei, die deutsche Sozialdemokratie einst und jetzt. 1-4. Jena, Eugen Diederichs, 1911.

———.
  Ferdinand Lassalle, eine Würdigung des Lehrers und Kämpfers, von Eduard Bernstein. Berlin, P. Cassirer, 1919.

———.
  "Selbstanzeige..." In *Neue Zeit*, Vol. 9, No. 2, 1891, p. 556.
Bernstein, Samuel.
  The First International in America. New York, A. M. Kelley, 1962.
Blanc, Louis.
  Organisation du travail. 9th ed. Paris, Au bureau du nouveau monde, 1850.

———.
  Organization of Work. Translated from the 1st ed. by Marie Paula Dickore. Cincinnati, University Press [c1911].
Blanqui, Jerome Adolphe.
  Histoire de l'économie politique en Europe, depuis les anciens jusqu'à nos jours, suivie d'une Bibliographie raisonnée des principaux ouvrages d'economie politique. Paris, Guillaumin, 1837.
Brazill, William J.
  The Young Hegelians. New Haven, Yale University Press, 1970.
Buber, Martin.
  Paths in Utopia. Translated by R. F. C. Hull. Intro. by Ephraim Fischoff. Boston, Beacon Hill [1958, c1949].
Carr, Edward Hallett.
  Michael Bakunin. Reissued with minor alterations. New York, Octagon Books, 1975.
Cole, G. D. H. (George Douglas Howard).
  A History of Socialist Thought. London, Macmillan; New York, St. Martin's Press, 1964-67 [v. 1, 1965].
Collins, Henry.
  Karl Marx and the British Labour Movement: Years of the First International, by Henry Collins and Chimen Abramsky. London, Macmillan; New York, St. Martin's Press, 1965.
Confino, Michael.
  Violence dans la violence: le debat Bakounine-Necaev. Paris, F. Maspero, 1973.
Cornu, Auguste.
  Karl Marx et Friedrich Engels: leur vie et leur oeuvre. [1. ed.] Paris, Presses Universitaires de France, 1955.
Cornu, Auguste.
  Karl Marx und Friedrich Engels, Leben und Werk. Berlin, Aufbau-Verlag, 1954-62.
Cunninghame Graham, R. B. (Robert Bontine), 1852-1936.
  A Vanished Arcadia: Being Some Account of the Jesuits in Paraguay, 1607 to 1767. New York, Haskell House, 1968.

Cuvillier, Armand.
Hommes et idéologies de 1840. Preface by Georges Bourgin. Paris, Librairie M. Rivière, 1956.
Dansette, Adrien.
Le boulangisme. Paris, A. Fayard [1946].
Dawson, William Harbutt.
Bismarck and State Socialism: An Exposition of the Social and Economic Legislation of Germany since 1870. New York, H. Fertig, 1973. Reprint of the 1890 ed. published by Swan Sonnenschein, London.

―――.
German Socialism and Ferdinand Lassalle: A Biographical History of German Socialistic Movements During this Century. 2d ed. London : S. Sonnenschein, 1891.
Der Bund der Kommunisten.
Dokumente und Materialien. [Ed: Herwig Forder et al. 1. Aufl.] Berlin, Dietz, 1970.
Dowe, Dieter.
Aktion und Organisation: Arbeiterbewegung, sozialistische und kommunistische Bewegung in der preussischen Rheinprovinz 1820-1852. Hannover, Verlag fur Literatur und Zeitgeschehen [1970].
Draper, Hal.
"Note on the Father of Anarchism," *New Politics* (NY), Winter 1969, Vol. 8, No. 1, p 79+.
Draper, Hal.
"The Neo-Stalinist Type," *New International*, Jan. 1948, Vol. XIV, No. 1.
Droz, Jacques.
Histoire générale du socialisme. 1st ed. Paris, Presses universitaires de France [1972-<78>].
Eckhardt, Celia Morris.
Fanny Wright: Rebel in America. Cambridge, Harvard University Press, 1984.
Encyclopaedia of the Social Sciences.
Editor-in-chief, Edwin R. A. Seligman; associate editor, Alvin Johnson... New York, The Macmillan Company, 1937.
Fedoseev, Petr Nikolaevich.
Karl Marx. Biographie [author collective: P. N. Fedosseiev (Director) et al. Transl. Hans Zikmund]. Berlin, Dietz, 1973.
Feuer, Lewis Samuel.
Marx and the Intellectuals: A Set of Post-ideological Essays. 1st ed. Garden City, N.Y., Anchor Books, 1969.
Foigny, Gabriel de.
La Terre Australe connu, c'est à dire la description de ce pays inconnu jusques ici, de ses moeurs et de ses Coutumes, par M. Sadeur. Réduites et mises en lumière par le soins et la conduite de G. de F. Vannes, Par Jacques Verneuil (in reality printed at Geneva by La Pierre), 1676.
Footman, David.
Ferdinand Lassalle, Romantic Revolutionary. New York, Greenwood Press [1969].
Freymond, Jacques, ed.
La Première Internationale. Textes etablis par Henri Burgelin [et al.]. Geneva, E. Droz, 1962-71.
Furet, Francois.
Marx et la Revolution Francaise. With an anthology of writings by Marx, edited and translated by Lucien Calvie. [Paris], Flammarion, c1986.

―――.
Marx and the French Revolution. Translated by Deborah Kan Furet; with selections

from Karl Marx edited and introduced by Lucien Calvie. Chicago : University of Chicago Press, 1988.

Gay, Peter.
The Dilemma of Democratic Socialism; Eduard Bernstein's Challenge to Marx. New York, Collier Books [1962].

Godwin, William.
Enquiry Concerning Political Justice and its Influence on Morals and Happiness. Facsimile of 3rd ed. by F. E. L. Priestly, Toronto, University of Toronto Press, 1946.

Guillaume, James.
Karl Marx, pangermaniste, et l'Association internationale des travailleurs de 1864 a 1870. Paris, A. Colin, 1915.

———.
L'Internationale: documents et souvenirs. Ed. Marc Vuilleumier. Geneva, Editions Grounauer, 1980.

H.
"Karl Marx. Interview with the Corner-Stone of Modern Socialism..." *Chicago Tribune*, Jan. 1879, p.7. (Datelined London, Dec. 18 [1878], T.W. Porter, ed. (Amer. Inst. for Marxist Studies, Occas. Papers, 10), NY, 1972. This reprint has some inaccuracies. The identity of H. is unknown. [MEW 34:513].

Harrison, Royden, ed.
The English Defence of the Commune, 1871. London, Merlin Press, 1971.

Hauser, Arnold.
The Social History of Art [Translated in collaboration with the author by Stanley Godman]. London, Routledge & Kegan Paul, 1968.

Hegel, Georg Wilhelm Friedrich.
The Philosophy of Right. Translated with notes by T. M. Knox. London, New York, Oxford University Press [1967].

Herwegh, Georg.
Einundzwanzig Bogen aus der Schwiez. Vaduz, Liechtenstein, Topos Verlag, 1977.

Hess, Moses.
Philosophische und sozialistische Schriften 1837-1850: eine Auswahl. Ed. Wolfgang Monke. Second and revised edition. Vaduz/Liechtenstein, Topos, 1980.

Höchberg, Karl.
Rückblicke auf die sozialistische Bewegung in Deutschland. Kritische Aphorismen von ***. In: *Jahrbuch für Sozialwissenschaft und Sozialpolitik*, Vol 1,1. Hälfte, 1879 (Zurich). Ed. Ludwig Richter [Karl Höchberg]. S. 75-96.

Höhle, Thomas.
Franz Mehring; sein Weg zum Marxismus 1869-1891. 2nd ed. Berlin, Rutten & Loening [1958].

Hook, Sidney.
From Hegel to Marx: Studies in the Intellectual Development of Karl Marx. Ann Arbor, University of Michigan Press, 1962.

Hümmler, Heinz.
Die Revolutionäre Opposition Rutter gegen Lassalle im Allgemeinen Deutschen Arbeiterverein. Rüten & Loenig, Berlin, 1963.

Hyndman, H. M. (Henry Mayers).
The Historical Basis of Socialism in England by H. M. Hyndman. London, K. Paul, Trench & Co., 1883.

Iggers, Georg G.
The Cult of Authority : the Political Philosophy of the Saint-Simonians. 2d ed. The Hague : Nijhoff, 1970.

Institut fur Marxismus-Leninismus beim ZK der SED.
Mohr und General; Erinnerungen an Marx und Engels [Ed. Institut fur Marxismus-Leninismus beim ZK der SED]. [Second corrected ed.] Berlin, Dietz, 1965.
International Encyclopedia of the Social Sciences.
David L. Sills, editor [New York] Macmillan [1968]-c1979.
International Workingmen's Association. 5th Congress, Hague, Netherlands, 1872.
The Hague Congress of the First International : September 2-7, 1872 : Minutes and Documents [translated by Richard Dixon and Alex Miller]. Moscow : Progress Publishers, c1976.

———.
The First International : Minutes of the Hague Congress of 1872, with related documents edited and translated by Hans Gerth. Madison : University of Wisconsin Press, 1958.
Kampffmeyer, Paul.
Changes in the Theory and Tactics of the [German] Social-Democracy, by Paul kampffmeyer. Translated by Winfield R. Gaylord. Chicago, C. H. Kerr, 1908.
Keeble, Samuel Edward.
Industrial Day-dreams : Studies in Industrial Ethics and Economics. New ed. London, Culley, [pref. 1907].
Kelsen, Hans.
Marx oder Lassalle. Wandlungen in der politischen Theorie des Marxismus. Darmstadt, Wissenschaftliche Buchgesellschaft, 1967.

———.
Sozialismus und Staat: eine Untersuchung der politischen Theorie des Marxismus. 3rd ed. Ed. Norbert Leser. [Wien] Verlag der Wiener Volksbuchhandlung [1965].
Koch, Jean Paul.
Quelques experiences collectivistes. 1947.
Koebel, William Henry.
In Jesuit Land, the Jesuit Missions of Paraguay. With an introduction by Mr. R. B. Cunninghame Graham. Fifty-five illustrations in halftone. London, S. Paul [1912?].
Kommunistische Zeitschrift, Probeblatt, nr. 1 [Sept. 1847].
Reprinted in: *Bund Kom.* 1:501 (incomplete), and in Grünberg, ed. *Die Londoner Kommunistische Zeitschrift.*
Köppen,K. F.
"*Noch ein Wort...*" in *Deutsche Jahrbücher* (Leipzig), 1842, p. 515.
Kropotkin, Petr Alekseevich.
Selected Writings on Anarchism and Revolution. Edited, with an intro., by Martin A. Miller. Cambridge, Mass., M.I.T. Press 1970, 1975 printing.
Ladendorf, Otto.
Historisches Schlagworterbuch. Hildesheim, G. Olms, 1968.
Lafargue, Paul.
Karl Marx, His Life and Work; Reminiscences by Paul Lafargue and Wilhelm Liebknecht. New York, International Publishers [1943].

———.
"Parliamentarism and Boulangism," *Labour Monthly* (London), Aug. 1958, p. 374+. Tr. of an article published in the Russian *Sotsial-Demokrat*, 1888.

———.
Souvenirs sur Marx par Paul Lafargue et Wilhelm Liebknecht. Paris, Bureau d'editions, 1935.
Landauer, Carl.
European Socialism: A History of Ideas and Movements from the Industrial Revolution to

Hitler's Seizure of Power. With Elizabeth Kridl Valkenier and Hilde Stein Landauer. Westport, Greenwood Press, 1976, c1959.

Larousse, Pierre.
Grand dictionnaire universel du XIXe siecle; francais, historique, geographique, biographique, mythologique, bibliographique, litteraire, artistique, scientifique, etc. . . . Paris, Administration de Grand dictionnaire universel [1865-90?].

Lassalle, Ferdinand.
Nachgelassene Briefe und Schriften. Osnabruck, Biblio Verlag, 1967.

Laveleye, Emile Louis Victor de.
The Socialism of Today. Translated by Goddard H. Orpen. London, Field and Tuer, 1885.

Lehning, Arthur.
"The International Association (1855-1859)." In: IRSH (Amsterdam), Vol. 3,1938.

Lewis, John.
Marxism & the Open Mind. New York, Paine-Whitman [c1957].

———.
The Life and Teaching of Karl Marx. New York, International Publishers [1965].

Lichtheim, George.
Marxism: An Historical and Critical Study. Columbia University Press Morningside ed. New York, Columbia University Press, 1982.

Lidtke, Vernon L.
The Outlawed Party: Social Democracy in Germany, 1878-1890. Princeton, Princeton University Press, 1966.

Liebknecht, Wilhelm.
Briefwechsel mit Karl Marx und Friedrich Engels. Ed. Georg Eckert. The Hague, Mouton, 1963.

Lipow, Arthur.
Authoritarian Socialism in America : Edward Bellamy & the Nationalist Movement. Berkeley, University of California Press, c1982.

Loubere, Leo A.
Louis Blanc: His Life and His Contribution to the Rise of French Jacobin-socialism. [Evanston, Ill.] Northwestern University Press, 1961.

Macfarlane, Helen.
"Democracy. Remarks on the Times [&c.]," *Democratic Review,* April, May and June, 1850.

Maitron, Jean.
Histoire du mouvement anarchiste en France (1880-1914). Paris, Société universitaire d'éditions et de librairie, [c1951].

Manuel, Frank Edward, ed. and tr.
French Utopias: An Anthology of Ideal Societies. Ed. with an Frank E. Manuel and Fritzie P. Manuel. New York, Schocken Books [1971, c1966].

Marx, Jenny (Mrs.).
"A Short Sketch . . ." In *Reminiscences of Karl Marx,* FLHP, Moscow, n.d.

Massing, Paul W.
Rehearsal for Destruction: A Study of Political Anti-Semitism in Imperial Germany. New York, H. Fertig, 1967 [c1949].

Mayer, Gustav.
Bismarck und Lassalle, ihr Briefwechsel und ihre Gesprache, von Gustav Mayer, [Berlin] J. H. W. Dietz [c1928].

Mayo, Henry Bertram.
Introduction to Marxist Theory. New York, Oxford University Press, 1960 [reprinted 1965].

McLellan, David.
Karl Marx: His Life and Thought [1st U.S. ed.]. New York, Harper & Row [1974, c1973].

———.
The Young Hegelians and Karl Marx. London, Melbourne [etc.]. Macmillan, 1969.
Mehring, Franz.
Geschichte der deutschen Sozialdemokratie. 12. aufl 1922.

———.
Karl Marx: The Story of His Life. Translated by Edward Fitzgerald. New York, Covici, Friede, 1935.
Mendel, Arthur P.
Michael Bakunin: Roots of Apocalypse. New York, Praeger, 1981.
Miller, Susanne.
Das Problem der Freiheit im Sozialismus: Freiheit, Staat und Revolution in der Programmatik der Sozialdemokratie von Lassalle bis zum Revisionismusstreit. Berlin, Bonn-Bad Godesberg, Dietz, 1977.
Money, J. W. B. (James William Bayley).
Java: Or, How to Manage a Colony. Showing a practical solution of the questions now affecting British India. London, Hurst and Blackett, Publishers, successors to Henry Colburn, 1861.
Mönke, Wolfgang.
"Über Mitarbeit Hess...". In *Wissenschaftliche Annalen,* Bd. 6, 1957, p. 316ff.
Morgan, Roger.
The German Social Democrats and the First International, 1864-1872. Cambridge, University Press, 1965.
Mumford, Lewis.
The Story of Utopias. With an introduction by Hendrik Willem Van Loon. Gloucester, Mass., P. Smith, 1959 [c1950].
Na'aman, Shlomo.
Ferdinand Lassalle. Hannover, Buchdruckwerkstatten, 1968.

———.
Lassalle. [2. Aufl. Hannover] Verlag fur Literatur und Zeitgeschehen [1971].
Noyes, P. H.
Organization and Revolution: Working-class Associations in the German Revolutions of 1848-1849, by P. H. Noyes. Princeton, Princeton University Press, 1966.
Oates, Whitney Jennings, ed.
The Complete Greek Drama; all the extant tragedies of Aeschylus, Sophocles and Euripides, and the comedies of Aristophanes and Menander, in a variety of translations, edited by Whitney J. Oates and Eugene O'Neill, Jr. ... New York, Random House [c1938].
Osterroth, Franz.
Biographisches Lexikon des Sozialismus. Hannover, Dietz [1960-.
Padover, Saul K.
The Karl Marx Library, vol. 3 (The First International). McGraw-Hill, New York, 1973.
Pataud, Emile.
Comment nous ferons la Révolution. Paris, Librairie illustrée J. Tallandier [1909].
Pisani-Ferry, Fresnette.
Le Général Boulanger. Paris, Flammarion, 1969.
Plekhanov, Georgii Valentinovich.
Anarchism and Socialism. Translated with the permission of the author by Eleanor Marx Aveling. London, Twentieth Century Press, 1906.

Proudhon, P.-J. (Pierre-Joseph).
Carnets de P.J. Proudhon / texte inédit et intégral établi sur les manuscrits autographes avec annotations et appareil critique de Pierre Haubtmann. Paris, M. Rivière, 1960-.

———.
De la justice dans la révolution et dans l'église; nouveaux principes de philosophie pratique adressés à son éminence Monseigneur Mathieu, cardinal-archevêque de Besançon. Paris, Garnier freres, 1858.

———.
La pornocratie; ou, Les femmes dans les temps modernes. Paris, A. Lacroix, 1875.

———.
Système des contradictions économiques, ou Philosophie de la misère. Paris, Garnier freres, 1850.

Pyziur, Eugene.
The Doctrine of Anarchism of Michael A. Bakunin. Chicago, H. Regnery [1968, c1955].

Ramm, Thilo.
"Lassalle und Marx," *Marxismus Studien.* (Ed. 1. Fetscher). Tübingen. Dritte Folge, 1960. (*Schriften der Evangelischen Studiengemeinschaft,* 6.)

Revol, René.
"François Furet, historien ou idéologue?" in *Cahiers Léon Trotsky* (Grenoble), June 1989.

Richard, Albert.
"Bakounine et L'International à Lyons 1868-70" *La revue de Paris,* Sept. 1, 1896.

Rosenberg, Arthur.
Democracy and Socialism: A Contribution to the Political History of the Past 150 Years. Translated from the German by George Rosen. London, G. Bell, 1939.

Rosenberg, Philip.
The Seventh Hero; Thomas Carlyle and the Theory of Radical Activism. Cambridge, Harvard University Press, 1974.

Röser, Peter.
"Aus den Aussagen von Peter Gerhard Roeser" [selections], in *New Mega* III, 3:740; note that this paragraph is not included in the selections from the same document ("From Peter Röser's Evidence") included in MECW 38:550-54.

Rossiter, Clinton.
Marxism: The View from America. 1st ed. New York, Harcourt, Brace, [1960].

Ryazanov, David.
The Communist Manifesto of Karl Marx and Friedrich Engels. With an introduction and explanatory notes by D. Ryazanov. London, Martin Lawrence, 1930 [Translation by Eden and Cedar Paul].

Sams, Henry W.
Autobiography of Brook Farm. Ed. Henry W. Sams. Gloucester, Prentice-Hall, 1974, c1958.

Schapiro, J. Salwyn (Jacob Salwyn).
Liberalism and the Challenge of Fascism: Social Forces in England and France, 1815-1870. 1st ed. New York, McGraw-Hill Book Co., 1949.

Schleifstein, Josef.
Franz Mehring: Sein Marxistisches Schaffen 1891-1919. (Schriftenreihe des Instituts für Deutsche Geschichte an der Karl-Marx-Universität Leipzig. Ed. Prof. Dr. Ernest Engelberg. Band 5) Berlin, DDR: Rütten & Loenig, 1959.

Schmidt, Walter.
"Karl Friedrich Köppen, Friedrich Engels und die Terreur in der Groaen Franz-

ösischen Revolution," in *Beiträge zur Marx-Engels-Forschung* 26, Berlin 1989, s. 15-23.

Seager, Frederic H.
The Boulanger Affair: Political Crossroad of France, 1886-1889 [by] Frederic H. Seager. Ithaca, N.Y., Cornell University Press [1969].

Semmel, Bernard.
Imperialism and Social Reform, English Social-Imperial Thought, 1895-1914. Cambridge, Harvard University Press, 1960.

Shelley, Percy Bysshe.
The Masque of Anarchy: A Poem. A type-facsimile reprint of the original ed., first published (together with a pref. by Leigh Hunt) in 1832. Ed. Thomas J. Wise. New York, AMS Press [1975].

Silberner, Edmund.
Sozialisten zur Judenfrage; ein Beitrag zur Geschichte des Sozialismus vom Anfang des 19. Jahrhunderts bis 1914. Arthur Mandel. Berlin, Colloquium Verlag [1962].

Somerhausen, Luc.
L'humanisme agissant de Karl Marx; preface by Bracke (A.-M. Desrousseaux) Paris, Richard-Masse, 1946.

Stafford, David.
From Anarchism to Reformism: A Study of the Political Activities of Paul Brousse within the First International and the French Socialist Movement 1870-90. [Toronto], University of Toronto Press [1971].

Stein, Lorenz Jacob von.
Der socialismus und communismus des heutizen Frankreichs. Ein beitrag zur zeitgeschichte von L. Stein ... 2 umgearb. und sehr verm. Aus. ... Leipzig, O. Wigand, 1848.

———.
The History of the Social Movement in France, 1789-1850. Translated by Kaethe Mengelberg. [Totowa, N.J.], Bedminster Press [1964].

Stirner, Max.
The Ego and His Own. Translated from the German by Steven T. Byington. Rev. ed., selected and annotated, and with an introduction by John Carroll. London, Cape, 1971.

Symons, Julian.
Thomas Carlyle: The Life and Ideas of a Prophet. Freeport, N.Y., Books for Libraries Press [1970, c1952].

Vahlteich, Julius.
Ferdinand Lassalle und die Anfange der deutschen Arbeiterbewegung. Reprint of the 1904 1st ed. Berlin, Dietz, 1978.

Venable, Vernon.
Human Nature, the Marxian View. Gloucester, Mass., Peter Smith, 1975, c1945.

Venturi, Franco.
Roots of Revolution: A History of the Populist and Socialist Movements in Nineteenth Century Russia. Translated from the Italian by Francis Haskell. With an introduction by Isaiah Berlin. New York, Grosset & Dunlap [1966, c1960].

Villetard de Prunieres, Charles Edmond.
Histoire de l'Internationale. Paris, Garnier Freres, 1872.

Wildhagen, Karl.
The New Wildhagen German Dictionary; German-English, English-German; an encyclopedic and strictly scientific representation of the vocabulary of the modern and present-day languages, with special regard to syntax, style, and idiomatic

usage [by] Karl Wildhagen [and] Will Heraucourt [Editors: Eva Ruetz and Richard Wiezell]. Chicago, Follett Pub. Co., 1965.

Willard, Claude.
Les guesdistes; le mouvement socialiste en France, 1893-1905. Paris, Editions sociales [1965].

Williams, Raymond.
Keywords : A Vocabulary of Culture and Society. New York, Oxford University Press, 1976.

Wilson, John, Rev., M.A.
Thomas Carlyle, the Iconoclast of Modern Shams: A Short Study of His Life and Writings. Paisley [Scot.], A. Gardner, 1881.

Wittke, Carl Frederick.
The Utopian Communist: A Biography of Wilhelm Weitling, Nineteenth-century Reformer. Baton Rouge, Louisiana State University Press [1950].

Woodcock, George.
Pierre-Joseph Proudhon: A Biography. London, Routledge & Paul [1956].

INDEX

abolishing the state, 107, 110, 122, 132, 174
Absolute Freedom, 113. 118
Accident Insurance Law, 74, 310
Address to the Communist League, 83
Adler, Victor, xiv
Alcoy, 163
Alexander II, 273
Alianza de la Democratia Socialista, 283
Allemane, Jean, 209
alliance, 55, 59–62, 64, 68, 136, 137, 141, 143, 144, 149, 150, 156, 159, 160, 162, 165, 166, 168, 183, 184, 225, 231, 232, 270, 276, 277, 279–82, 282, 283, 283, 285, 290, 294, 295, 299, 307, 315
Alliance of Revolutionary Socialists, 280
anarchism, xi, xii, xiii, 41, 107, 109–16, 119–22, 124, 126, 128–33, 137, 140, 146, 147, 149, 150, 152, 156, 157, 165, 169–71, 173–75, 212, 270, 272, 273, 274, 277, 278, 291, 297, 299
Anarchism and Socialism, 152
anarchist, xii, xiii, xxii, 41, 107–12, 114, 116, 119, 122, 123, 124, 126–39, 141–54, 156–58, 160–74, 270, 272, 273, 275–78, 284, 286, 288, 289, 292, 293, 295, 298, 301
anarchy of production, 85, 86
anti-Germanism, 291, 292, 298
anti-Semitism, xiv, 60, 193, 208, 282, 291, 292, 293, 295, 296, 298, 300, 303, 310
Anti-Socialist Law, 61, 73, 91, 99, 100, 106, 165, 264, 265, 309, 310, 311, 313
antipoliticalism, 109, 110
antistatism, 107–09, 111–14, 118, 120, 126, 128, 171, 172
apotheosis of the state, 46
Appeal to the German Workers, 261
Appeal to the Russian Nobility, 274
Arbeiter-Zeitung, 260
Archives Bakounine, 271, 288, 295, 303
Ashley, Lord, seventh Earl of Shaftesbury, 183
Association for Social Politics, 76
ateliers nationaux, 43
Auguste Comte, 193, 216

Babeuf, François Noël (Gracchus), 116, 130
Bakunin, Mikhail, xi, xvii, xviii, xxi, xxii, 9, 14, 37, 41, 98, 107, 111, 112, 114, 117, 124, 128–31, 134–37, 140–47, 149–56, 158–62, 165–68, 170, 270, 271–79, 280–84, 284–88, 289–304
Barcelona, 136, 208, 283
Basel Congress, 136, 280, 282, 292, 293, 296, 297
Bastiat, Frédéric, 46
Bauer, Bruno and Edgar, 113, 117
Beamtenstaat, 65, 66
Bebel, August, 30, 50, 67–69, 71, 72, 77, 92, 93, 98, 100, 101, 104, 105, 106, 173, 193, 226–28, 262, 264, 265, 268, 312, 316
Becker, Bernhard, 62
Becker, J. P., xxii

365

Bentham, Jeremy, 108, 112, 115
Berlin, Isaiah, 203
Berneri, Marie Louise, 109
Bernstein, Eduard, 47, 72, 217
Bernstein/Engels (joint production titled *Ferdinand Lassalle as a Social Reformer*), 47–49, 52, 53, 56, 58, 242, 244, 255, 256, 262, 266, 268, 269
Bibliothèque Nationale, 272
Bignami, Enrico, 166, 167
Bismarck, Otto von, 52, 54–57, 59–64, 67, 68, 73–78, 80, 81, 83, 86, 87, 88, 91–95, 97–99, 101, 102, 104, 165, 178, 206, 221, 224, 233, 235, 236, 258, 265, 273, 298, 299, 308, 309, 309, 310, 313
Bismarckian Bonapartism, 49
Bismarckian socialism, 41, 42, 45, 78, 97, 98, 104, 178, 193
black cabinet, 170
Blanc, Gaspard, 162
Blanqui, Louis Auguste, xi, 2, 130
bloodsucker people, 296
bodyguard proletariat, 67, 74
Bologna, 168, 296
Bonaparte, Louis (Napoleon III), 46, 67, 221, 273; "socialist experiments" of, 46
Bonapartist socialism, 5, 45, 46, 76
Bonapartists, 206, 220, 230
Book of the Kahal, 296
Bucher, Lothar, 258
Boulangeo-Blanquists, 210, 212, 220, 230, 231
Boulanger, Georges, 204, 206–11, 213–16, 218–28, 230–36
Boulangism, 204–11, 213–16, 218–22, 225–30, 233, 234
Boulé, 211
Bourbon monarchy, 182
bourgeois anarchism, xiii, 115, 121, 122
bourgeois socialism, 31, 122, 178
Brafman, Jacob, 296
Bray, J. F., 110
brothels, 87
Brousse, Paul, 98, 209, 225, 227
Bucher, Lothar, 258
Buchez, Philippe Joseph Benjamin, 8, 9, 42–44, 51, 181
Bulletin de la Fédération Jurassienne, 282

bureaucratic state, 62, 65
Bürgers, Johann Heinrich Georg, 247, 252

Cadettists, 209, 210, 213, 214, 219, 223, 225, 227
Caesarism, 54, 56, 57
Cafieroarlo, 149, 171, 172, 290
Cains, 38
Calvié, Lucien, xvi
capital punishment, 141
capitalist statification, 85, 89
Caprivi, Leo von, 73
career-socialism, 79
Carlyle, Thomas, 185, 188
Carr, E. H., xviii, xxiii, 140, 145, 153, 159, 161, 162, 272–75, 277, 280, 281
Cavaignac, Louis Eugène, 273
Charles V (Holy Roman Emperor), 60
Charles XV (Sweden), 162, 274
Chartism, 38, 61, 183, 185, 186, 188, 189, 192
Christian communities, 34
Christian socialism, 181, 193, 291
Circular Against Kriege, 38
civil society, 49, 51, 89, 108, 120, 121, 180
Civil War in France, The, 18, 172, 195
class peace, 74
Class Struggles in France, The, 127
Clemenceau, Georges, 205, 209
clerical socialism, 181
Cluss, Adolph, 200, 249, 251
Cobbett, William, 188
collective capitalist, 87, 88
Collet, D., 203
Cologne Communist trial, 263
combinations, 64, 65
Committee of Public Safety, 140
Communards, 206
communism, 1, 2, 12, 20, 35, 38, 39, 46, 64, 82, 83, 91, 96, 101, 102, 112, 114–16, 118, 153, 167, 168, 176, 177, 181, 182, 186, 247, 250, 276, 293, 296, 309
Communism of the Rheinische Beobachter, The, 64, 182
Communist Confession of Faith, 36
Communist League, 18, 37, 38, 83, 108, 158, 246, 249, 251
Communist Manifesto, 1, 2, 13, 18, 23, 25,

Communist Manifesto (continued)
35, 69, 105, 121, 122, 126, 159, 176, 180, 185, 189, 192
communitarian lie, xvi
compulsory physical labor, 167
Comte, Auguste, 192–95, 216
Comtism, 193–96, 216
concept of the state, 47–49, 111, 300
Condition of the Working Class in England, The, 112, 183, 188
"Confession," 36, 243, 273, 292
Confino, Michael, 272, 283
Coningsby, 183
Conservative party, 206
contending ruling classes, 50
cooperatives, 4, 42, 51, 52, 63, 68–70, 101, 109, 260, 315
Cordova, 164
Cornu, Auguste, 116
Council of the Commune, 145
Count Lavagna, 243
Cournet, 286
Crédit Mobilier, 5, 45
Critical Critics, 117
Critique of the Gotha Program, 69, 70, 264, 317, 318
Cromwell, Oliver, 188
cult of the state, 46, 49
cultural anarchism, 169
Cuno, Theodor, xxii, 153, 156
Czar Nicholas, 57, 273

Dammer, Otto, 261
Daniels, Roland, 247, 255
Danton, Georges-Jacques, 188
"Democracy of dunderheads", 33
Democracy, the, 83, 177, 181, 214
Democratic Association, 20, 158, 159
Democratic Review, 189
democratic socialism, xii, 75
De Paepeésar Aimé Désiré, 162
Der Staatssozialist, 76
Deutsch-Französische Jahrbücher, 11, 177, 181
Deutsche Jahrbücher, xiv
dictatorship, xi, xvi, 55–57, 67, 109, 129–31, 136, 144, 147, 160, 165–67, 195, 204, 207, 210–14, 219, 222, 223, 229, 258, 263, 264, 270, 273, 289, 291, 299, 301, 303
dictatorship of the proletariat, 131, 264
Diderot, Denis, 34

"Die Freie," 113
Die Quintessenz des Socialismus, 80
Diplomatic Review, 197, 203
Directorate, 280
Disraeli, Benjamin, 183
dissolution du gouvernement, 127
Don Carlos (Schiller's drama), 60
Drumont, Edouard, 208, 291
Dühring, Eugen, 4, 5, 7, 8, 15, 31, 32, 79, 82, 84–86, 89, 90, 173

Eccarius, Johann Georg, 27, 28
Ego and Its Own, The, 111
Eisenachers, 50, 67, 68, 71, 72, 262, 306
Ely, Richard Theodore, 76
enemy of humanity, 28, 38
enemy of the party, 39
Enragés, xvi
étatisme, 44
Eternal Justice, 26, 27, 32

Fanelli, 281, 282
fare da se, 289
Farga-Pellicer, 282
fascism, 177, 185, 204, 271
Fatherland, 62, 299, 312
Faucher, Julius, 124, 158
Faure, Sébastian, xii
federalism, 128, 277
Ferdinand Lassalle as a Social Reformer, 47
Ferdinand Lassalle und seine Bedeutung für die Arbeiterklasse, 262
Ferdinand Lassalle, Eine Würdigung, 262
Ferry, Jules, 205, 213, 223, 225
feudal socialism, 64, 65, 176, 178, 180–82, 185, 192, 193
Feuerbach, Ludwig, 34–37, 187
Fiasco at Lyons, 140
Fichte, Johann Gottlieb, 47, 76, 116
First International, xviii, xx, 27, 169
Fleurus (battle of), xiv, xv
Footman, David, 242, 244, 248, 250, 253, 259
Frankfurt Assembly, 23
Franz von Sickingen, 54, 60, 178, 256
fraternal union of peoples, 25
Fraternité, 27, 190
Frederick the Great, 75
Free, the, 12, 113, 114, 117, 121, 166, 290
free enterprise, xiii, 114
free labor, 114

Free Press, 197
free trade, 114, 190, 310
freedom, 17, 24, 25, 27, 48, 56, 91, 113, 114, 117, 118, 126, 133, 136, 137, 142, 144, 146, 150, 152, 158, 166, 172, 174, 175, 187, 188, 198, 212, 243, 245, 247, 270, 279, 280, 284, 289, 290, 292, 295, 303
Freiheit, 99, 157
French Legitimists, 181, 182
French Revolution, xiii, xiv, xv, xvi, 178, 202, 227
Frese, Julius, 58
Friedrich Wilhelm III, 87
Friedrich Wilhelm IV, 179
Friscia, 281, 282
Fritzsche, F. W., 261
Frohme, Karl, 48
Furet, François, xv

Gambuzzi, 289
Gargantua, 133
Garibaldi, Giuseppe, 142, 143, 257
Gemkow, Heinrich, 205
General Council of the International, xviii, xix, xxii, xxiii, 27, 29, 45, 135, 148, 150–52, 155, 161, 163, 166, 167, 195, 196, 275, 276, 277, 280, 281, 283, 284, 286, 288, 289, 293, 296, 299, 303
General German Workers' Association, 55, 252, 259
German Empire, 59, 92, 299, 307, 310, 312, 313
German Ideology, The, 4, 5, 36, 112, 114, 119, 121
German Social-Democracy, 46, 165, 309
German Workers Educational Association, 158
Germany: A Winter's Tale, 24
Gerth, Hans, xvii
Gesamtkapitalist, 87
GGWA, 55–57, 62, 258–60, 262, 263
Girardin, Emile de, 8, 122–25, 127, 128
Girondins, xvi
Gotha, 50, 67–70, 264, 306–308, 317, 318
Granger, Ernest, 210–13, 218, 231
Grün, Karl, 2, 8, 36, 125
Grundrisse, 46, 127, 179

Guesde, Jules, 211–16, 223, 224, 230, 231, 234
Guesdists, 204, 205, 211, 213, 215, 216, 226–28, 231, 234
Guillaume, James, xviii, xix, xxi, 128, 162, 163, 165, 168, 278, 281, 282, 283, 287–91

Hague Congress, xvii, xviii, xxii, 30, 143, 153, 158, 168, 271, 272, 280, 282–84, 288, 289, 291, 295, 298, 301
Hales, John, xxiii
Harney, G. J., 192
Hatzfeldt, Sophie von, 55, 57, 243–45, 247–49, 253, 254, 264
Hebrew Melodies, 60
Hegel, G. W. F., 12, 45, 47, 49, 111, 117, 118, 135, 194
Heine, Heinrich, 60, 182, 291
Held, Adolph, 76
Heraclitus, 47, 256
Herder, 35
Herzen, Natalie, 271
Hess, Moses, 8, 9, 36, 111, 115–18, 186, 292, 293
Hins, Eugène, 277
Holy Family, The, 13, 35, 36, 119, 183
Höchberg, Karl, 21, 26, 53, 79, 80, 93, 104, 106
Holy Inquisition, 43
hommes déclassés, 165
Horner, Leonard, 33
Housing Question, The, 46
How We Will Make the Revolution, 110
Huber, V. A., 57
humanism and love, 34, 36
humanistic socialism, 35, 36
Humanity, 26, 28, 33–40, 48, 54, 132, 155, 156, 163, 299
Hutten, Ulrich von, 178
Huxley, Thomas Henry, 194

Idée Générale de la Révolution au XIXe Siécle, 126
Idiotismus, 115
Imperative Mandates at the Hague Congress, 288, 291
Imperial Regency, 125
Imperial socialism, 45
Imperialism, 101, 195
"Indifference to Politics," 110, 157

"Indirect Taxation," 48
"Instant Abolition," 132, 140, 150, 163
International Alliance of Socialist Democracy, 276
International Alliance of the Socialist Democracy, 137, 282
International Brotherhood, 160
International Brothers, 165, 166, 280
International Working Men's Association, 143, 285
Invisible Dictatorship, 289
iron law of wages, 52, 97

Jacobin Club, 34
Jacoby, Johann, 297
Jehuda ben Halevy, 60
Jesuits, 149, 168, 243, 293, 302, 303
Jesuit methods, 302, 303
jesuitical discipline, 168
jeune France, 155
jeunesse sans issue, 165
Joffrin, 209
joint-stock companies, 85–87, 95
Jones, Ernest, 38, 192
Journey Through Utopia, 109
June Days, 43, 273
Junker, 55, 57, 75, 89, 93, 103, 311
Junkerdom, xiv, 64
Jura Bulletin, 288
Jura Federation (of the First International), 165, 168, 287–89
Justice and Morality, 22, 28–30

Kammergericht, 48
Karl Marx, Pangermaniste, 281, 282
Katheder-socialists, 46, 75–78, 80, 84, 90, 98
Kathedersozialisten, 76
Kautsky, Karl, 72, 77–80, 82, 101, 264, 266–68, 315, 317, 318
Kautsky, Louise, 267
Kelly, Aileen, 304
Kelsen, Hans, 174
King of Prussia, 30, 180
Klein, W., 246
Köppen, K. F., xiv
Kolokol, 273
Kriege, Hermann, 38, 39
Kropotkin, Petr Alekseevich, 124, 125, 170
Kugelmann, Louis, xix, xx, xxi

L'Atelier, 43
L'Intransigeant, 208
La France Juive, 208
La Plebe, 166, 167
La Solidarité, 162
Labor Parliament, 43
Labour's Wrongs and Labour's Remedy, 110
Laisant, A. C., 208, 216
Lamennais, Félicité Robert de, 181
language of gods, 25, 26
Lassalle, Ferdinand, 9, 42, 45–66, 68, 70–72, 75, 77, 79, 80, 97, 98, 101, 173, 174, 178, 217, 241–69, 273, 293, 306, 307, 309, 312, 313, 315, 316, 317, 318
Lassallean, 41, 42, 45, 47–52, 55, 56, 59–61, 63–70, 75, 80, 97, 98, 100, 241, 252, 261, 263, 266, 268, 306, 307, 315, 316
Lassalleans, 43, 44, 48, 50, 61, 62, 65–70, 72, 182, 262, 264, 267, 306
Latter-Day Pamphlets, 186, 188
Lavrov, Petr Lavrovich, 117
Le Libertaire, xii
Le National, 51
Leclerc, xvi
legitimists, 181, 182, 206
Lehning, Arthur, 271, 272, 282, 283, 287, 303, 304
Lewy, Gustav, 250–56
les services publics, 98, 209
Libertarian, xii, xiii, 5, 23, 134, 143, 145–47, 270, 295, 302
libertarian socialism, xii
Liebknecht, Wilhelm, 50, 217, 227, 316
Lidtke, Vernon L., 72
Lindau, Paul, 258, 259
"livery of loyalty," 57
List, Friedrich, 76
Lucraft, Benjamin, xxiii
Luxembourg Palace, 43
Lyons, xxi, 140, 141, 216, 278, 284
Lyubavin letter, 301

Macfarlane, Helen, 189
MacMahon, Marshall Patrice de, 206
Manchester, 43, 48
Manchesterism, 75, 95
Manners, John, 183
Manifesto of the Three Zurichers, 53, 80, 93, 106

Manifesto of War Against the World, 243
Marquis Posa, 60
Marr, Heinrich Wilhelm, 295
Marrast, Armand, 51
Marx, Francis, 199
Marx, Eleanor, 47, 84, 171, 267, 268
Mathiez, Albert, xv
Mazzini, Giuseppe, 28, 45
Macartney, George, 151
Mayer, Gustav, xviii
medievalism, 182, 192
Meyer, Rudolph, 76
Mill, John Stuart, 186
Ministry of Agriculture, 75
Miquel, Johannes, 65
mob, 53
monarchical socialism, 41, 76, 80
monarchist, 48, 56, 59, 62, 66, 79, 312
More, Thomas, 177
Muraviev, Michael, 296
Mutual Credit Society, 129
mutualist, 128, 157

Napoleon I, 273
Napoleon III, 30, 45, 57, 140, 158, 162, 179
Naquet, Alfred, 208, 216
Narodnik, 276
National Guards, 141
national workshops, 10, 43
nationalization of the railways, 74, 83
Nechayev, Sergei Gennadyevich, 137, 167, 271, 274, 283, 300-303
"negative acrid individualism," 56
Neuchâtel, 304
Neue Oder-Zeitung, 249
Neue Rheinische Zeitung, 181, 245, 248
Neue Rheinische Zeitung, politisch-ökonomische Revue, 122, 127, 188
Neue Zeit, 80, 266, 267, 314, 315, 317, 318
New York Daily Tribune (NYDT), 32, 43, 45, 83, 198, 199
New Yorker Volkszeitung, 173
Nicholas I, 273
Nietzsche, Friedrich, 242
Nigger Question, The, 186
nonproletarian socialisms, 181

Oastler, Richard, 61
O'Connor, Feargus, 192, 193

Obolensky, Zoe Princess, 275
Odger, George, xxiii
On Authority, 135, 138, 139, 143
Oncken, Hermann, 262
Oppenheim, H. B., 76
opportunism, xi, 42, 50, 68, 147, 161, 162, 170, 207, 218, 221, 223, 228, 231, 232, 235
Opportunists (French Political Party), 66, 205, 206, 209, 213, 215, 221, 222
Organisation du Travail, 44
organization of labor, 51, 99
Orleanists, 206
Our Committee, 167
Owen, Robert, 110
Owenite, 27, 181, 185, 186

Padover, Saul K., xx
Palmerston, Lord, 197
Paris Commune, xxii, 43, 45, 121, 142, 143, 172, 196, 205, 207, 285
Parkinson, Northcote, 76
parliamentarism, xi, 207, 209, 221, 222, 229-31, 236
Past and Present, 185-87, 189
Peace League, 159, 160, 275, 276, 279, 281
peasantry, xi, 103, 109, 161, 165, 270
People's Cause: Romanov, Pugachev, or Pestel?, The, 273
People's Party, 50, 58
Péreire brothers, 208
Perfect Liberty, 133, 141
permanent revolution, 181
Perret, Henri, 135
Perronharles, 280, 281
personal dictatorship, 56, 129, 166, 195, 258
petty-bourgeois socialist, 42
philanthropic Tories, 183, 187
Philip II, 60
Philippe, Louis, 56, 182, 273
Philistines, 10, 122, 188, 194, 223
Plekhanov, G. V., 15, 152, 171
police state, 48, 99
Political Justice, 112
Positivism, 193, 194, 216
Positivist Club, 194
Possibilists, 98, 209, 211, 213, 215, 216, 223, 225-28, 231, 232, 236

Pranger, R. R., 174
Prince Jerome, 273, 274
principle of authority, 127, 131, 132, 135, 137, 139–41, 144
professorial socialism, 76
Progressives, 63, 64, 260, 261, 311, 315
Protocols of the Elders of Zion, 296
protofascist, 204, 205, 216
Prussian absolute monarchy, 48
Prussiandom, 91
Prussian Military Question and the German Workers, The, 61
pseudosocialist, 46
Putschists, 142

Quintessence of Socialism, The, 80

Rabelais, 133
Radical party, 205
Rappoportharles, 194
reactionary anticapitalism, 177, 192, 193
reactionary socialism, 176–78
reactionary socialists, 46, 178
reform versus revolution, xi
reformism, xi, 43, 44, 50, 53, 54, 65, 66, 69, 98, 105, 110, 174, 177, 307, 311, 315
Regiments of the New Era, 191
Reichstag, 59, 72–75, 77, 92, 103, 104, 106, 165, 261, 264, 308, 309, 311, 316
Reign of Terror, xiii, xiv
religion of Love, 36, 38
Republican Party, xiii, 111, 205, 227, 235
Reuchlin, 35
Revisionism, 47, 48, 54, 173, 262
Revolution (1848), 20, 23, 37, 51
Reybaud, Louis, 176
Rheinische Beobachter, 64, 182
Rheinische Zeitung, xiv, 11, 113–16, 181, 245, 248
Ricardian socialist, 110
Ricardo, David, 16, 52, 77
Richard, Albert, 61, 278, 282, 284, 295
Rimini Congress, 288
Rittinghausen, 278
road to power, xi
Robespierre, Maximilien, xv, xvi, 43
Rochefort, Henri, 208, 210

Rodbertus, Johann Karl, 17, 18, 52, 53, 77–80, 99, 178
Ronsdorf Address, 56
Röser, Peter Gerhard, 246, 247
Roscher, Wilhelm, 76
Rothschilds, 296, 297
Roux, Jacques, xvi
Royal Maritime Company, 87
royal porcelain factory, 87, 96
Royal Prussian government socialism, 63, 64, 182
Ruge, Arcold, 113, 125, 181

Saint-Imier, 290
Saint-Simonian school, 43
Schäffle, Albert, 80
Schiller, Johann Christoph Friedrich, 60
Schlüter papers, xvii
Schmidt, Walter, xiv
Schmoller, Gustav, 76, 307
Schnaebelé affair, 207
Schramm, August, 21, 53, 79, 80
Schulze-Delitzsch, 51, 66
Schweitzer, Johann Baptist, 61–66, 260, 309, 315, 316
Schwitzguebel, Adhémar, 282, 291
secret dictatorship, 160, 289
Sentimental socialism, 22, 23, 25, 40
sentimentality, 22–24, 38
Serraillier, 302
Sheffield Free Press, 197
Shelley, 118
Sickness Insurance Act, 74
Silesian weavers, 118, 180
Shaw, George Bernard, 37
Simon, Ludwig, 125
Slavic Section of the International, 288
Smith, Adam, 108, 118
Smithiasmus, 75
Soboul, Albert, xv
Social Monarchy, 50, 55, 58, 99, 273, 310, 313
Social Question, 50, 51, 73, 75, 76, 109, 122, 128, 208
Social Republic, 62
Social-Democracy, xii, 45, 46, 53, 66, 72, 77, 78, 80, 94, 99, 106, 165, 169, 261, 262, 309, 310, 311–316
Social-Democrat, 48, 60
Social-Democratic, 41, 71–74, 76, 77,

79, 81, 92, 104, 153, 169, 170, 214, 227, 228, 266, 305, 306, 311, 312, 313, 316
Social-Democratic Party, 41, 72–74, 76, 77, 79, 92, 214, 227, 228, 266, 306, 311, 312
Social-Demokrat, 61–63, 66
Social-Fascism, 271
Socialism and Taxation, 122
socialism of fools, 193, 208
socialism of the chair, 41, 76
Socialism Utopian and Scientific, 2–5, 7, 16, 19, 85–87, 97
Socialisme Collectiviste et Socialisme Libéral, 208
socialization of production, 85, 87, 89
Society of the Rights of Man, 209
Sorge, Friedrich Adolph, xvii, xix, xx, xxi, 266
South German People's Party, 50, 58
Sovereign Individual, 131, 133, 144
Sozialdemokrat, 73, 80, 94, 100, 104, 173, 231
St. Martin's Hall, 196
Staatssozialismus, 41, 78
Stalinoid, xvii
state capital, 62, 83
state cultism, 44
state mystique, 54
state-aid, 50, 52, 63, 66, 67, 69
State-Caesarism, 54
state-capitalism, 45, 84, 89, 93
state-cultism, 48, 58
state-slavery, 49
state-socialism, xii, 41–45, 47, 53, 54, 64, 66, 67, 70, 72, 73, 76, 77, 79, 80, 81–84, 88–90, 92, 93, 95, 97–104, 106
statification, 83, 85–87, 89–97, 100, 102, 103, 209
statification equals socialism, 87
statism, 34, 44, 124, 152, 160, 298, 317
Statism and Anarchy, 124, 152, 160, 298
Status Quo in Germany, The, 65, 180
Stoecker, Adolph, 193, 291
Strauss, D. F., 187, 189
Study on the German Jews, 292
Stuttgart parliament, 125
Sue, Eugene, 183
Sybil, 183

Ten Hours Bill, 183

terror and terrorism, xiii, xiv, xv, xvi, 143, 170, 318
Theories of Surplus Value, 77
Thermidoreans, xvi
Thousand Year Reich, 64
tobacco monopoly, 74, 91, 93, 95–97
Tölcke, Karl Wilhelm, 62, 75, 268
Tönnies, Ferdinand, 194
Tory Chartist, 61, 183
Tory Democracy, 61
Tory Radicalism, 61, 76
trade unions, 52, 63–65, 67, 120, 154, 196
"Transformation of Communism into Love-mongering," 38, 39
True Socialism, 25, 26, 36, 37, 116, 180
Tucker, Benjamin, 111
Turkey, 198

universal suffrage, 20, 51–55, 59, 60, 119, 172, 231
University of Chicago, xv, 111
Urquhart, David, 196–203
Urquhartites, 199, 202
utilitarianism, 112, 115
Utin, Nikolai Isaakovich, 145, 167, 276

Vahlteich, Julius, 51, 57, 261, 262
Vaillant, Edouard, 210, 211, 213, 224, 230
Verein für Sozialpolitik, 76
Verstaatlichung, 86, 98
"vieillerie St. Simoniste," 160
Villetard, Edmond, 29
Voden, Alexei Mikhailovich, 117
Vogt, Karl, 125
Volksstaat, 80, 245
Vollmar, Georg, 73, 98
Vorwärts, 24, 80, 267, 308

Wagner, Adolph, 72, 76–78, 80, 84
Wagener, Hermann, 76, 103
Warren, Josiah, xiii, 111
Wealth of Nations, 118
Weimar, 74, 260
Weimar Republic, 74
Weitling, Wilhelm, 37, 38, 108, 109
Weston, John, 27
Whigs, 187
Wilhelm I, 60, 73, 312
Wilhelm II, 313

Woman and Socialism, 173
Workers' Educational Association, 260
Workers' Program, The, 48
workers' state, 41, 44, 69, 105, 120, 132, 137, 162, 278

Yellow Peril, 292
Young England, 179, 181–85, 187
Young Germany, 118

Zeus, 141